THE
BRITISH
COUNCIL

THE
BRITISH
COUNCIL

The First Fifty Years

*Frances
Donaldson*

JONATHAN CAPE
THIRTY BEDFORD SQUARE LONDON

First published 1984
Copyright © 1984 by Frances Donaldson
Jonathan Cape Ltd, 30 Bedford Square, London WC1

British Library Cataloguing in Publication Data

Donaldson, Frances
The British Council
1. British Council—History
I. Title
062   DA20

ISBN 0–224–02041–2

Typeset by Gloucester Typesetting Services
Printed in Great Britain by
Butler and Tanner Ltd
Frome and London

Contents

PART THREE: Epilogue

Appendices

Illustrations

Photographers

Preface

The whole of the research for this book was done by Dr Harriet Harvey Wood. Dr Harvey Wood has been a member of the British Council staff for most of her working life, and her father was the Council Representative in Scotland from 1940 to 1950 and later Representative in Paris and Rome. She probably knows more about the British Council than any other living person, and I have had the benefit of this knowledge as well as of her labours.

By reading this book, anyone can see the weight of her research, but I have to thank her for services which are less obvious. She has all the qualities of a good editor – the most important of which is to have the courage of one's own opinions. It is easy to say when something is wrong; the number of people who are prepared to make an unequivocal statement in the early stages of a book that something is right are very much fewer than might be thought. I have profited enormously from Dr Harvey Wood's views, even more from her willingness to comment on mine and I have very much enjoyed working with her.

My thanks to Sir Charles Troughton, Chairman of the British Council, and Sir John Burgh, Director-General, for kindness and consideration well beyond the demands of our professional relationship.

So many members of the Council's staff, past and present, have been willing to spend time to help me that I cannot name them all. Among the retired staff, those who have allowed me to quote from unpublished papers or recorded conversations include Richard Auty, Henry Croom-Johnson, Norman Daniel, Morris Dodderidge, Professor Michael Grant, Stanley Hodgson, James Livingstone, James McDonaugh, Miss Enid McLeod, Harold Oxbury, Dr Leslie Phillips, Reginald Phillips, T. F. S. Scott, the late Richard Seymour, Mrs Lilian Somerville, Dr Margaret Suttill, Irvine Watson and Professor George West. I am indebted to A. J. S. White, not only for talking to me and allowing me to quote from his unpublished memoirs, but also for the use I have made of his short history of the Council's first twenty-five years, the only other history of the Council so far produced.

I have received help from far more of the serving staff than I can record here (and have unknowingly made demands on many others); I am grateful for the willing assistance I have had from all of them, and especially to the Representatives and their families and staff who looked after my husband and me on our overseas visits. I must particularly acknowledge the special help I have received from Roderick Cavaliero, Trevor Rutter, Keith Hunter, Richard Joscelyne, James Took, Robin Twite, Stewart Smith, Raymond Adlam, W. E. Moss, Mary Wane, Malcolm Dalziel, Henry Meyric-Hughes, Oliver Siddle, E. J. Rayner, John Coope, Roy Mayo, Angela Rice, Juliet Gayton, Wendy Barnes, Mrs Sukla Mitra and Mrs Romola Majumdar in Calcutta, and Mrs Sushma Bahl in Delhi. Among members of the Council's Board, past and present, who have allowed me to interview them, I owe particular thanks to Lady Albemarle and Lewis Robertson.

Since so much of my information necessarily comes from members of the British Council's staff, past or present, what becomes of impartiality? Obviously someone willing to spend three years on a book about an institution of this sort must be in some degree partial to it in the first place. Yet this is a history covering fifty years, to write which I have had access to papers from many other sources and interviewed a great many people. I have not consciously suppressed any information I thought relevant and, to the extent permitted, I have quoted direct from official or other papers. I have not taken much trouble to disguise my views but I have tried to present the information so that the reader can form his own.

I have to thank Lady Leeper for permission to quote from her late husband's letters to his father and sister and from the article in *The Contemporary Review* on pages 11 and 12; Henry Moore for permission to quote from his letter to the Prime Minister on page 311; A. D. Peters & Co. for permission to quote from Dame Rebecca West's letter to Colonel Bridge on pages 38–40; Samuel French Ltd for permission to quote from Ian Hay, *Peaceful Invasion*, on pages 117, 118 and 119; and Lord Lloyd for letting me see relevant papers in his father's collection at Churchill College, Cambridge and for giving permission for the use of a photograph from the collection (Plate 4). I must express my gratitude for the help of Miss Marion Stewart, of Churchill College, when I went through the Lloyd papers, and thank the Librarians of the House of Lords Library for their patient and courteous response to the many demands for parliamentary papers made by my husband on my behalf.

I must acknowledge the important help I have had from Dr Philip Taylor's book, *The Projection of Britain*, and Dr Diana Eastment's unpublished doctoral thesis, 'The policies and position of the British Council, 1939–1950' (University of Leeds), which she very kindly allowed me to read in its final draft.

Most of the illustrations are from the British Council's own archives and I thank the archivist for her assistance. For kind permission to use other illustrations I am grateful to Camera Press for nos 7 and 10, The Press Association for no 9, and Universal Pictorial Press Agency for nos 8 and 14.

Finally I must thank the officials of the Foreign and Commonwealth Office for giving me access to their records, especially those not yet in the public domain. Without this permission, and the courtesy and helpfulness of the staff of the FCO Records Branch, this book could not have been written.

July 1984   FRANCES DONALDSON

Introduction

The year 1984 is the fiftieth anniversary of an institution which began its life under the title of 'British Committee for Relations with Other Countries'. The word 'Committee' was soon replaced by that of 'Council', and in 1936 the Foreign Office officially announced that 'in view of the numerous criticisms, The British Council for Relations with Other Countries has decided to abbreviate its title and to style itself "The British Council" '.

Today the British Council is known and has devoted friends in most of the countries of the world. Yet, in its corridors they constantly bewail the fact that ninety-nine out of every hundred of its own countrymen have never heard of it, while, of those who have, very few have a clear idea of what it stands for. Retiring as Chairman in 1976, at a time when the Council had for forty-two years shown an astonishing capacity for development and growth, as well as much evidence of its adaptability, Lord Ballantrae said: 'I remain baffled by the problem of how to get our work better known in this country, where, except in small specialised circles such as universities, ignorance about it is abysmal.'[1]

The truncated title, forbidding as well as inexplicit and inexpressive, must contribute to this ignorance. The impression is of one of those vague areas of political or possibly legal life which are genuinely functional but too arid for the consideration of the ordinary man. So it cannot be said too soon that the business of the British Council is not merely relations with other countries but cultural relations. A statement of its early aims and objects reads as follows:

To promote abroad a wider appreciation of British culture and civilisation, by encouraging the study and use of the English language, and thereby, to extend a knowledge of British literature and of the British contributions to music and the fine arts, the sciences, philosophic thought and political practice.
To encourage both cultural and educational interchanges between

the United Kingdom and other countries and, as regards the latter, to assist the free flow of students from overseas to British seats of learning, technical institutions and factories, and of United Kingdom students in the reverse direction.

To provide opportunities for maintaining and strengthening the bonds of the British cultural tradition throughout the self-governing Dominions.

To ensure continuity of British education in the Crown Colonies and Dependencies.[2]

If allowance is made for the change in status of the Crown Colonies and Dependencies and of their consequent relationship to Great Britain, these words still serve as a fair description of the aims and objects of the British Council.

In 1934 there was nothing new in the idea that the language, litera-ture, art, science and way of life of a nation might be spread abroad as a means of encouraging understanding and goodwill on the part of others. Indeed Great Britain was almost alone among the leading Euro-pean nations in not acting upon it. Both the French and the Germans had treated it as an important part of foreign policy since the latter half of the nineteenth century, although their motives were subtly and characteristically different. To quote an earlier writer on the subject of the French:

The French, having from the cradle been encouraged by their parents to assert themselves, *de se faire valoir*, being convinced that since the age of Pericles there has existed no type of civility comparable to that evolved during the reign of Louis XIV, have in all sincerity regarded it as their mission to spread latin culture across the globe and to im-part to untutored savages the logical intelligence of Descartes and Pascal, or the orderliness of Racine's careful style. For them, in this respect, pride and philanthropy are nobly fused. Even the Italians, who rely for their prestige upon a magnificent past rather than upon present proportions of wealth and power, have striven to extend their influence by communicating to others the beauty of their language and the glamour of their intellectual and artistic achieve-ment.[3]

From the nineteenth century the French Government had given subsidies to the schools of the French Roman Catholic missionaries in the Mediterranean Basin, as well as to the hospitals and agricultural institutions, and in the twentieth century they extended their work by establishing lay schools and at the same time enlarging their sphere of influence to take in the countries of the West and South America. Splendidly equipped institutes for higher education were established in Florence, Rome, Athens, Cairo and Damascus. 'Nos universités et nos écoles à l'étranger sont de véritables foyers de propagande en faveur de la France,' declared a report on the Estimates for the Foreign Services for 1920. 'Elles constituent une arme aux mains de nos pouvoirs publics.'[4] A private society called the Alliance Française, established in 1880, promoted the teaching of the French language through groups organised in many parts of the world to carry out a programme of schools and libraries and to arrange lectures and exhibitions of art and so on. This society grew to be of the first importance. By 1933 Sir Charles Mendl, Press Attaché at the British Embassy in Paris, reported that the Alliance Française was by far the largest, best organised and most powerful instrument of cultural propaganda which France possessed, subsidised by the Ministries of Foreign Affairs, National Education, and of the Colonies, by the Governments of the various French Colonies and Protectorates, by the City of Paris and by a number of Conseils généraux throughout France; and with an expenditure of something like six million francs a year.[5]

Writing at about the same time, Russell Galt of the American University in Cairo concluded a pamphlet on the difference between French and English educational philosophies in Egypt with the following sentences: 'In Egypt England had an army, — the French an idea. England had educational control — France, a clear educational philosophy. Because the French did have such an organized philosophy and the English did not, the French pen has proved mightier than the English sword.'[6] And an appropriate appendage to these words may be found in the experience in 1981 of a member of the staff of the British Council who, having replied in some detail to a request from a compatriot for information as to what this body stood for, was surprised to receive the reply: 'Oh, I see. Rather like the Alliance Française.'

The Germans were neither later nor less active in the field, although initially their motives were rather different. They wished to maintain the spirit of Germanism (Deutschtum) in the millions of Germans living outside the Reich.

In the larger cities abroad in which the Germans have organized themselves into colonies of a corporate character, especially in the East, there often exist (as in Constantinople, Cairo, Belgrade, Bucharest, and many other places in Rumania, and also in Athens, Rome and Genoa) special school organizations in which the instruction is given in the mother tongue. Experience has shown that these institutions offer the best means of keeping the children of German descent from becoming denationalized, especially the children of the poorer families. They also make it possible to give these children the benefits of the German language, a German education, and the German point of view ... The support of these institutions is certainly the affair of the Reich.[7]

However, like the French, the Germans believed also in the importance of their national contribution to civilisation and to the richness of the culture of the world. After the First World War and again after the Second, they had the further motive of wishing to re-establish themselves in the eyes of other countries.

The Italians, if not as active as the French, had shown that they recognised the spread of their language and culture as a matter of first class importance and in the Dante Alighieri they had an institution roughly the equivalent of the Alliance Française. In 1935 it was reported that, although neither the figures for membership nor the number of committees abroad of the Dante Alighieri compared with those of the French, both were steadily increasing. In a report to the Foreign Secretary, Sir Samuel Hoare, Sir Eric Drummond, British Ambassador in Rome, wrote in 1935:

> How far Italy's propaganda expenditure brings in a material or spiritual return proportionate to the outlay is naturally a question of opinion. There is, however, no doubt that the Fascist Government consider it well worth while to allocate .3 per cent of their total expenditure to preserving the Italian character of at least some of the emigrants settled in foreign lands and to advertising to the world at large the cultural legacy of ancient Rome and the progress in various fields to which the Fascist revolution has inspired the new Italy.[8]

It is nevertheless doubtful whether the utilitarian British would have been influenced by these examples but for one thing: by 1935 the attitude in the East and in South America of both the German and the Italian Governments was discernibly hostile to Britain and damaging to her interests. In the atmosphere of the time the idea that a truer understanding of Great Britain might be contributed to by a non-political, educational programme, specifically designed to spread knowledge of the English language and of British arts, science, parliamentary institutions, technological achievements and way of life held out some, if only a small, attraction.

Conceived too late to bear much on the immediate issues for which it was formed, and with too small a grant from the Foreign Office, the British Council nevertheless proved itself a weapon so easily adapted to the changing circumstances of war and its aftermath, a tool so appropriate to the continually altering and diminishing role of the erstwhile Mother Country, that in 1980–1 it was responsible for the administration of a total budget of £123.2 million. Of this, £31.5 million was from the Foreign Office as its contribution to the basic operating budget, £64.7 million from the Overseas Development Administration as its balancing contribution towards the basic operating budget and towards its expenditure on certain aid programmes in developing countries, £14.2 million from contracts with international agencies, overseas governments and so on, and £12.8 million from direct earnings on educational programmes.[9] Its activities in that year ranged from the teaching of English to 142,764 students in its own centres and, in association with Institutes and Anglophile societies abroad, to 100,000 more, to what is known as a Paid Educational Service, by which, for example, it contracted with the Government of Sri Lanka to train about 50,000 members of the construction industry in a great variety of crafts such as carpentry, bricklaying, electrical wiring and so on, at a cost of £1.8 million to be paid for by the World Bank. Fifty drama and dance tours ranging from the National Theatre and the Covent Garden Ballet to small theatre workshops were sent to countries in all parts of the world, while exhibitions of the work of artists ranging from Henry Moore to students of the Royal College of Arts were sent to many countries in Europe, to New Zealand and the United States, to Brazil, Thailand and Korea.[10]

The British Council has never escaped the ills which, during the whole of its career, have afflicted Britain; indeed it might be said to have had more than its fair share. Constantly asked to change course in response to the different ideologies of different Governments, and inevitably a victim of the cycle best described as Stop-Go, it has sometimes been forced to cut projects so recently entered upon that, not merely has no return either material or psychological been earned, but actual damage to its prestige has resulted. Neither has it ever been immune from criticism. So many Governmental inquiries have been conducted upon it that it is a cliché among the initiates to complain that it cannot thrive 'while so constantly pulled up by the roots to see how it is getting on'. The analogy is not completely apt, and, if the comparison with a plant is to be used, it would be truer to say that it thrives less well for being constantly pruned and re-trained. The Reports of all these inquiries will be dealt with in the appropriate place and only one need be mentioned here, that of the Central Policy Review Staff (the Think-Tank) in 1977, which also takes its name from its Chairman, Sir Kenneth Berrill. (This review was not of the British Council alone, but of Overseas Representation.)

The body of the Report makes difficult reading because it is written in that lingo, unfortunately affected by many people other than economists, which seems to be the result of a belief that if words such as 'of' and 'on' are eschewed altogether, and strings of nouns used as adjectives, an economical prose will result. There is great fondness for phrases such as 'co-located', 'Sectoral [sic] expertise', 'non-developmental educational co-operation' and so on; and also for such umbrella expressions as 'cultural manifestations' – which a close reading suggests means exhibitions of the creative and performing arts, but which to the uninitiated might be intended to cover anything from the English language to bricklaying in Sri Lanka. A substitute for thought, this hideous jargon is also a recipe for sending the reader to sleep.

Nevertheless, however obscure the body of the Report, there is no doubt about the meaning of the conclusions. The authors put forward two options and express the opinion that there is much to be said for the former. This is, in effect, that the British Council (and other small agencies) should be abolished altogether, and the work done by it be spread among new and existing agencies. The second is that it should be retained in a much reduced form, undertaking chiefly educational recruitment, while its overseas representation is incorporated into diplomatic posts; and that its educational and cultural staff, overseas and in London, should be considerably reduced.[11]

The object of referring to the Berrill Report here is not to refute its conclusions, because this was forcibly and conclusively done when it appeared, by both Houses of Parliament and the British press, where it was almost unanimously rejected and often derided, and also by innumerable foreigners and heads of foreign institutions who wrote to explain the harm that would be done in their countries if these recommendations were carried out.

There are, however, two other reasons for mentioning it. The first is that, taken by themselves and out of the context of the ensuing debate, these recommendations remain as a stick always ready for the use of the old enemies of culture. The second, and more important, is that, during the whole of the research and writing of this book, they have continually served as a point of reference for the author as well as a mild source of amusement; and this advantage has seemed worth sharing with the reader.

For the small Committee conceived fifty years ago remains autonomous, but has become one of the arms of our diplomacy. In most countries it operates at different levels of society from the Diplomatic Service, and in modern conditions is none the worse for that. In common with other bodies of its size, complexity and importance, it can never escape some criticism, and we are right to complain where it falls below the standard of excellence visualised by its founders. Nevertheless, the British Council is one of the great institutions of this country, and its history is a part of ours.

PART ONE

1934-53

I

The Case for Cultural Relations

More than one writer has attempted to explain why the British took
so long to accept the necessity for some institution to undertake cultural
propaganda, even if it were to be regarded only as an essential presence
on a scene otherwise totally occupied by others. Thus Harold Nicolson
attributes our failure in the nineteenth century to an arrogant reticence
based on the training to regard all forms of self-display as obnoxious.
'If foreigners failed to appreciate, or even to notice, our gifts of inven-
tion or our splendid adaptability, then there was nothing that we could
do to mitigate their obtuseness. The genius of England, unlike that of
lesser countries, spoke for itself.'[1] In the same article he wrote:

> It might have been supposed that the first months of the South
> African War, when we woke up to find ourselves encompassed by
> sudden jealousy and malice, would have disturbed this flattering
> dream. Having momentarily been roused from our slumber by a
> sudden nightmare, we turned round upon our pillows and relapsed
> once again into the somnolence of the *Superbia Brittanorum*.[2]

In 1935 in an article in the *Contemporary Review*, R. A. Leeper
expressed himself on the same subject in the following way:

> We ourselves read with interest the books that others write about
> us, and note with equal condescension their errors of fact or judg-
> ment or the shrewdness of their criticism; only rarely are we annoyed
> by either. We are perhaps dimly aware that our habits of thought
> and action are often extremely irritating to foreigners, but our
> equanimity is hardly ruffled when they show their irritation, and for
> that very reason we make little effort to correct its cause. For example,
> the criticisms of our foreign policy which appear in the newspapers
> of other countries are seldom answered in our own, no matter how
> malicious or misinformed we may consider them. As for taking

positive steps to explain our aims and achievements, that we regard as undignified and unnecessary. Good wine, we optimistically feel, needs no bush.

The average Englishman, even though he may not admit it openly, is at heart rather proud of this attitude. He persuades himself that it springs from some superior quality peculiar to Britain, from a spirit of detachment which the circumstances of our history have developed more maturely here than elsewhere. He would be incredulous or even mildly shocked were he told that this attitude was due, at least in part, to mental indolence and lack of imagination, and only if he were fully convinced that it was materially damaging his interests would he take steps to correct it.[3]

It is relatively hard to recognise ourselves today in the passages from these two writers, but they probably give a true picture of the attitudes prevailing at the time. However, the failure after the First World War to attempt any kind of cultural propaganda to other countries was more the result of conscious decisions than would appear from these quotations.

There were two contributory causes, the first of which is touched upon by Leeper in his last sentence. The British would not, and in the event did not, embark on any programme of this sort until they were convinced that it was materially damaging to their interests not to do so. Their scepticism about the value of spreading such intangibles as language, literature, the arts and civilised values was almost as complete as the French belief in it, while the national tendency to philistinism was stronger in the period between the two wars than at any other time. The education of the upper class males was among the best, if not the best, in the world, although the philosophy of the public schools was still dominated by an excessive emphasis on the physical, mental, even spiritual value of sport. English females, including those of the upper classes, were often barely educated at all, while the state education of the bulk of the population was probably the worst of any civilised country. Alone among leading European nations, England had no national theatre or state opera company, gave no state subsidy to the arts, while Shakespeare was seldom performed in the capital city of his own country for fear of emptying the theatre. The British did not reach for a revolver at the mention of the word culture, but they turned off the radio and shut their books. Then, as always, they got the Treasury they deserved.

The second reason was less obvious. It was the British themselves who, in the First World War, established for general use the most sinister of several meanings for the word propaganda. As one writer on the subject of war-time dissemination of news has put it:

> Information was not only restricted, it was also structured. Much of what reached the public was distorted and exaggerated for propagandist ends, through the activities of newspaper proprietors and editors. They often subordinated their responsibility of providing accurate information to other obligations which were to do with carrying out their patriotic duty; the duty to persuade men to fight, to keep up morale, to inspire patriotism and continually to degrade the enemy.[4]

Early in 1918 newspaper proprietors gained an even more direct control of war-time propaganda. A new Ministry of Information was set up under Lord Beaverbrook to deal with propaganda to allied and neutral countries, and Lord Northcliffe was appointed Director of Propaganda to Enemy Countries (an appointment made, according to A. J. P. Taylor, for the purpose of keeping the Northcliffe papers on Lloyd George's side).[5] British propaganda was extremely efficient and not always false. Lord Beaverbrook was the first to use photography and the cinema and the first to commission leading artists to paint scenes of war. Nevertheless, it was often conducted with a ruthless disregard for the truth. In later years it would be much admired by Hitler who praised British and American propaganda for picturing the Germans only as barbarians and Huns, thus preparing their soldiers for the horrors of war and safeguarding them against illusions; and he wrote that the English understood in a marvellous way that in propaganda there should be no half measures between love and hate, right and wrong, since these give rise only to doubt. He was to base on these ideas his own propaganda of the big lie, consistently told.

The British themselves, and particularly the Americans, looked back on their war-time propaganda with extreme distaste. As late as 1929 we find Angus Fletcher, head of the British Library of Information in New York, writing to Sir Arthur Willert, head of the News Department of the Foreign Office, to protest against the use of the word 'propaganda' in official documents: ' ... it never fails to disturb me because over here it has now only the debased meaning of a sinister activity. It is a good word gone wrong – debauched by the late Lord

Northcliffe.'[6] In a debate in the House of Commons Harold Nicolson said, 'During the war we lied damnably,' and, when interrupted, repeated, 'No, damnably, not splendidly. I think some of our lies have done us tremendous harm and I should not myself like to see such propaganda again.'[7]

It is hardly surprising, therefore, that for many years anything which smacked even faintly of organised publicity should be regarded in official circles with extreme wariness.

At the end of the war both Lord Beaverbrook and Lord Northcliffe wished to continue the work of propaganda at least until the peace treaty was signed, but the opposition to it was already too great and at the end of 1918 the war-time ministries were closed down and such of their work as it was considered necessary to continue returned to the Foreign Office. In order to avoid the use of the word propaganda, the Department created to deal with it was named the News Department and this was put under the direction of Sir William Tyrrell, later Ambassador to Paris. The work of the Department was to receive, collect and dispose of all information from abroad, and to issue information both in this country and outside it. The head of the Department would be responsible for dealing with the press and would 'superintend and control the Establishment abroad and would advise as to the countries to be dealt with, the nature of the work to be done, and the personnel to whom it should be entrusted.'[8] It was to receive a budget of £100,000 a year, a reduction of 95 per cent on the budget previously allowed the two propaganda Ministries. To the News Department was joined the Political Intelligence Department, although this was shut down in 1920.

The work of the new Department was to be strictly limited. A memorandum from the Treasury to the Secretary of State for Foreign Affairs stated:

> My Lords recognise that it is not at the present moment practicable to terminate altogether the system of propaganda and the expenditure which it involves. On the other hand, the case is admittedly one in which it is necessary to move tentatively and experimentally: and My Lords trust that the Secretary of State will keep the question under close observation and will discontinue any particular type of propaganda so soon as experience shews that it is not productive of valuable results ... They understand that his primary object is to correct misapprehensions as to the policy and actions of His Majesty's

Government and to supply accurate information either to the
Foreign Press or to well-wishers of this country abroad: and They
admit that there is much to be said for the publication of explanations
of this kind. On the other hand, They would point out that there is
some danger that this object may imperceptibly be transformed into
a general desire to spread British culture throughout the world: and
They do not think it would be possible to defend in Parliament or in
its Committees expenditure on such a purpose – to which it would
not be easy to assign definite limits.[9]

Not everyone was entirely satisfied with a complete withdrawal
from the cultural scene, however, and in 1919 the then Foreign
Secretary, Lord Curzon, appointed a Committee to consider by what
means His Majesty's Government might (1) foster a greater spirit of
solidarity among British communities abroad, and (2) make British
ideals more generally known and appreciated by foreign nations. This
Committee sat under the Chairmanship of Sir John Tilley and reported
in 1920.[10]

The Tilley Report is interesting today. ts terms of reference include
matters which are outside the scope of this book, but it is surprising to
find so many of its recommendations, although well-known to students
in the field of cultural relations, stated so definitely and so cogently as
early as this. It urges a policy for schools for British and foreign children
abroad, and suggests that at least in South America, China, Egypt and
Constantinople a *prima facie* case already exists for sending experts to
report on the possibilities and probable costs of establishing them. It
alludes, as every writer on the subject always would, to the Alliance
Française and suggests some British equivalent, proposes Institutes in
foreign countries where lectures on English literature, history and art
might be given and where libraries and reading rooms would contain,
not merely books, but leading English periodicals and newspapers, and
it asks for facilities for the reception and education of foreign students
at British universities and technical schools. In short, the Tilley Report
was a blue-print for the British Council.

After the Treasury had rejected it, the Foreign Secretary, Lord
Curzon, sent it with a covering memorandum to the Cabinet, since
he said he believed it was a matter for the Cabinet to decide whether the
report should be shelved 'or a more generous policy adopted'. The
Cabinet took the same view as the Treasury and nothing was heard
officially of these matters for more than ten years.

The necessity for some kind of self-advertisement was nevertheless so apparent that it gave rise in the latter half of the 1920s and early 1930s to several private initiatives. The Travel Association was formed in December 1928 under the chairmanship of Lord Derby, with the primary object of capturing some of the ever-increasing tourist trade. But it had the secondary objective of promoting our export trade through a knowledge of Britain, British culture and British goods. 'The visitor who comes over here reads our newspapers, shares our recreations, talks with our people and makes friends with many of whom he keeps in touch afterwards ... Such a person recognises the common interests of nations ... In fact, he becomes an ambassador of this country.'[11]

A second body of some importance was the All People's Association, an international institution, drawing funds from and doing publicity for its member nations.

During the whole of this period evidence grew of the damage done to British interests by the increasingly hostile propaganda of other countries as well as of the size of the budget devoted elsewhere to cultural propaganda. In 1929 the Foreign Office estimated that the French Government was devoting to it the equivalent of £500,000, the Germans £300,000 and the Italians only slightly less.[12] The British contribution to any similar programme was nil. Philip Taylor,[13] however, believes that the Treasury were first persuaded to accept the need for some form of cultural propaganda by two other events of 1929.

The first of these was the entry into the News Department of the Foreign Office of a young Australian named Reginald (Rex) Leeper. The speedy establishment of the British Council as a national institution is generally believed to be the result of the energy, drive and extraordinary persistence of Lord Lloyd. But, if Lloyd must be given credit for the early development of the small committee of 1934 into a body with adequate finance and widespread functions, Leeper was its architect.

Born in 1888 in Sydney, Australia, he was the son of Alexander Leeper, a distinguished classical scholar and Warden of Trinity College, Melbourne. As a young man, he went with a scholarship to New College, Oxford. In the First World War he returned to England from India but, because he had had dysentery, was unfit for war service. He was an excellent linguist and, because of his knowledge of Russian, his brother Allen, already here, was able to get him a job in the Intelligence Division of the Department of Information. A year later he was transferred to the Foreign Office Department of Political Intelligence and in 1920 appointed permanently to the Diplomatic Service of the Foreign Office. In 1929, as we have already seen, he was transferred to the News Department and in 1935 became its head. The following description was written by Kenneth Johnstone, who worked with him almost from the beginning and knew him well.

> It is one of the Council's uncounted blessings that its birth took place at a time when Government regarded cultural work only as a potentially useful sideline. It is another that its first Foreign Office sponsor was the least empire-building of officials, content to sift and choose the leaders for his enterprise, to listen to their ideas and, having approved, to press their policies and their modest financial requests. He knew to a hairsbreadth what would get through. Although himself gentle, reserved and unemotional in manner, he was able to attract and enlist men of much fiercer character. They appreciated his shrewd political judgement, his tactical skill, his frankness, friendliness and humour and above all his absolute steadfastness of principle and his quiet but unyielding defence of what he saw as the general interest ... Looking back, it is astonishing to find that the years during which he was directly concerned with the Council, though all-important in its history, were in fact so few – from the germination of the original idea in 1934 until 1939 ... But in those five years he had seen the Council firmly set in the shape which has ever since distinguished it. Its close connection with Government but non-official character, its interest in English teaching, its display of British cultural achievement abroad, its students and visitors programmes, all owed something to his initial selection.[14]

To this account should be added that Leeper was a friend and adherent of his chief, Sir Robert (later Lord) Vansittart, Head of the Foreign Office, who in the public mind stood as the champion of all those who opposed the Government policy of appeasement.

Yet, if in the long term Leeper's transfer to the News Department was the single most important event of 1929, Philip Taylor is right in saying that more significant at the time were the recommendations of the D'Abernon trade mission to South America.[15]

The D'Abernon Report makes gloomy reading today. In an introductory chapter it is explained that, although in the last half-century Great Britain had become involved in the economic fortunes of the

South American Republics through the investment of millions of sterling in railways, land and waterworks, and, in consequence, had earned a position of exceptional favour, almost no advantage had been taken of this. In old established businesses we had retained our position, but in new undertakings and particularly in aviation, road construction and motor transport we had been completely outdistanced by others. The reasons for this were given as lack of investment, lack of adventurousness, and 'a persistent adherence to what Great Britain thinks good, to the exclusion of what South America wants'.[16] This part of the Report might have been written yesterday.

Equally melancholy and more immediately relevant is the final chapter of the Report, entitled 'The Commercial Importance of Cultural Influence'. The authors remark that it cannot be said 'that we have sufficiently understood the direct relation between culture and trade', and they devote considerable space to the cultural influences of France, America, Germany and Italy. Referring to the Argentine Association of English Culture, formed in 1928 to take and encourage steps which would spread knowledge of the English language and culture, they say that it has had considerable success but that the tuition fee is too small to pay the teachers' salaries and that the permanent income from membership fees and subscriptions from British firms is 'nothing like enough'.

> For want of funds the Association has not yet organised any lectures or invited official lecturers from the universities of this country. It is unhappily true that, owing to want of interest and support on our part, British education does not yet enjoy very high favour in Argentina. The Universities send to France, Germany, Italy and Spain for professors: never to Great Britain.[17]

In a later passage, having said that 'we have not been sufficiently active in the exercise of British cultural influence', they go on to ask for the co-operation of British brains in agricultural science and the prevention of tropical disease, for more books, more frequent visits by theatrical companies and for the display of more and better British films.

> To those who say that this extension in influence has no connection with commerce, we reply that they are totally wrong; the reaction of trade to the more deliberate inculcation of British culture which we advocate is definitely certain and will be swift.[18]

1 Sir Reginald Leeper

2 Lord Tyrrell of Avon, Chairman, 1934–6

3 Lord Eustace Percy (later Lord Percy of Newcastle), Chairman, 1936–7

4 Lord Lloyd of Dolobran, Chairman, 1937–41

5 Sir Malcolm Robertson, Chairman, 1941–5

6 General Sir Ronald Adam, Bt, Chairman, 1946–55

8 Lord Bridges of Headley, Chairman, 1959–67

7 Sir David Kelly, Chairman, 1955–9

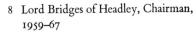

The Report states that, although it has for long been the custom for young South Americans to be educated in British schools and universities, the numbers coming to England are steadily decreasing, because 'many South American families are today sending their sons to other countries', and they suggest that this whole question should be studied by the Board of Education and others with a view to attracting South American youths to Great Britain. 'To make this country a training ground for the foreign student cannot but be of advantage to our export trade.'[19]

Finally they ask for better facilities for tourists and for an improved news service.

The views expressed in the D'Abernon Report received endorsement by the Prince of Wales when he returned from a visit to South America in 1931. He had been much struck by the failing influence and lack of initiative of the British. Even more important, warnings of the aggressive spirit of the propaganda of other countries could no longer be completely ignored. In December 1930 the Treasury reversed a long-term policy and informed the Foreign Office that an annual grant of £2,500 would be made for British cultural activities.

On 19 February 1931 Rex Leeper wrote to his father:

We have taken over a new sphere of activity – known, for want of a better name, as 'cultural propaganda'. We have got from the Treasury a considerable sum of money to spend on it and it is keeping me pretty busy. It consists largely of promoting the knowledge of British art and literature etc. abroad and of finding lecturers on various English subjects to deliver lectures in different capitals.[20]

On 26 March 1931, he wrote:

We have just secured Masefield to lecture on English poetry both at Angora and at Athens. We told him that at the former place the standard of intelligence would not be high, while at the latter it would be. He will vary his lecture accordingly.[21]

Unfortunately, but true to a pattern endemic in this country and particularly in the world of culture and the arts, this small beginning was soon cut back, and in September we find him writing:

At the beginning of this financial year we had at last succeeded in obtaining a sum of money from the Treasury ... and it is therefore very disappointing that the whole work has now had to be suspended only a few months after we had begun ... The FO like all Government departments is economising as much as possible. We have sacrificed the whole of our funds for cultural propaganda and salaries and allowances have been cut ... [22]

By then, however, £722 17s. 5d. of the £2,500 annual grant had already been spent, and in a Foreign Office memorandum the following remarkable account of the return for this money is given.

A series of Talks had been prepared by eminent writers on various subjects, and arrangements made with certain countries – notably Belgium, Denmark, France, Portugal, the United States of America and Yugoslavia – for these talks to be broadcast through their local stations, and in addition an English programme had been prepared for the Bucharest Broadcasting Station. Gifts of books had been made to various libraries and educational and other institutions in Austria, Bulgaria, Chile, China, Denmark, Egypt, Ethiopia, France, Germany, Greece, Italy, Latvia, Mexico, Holland, Norway, Persia, Peru, Poland, Portugal, San Domingo, Siam, Spain, Sweden, Syria, Turkey and Yugoslavia. Reports received from these various centres invariably indicated that the gifts had been much appreciated, and it was confidently believed that this was an effective and inexpensive form of cultural propaganda. A lecture tour in Bulgaria was arranged for Professor J. L. Brierly, Chichele Professor of International Law at the University of Oxford. In addition there were other miscellaneous activities which had been found to be desirable and which it was believed furthered British cultural aims abroad.[23]

In the following May the Treasury restored the small grant and Leeper wrote to his father: 'I am now in correspondence with our Embassies and Legations to get the thing going. This work interests me particularly, as it is so constructive and I think I can claim the credit for the whole initiative.'[24]

The Committee on the Education and Training of Students from Overseas was formed in 1933, and its Chairman, Sir Eugene Ramsden, visited Denmark, Sweden, Finland and Norway. In his report afterwards, he began by saying that he had been assured that, apart from the psychological influences of a foreign education, 'the personal contacts formed, and the familiarity with the products which is established during courses of practical training had often caused business men to turn to the countries in which they had received their training for supplies of machinery etc.'. He then referred to the influence gained by other countries, and in particular Germany, through a policy of encouragement to students, and went on to say that students were deterred from coming here by the fees charged in the United Kingdom and the general cost of living, by lack of information as to what we were prepared to offer, by lack of knowledge of any of our universities except Oxford, Cambridge and London (our provincial universities had hardly been heard of), by the difficulty of finding firms to take trainees, and finally by the drastic restrictions imposed by the British authorities on foreign students wishing to become trainees in industry or commerce. In paragraph 10 he quotes the Director of the Commercial College of Stockholm:

> The Director told us that the college has four travelling scholarships of about 3,000 Kroner each to enable students to go abroad for 1½ years to obtain practical commercial training, but that during the last 15 years it had not been possible to arrange for one of these students to carry out his or her training in Great Britain.[25]

This Report was to have far-reaching effects.

By now requests for some promotion of British culture, the establishment of British schools, greater facilities for students to visit England, for books and periodicals, for English teaching, for lecturers and films, for aid for local societies, were coming from all over the world. Of the following examples, the first, from the High Commissioner to Egypt, Sir Percy Loraine, is one of the most important and the most famous papers in the history of cultural relations.

Sir Percy remarked in an introductory passage that, although he would confine himself to a discussion of conditions in Egypt, the story he had to tell was the same in other parts of the Near East, in Arab countries and in Persia, and he went on to a short account of the history of France in the Near and Middle East, in which he said that it should be borne in mind that the 'Gesta Dei per Francos' was the mediaeval, knightly equivalent of the irritatingly complacent refrain of the modern French bourgeois: 'La Mission civilisatrice de la France en Orient.' He then said:

The failure of England to make use of the forty years from 1882 to 1922 to create for herself a strong cultural position in Egypt is one of the most extraordinary phenomena of our illogical Imperial story ... The net result is that the declaration of Egyptian Independence in 1922 found France still predominant in the cultural field.[26]

In the second half of this memorandum, Loraine outlined a policy for the future, which included the development and maintenance of British schools, both for the education of the British and to increase the number of Egyptian and other oriental boys and girls educated in British institutions. (In an earlier paragraph he had stated that for every Egyptian receiving an English education in 1930-1, nine were receiving a French, while between 1927-8 and 1930-1 the number at British schools diminished by 10 per cent and at American by 2 per cent, while those at French schools increased by 10 per cent and those at Italian schools by 20 per cent.) He remarked that the absence of a British university in the Near East is 'one of the more remarkable lacunae in our Eastern history'. (There was a French university at Beirut and there were American universities in Beirut and Cairo. Governments under our aegis, such as those of the Sudan and Iraq, had to send pupils to the American University at Beirut since there was no British university within easy reach.)

He asked for a British Library of Information with a central establishment at Cairo and later with branches in other capitals of the Near East, cultural features to be added; for films of current events to be shown on the screens of Egyptian cinemas; for an extension of the Boy Scout movement, although he remarked that this would have to be made considerably more attractive and reorganised on the lines of the Italian Balilla (a Fascist 'Boy Scout' organisation); for English lecturers to balance the continual stream of French *conferenciers* passing through Egypt; for the encouragement of Egyptian students in the United Kingdom ('At present it is difficult to get an Egyptian into an English University. I of course realise there are difficulties in this respect owing to the overcrowding of universities. However, France makes no such difficulties and every Egyptian student is welcomed there.'); and finally he suggested an unofficial board, to deal with all these matters, with representatives of the Treasury, Foreign Office and Board of Education on it.[27]

Almost equally persuasive was a memorandum from C. G. Hardie of the British School in Rome in which, after making some of the same points, he wrote:

> The resources of the British [architectural] schools in Rome and Athens are not sufficient for their efficient internal working and ... other nations much less rich than Britain and the Empire and not only among the 'Great Powers' but even such as Roumania and Hungary, have estimated much more generously the needs of their institutes. They have seen that to spend not enough is to waste it on the means without attaining the ends.[28]

And in a later paragraph,

> I have so far discussed the British schools in Rome and Athens from the point of view of their internal efficiency as a part of the English system of university education. But it would be a mistake even from my limited point of view to ignore another aspect of them, their relation to their environment, their representation of Britain and the British Empire in the eyes of the Italians and the Greeks and of the sister foreign institutes. The Italians and the Greeks regard the foreign Institutes in their capitals not only as a compliment to themselves, but as an index of the importance of the nation which maintains them, as a kind of national propaganda, not in any bad sense of the word which we now tend to associate with Germany and Italy.[29]

Of all the interventions of the time, however, probably the most appealing was that of a young Englishman named George West. He was a lecturer in English at King's College, London. In 1933 it was suggested to him that he should seek experience at some other university and, unable because of the depression to find work in an English university (there were 710 applications for posts at Manchester alone in that year), in 1934 he accepted a post as lecturer in English at Coimbra University in Portugal with the personal motive of perfecting his knowledge of the Portuguese language.

At Coimbra he found three Institutes for the promotion of French, German and Italian culture and a Spanish Room. No attempt had been made by the British or the Americans to support the University, although an appeal had been made to the USA. It was not possible for any Portuguese student to take a degree solely in English, but in English and German only. The curriculum was such that the first three years of a four year course were devoted to both languages but the fourth year, in which the student worked on a dissertation which would enable him to receive his licentiate, the English language was dropped and only the German taught. Worse still, the so-called 'English' Room, cold and cheerless and in the basement, was permanently locked. George West managed to get it open and discovered a catalogue of 250 English books, of which more than half were missing.

He found that the students were genuinely anxious to learn English and, because of the ancient alliance between Britain and Portugal, had a natural sympathy for Britain and the British. 'But there were no books, no periodicals, no music ... in fact no promotion of British culture to be seen anywhere.'[30] West, on his own initiative and without an appointment, travelled by train to Lisbon and succeeded in seeing Sir Claud Russell, the British Ambassador. In ten minutes he rapidly outlined the situation, pointing out the disservice done to Britain by the failure to compare with other nations in the promotion of their culture at the University of Coimbra from where, he pointed out, the leading citizens of Portugal came to occupy positions of distinction, many of them in the Government.

Sir Claud Russell listened to him in silence and when West stopped talking he still said nothing. For the first time uncertain and rather embarrassed, the young man repeated some of what he had just said. This time the Ambassador spoke. 'Do you find it rather cold in Coimbra, Mr West?' he asked, and for the rest of his life Professor West pondered the meaning of this question. But Russell nevertheless sent him immediately to the British Consul, Henry King, who asked him for a written report.

This report formed the basis of a memorandum which King sent to the British Ambassador, to the Foreign Office, to representatives of British firms with interests in Portugal, to the British Chamber of Commerce in London and to the Chancellors of the Universities of Reading, Leeds, Manchester, Cambridge, Birmingham, Sheffield, Bristol, Edinburgh, Aberdeen, St Andrews, Glasgow and Belfast. To the Universities of London, Oxford and Liverpool it was suggested that, in view of their own Portuguese Departments, some sort of association with Coimbra might be effected.

Within a few days forty copies of West's memorandum had arrived at the Foreign Office, all from different sources. The pressure for some institution to undertake cultural relations was becoming irresistible.

Concurrently with these events there was also much activity in

London. From a memorandum dated 18 June 1934 and signed R. A. Leeper, we learn that the Foreign Office had taken the initiative in suggesting that an unofficial Cultural Relations Committee should be set up.

> The members of the committee will be assisted by liaison officers from the Foreign Office, the Board of Education and the Department of Overseas Trade. Their functions will be twofold: (1) to collect money from private individuals and from industry; (2) to decide on the policy governing the distribution of the money they obtain. They will also decide to what private organisations the money will be allotted for carrying out any particular work that they may recommend.[31]

The memorandum continues by saying that while no hard and fast rule can be laid down about the societies through which 'our propaganda is conducted', full support will naturally be given to institutions teaching English, such as the British Institutes in Paris and Florence, and the similar bodies in South America. It then goes on to argue at some length for close contact with the All People's Association (APA), an organisation with branches in fourteen European countries but with headquarters in London.

> In each country where it is established there is a National Council whose function is to promote direct cultural relations with other countries. The British National Council, for example, with which alone we are directly concerned, conducts British cultural propaganda with other countries on a basis of reciprocity, sending out British speakers abroad and bringing foreigners here both to lecture and to meet people of similar interests in this country. It also establishes English libraries abroad, and in the near future it intends to inaugurate a scheme of prizes and scholarships for proficiency in English. The fact that the whole organisation is on an international basis in no way impedes the purely national activities of each National Council, and the very fact that its basis is wide should in the long run render its activities more effective.[32]

Leeper therefore argued for and in fact secured very close co-operation with the All People's Association and, when at the end of June the Committee of International Understanding and Co-operation came into being, its Chairman was Sir Evelyn Wrench, also Chairman of the APA. Very little is known of this Committee, so clearly a forerunner of the British Council, except that its life was short. Nor would it be of much interest today but for the light its history throws on the character and actions of Rex Leeper, which were to prove of such importance to the later body.

Leeper once told his wife that when he first went to the Foreign Office anything remotely connected with culture was marked 'Bring up in six months' and shelved.[33] For many years he struggled to promote the idea of international cultural relations and he was always determined that these should be kept clear of short-term commercial ambitions. In the article already quoted, Kenneth Johnstone says of him: 'It was part of Leeper's persuasive genius to combine within a single organisation bodies like Sir Eugene (later Lord) Ramsden's Students Committee and Philip Guedalla's Ibero-American Committee, which led independent lives under highly individual chieftains.'[34] Such evidence as remains suggests that this remark, true as far as it goes, does less than justice to the ruthlessness with which Leeper rid himself of persons or organisations which seemed to threaten his own policy. During the five-year period of which Johnstone speaks, he kept complete, if not always open, control of the direction of policy and withstood all efforts to convert it to the immediate interests of commerce and industry. Without him the British Council might easily have foundered in its early days because, as he was well aware, it could never satisfy expectations of speedy material returns.

If not much is known of the earlier Committee, such details as remain tend to add to the confusion. What is certain is that, in the belief that he had full Foreign Office support, Wrench not merely went to considerable expense in taking a house in Arlington Street to accommodate staff extra to the needs of the All People's Association, but also agreed to provide some of them. In a letter to W. E. Rootes, a member of the Committee, C. M. Pickthall, of the Department of Overseas Trade, said:

There is just one further point that you ought to have in mind. If this Committee is accepted, Wrench will provide clerical staff and the services of Colonel Bridge, his right hand man, free of cost for the first year, and that means that we get all the secretarial use of APA, plus accommodation for our meetings, without paying for it for the first year. Wrench has suggested that in return for this, when we get going, we should make some contribution to be agreed on later, towards the overheads of APA, and to contribute towards the establishment of one or two APA branches abroad in countries where the Foreign Office wish to see them formed.[35]

The minutes of the second meeting of the Committee also confirm that Sir Evelyn Wrench offered the services of Lieut.-Colonel Bridge, Secretary-General of the All People's Association, to act as Hon. Secretary to the new Committee, a detail of some interest since Colonel Bridge was later to become the first Secretary-General of the British Council. Philip Taylor, following an account written a year later by L. A. de L. Meredith of the Travel Association, suggests that Wrench, on Leeper's recommendation, appointed Bridge to help his staff at the time he took the house in Arlington Street, which in view of the above is clearly incorrect. Leeper might have recommended Bridge to Wrench earlier because the two were old friends, Bridge having been Military Attaché in Warsaw when Leeper was First Secretary and Cultural Attaché; and Taylor may therefore be correct in surmising that Leeper saw in his appointment a 'means of checking Wrench's growing preference for industrial and private support over that of the Foreign Office'.[36] Lady Leeper, however, believes that Leeper found Wrench too vague and inefficient for the tasks he had in view.[37]

Whatever the truth of all this, within a few months, the life of the Committee was brought to an end by what must surely be one of the briefest and least conciliatory letters of its kind ever written:

Dear Evelyn

Vansittart [Permanent Under-Secretary to the Foreign Office] has asked me to write and tell you that he has reconsidered the problems which led to the formation of a Cultural Relations Committee last July.

Since the idea was first put forward difficulties have arisen with other societies and he has therefore decided to dissolve the Committee and to start afresh on different lines in consultation with other departments concerned.

He has asked me to thank you for your willingness to serve on the former Committee.

Yours sincerely
R. A. Leeper.[38]

This letter was written on 5 November 1934. On 14 November Leeper informed the Foreign Secretary of the formation of an as yet unnamed committee under the chairmanship of Lord Tyrrell, and on 5 December there took place its first meeting at which it was agreed that it should be called 'The British Committee for Relations with Other Countries'.

2

Early Days

The inaugural meeting of the British Council took place on 2 July 1935 at St James's Palace, HRH The Prince of Wales having agreed to become Patron. Lord Tyrrell (lately Ambassador to Paris and formerly Head of the News Department in the Foreign Office) had been appointed Chairman with executive powers, and Lord Riverdale Vice-Chairman. The list of the members of the Governing Board strikes one, as it would continue to do throughout the history of the British Council, by the distinction of the names included in it. (See Appendices 1 and 2.) The only members of the original board whose names need concern the reader were Lord Lloyd, Dr John Masefield, Philip Guedalla, Sir Eugene Ramsden (later Lord Ramsden), W. E. Rootes (later Lord Rootes), Mr (later Sir) Stanley Unwin, R. A. Leeper for the Foreign Office and C. M. Pickthall for the Department of Overseas Trade. Lieut.-Colonel Charles Bridge had been appointed Clerk to the Council, later termed Secretary-General.

Lord Tyrrell opened the proceedings at St James's Palace with an account of the work of the past seven months. He said:

> We have been encouraged in our undertaking by a small grant from the Treasury of £6,000, by the active collaboration of six other Government Departments besides the Foreign Office [the Colonial Office, the Dominions Office, the Board of Education, the Department of Overseas Trade, the Scottish Education Department and the Board of Trade], and by generous donations from Viscount Wakefield of Hythe, Sir Herbert Grotrian and Mr William Graham — while one or two leading industrial firms and publishers have already given practical effect to their sympathy in the form of contributions, and the Book and Music Publishers' Associations have lent us valuable moral and material support.[1]

He then went on to say that with the small funds at their disposal the

Council had been able to do little more than lay the foundations of their future work, although a party of Swedish landowners and gardening experts had been brought to this country, as well as teachers of English and students, including technical students, from Norway, Sweden, Finland and Denmark. Steps were being taken to encourage a further flow of students from overseas for general and technical education by scholarships and fellowships and by making better known the facilities provided for them in our universities.

> The importance of assisting the growing use of the English language in Poland and in the Baltic States is receiving our attention, while in Portugal, aided by the generous response to a local appeal to British firms trading to that country, English departments in the two leading Portuguese Universities are in process of formation, to which the Council hopes to lend its active support.* The same may be said of the British Institutes in Florence, Paris and Buenos Aires, which will form the models for those Institutes which the Council desire to be instrumental in establishing throughout the world ... [2]

He wound up by saying that the Council looked forward to fruitful collaboration with other bodies with similar aims and by thanking the Prince of Wales 'for the appreciation you have shown of the national importance of our work by agreeing to become our Patron'.

In reply the Prince said that of all the Great Powers this country was the last in the field in setting up a proper organisation to spread knowledge and appreciation of its language, literature and art, science and education and he gave a by now well-known analysis of the probable reasons for this. He said that the basis of our work must be the English language, and referred to our lack of appreciation of the importance of an educational philosophy. He continued:

> Before I finish I should like to say a word or two about two other organisations with which I am connected, and whose objects to a considerable degree coincide with those of the Council. The first is the Travel Association, which has been doing excellent work and

---

* According to Professor George West, £2,000 had been received from the recipients of the memorandum sent out by himself and the Consul General in Lisbon, Henry King, and in addition promises of gifts, books, periodicals and equipment had been received.

with which I feel we should co-operate most carefully in the department which it covers. The second is the Ibero-American Institute, in
which I have a very special interest, since it is the direct outcome of
my last visit to South America. To my mind the work which it has
been doing exactly corresponds to that which we wish to do all over
the world, and I sincerely trust that means will be found by affiliation
or otherwise to ensure its intimate co-operation with the Council, of
which it should be something in the nature of a local offshoot.[3]

The Prince of Wales wound up by expressing thanks to those individuals and firms which had already provided funds and urged others to
do the same. Of the two other bodies to which he referred, the work of
the Travel Association has already been explained[4] and it is true that the
Ibero-American Institute, which was formed in 1932, was undoubtedly
inspired by his accounts of his visit to South America in 1931. On his
return he had set the precedent for a custom, now well established, by
which Royal Princes draw the attention of British industrialists to their
failings; he had endorsed the findings of the D'Abernon Report and
pointed out that we had done little in South America to make the
people realise that we have a culture equal to that of other European
nations. 'South Americans are attracted to pursue their studies in
engineering and technical education rather to Continental countries in
Europe.'[5]

The second of the two institutions to which he referred, the Ibero-
American Institute of Great Britain, was chiefly responsible for the
administration of the Prince of Wales scholarships, which brought
Argentinian scholars to Oxford (four were in residence by 1934), and
it undertook the interchange of lecturers between the two countries.
These lectures were primarily of a literary character, one of the most
important occasions being when Compton Mackenzie accompanied
the Director, Philip Guedalla, on a tour of Buenos Aires, Rio de
Janeiro, Sao Paulo and Montevideo. In 1934 the Ibero-American
Institute inspired the establishment of a Brazilian Society of English
Culture at Rio de Janeiro and of a Paulista Society of Cultural Relations
with England at Sao Paulo.* It remained autonomous in 1935 and

---

* The South American terms are apt to confuse an issue which in itself needs
explanation. In the British Council (as at Florence and in Paris), the word Institute
is used to denote that teaching is done on the premises. There are a number of
Council headquarters and offices abroad which have large libraries and a hall for
lectures and so on, and from which extramural teaching is organised, but these are

continued to administer the Prince of Wales scholarships, but all other activities, such as financial grants to the Anglophile societies, the supply of books and periodicals to these and to schools and universities, were funded and administered by the Council itself. The main interest of the Ibero-American Institute here is that its Director, Philip Guedalla, ' "doubled in brass" as simultaneously Director of the Institute and Chairman of the Ibero-American Committee of the British Council'.[6] In 1938, the Institute ceased to exist, the Council taking over its work, and in 1945, after the death of Guedalla in 1944, the Ibero-American Committee was also wound up.

The air of authority and confidence with which the inaugural meeting was conducted was not at the time warranted by the facts. The Treasury grant for the year 1935–6 was £5,000, and at its first meeting the Council gave thanks to Mr W. E. Rootes, who had guaranteed up to £5,000 — this in a year when, according to one estimate, the French, German and Italian Governments were each spending something like £5 million sterling on cultural propaganda.[7] However, the principle had been firmly laid down that success would depend on quality not quantity (there was, in fact, evidence that the lavish expenditure of the other leading European nations was to some extent counter-productive, since it was easily recognised as propaganda and as such resented), while there was still a belief that the leaders of industry would expect sufficient benefits from the work of the new committee to contribute significantly to it. This hope was dashed by Counsel's opinion, given on 8 July 1935, that 'subscriptions made by traders to the company could not be deducted in the computation of their profits as liable to income-tax; such expenditure could not be properly regarded as expenditure wholly and exclusively incurred for the purpose of earning the profits. Any hope of encouraging subscriptions on this ground should be abandoned'.[8] Meanwhile, the Government had increased the grant to the Council in 1935–6 to £15,000, while Lord Eustace Percy (who had succeeded Lord Tyrrell as Chairman in May 1936) on his own retirement in July 1937 was able to report a further increase from £15,000 to £30,000, with a supplementary estimate to Parliament of a further

---

not called Institutes. In Lisbon the British Council and the British Institute occupy different buildings but both belong to the Council: in Paris the British Council and the British Institute occupy the same building but they are not part of the same organisation. The Ibero-American Institute was merely a small administrative organisation based in London, while on the other hand the activities of the South American Societies (*Culturas*) did (and do) include teaching.

£30,000 which would provide a total grant-in-aid of £60,000.

Consequently, the years before the war were not wasted. The report for the first nine months' work (2 July 1935 to 15 March 1936) stated that permanent premises at 32 Chesham Place, Belgrave Square had been presented to the Council by its Honorary Treasurer, Sir John Power, and showed the Council primarily concerned with setting up an administrative structure and with proposals for its future work. A small Executive Committee had been set up in March 1935 and in November of that year the Finance and Agenda Committee was established to take urgent decisions and to prepare agenda for the Executive Committee, thus enabling representative and distinguished people, who could not give full time, to serve.

The most urgent task of the first years was the setting up of specialist committees. These were to become a permanent feature of the structure of the British Council, although today these have a purely advisory function whereas in 1935, in the absence of money and staff, they acted as working committees. In addition to the Ibero-American Committee, already mentioned, the first year saw the formation of the Education Committee, the Students Committee, the Fine Arts Committee, the Lectures Committee and the Books and Periodicals Committee. (See Appendix 4.)

The Education Committee, which had a sub-committee under Lord Lloyd to deal with the special problems of the Near East, was the most important. Its task was to consider the means of increasing the facilities for teaching English in foreign schools and universities. The Report stated that 'assistance is being given to British schools abroad and Foreign-British Societies are being helped to develop the English classes which most of them organise. Particular attention is being given to the work of the British Institutes in Paris, Florence, Buenos Aires, Rio de Janeiro, Sao Paulo and Montevideo, and the foundation of similar institutes elsewhere is under consideration.'[9]

In a memorandum sent out as a guide to Foreign Office Missions, Rex Leeper had earlier proposed that support should be given to Foreign-British Societies 'which should be encouraged to stand on their own feet and not be entirely dependent on official assistance':

It will no doubt be found that many of these societies, whether they be purely local or branches of a bigger organisation, are but feeble bodies with the wrong people in charge and little independent initiative. Even so, they should not be condemned or neglected, but every effort should be made to assist them, and reports on what is required for them should be furnished to the Foreign Office. The growth of such societies is likely to be slow, and it is important to foster them gradually.[10]

Of the British Institutes already existing overseas, perhaps the most important is the one in Florence, not merely because it was an early and a long-term recipient of British Council grants, but also because it is often regarded as the model for all later Institutes. The large British colony in and around Florence had for some years cherished a wish to establish an Institute on the lines of the French Institute there, founded as early as 1908; and in 1917, with support from the Ministry of Information, this plan was realised by a group of Italian and English scholars, prominent among the latter being Mr and Mrs George Trevelyan, Mrs Aubrey Waterfield, William Hulton, Edward Hutton and Herbert Trench. To Lina Waterfield (born Duff Gordon) more than to anyone else the credit for the foundation is given. Its first director was A. F. Spender, the uncle of Stephen Spender.

The aims of the Institute were to promote intellectual relations between the two countries and it had and still has advantages not given to any of the later Institutes. Splendidly housed, for many years in the sixteenth-century Palazzo Antinori and later by the generosity of its Vice-Chairman, Sir Harold Acton, in the Palazzo Lanfredini, it soon acquired, through the discernment and the generosity of its patrons, a library which was recognised as by far the most important for the study of English literature and history in Italy, as well as a large and valuable art library. In 1923 it received a Royal Charter. After the war and the demise of the Ministry of Information, it relied for its funds almost entirely on its earnings and on the generosity of private patrons.

Its most important function was the teaching of English to students of all kinds – to those who wanted merely a knowledge of English for business purposes, to others who wished to take English literature for their university studies, and to still others who wished to acquire a teacher's diploma. Since the object of the Institute was to promote an interchange between the two countries of language, literature, art history and philosophy, classes were also held in Italian for English-speaking people whenever these could be formed. Bursaries were given and scholarships to Italian students wishing to visit Britain, while the Institute ran a Summer School as a refresher-course for teachers of English from all parts of Italy. From the very beginning the demand for

English teaching proved great, although the numbers at the Institute went down as the teachers it had trained began to teach.

The Florence Institute was always short of funds and in order to raise money it allowed the use of the library and reading rooms to the local British colony on the payment of subscriptions. This practice is also sometimes adopted by the British Council, but it is rare for British expatriates to be so thick on the ground or so deeply dependent on the Institute for intellectual pursuits. According to both public and private statements of its directors and staff (past and present), there has tended in Florence to be some division of interest between the British members and the Italians, and a tendency among the former to regard the Institute in the light of a club run for their benefit. The British Council may never have achieved quite the academic distinction of the British Institute at Florence, but they have avoided its slightly dilettante air.

In 1935 the Institute in Florence was enabled to keep going in spite of the Abyssinian war and the application of sanctions by the countries of the League of Nations, only because of the pro-Fascist sympathies of its director, Harold Goad. Nevertheless it was an obvious and immediate object for the support of the British Council. The Council began with a grant of £200 paid annually and in 1937 increased this considerably, subscribing to a pension fund for teachers, to an increase in their salaries and for an assistant to the director. According to figures given by Ian Greenlees, its fourth director, the grant from the British Council was raised to £1,050 a year in 1937, and to about £1,500 a year, in 1939. In 1945 the grant was renewed but 'varied in concertina fashion from £1,000 to £7,000'.[11] In 1977 it was commuted for a final once-for-all grant of £12,000.

In 1930, Harold Goad, unable to interest the Board of Governors of the Florence Institute, started at his own expense a small branch of the Institute in Milan and in 1938 another in Rome. After the war these were absorbed by the British Council, who run them today.

There were also at that time Institutes in Paris (this has remained independent), in Buenos Aires, in Rio de Janeiro and in Montevideo, and the survival of the British Council is before anything else bound up with the formation of teaching institutes all over the world. For, from first to last, in all the fifty years of its existence, it has been proved again and again that, under-valued and under-nourished, sometimes encouraged but as often cut, compelled by changing circumstances and the vagaries of different Governments constantly to alter course, it has nevertheless always possessed one golden egg — the English language.

The Books and Periodicals Committee took over from the Foreign
Office the distribution of English literature of all kinds to Foreign-British
societies, foreign universities and schools. Its aims were to build up
general libraries of English books (by July 1937 presentations had been
made to 97 institutions in 37 countries), to supply British scientific and
technological books to specialist libraries (20 presentations in 11 countries), to increase the circulation of British periodicals (2,800 general,
learned, specialist and technical periodicals to 663 institutions in 51
countries) and to supply bibliographical information. One long-lived
and interesting innovation of these years was the Overseas Book Review
Scheme which lasted until 1982 and through which English books
were sent to foreign periodicals for reviewing. The intervention of the
British Council between the publishers and the foreign critics inspired
confidence in the selection of books sent and an encouragement to
consider them for review.

The Books and Periodicals Committee was chaired from 1936 by
Stanley Unwin, who was at that time Vice-President of the Publishers
Association and came on to the Executive Committee of the Council
as its nominee. The Publishers Association had agreed earlier that the
British Council should be entitled to buy books at trade prices provided
they procured them direct from the publishers, a decision of great and
obvious importance. Stanley Unwin also initiated the publication of a
number of pamphlets on special subjects in a series called *British Life and
Thought*, which could be bound together in a single volume for
libraries.[12] Here in his own words is an account of how he organised
this:

> It was decided that [the pamphlets] should be produced ... under
> my supervision and that half a dozen leading publishers should be
> invited to tender for the work of distribution on a commission basis;
> that is to say, that the copies would be printed with the selected
> publisher's imprint: that they would sell all they could to the book-
> sellers and hand over the proceeds to the Council less a commission.
> It is seldom that such a commission adequately covers the publisher's
> overhead, let alone shows a profit, so that it was not surprising that
> one or two of those approached refused to tender. Messrs Longman
> were appointed and they have been the Council's most efficient
> publishers ever since.[13]

In 1936 the Council issued a handbook called *Higher Education in the*

United Kingdom which gave information on such matters as the requirements for admission to a university, at which universities particular
schools could be found, fees and the cost of living, details of technical
and commercial institutions, special courses for overseas students and
vacation courses, and also on hostels and social life. Immediately 4,500
copies were distributed and the handbook, now in its eighteenth
revised edition, has been kept in print for fifty years.

The Joint Films Committee of the British Council and the Travel
Association was less successful because of a complete dearth of suitable
films. H. P. Croom-Johnson, an early member of the British Council
staff, wrote to Colonel Bridge:

> I feel that the Committee is apt to underestimate the mentality of
> foreign film audiences. Guedalla remarked that 'We are trying to
> place ourselves in the position of a low-class Maltese tobacconist'.
> Admittedly this was flippantly meant, and the Committee are right
> in remembering that to many film audiences abroad the sound com-
> mentary will be incomprehensible and must largely be disregarded.
> Against this, however, should be remembered the verdict of the
> Finno-British Society which roundly condemned as very poor two
> films sent them recently by the Travel Association. By 'playing
> down' to film audiences we shall not gain the interest of the un-
> intelligent (who don't matter to us any way) and shall lose the
> sympathy and interest of the intelligent anglophil students and the
> moderately intelligent newspaper readers at whom we should
> presumably aim.[14]

An attempt to co-ordinate with the BBC (by a Joint Committee of
the Travel and Industrial Development Association and the BBC)
failed for a different reason. Neither the Foreign Office nor the British
Council seemed at this date to have any conception of the national
importance and great future of the BBC. Thus Leeper once suggested
to Vansittart that, in view of the fact that both bodies were engaged in
cultural propaganda, the British Council should receive a small proportion of the BBC's grant.[15] And in fact in 1935 Sir Robert Vansittart
warned the BBC to 'avoid talks put on by the BBC having the appearance of being directed expressly "at" the United States'.[16]

Two other Committees did important work at the time. The Music
Committee under the chairmanship of Ernest Makower sent Myra
Hess to Norway, Denmark and Sweden, Thelma Reiss and John Hunt

to Lithuania, Finland, Poland, Latvia and Estonia, and Keith Faulkner and Cyril Smith to Czechoslovakia, Hungary and Yugoslavia. Fifteen sets of gramophone records were issued to broadcasting companies which arranged concerts in many countries. In addition, this committee brought a group of European music critics on a visit to London where, if the number of musical events was probably fewer than in any other European capital city, the quality of what they heard was nevertheless high. This included concerts by the London Symphony Orchestra under Landon Ronald, the BBC Symphony Orchestra under Adrian Boult and the Royal Philharmonic under Hamilton Harty, all at the Queen's Hall. They saw a performance of the Sadler's Wells Ballet at which the orchestra was conducted by Constant Lambert, they travelled to Oxford to hear the New College Choir under the organist and choirmaster Sydney Watson, and attended a People's Concert at the London Museum where the soloists were Edwin Fischer (pianist) and Emanuel Feuermann (cellist). Most of these performances owed much to the generosity and enthusiasm of private persons and the People's Concerts, at which a nominal admission of 6d. was charged, were paid for entirely by Mr and Mrs Ernest Makower.

The Lectures Committee was chaired by the Poet Laureate, Dr John Masefield, and in its first two years lecturers were sent to almost every country in Europe. Those lecturing in the first year included Philip Guedalla, R. F. Harrod and Rebecca West, and in the second, Robert Byron, Kenneth Clark, Stephen Gaselee, Bruce Lockhart, Lionel Robbins, Josiah Stamp, William Teeling and the Rt Hon. W. Wedgwood Benn. There is in the files of the British Council a twenty-six page letter from Rebecca West to Colonel Bridge, describing the tour she made in Austria, Yugoslavia and Greece. This has the double interest of describing the difficulties of travelling for the British Council in the days when all arrangements were made from London and it had no Representatives abroad, and of suggesting that the experiences she had then, although in many ways so rigorous, remained in her mind and exerted sufficient strength to inspire a second tour, resulting in *Black Lamb and Grey Falcon*.

She begins by saying that she had assumed the journeys would be undertaken in reasonably comfortable trains, that she would get enough sleep and that the lectures she had arranged would be suitable for the audiences, 'and I am sure the Council made the same assumptions'.[17] But in Vienna, where she began, she said there was a plethora of lectures, and she thought cultural propaganda should be handled by

universities and learned societies 'by the lending of distinguished lecturers to give series of lectures', because the isolated lecture by a person
of less than international standard did not do much to help Anglo-
Austrian relations. Next she went to Ljubljana, which she wrote was
the only properly planned part of the entire tour, but where three
circumstances made it of doubtful value to send English lecturers. These
were that the population understood very little English, had read no
English books apart from 'some battered relics in the Club library',
had read few books in its own language and had no general idea of
literature. 'One cannot get up on a platform and in fifty minutes break
the news of what literature is to an uninstructed public.'

After Ljubljana the arrangements deteriorated so much that she spent
hours on uncomfortable trains, many of which might have been
avoided if her journeys had been properly planned, getting little rest
and not enough sleep to be able to do her best, while there were often
no proper arrangements for her lectures.

I found [she wrote] that the Legation people in Belgrade believed
Dr Popovic to be a competent person, but I most emphatically dis-
sented. I could not rest the next day after I got back from Athens,
because he had made a number of futile appointments without consulting me, and said 'it would be awkward' to cancel them ... There
were other annoyances too trivial to relate, but distinctly trying to
the nerves. If I had been fit I could have dealt with this half-wit in
my stride; as it was I cannot conceal from myself the fact that I
allowed these things to submerge me and did not give as good a
lecture as I would have wished ...

I think you will agree with me that the tour I have described was
not ideal. It seems to me to have been badly planned from every
point of view. Granted that I had to visit the places I did visit —
Ljubljana, Zagreb, Split, Dubrovnik, Sarajevo, Sofia, Nish and
Athens — the obvious order in which I should have visited them if
I was not to fall dead in my tracks was, Ljubljana, Zagreb, Sarajevo,
Belgrade, Nish, Sofia, Athens, and then by boat, Dubrovnik and
Split. But it was not really worth your while to send me to Split or
Dubrovnik, since there is no lecture public there, nor to Athens since
there are enough lecturers there already. The only places I really
needed to go to were Zagreb, Sarajevo, Belgrade and Sofia; and
since it is on the way I could have stopped at Nish, and could have
travelled a further few hours to Skopje, where there is a struggling

University, and as yet very little English influence. Then you would have saved the railway fare in Greece and the Hotel there, and at Split, and at Dubrovnik; and with a small part of that money I could have spent an extra day or two in each of the places I visited, which would have enabled me both to do my work and to keep fit for it.[18]

The moral, Rebecca West wrote, was that you cannot organise a Yugoslav tour from London. But she also said this:

I found everywhere that there was a substantial residue left of the pro-English feeling that began in the war; and since the French influence is so rapidly fading there is an appetite for culture and liberalism which will be unsatisfied unless we take steps to fill it. It is a field worth cultivating.[19]

Of the original Committees, only the Music and Fine Arts remain today; the others have changed in name or in function. They have proved a great source of strength to the Council since they have always contained men who were the leading authorities on their subject and who were able, not only to give expert advice, but also to secure backing from the Council from outside. Theoretically only advisory, they have often been responsible for initiating new ideas.

Lord Tyrrell, the first Chairman of the British Council, was succeeded in 1936 by Lord Eustace Percy (later Lord Percy of Newcastle, and first Rector of King's College, Newcastle). Lord Eustace had been Minister for Education in 1924 and Minister without Portfolio in the National Government in 1935. He remained only for fifteen months and, because his period in office was short and his personality overshadowed by that of his immediate successor, his contribution to the Council is sometimes underestimated. He has to be given some of the credit for the speedy setting up of the advisory Committees and he achieved very important benefits for some categories of teachers. Because French, German and Italian teachers were part of a state system, the British were at a great disadvantage in recruiting teachers for overseas since, unlike their foreign colleagues, these had no assurance of pensions, promotion or even a job on their return. They went on short-term contracts, entirely at their own risk. Lord Eustace set up an Advisory Committee respresenting Government Departments, local education authorities and associations of teachers and schools. As a result, teachers serving in recognised schools abroad were able to continue in a contributory service (i.e. rank for pension), while their foreign service would count towards an increase of salary. Even more important, local education authorities and the Headmasters' Conference undertook to find employment for them on their return. Teachers not in recognised schools went at their own risk.[20]

Behind the scenes, the evidence suggests that there was a continuing struggle for power. The line-up seems to have been Rex Leeper and Colonel Bridge for the Foreign Office against on the one hand Meredith of the Travel Association and on the other W. E. Rootes, Philip Guedalla, Arthur Mullins (who had succeeded Pickthall at the Department of Overseas Trade) and possibly others. As early as 14 March 1935, Leeper had written to Vansittart:

> I am far from satisfied with the way the British Council is developing. The Treasury has given us £5,000 which is far too little for our purpose; for the rest of the money we require we are at present relying upon industrial firms. On account of that the Board of Trade and the D.O.T. [Department of Overseas Trade] have urged us to increase our industrial representation on the Council with the result that half the members are industrialists. The D.O.T., backed by the industrialists, have seconded one of their own men to the Council with the title of Industrial Commissioner. This preponderance of the industrial element in work which is essentially cultural is not at all what I like, but I have not been able to oppose it so long as we have to rely on industrial firms for the major part of our funds. A D.O.T. man is to do the canvassing and I very much fear that if Industry supplies the money, it will also want to call the tune.
>
> For my own part I have very little faith in the vision or imagination of our industrialists. They will be influenced mainly by the desire for commercial rather than political results and I am convinced that our aim should be political rather than commercial and that the Foreign Office should have the major say in the policy of the Council. I foresee, however, that the Foreign Office will not be able to assert itself fully unless we are able to find the main portion of the funds, i.e. unless we can find a few private individuals to endow the Council on an adequate scale as Mr Lionel Curtis has succeeded in endowing Chatham House for work which is very much less important to this country as a whole ...
>
> The main difference between the Foreign Office view and that of

the industrialists is this. The latter wish to concentrate on those countries with which they hope to increase their export trade, while we are concerned with increasing British influence in those countries which are important to us politically. In my view the part of the world which matters most to us for the next few years is Europe and the Near East. If we could strengthen our influence very considerably in these countries with adequate sums at our disposal we could use our cultural work as a very definite political instrument. This work should go hand in hand with our foreign policy and quite definitely the Foreign Office should be the advisers to the Council.[21]

Then on 18 July 1935 he wrote to Bridge:

You and I started this thing together and you and I have really done the whole job. I have done the touting outside and the lubricating inside while you have been steadily building up the whole structure from within ... I believe that this is going to grow into something really big, and you and I are going to have the chief say in it ... [22]

On 11 April 1936 we find him writing again to Bridge:

I tried to get away with too much at the last meeting of the B.C. and I quite see why they resisted. But I don't think it was altogether a failure, as I have made them tackle the question of strengthening the staff seriously at last. So long as the staff remains inadequate, the close supervision and interference of the Committee is justified. That will be relaxed and mitigated as the staff develops in such a way as to take things more into its hands. You and I therefore must now concentrate on the question of staff and we should do so quickly. Let us work out some scheme, even if it can't be realised at once in its entirety, for dividing the work of the staff. I would suggest something like this:

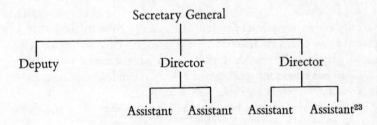

This design is not unlike the present organisation of the senior staff of the British Council, if one substitutes Director-General (with executive powers) for the Secretary General. Rex Leeper then defined the duties of these officials, particularly those of the Deputy Secretary, and continued:

> He would then deal direct with members of the Council instead of this being left to the junior assistants as hitherto. People like Guedalla will not be able to bully an older man of some standing as they can Adie and Croom-Johnson.[24]

And he ended his letter by saying 'last week's meeting showed me that reform of the Council will have to be tackled from below and not from above'.

Leeper's attempt to keep matters entirely in his own and Colonel Bridge's hands did not go unremarked, and there was immediate opposition. The first to take offence was Meredith of the Travel Association. Writing to his Chairman, Lord Derby, he complained of a lack of consultation, of Colonel Bridge's behaviour to him, and of duplication 'of our own special activities, including film work, photographs for reproduction etc' and he said: 'We have tried to work with them, but whether of ineptitude or malice prepense, I think a bit of both, on their part, we found it difficult to do so ... '[25] Meredith went on to say that Philip Guedalla was also exceedingly angry and complained that Bridge and Leeper had sent circular instructions to Embassies and Legations in the countries with which he was specially concerned without informing him. Guedalla had insisted on being put on the Executive Committee of the Council and advised Meredith to do the same.

These difficulties were solved, at least temporarily, by a seat on the Executive Committee being given, not to Meredith, but to Lord Derby. However, there were also signs of insurrection on the Executive Committee itself. The letters between its members are written so much in terms of 'our mutual friend' that it is not possible to be sure of the whole of their meaning today. Thus: 'You will naturally understand that it was impossible for me to bring the matter up to you at the Committee meeting for reasons which you were good enough to appreciate.'[26] There seems to be little doubt, however, that, although the relations with Leeper remained cordial, they were gunning for Colonel Bridge. K. R. Johnstone, who worked for Bridge, has left the following description of him:

> In addition to the energy and exactitude of a first-rate staff officer,
> the courtesy and knowledge of the world expected of a Military
> Attaché and the dash and choler proper to an Irish Cavalryman, he
> possessed in a high degree what a French writer has called 'that in-
> definable mixture of devilry and charm which is the Celtic spirit'.
> In an enterprise which might so easily have lost itself in vagueness or
> foundered in a welter of bright ideas and conflicting pressures, he
> insisted on order and on action. It was he who, among other things,
> first established the Council's budget on its twofold basis of countries
> and subjects and on a basis of territorial priorities. These distinctions
> may seem obvious enough now, because we have grown accustomed
> to them; they were a good deal less self-evident then.[27]

Nevertheless even his best friends admit that Colonel Bridge was a
difficult man and one with a very hot temper.

On 13 November 1936 W. E. Rootes wrote to Lord Riverdale:

> This meeting is being called for the express purpose of engaging
> additional personnel in connection with appeals, and we have been
> asked to submit names. The suggestion we are now discussing is, of
> course, an entirely different proposition in so far as it brings in a
> number one. Therefore arrangements will have to be made for
> Colonel Bridge to leave the meeting, otherwise he will sit fast
> throughout.[28]

Earlier (13 October 1936) Philip Guedalla had written to Rootes with
a refreshing lack of guile: 'The more I think about it, the more convinced I am that the British Council has got the right job and the wrong
people.'[29]

This correspondence ceases in May 1937 with a letter from Guedalla
to Rootes in which he says:

> At the Finance and Agenda Committee this morning Percy spoke to
> us privately of his own intention of leaving the Council at some
> future date and of the nomination of a successor by the Foreign
> Office. This, it seems to me, is the moment for the practical men to
> find some means of indicating to Van [Vansittart] or elsewhere their
> views as to a working successor.[30]

We know, however, that Colonel Bridge remained in position and that the British Council was never sufficiently well supported by industrialists for there to be any alternative to the Foreign Office grant and therefore its control. We may also guess that the views of Rootes and Guedalla became progressively less important because the successor to Eustace Percy was Lord Lloyd.

3

Lord Lloyd

When Rex Leeper heard that Eustace Percy intended to resign the chairmanship of the British Council, he drove down to Chartwell to ask Winston Churchill to take his place. Churchill, who replied that he thought he might be wanted for other things, suggested Lord Lloyd. Lloyd is remembered as the man who, by his energy and resource and by his contacts with men of power, achieved permanent recognition for the role of cultural propaganda in the foreign policy of the country, and strengthened and stabilised the administration of the British Council in London, while extending, widening and giving real purpose to its activities overseas. Fifty years have passed and the name of Rex Leeper is known only to the few who still remember the earliest years of the British Council, but that of Lord Lloyd has legendary significance.

George Lloyd was a member of the Quaker family which founded Lloyd's, Lloyd's Bank, Stewart & Lloyd's Iron and Steel works and the Lloyd-Triestino shipping line. He had had a conventional upper class education at Eton and Trinity, Cambridge. At Eton he coxed the Eight and became a member of the very exclusive Eton Society (Pop), his classical tutor being Mr Donaldson.* At Cambridge he also coxed the University boat to victory in 1899 and 1900.

He might have been expected to take one of the many openings available in his own family's businesses and in fact he did begin his working life in Lloyd & Lloyd, steel tube makers, but in 1905, for reasons his biographer is unable to explain, he left the business world and entered public service, first travelling as King's Messenger to Constantinople and then becoming honorary attaché at the British Embassy there. He had plenty of money and privately as well as professionally he travelled extensively in India, Turkey and the Middle East, not merely on well-known routes but in the native caravanserais and on uncharted territory. In 1907 he was appointed Special Commissioner to inquire

---

* The father-in-law of the author, a point of almost no interest to anyone else.

into the possibilities for British trade in Turkey, Mesopotamia and the Persian Gulf. As a result, when he rose to leading positions, first as Governor of Bombay and then as High Commissioner to Egypt, his authority was unusually well-informed. He was a Conservative Member of Parliament from 1910 to 1918 and again from 1924 to 1925, his term being cut short both times – by the First World War and by his appointment to Egypt. He received a knighthood in 1918, and was created 1st Baron Lloyd of Dolobran in 1925.

In character and temperament he was the product of a generation whose emotional attachments and moral outlook are now so much outgrown as to be barely comprehensible. His biographer speaks of 'the well-informed, yet romantic imperial patriotism that was fashionable at the time' and tells us that, after hearing Joseph Chamberlain at Birmingham, Lloyd became an immediate and passionate convert to the cause of Tariff Reform. 'The imperial flavour of the plan made a vivid appeal to his imagination ... From that moment his faith in Tariff Reform never wavered, and substantial reinforcement was given to the influences drawing him towards the public service of the Empire.'[1]

Lloyd has been described as 'an Imperialist of the Curzon type'[2] and there is no doubt that he shared with Curzon a belief in 'that noble work which I firmly believe has been placed by the inscrutable decrees of Providence upon the shoulder of the British race'.[3] He was completely courageous and he had that heroic patriotism which, like imperialism, was one of the casualties of the Great War. Writing of him in 1914, a friend said: 'He has lost all sense of proportion in his burning desire to get somewhere where he can expose himself to physical danger. At the moment he would much rather be a Tommy in the trenches than Generalissimo in Cairo. He wants to be shot at ... '[4]

He fought in Egypt, Turkey, Arabia and Palestine. He helped defend the Suez Canal against the Turks and he saw fighting on the beaches at Gallipoli. He was one of a band who helped T. E. Lawrence organise the Arab armies and he often rode alone with Lawrence on raids on the enemy outposts. He was mentioned six times in despatches and awarded the DSO.

In appearance he was small and dapper and, in daily life, bowler-hatted. In some of his photographs he looks like a caricature of an age that by 1935 was already gone. But James Lees-Milne, who was devoted to him, speaks of his 'tight resilient build', and his 'fidgetty charm', and he tells us that Lord Fitzalan said of him that 'he never knew a greater patriot or more honourable man', and Lady Milner 'he was the only person in the world she respected so much that she would have gone to him from wherever she happened to be, at a whistle'.[5] He was very religious and, in spite of his antecedents, an Anglo-Catholic, but his most noticeable characteristics were his prodigious energy combined with the compulsive need to overwork which was thought by many people to have been responsible for his early death. James Lees-Milne writes:

> Without doubt the tragedy of Lloyd's career to my mind was his hallucination that he was everlastingly pursued by the furious Erinyes in retribution for opportunities lost, and hours misspent on false anagogical trials, an hallucination that the shears of Atropos were hot on his heel and that the faster he ran from them, the further they would keep their distance. Moreover I fear he never quite made up his mind what the Grail was for which he so passionately yearned — self-fulfilment? imperial glory? the betterment of mankind? union with God? — and which, distracted by countless conflicting, psychic will-o'-the wisps, he surely did not ultimately attain. If only he could have slackened the lunatic flight and chase, the exhaustion of which prematurely killed him.[6]

Lloyd overworked his staff as he did himself but he ensured their devotion by the strength of his personality and charm and by a direct-ness and friendliness of manner which sprang from a large nature and an unforced belief in the spiritual equality of his subordinates. K. R. Johnstone said of him: 'As a leader, perhaps, his greatest gift was his ability to enter sympathetically into projects which lay beyond his personal tastes or experience and to give a free hand in their execution.'[7] And A. J. S. White, who, like Johnstone, worked for him said:

> As for the staff, we existed to carry out what he had decided to do. This was not as simple as it sounds for he was not easy to work under. He had very unorthodox principles of administering. His great idea was: get on with the job and clear up the mess afterwards. When he wanted something done he tended to send for the person who would actually send the telegram and leave it to him to inform the seniors who had been side-tracked.[8]

White also said that Lloyd knew exactly 'when to bully and when to cajole'[9] and certainly he had no difficulty in endearing himself to his staff. 'Good-bye,' he said once to George West, who was leaving for Portugal. 'Drive a wedge between the Germans and the Italians and I want every German out of there by Christmas.'[10]

Lloyd was very talented. The prose of few public men survives the gradual loss of interest in the events that they record, but the two volumes of Lloyd's *Egypt after Cromer* remain immensely readable, not merely for the strong (if arguable) material content but for the suppleness, vigour and wit of the style. His friend, T. E. Lawrence, who seems to have disagreed with some of his opinions, wrote to him:

If only you didn't keep yourself so neat always. The book is too judicial, too sober, too good. (At this juncture let me remind you of the eleven hats — for the Court, for the Play, for the walk-round-the-Park, for the train, for grouse-shooting, for golf, for the House of Commons, for the pictures — which are to be counted on the marble table to the right of your hall door. They are significant.)

But he also wrote, 'You can write pages of moving, sonorous, and yet nervy prose. It is a very good book. Egypt has been fortunate in her historians.'[11]

However, the most conspicuous of all Lloyd's remarkable characteristics was that, although so much at ease with men of different race and at different levels of society, his natural habitat was among the great. 'He would fly', Harold Nicolson said, 'from capital to capital, interviewing kings, dictators and ministers ... '[12] And this was true. In or out of power, at home or abroad, he went straight to the top. His friends included Winston Churchill and Lord Halifax, and, although regarded as a reactionary Tory, he could generally secure the co-operation of the Opposition leaders, Clement Attlee and Archibald Sinclair, on non-political matters. There would have been no possibility that the British Council could have secured a leader of this quality and stature but for the fact that in 1931 Lloyd had been sacked from his post as High Commissioner to Egypt by the Labour Foreign Minister, Arthur Henderson, in a most public, humiliating and unmannerly way.

George Lloyd may not have believed, as Curzon did, that the subject Eastern races were not merely politically uneducated but ineducable, but he undoubtedly believed that their education could only be slow and must be undertaken with extreme patience and in the fullness of time.* He believed that the job of the British was to administer the countries under their control for the benefit of the masses of people, and that nationalism was usually confined to a few militant agitators who, far from bringing greater happiness to their subjects if they achieved power, would probably be responsible for bloodshed and certainly for widespread maladministration, poverty and hunger. He spoke of the 'devil of self-determination', and he wrote:

> It is hard enough in the numerous discussions that take place upon our Imperial problems to discern any voices raised on behalf of the mass who live under our Empire. When we are considering whether we should relax our rule further, the question whether the step will promote their welfare is simply not debated.[14]

Again:

> People who are attracted by the purely material appeal of a policy of 'cutting losses' can shelter themselves behind the moral value which a policy of 'self-determination' appears superficially to possess. Those who are naturally inclined to run after misty ideals find themselves strangely re-inforced by their natural enemies, the self-interested cynics.[15]

Holding these views and being at the same time a brilliant administrator, and having greater knowledge of the countries in which he served than those at home, Lloyd was often that most unpopular of men, one who was right at the wrong time. His colossal achievements in Bombay, the Back Bay development scheme, said to be the equivalent of the housing of a quarter of a million people, and the Lloyd Barrage, which turned Sind from a desert into a fertile and remunerative province, were undervalued in India because of what was sometimes regarded as his lack of sympathy with the Reformed Constitution and his failure to advance the powers of the Legislative Council fast enough.

In a review of Forbes Adam's biography, James Lees-Milne says: 'The 'twenties and 'thirties exhaled a fog of cynicism that permeated the very arteries of social and public life', and Lloyd might well have agreed with him. Yet if true at all, this was true only of a small section

---

* 'Where Curzon differed from more visionary administrators was in holding that the incapacity of the Indian for self-government was impervious to education and thus permanent.'[13]

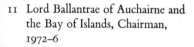

9 Lord Fulton of Falmer, Chairman, 1968–71

10 Sir Leslie Rowan, Chairman, 1971–2

11 Lord Ballantrae of Auchairne and the Bay of Islands, Chairman, 1972–6

12 Sir Charles Troughton, Chairman, 1976–84

13 Sir Paul Sinker, Director-General, 1954–68

14 Sir John Henniker, Director-General, 1968–72

15 Sir John Llewellyn, Director-General, 1972–80

16 Sir John Burgh, Director-General, 1980–

of the population who had lost power as a result of the war. The youth of this generation were often passionately idealistic but they were in search of new gods. Their cynicism lay only in a profound disbelief in the values of the past. Many of them saw Lloyd as the friend of Franco who associated himself with Winston Churchill's opposition to the India Bill.

In Egypt Lloyd actively opposed the views of the Foreign Office. He was convinced that a compromise solution to the negotiations for a new Treaty of Alliance with Egypt would fail because Mahmoud Pasha, the Premier and a moderate, had not the power to ensure its acceptance. In this situation he believed that, providing he was ultimately loyal to an agreed decision, it was his duty to express his views as straightforwardly and as forcibly as he could. The Foreign Office found him obstructive (the fact that he proved right did nothing to alter their view). In June 1929, Lloyd was astonished to receive a letter from the new Foreign Secretary which virtually forced his resignation and to hear Henderson, in answer to a question by Winston Churchill in the House of Commons, complain that he had been responsible for 'a stream of dissatisfaction of which it could be said, normally it was restless, very frequently it was turbulent, never smooth, and never clear', and ask:

> Could we contemplate going forward with the policy that eventually we hoped to submit to the House, with any degree of confidence, if this marked determination to misinterpret, or ungenerously to misapply, that characterised the views of the High Commissioner during the last few years were to continue?[16]

These charges were never substantiated but they brought a temporary end to Lloyd's administrative career. He felt less bitterly about this unexpected and public criticism than he did about the previous Foreign Secretary, his friend, Austen Chamberlain, who never at any time attempted to defend him against it. What was admirable, however, was that he lost little time bewailing and took in his stride something that might have finished the career of a lesser man. He devoted his energies to what came his way. By 1937 he had already done much good work as President of the Navy League, and in the British Council he found an outlet for his energy and talents which gave satisfaction to his romantic Imperialism without providing scope for his intolerance of radical philosophy.

It is usual to assume that once Lord Lloyd's name was suggested, Leeper accepted it enthusiastically. 'He would have Lloyd,' a diplomat who knew them both once said. This, however, is not true. Writing from the Foreign Office to Bridge at the British Council, Leeper told him that, in addition to Churchill, Eustace Percy had recommended Lloyd as his successor and continued:

> Went through all the objections — political, personal etc. He maintains that they are less important than I imagine and are becoming less so. He also says that he knows that I will find him easy. I then raised another point. I said I would only agree to his appointment after I had made it clear to him and secured his agreement that he should not remove any member of the staff or make any appointments himself. Percy said that this was essential and that he would say the same thing to him viz. that he must regard the Council so far as staff is concerned as a Govt. dept. in which the staff had security of tenure and for which the Chairman could make no personal appointments. In other words that side of it must remain under my control as F.O. representative. Percy said he would back me completely over this. The Chairman must be like a Minister who does not choose his own staff.
>
> I also talked about you. Percy didn't anticipate any difficulties between you and Lloyd. I said there would be none provided that Lloyd backed you and dismissed the idea of introducing any friend of his own ...
>
> I am writing this to you at once before even speaking to Lloyd. I do not intend to offer the job to Lloyd until I have a clear understanding from him as regards staff and his full and frank co-operation with the staff. He will have to take the Sec. Gen. completely into his confidence. There must be no repetition of what has been happening hitherto ... [17]

On 8 July Leeper wrote:

> It was only with considerable difficulty that I got the P.M.'s approval in time to talk to Lloyd. I went straight to the point. I told him that tomorrow Eustace Percy would get a letter from the Sec. of State nominating him [Lloyd] as the new Chairman. Would he take it? He demurred to 2 years and asked for 3. He said that if he gave his time and energies to the work he would like more than 2 years in

order to register results. He felt it would be hard to be pushed out just when the fruit was ripening. I agreed to the 3 years.

I then got on to the question of staff and organisation. I told him why I wanted it run more or less as a Govt. dept. with the staff having the same kind of status as Civil Servants. I said that the relation between the Chairman and the Sec. Gen. should be the same as that between a Minister and his Permanent Under Sec. He agreed and said he couldn't conceive any other relationship. I said I mentioned it particularly because Percy had shown the opposite tendency and kept many matters entirely to himself. He said he would certainly take you completely into his confidence. I then talked to him a good deal about you and some of the difficulties there had been in the beginning owing to the fact that W[illiam] T[yrrell] never stood up to the different Chairmen of Committees. He said he had no doubt that you and he could work well together. There were two main things he wanted 1) loyalty 2) hard work. Given that no real difficulties should arise. The staff might say after three months, 'This damned fellow is giving us too much to do'. In which case, I replied, they would need extra help.

I told him that he would find in you to 100% the two qualities he wanted. He would have complete loyalty from you provided he told you everything and consulted you. 'That I will certainly do. I don't mind if Bridge disagrees, but when he does I want him to say so to my face. I don't mind people saying things behind my back if they say them also to my face.' Very nice sentiments.

I told him that I felt some of the Chairmen of Committees might feel that he was only interested in the Near East and I thought it was essential for him to show at the outset that his interests would embrace all the activities of the Council. This also he promised.

I then tackled him on the question of Guedalla and the I.A. Institute. We hadn't time to go into this in detail, but I found that he had no idea there was such a pseudo-independent body. He only knew of the Ibero-American Committee of the Council. He said he thought this quite ridiculous. He asked a good many questions about the different Committees. On the subject of the Lectures Committee he agreed to take it over and then see if he could kill it and leave it to you as it was formerly.

I didn't have time to cover all the ground, but so far as we went I met with no opposition on any point ... He said quite frankly that he would have to sit down and get to know the whole work of the

Council. He assumed that it would mean being at Chesham Pl. most days and I said that I hoped very much that he would ...

One of his defects as you know is that he has too many things in his mind at the same time and he switches off to something else before the matter in hand is disposed of. He has to be brought back to it quietly but firmly. He is very flattered at being offered the job and said he hoped he wouldn't disappoint me, as he wanted to work in the closest possible touch with me.

I am to have a further talk to him in a day or two.[18]

In the meantime Lord Lloyd recorded certain other conversations. The first was between himself and the Prime Minister, Neville Chamberlain, who, he said, had given him an assurance when he accepted the invitation to become its Chairman, that he regarded the British Council as a permanent body, forming part of the country's organisation for National Defence, and, secondly, that he accepted his clearly expressed intention to demand from the Treasury annually increasing sums for the development of the Council's programme. He had then, with the Prime Minister's permission, spoken to the Chancellor of the Exchequer on the same subject and Sir John Simon had promised that his agreement with these principles should be recorded in writing at the Treasury.[19]

4

Pre-war Development, 1935-9

By the time Lord Lloyd was appointed Chairman of the British Council, the general lines both of its organisation and of the work it was expected to do had already been successfully laid down. It would be untrue to suggest that he played no personal role in the extension of this work or took less than a detailed interest in its day-to-day development. On the contrary, A. J. S. White tells us that he soon had the Executive Committee and all other organisations 'completely under his control', and there is much evidence of his personal initiatives in all departments. In addition, he not only undertook long tours of investigation into the needs and opportunities for extending British culture in the Middle East and in Europe, but he encouraged members of his staff to undertake similar tours in other countries.

Nevertheless, his major achievements were the speed with which he enlarged the whole conception of the role of the British Council, the success with which he pressed for increased grants with which to meet its objectives, the determination with which he defended it against various attempts either to diminish the area of its responsibility or even to take it over, and finally the feat of establishing it permanently as an autonomous and independent body.

If one isolates the papers recording the history of the British Council up to the outbreak of war in 1939, with their constant reiteration of the themes of quality and the need for slow growth towards a long-term objective, they give a picture of out-of-this-world innocence which suggests that the officials of the Foreign Office and the many distinguished men serving the British Council were all equally unaware that a war of unknown proportions was now almost upon them. This, however, is a question of perspective and indeed one cannot understand Lloyd's demands for money or the uses he put it to, unless one is aware that his major preoccupation was to increase British influence in areas vital to her interests in the event of war. He believed that control of the eastern end of the Mediterranean was a vital link in Imperial communications, just as he visualised the importance that Cyprus and Malta, and, at the west end, Portugal might assume. In 1936, even before becoming Chairman, he had toured these areas and had added to his already considerable knowledge of them much detail of their educational needs. He rightly understood that his first task was to secure an increase in the annual Treasury grant sufficient to meet the requests already being made on the British Council and to allow for expansion.

Even before Lloyd's appointment, Lord Eustace Percy had, in November 1935, submitted an estimate for an increased grant of about £100,000 a year in addition to capital grants of £75,000. In a letter to the Foreign Secretary, dated 8 June 1937, he said that, although this amount would not have met all the demands being made upon the Council, it would have enabled an effective appeal for public support to be launched with Government backing. He wrote: 'I am afraid that the increase of the Treasury grant from £15,000 to £30,000, though I am genuinely grateful for it, is useless for the purpose.' He added that he felt 'there is something unreal about these negotiations.'

For the truth is that the original conception of the Council's functions has been superseded by another. The Council is no longer expected merely to rescue British prestige from neglect; it has to defend that prestige from deliberate attack. The political motive has become overwhelming; the 'bread-and-butter' motive, always rather shadowy, has receded into the background. The effect of this change on the Council's position is almost ludicrous. It is supposed (to mention only one aspect of its work) to be doing at least something towards making good the ground of British influence in Egypt, in the Eastern Mediterranean and in Portugal against Fascist cultural penetration; and it has to perform these tasks with resources no more than sufficient to enable it to conduct Pleasant Sunday Afternoons for Anglophils in Gothenburg and Helsingfors. The attack it has to meet is an attack on the British Government; yet it is still expected to meet the attack mainly by appeals for private subscriptions.[1]

He argued that small Treasury grants on more or less definite estimates submitted in advance were the wrong way to finance this kind of work.

H.M. Representatives in each country have to ask themselves, not

what is necessary to establish British influence, but what they can do
with one or two thousand pounds ... If H.M. Government desire a
sound and well-balanced policy, they had much better tell the
Council that they are prepared to contemplate an eventual annual
expenditure of x hundred thousand pounds and require the Council
to submit to them a full statement of the steps by which it proposes
to work up to this maximum.[2]

In sending this memorandum on to Sir John Simon, Anthony Eden
said that he wished to give his wholehearted support to a supplementary
of £50,000 (which had not been excluded in the first place) and he
wrote that he was being urgently pressed by Ambassadors and Ministers abroad to do more and that this work had become of real political
importance. 'It is primarily a Government responsibility and experience
has shown that until the Government put their hands in their pockets
to a much larger extent than hitherto, we shall not induce private
individuals to do so.'[3]

These pleas produced a supplementary of £30,000 (not the hoped-
for £50,000), bringing the total of 1937-8 to £60,000. Experience was
to show that private individuals would in no circumstances make contributions which bore any relation to the total needs. Lord Lloyd had
secured a gift of £50,000 from a private donor but this was almost the
only sum of any consequence ever to be raised.

Although Lloyd lost no time in fulfilling his promise to press for an
increased grant, and his demands were consistently backed by the
Foreign Secretary, there was agreement that no attempt should be made
to rival the enormous sums being spent by the axis powers – one
estimate now put German annual expenditure on propaganda at the
equivalent of £5 million and Italian at £2 million[4] – or to make any
direct reply to hostile attacks. The answer, however slow, must be
merely to give an opportunity for foreign nations to learn the truth.
In a speech quoted by Colin Forbes Adam, Lloyd said:

Our cultural influence is, in fact, the effect of our personality on the
outside world ... What mosts interests the outside world, beyond
the fact of our power, is the use to which that power will be put.
The answer to that question lies deep in our national character – a
character which many, even of our friends, have misunderstood, and
our opponents have been concerned to misinterpret. All the more
reason that we should give the world free access to our civilisation,

and free opportunity to form its own judgement on our outlook and motives ... We have in many places a wary and critical audience to convert, but our opponents lack of discretion has worked largely in our favour. Everywhere we find people turning with relief from the harshly dominant notes of totalitarian propaganda to the less insistent and more reasonable cadences of Britain. We do not force them to 'think British', we offer them the opportunity of learning what the British think.[5]

And, if the concluding sentence sounds a trifle sententious to the modern ear, the complete *volte face* in the Government attitude to cultural propaganda was at least in part due to the immediate response to the small beginnings made by the British Council, which suggested that in many countries, in a situation where the German agents were instructed that all disturbances in the good relations between other States were indirectly to the advantage of Germany, and the Italians and Russians as well as the Germans were representing this country as both an effete, declining force and as a ruthless colonial power, there was genuine anxiety to escape such oppressive and one-sided propaganda and to hear from the British themselves.

Lloyd backed his requests for extra money each year with so much detailed explanation of how he proposed to use it that his annual demands assume the proportions of progress reports. In December 1937, asking for an increase in the grant for the following year (1938–9) of £50,000 – from £60,000 to £110,000 – he proposed an increased distribution of English books and periodicals which had proved 'one of the most effective and enduring of our activities', and additions to the programme of student bursaries, post-graduate scholarships and prize visits.[6] He said that a Chair of English was proposed at the University of Debrecen, 'strongly recommended by our Minister in Budapest', and a Readership of English at Sofia University, the reader to be charged with the supervision of all the Council's work in Bulgaria, and mentioned provision for the Byron Chair of English at Athens University, 'for which the funds have been privately guaranteed for 3 years'.*

In asking for an increase in the sum proposed for the Lecture

---

* The Byron Chair was established in 1937, to mark the centenary of the University of Athens. The first incumbent was H. V. Routh. It continued to be subsidised by the Council until 1963.

programme, he complained of the difficulty of persuading distinguished speakers to give up their time. 'We may be driven — very reluctantly — in the future to offering fees to Lecturers.' He asked for additions to the fine arts ('which cannot be regarded as excessive in view of the very important exhibitions in Venice and New York which the DOT has invited us to organise and the desirability of arranging exhibitions in the Northern Capitals and in the Balkans'), to the musical and visual programmes and for the entertainment of visitors from the Near East, and here he mentioned the recent successful visit of Egyptian journalists. He wanted money for the Joint Committee on Films which had been set up in collaboration with the Travel Association,★ and to send an Inspector of British Schools to the Argentine.

He explained that the proposed heavy increase in expenditure in the Near East was due 'to the urgent need for ... work in that area, which is constantly being represented to me by your Department', and he asked for an addition to the grant for the Anglo-Egyptian Union and for the Anglo-Hellenic League. 'The first is a new venture strongly recommended by the Ambassador at Cairo, and the second the mainspring of most of our activities at Athens.' The largest figures were for schools in Cairo, in Constantinople and (provisionally) at Jerusalem, and for bursaries for students from Egypt, Greece, Turkey, Iraq, Cyprus, Malta, Transjordan, Iran and Afghanistan.

Finally additions were needed for increases to the senior staff already agreed, for a superannuation scheme 'still under examination by the Government Actuary', and for a Reserve Fund to take account of changing political circumstances.

The increase to £110,000 was agreed to; the final expenditure out of Government grants for that year (1938–9) was in fact £130,500, while the total expenditure was £178,466, the balance coming from receipts from teaching, sales of publications and donations.

However, Lloyd was not content for very long, and in December 1938 he asked for a grant of £275,000 for the year 1939–40, saying that he had not forgotten his undertaking not to recommend expenditure in excess of that with which the Council could adequately deal.[7] In this letter we hear for the first time of the appointment of special Representatives overseas, Mr C. A. F. Dundas having been appointed British Council Representative in Egypt, working independently of the

★ In December 1938 Lloyd succeeded Lord Derby as Chairman of the Travel Association, thus ending friction between the two bodies.

Embassy, and Mr Egerton Sykes in Poland.* Also mentioned is a sum of 'from £28,350 to £32,000 due to Rent and Rates of new offices and increased running expenses'.†

One of the most important items in the estimates was the large increase for Institutes and Societies caused by the growing demand for knowledge of the English language.

> I would mention in this connection the very encouraging results which have attended the opening of Institutes of English Studies at Cairo, Alexandria and Lisbon, and the dramatic and indeed embarrassing success of the Institutes of English Studies in Athens and Bucarest, in which places the over-worked teaching staff whom the Council have sent out are literally unable to deal with the thousands of enthusiasts clamouring for admittance. I was myself present at the inauguration last month of the Institute in Lisbon and can testify to the impression which this made upon our Portuguese allies and the misgivings to which it gave rise among the Germans. In Malta too we have established an Institute in the ancient 'Auberge d'Aragon' ... In Bucarest it was the pressure of impatient students which forced us to open the Institute of English Studies before we were really ready and in a building scheduled for early demolition. But the Mayor of Bucarest, at King Carol's request, has now signified his intention of presenting land to the Council for a building, similar to the French and Italian, to house all our cultural organisations. In Belgrade also a scheme is well advanced for the foundation of an Institute ... [8]

He reported great successes in the bursary system; in a prize visit scheme for foreign children successful in an English essay competition; and, in particular, in securing the appointment of British professors or teachers to foreign academic institutions. 'This is an important feature of our work and provides us with a local representative to look after our interests.' There were increased demands for the fine arts and for hospitality (successful visits had been paid by parties of editors from Denmark and Sweden, architects from Argentina and doctors from

---

* George West was appointed with approximately the same duties to Portugal where an Institute had been opened in Coimbra in June 1936. A new Institute wa opened under his direction at Lisbon in November 1938 but until 1941 he was no termed Representative.

† Having to find larger quarters, the Council moved in 1938 to No. 3 Hanove Street.

Chile, the last two of whom were visiting Germany at the expense of the German Government). He said he was much concerned with the 'ill-success' attending efforts to place the production and dissemination of British prestige films and he put in an increased estimate in order to be able to effect an improvement.

His request for £275,000 for the year 1939-40 initially appeared to be successful. However, two months later, in February 1939, he was told confidentially by Rex Leeper that it was proposed to cut £54,000 off his estimates. He then appeared personally before Lord Halifax (who had succeeded Eden as Foreign Secretary when the latter resigned in 1938) and gave such a display of intransigence in his demands that he not merely secured the restoration of the proposed cut but (history would appear to show) made his friend Lord Halifax view with apprehension any repetition of such visits.

He was aware, he said, that even with the contemplated reduction the figure proposed would be £80,000 in excess of that for the current year but he wished to explain what it would mean in terms of reduced activities. He mentioned 'our new venture, *Britain Today*,★ increased appropriations for students' scholarships, principally from Iraq, Greece, Afghanistan and Siam and for books and periodicals, 'perhaps the most enduring form of all the work we undertake', and then he turned to allocations for lecturers and teaching posts.

The latter is forced upon us [he said] by the enthusiastic success we have achieved. One example will serve to illustrate what I mean. The Institute of English studies in Athens, which started less than a year ago with a few hundred pupils, is now dealing with 3,500 and has a waiting list of 1,500 students. In the last few weeks – even while our estimates have been under discussion – we have been compelled to send out four new teachers to help the four already there, who in addition to their purely academic duties have been performing those of special constables in maintaining order amongst the unruly crowd of would-be pupils, unable to find a seat in the Institute class rooms. Much the same is true of Bukarest where we have 2,000 pupils and Cairo only just started has 600, and a waiting list of 500 students.

★ *Britain Today* was a small fortnightly publication, usually containing an editorial and three articles written for the foreign reader on subjects which might be expected to interest him. There were four pages of illustrations and sixteen pages of reading matter. It was distributed on a very wide scale.

Insisting that the proposed cut would 'cripple' the drama programme, he referred to the triumphant success of the Old Vic Theatre Company in performances at Oporto, Lisbon, Milan, Rome and Naples, where not merely had the houses been packed but the enthusiasm of audiences and critics had shown beyond a doubt the value of this particular item. He wound up by saying:

I should like to remind H.M.G. of one factor. Throughout the Middle East the Germans are steadily pushing forward their economic drive. That is well known. What is not so easy to realise is that this economic drive is accompanied by a violently active cultural drive, an important feature of which is the provision of facilities for bringing students in large numbers to Germany, not only for their academic, but also for their technical and political education. If we are now not only [not] to press ahead but actually to recede from works we have undertaken of bringing these students to England – to study *our* methods, *our* economics and *our* ideals, then we must not be surprised if in six or seven years' time we wake up to find the whole of this area Nazified nationally, spiritually, economically and militarily.[9]

Then, after mentioning the impact of the German and Italian 'not to say Japanese' attempts at economic and cultural penetration of South America, he said that if the Chancellor of the Exchequer would not reconsider his decision he wished to place on record what he had already said in person the year before that 'as the work of the British Council is of a continually expanding nature, I may, in addition to increased allocations at the commencement of each financial year, find myself bound to ask in each year for a further supplementary estimate to meet any special needs as they may arise.'[10]

The cuts were restored. The grant for 1939–40 was £330,249, while the Council's general revenue from other sources was £21,110 (a figure lower than the year before, in which part of the donation of £50,000 had been received, but high in relation to previous and immediately subsequent years). In a letter to Halifax to thank him for 'backing up my plea', Lloyd said:

I believe more and more, as I immerse myself in this strange but absorbing work, that it is worth armies battleships & aeroplanes and that its effects – unlike those agencies' is both lasting and beneficial. For instance I think I could show you that for £6000 p.a. I could guarantee to get rid of hostile Italian influence in Malta & to make that fortress *permanently* British in sentiment & aim and so on, da capo.[11]

The restoration of funds was not achieved without provoking hostility. At the Treasury Edward Hale had serious doubts.

The rapid growth of expenditure on this service cannot but give rise to anxiety, since, once it is agreed that public funds should be spent on 'the promotion of a wider knowledge of Great Britain and the English language abroad and the development of closer cultural relations between Great Britain and other countries', there is practically no limit to the amount that might be spent.[12]

He also thought that as long as the British Council was controlled by people of moderation 'our propaganda may remain harmless, though expensive; but the organisation which is being built up might be a most dangerous weapon in the wrong hands'. And he remarked that the sort of control which could be exercised departmentally would not do much to check the growth of 'this horribly vigorous sapling'.

Hale's fears are a matter of history, but the British Council acquired one terrible enemy at this time whose powerful influence it has never managed to shake off.

Lord Beaverbrook was one of the few deliberately wicked men in British history. Others have done more harm but few have done it intentionally. It is well-known that Beaverbrook used his newspapers to push causes and men he cared for and to blacken those he disliked, and there is ample evidence that blanket instructions were sometimes given to his editorial staffs to lose no time in diminishing, even traducing, the latter. By this means he corrupted both those who served him and those who feared him. In 1939 it became apparent that the British Council had become a target for his relentless wrath.

Various reasons have been put forward for this. Many people believe he had a personal grudge against Lord Lloyd who might have been useful to him in his Empire Crusade, a campaign he conducted in his newspapers and on platforms. According to his biographer, Lloyd disagreed with some of Beaverbrook's policies and still more with his methods and consequently gave only lukewarm support. Beaverbrook might well therefore have attacked the Council initially as a means of getting at Lloyd, but this would not sufficiently account for the fact that he sustained the campaign at a very high level long after Lloyd's death. To explain this it is not really necessary to look for reasons outside his own temperament and character. One of his earliest biographers, Tom Driberg, who knew him long and well before he gave him mortal offence with his book, wrote as follows:

> The British Council, as is well-known, shares with the Arts Council and the British Information Services the honour of exciting in Beaverbrook and (by infection or instruction) in his newspapers the sort of blind fury which used to make Marshal Göring reach for his revolver when he heard the word 'culture'.[13]

He also wrote:

> It is by the accumulation of anecdotes that his [Beaverbrook's] character can chiefly be displayed, for one simple reason, essential to the understanding of his career and personality: he is primarily concerned not with ideas but with persons — with persons as companions or as enemies, as subjects for journalistic or political manipulation, or, empirically, for their usefulness. His habitual indifference to abstract ideas has already been mentioned; it is, indeed, not merely indifference but positive apathy. This is no doubt why such institutions as the British Council seem to him futile and wasteful: the want of critical balance in this attitude is shown in his almost complete ignoring of the Council's operations in British territories overseas, which even he might be expected to find praiseworthy.[14]

A. J. P. Taylor, having earlier in his book given an account of services to propaganda in the First World War said: 'Beaverbrook might even claim to be the remote progenitor of the British Council, an institution later held in low esteem by the Beaverbrook press.'[15]

Lord Beaverbrook began a campaign in 1939 that he would continue intermittently until the end of his life. One of the Council's most able officers speaks of its 'terrorisation' by the Beaverbrook press and says:

> This produced a quite false caricature which pursued it everywhere — a shadow of which the Council became abjectly afraid. The image was one of a bunch of effete and ineffectual amateurs, precious cultural dilettantes, who were damaging Britain's robust picture of itself abroad as tough, no-nonsense, islanders who did not dabble in

the effeminate cultural pseudo-intellectualism better left to funny
foreigners (such as the decadent French).[16]*

In matters which the public understood or on which they had strong
views, such as politics or war, Lord Beaverbrook never achieved the
power over their mind he strived for. Politicians feared and hated the
personal attack but soon learned that in a General Election the public
read the Beaverbrook press but voted as they pleased. In the field of
culture, the majority were only too ready to be convinced, while at
almost every level of intellectual attainment there were those who were
vulnerable to persuasion. In what Richard Auty has described as 'a
deeply philistine country – with, paradoxically, one of the great cul-
tures of the world',[17] even among men of considerable culture themselves, there could be found few MPs, editors, publishers or impresarios
entirely immune to these attacks.

Beaverbrook concentrated on the simplest themes, the easiest of
which was that expenditure on culture was a waste of money, and these
he rendered in his own terms. Thus:

> Which is the best propaganda for us – the roar of ... British bombers
> and fighters, or the melody of madrigals broadcast by the British
> Council?
> If we saved the money wasted by the Council, we could have three
> extra squadrons of fighters to join the display.[18]

At that time the word 'madrigal' was by itself enough to provoke
hostility in many a British breast.

A matter on which he trained his fire day after day, week after week
through the summer of 1939 was the visits of foreign newspaper editors
to Britain. The following is only one example of dozens of articles all
saying more or less the same thing.

> I have been investigating the finances of the British Council, which
> exists 'to make the life and thought of the British peoples more
> widely known abroad' and which has been given £250,000 by the
> Government to spend this year.
> They began spending in 1934. By the end of this year they will
> have spent £430,500 of taxpayers' money.

* Richard Auty is speaking of the period of the late 1940s onwards and is too young
to remember that this began and was almost equally damaging in 1939.

Six Spanish editors who have just gone home have cost £1,000.
This is how the money went.

They stayed for a fortnight at the May Fair Hotel, Berkeley Street.
They drove hundreds of miles in hired limousines. They flew to
Birmingham in specially chartered planes. They visited the Fleet at
Portsmouth, the Army at Aldershot, and the Air Force at Alton
(Hants). When I met them just before they left each sported a white
carnation. They cost a shilling each. The British Council paid. They
were drinking their favourite cocktails. The British Council paid.

They were not entertained to a farewell dinner at the May Fair.
They were entertained to a farewell dinner at Claridges, which is an
even more expensive hotel.

Ex-King Alfonso used to stay there. Cost? More than £30.[19]

The visits of foreign editors received attention from one or other of
the Beaverbrook papers again and again in the summer of 1939, sometimes in articles like the one just quoted, sometimes in shorts as, 'You
pay for cocktails and carnations on the British Council bill.'

The theme, as one might expect, was well-chosen. Ignoring the
language teaching, the eager students, the books and periodicals, lectures, music, drama and art, only the visits of the newspaper editors
received attention. And, reading these old articles today, one becomes
conscious of doubts about the value of these visits oneself. Yet in war-
time it was to become a hard fought issue between the British Council
and the Ministry of Information as to which should have the duty of
entertaining foreign journalists.

Very little attempt was made to counter this propaganda. Colonel
Bridge wrote a rather weakly sarcastic letter of inquiry as to which
editor was meant when Brendan Bracken was quoted in the *Daily
Express* as saying in the House of Commons that the British Council
has spent money on entertaining the editors of a railway guide and a
hairdressing journal; and in 1940 Lord Lloyd wrote to Lord Beaverbrook ('My dear Max') asking to see him in order to convince him of
the real value of the Council's work.[20]*

Very few Britons, as has been said, even know what the British
Council is or what it does, but among those who do and are old enough
to remember Lord Beaverbrook, even among those who would most
angrily reject the charge of being susceptible to his influence, there are

* A meeting did take place and may even have had a very temporary effect.

some who still believe it can be described in such terms as 'a bunch of third-rate poets'.*

Most serious of all has been the effect on the Council itself. Its staff is perforce recruited from the British and throughout its history it has been able to attract the services of original and talented people who have been unconcerned with this consistent, cleverly-directed attack; but the propaganda has in general had an appallingly weakening effect. Lord Beaverbrook died twenty years ago, but at the time of writing it is almost impossible to be in the company of a British Council officer of any length of service without his name coming up.

In the period immediately following that spoken of here, he, like everyone else, had other things to think of, but his name must occur again and again in the history of the British Council because, through the late 1940s and in the 1950s, he continued to pursue it with inexplicable venom.

* Writers actually employed by the Council at one time or another include John Betjeman, P. M. Hubbard, Francis King, Edwin Muir and Bernard Spencer; among those employed on contract to lecture or teach have been Edmund Blunden, D. J. Enright, John Fowles and Anthony Thwaite.

5

Struggle with the Ministry of Information

Writing to his step-mother in July 1939 about the announcement of a skeleton Ministry of Information to plan organisation in case of war, Rex Leeper said:

> I have of course been mixed up with plans for a Ministry of Information ever since its first inception in 1935 at the time of the Abyssinia War. Meanwhile as you [know] I have been doing a steadily developing [amount] of foreign publicity work. In fact practically everything that has been done has been on my initiative. I have however been limited by lack of staff and lack of funds. All this has now changed. Both staff and funds can be got. I therefore proposed to Halifax and Hoare to enlarge my department and to change its name. They agreed and I obtained 13 extra staff from the Treasury. [Illegible sentence.] But it should not be under me but under Perth [who had recently retired from the post of British Ambassador to Rome]. That was accepted by the Cabinet and announced in Parliament.
>
> To me this was a bit of a blow. Previously I had [worked?] on my own, merely [communicating] direct with Halifax when necessary. I now have a new master put over me, who had never had any experience of the work. Further it meant that my hopes of promotion in the FO seemed to be eliminated. For some weeks now I have been working with Perth. I ... find him pleasant, considerate and very hard working himself. He has been given far more authority than I ever had and I can now get done all kinds of things which before wouldn't be possible.[1]

By now Rex Leeper was beginning to slip out of this history. According to Philip M. Taylor he had been consistently outspoken in his opposition to the policy of appeasement. As long as Robert Vansittart and Anthony Eden were respectively Permanent Under-Secretary of State and Secretary of State for the Foreign Office, this was acceptable, but, when they left, it was inevitable that his views would not recommend him to the subsequent regime, although Taylor says that the precise reasons for what he calls his 'move sideways to take charge of the purely propaganda side of the News Department's work' which took place soon after, nevertheless remain vague. Taylor also says:

> In 1938, Leeper was charged with the task of reconstituting the Political Intelligence Department of the Foreign Office, and he also became involved in the preparations then under way for 'black' propaganda in wartime. It thus comes as no surprise to see him emerge in 1940 as the head of the Political Warfare Executive housed at Woburn Abbey.[2]

Rex Leeper insisted on continuing as the Foreign Secretary's representative on the British Council until after the first winter of the war when he found that his absence in the country and his new duties prevented him from giving it sufficient attention. He therefore appointed Mr Anthony Haigh to act as his understudy at the Foreign Office. In 1943 he was appointed British Ambassador to Greece, first in exile in Cairo and then in Athens, and in May 1946 he was appointed to the Argentine. He retired in 1948 and, although he continued to take an interest in the British Council (he was Vice-President, a purely honorary appointment, from 1948 until his death in 1968), he never attempted to regain any influence on it.

The history of Lord Lloyd's struggles with the wartime Ministry of Information must be told, because, without his determination not to give ground, it is unlikely that the British Council could have survived that Ministry's bid to take it over.

On 17 February 1939 a meeting took place at the Treasury which was attended by three members of the skeleton Ministry of Information, Leeper for the Foreign Office and Edward Hale for the Treasury. At this meeting it was agreed that in an emergency (the accepted synonym for war) the Council should cease to exist. The Ministry of Information would assume all its functions and responsibility for the salaries of such staff as had contractual rights until these expired, although certain measures would be taken to make it easy to resuscitate the Council after the war, assuming that to be the future policy of the Government.[3]

The only thing surprising about this meeting is that, when informed, Lord Lloyd agreed to its conclusions. However, there would be several occasions in the future when Lloyd's agreement was thought to have been achieved, only for his later opposition to be as determined as it was unexpected and for him to take his opponents by storm. Whether this initial agreement was due to a considered policy or to a momentary loss of concentration because of the innumerable subjects he always had on his mind is not certain, but the latter seems the more likely. In this case he seems originally to have been genuinely without a policy for his own or the Council's role in war. This situation did not last long, however, and in a letter to Hale of the Treasury, dated 17 October 1939, A. P. Waterfield of the Ministry of Information records the sequence of events which followed Lloyd's apparent agreement.[4]

He first consented to enter the Ministry of Information himself, to take charge of the Directorate of Foreign Publicity. Subsequently he withdrew and decided to retain his position as Chairman of the Council. From then on he pressed first that the Council should be allowed a more active and independent part in the war than had been previously contemplated, and secondly for it to be transferred from the Ministry of Information back to the Foreign Office. On this point, Waterfield remarked that he believed this proposal was not merely because Lloyd thought he could do better under the Foreign Office but because of 'the (not unreasonable) desire of the Council to clear themselves of the imputation that they are tarred with the propaganda brush of the Ministry'.[5]

In this letter Waterfield said that he feared 'We must accept as inevitable the retransfer to the Foreign Office of the responsibility for the British Council', a signal triumph for Lloyd, since it gave him freedom to conduct a running battle with the Ministry of Information about the conflicting roles of the two bodies and ensured that the Council was under the aegis of the Minister who had an interest in its survival rather than its suppression and who was also the more powerful of the two.

In the summer of 1939, the Council's Executive sought the grant of a Royal Charter. This was a tactical move, although one that had been considered as early as 1936. If once secured, the Charter would be a defence against attempts to abolish the Council against its will. The move was immediately opposed by the Treasury, Hale (always alive to the opportunities for aggrandisement which lay behind these attempts) remarking, 'I am not particularly anxious to proceed with this now, in order not to commit ourselves further than we already are to the continuance of the British Council in its present form after the war ... '6

The Foreign Office capitulated to the Treasury at this time in view of the difficulties in war, but Lloyd declared his intention to 'return to the attack', and, by persistence and, most important of all, by securing the 'warm support' of the Foreign Secretary, he was able to report to the Finance and Agenda Committee of 13 August 1940 that the Chancellor of the Exchequer had now withdrawn his objections.7* In October the British Council was granted its Royal Charter, establishing it 'as a permanent institution of the realm' and setting 'a seal upon the labours of the pioneers who have carried it from small beginnings to its present wide sphere of influence'.9

While these negotiations were going on, Lloyd was concentrating on obstructing the predatory intentions of the new Minister of Information, Sir John Reith, an opponent of equal obstinacy but one who seems at first to have underestimated the quality of the forces against him. Having lost control of the Council, Reith set about achieving agreement on the divisions of tasks into those which properly fell to it in war-time and those which were exclusively in the domain of the Ministry of Information. The obvious and agreed compromise was that the Council should continue to be responsible for work which was purely educational or cultural, while responsibility for all political propaganda went to the Ministry. The battle area lay in the no-man's-land between, since in such matters as films, lectures, hospitality, and the supply of periodicals and books, the line of demarcation between cultural and political matters proved insufficiently defined. Sir John's difficulty was much increased by the fact that in so many of the controversial areas, the Council had an existing organisation already in the field (Lloyd instructed his staff that: 'It is important ... never to admit, in our correspondence with M of I, that it is not possible to distinguish the borderline between cultural and political propaganda in wartime — that has always been their contention on which they based their attack on the Council, and we have always denied their thesis with the result that we are distinct.')10 The battle continued at all levels for several

---

* In a letter to Leigh Ashton of the Ministry of Information dated 15 November 1939, on the subject of the Royal Charter, Colonel Bridge said that the Executive Committee had been advised that as matters stood they were legally liable for the Council's torts ('I believe this is the correct expression'), and the matter was therefore brought up at every meeting.8

months but came to a head in interchanges which took place in February 1940 between Reith and Lloyd.

On 6 February, Reith wrote to Lloyd summarising his view of a conversation which had apparently taken place between them a few days before. In this he said he was very glad that they had been able to have 'a friendly and full interchange of opinion', and 'I hope we may be able to come to an arrangement satisfactory to all parties concerned'.[11]

He said that, although, when the Foreign Office resumed control, it had seemed to be on the understanding that the Council would confine itself to cultural activities, 'keeping the Ministry informed of all it was doing and proposing to do', this arrangement had not worked satisfactorily. He expressed the opinion that the best course would have been for the Council to come into the Ministry and that this might have been done with an understanding on various points 'which would safeguard your postwar interests and independence, unprejudiced by contact with propaganda in war'. And he went on:

> It is impossible, for instance, to say where cultural activity ends and propaganda begins, and surely all the Council's activities have in fact an underlying propaganda significance and orientation. Further, however clearly you deny propaganda motive or Governmental control, I should have doubted this being credited abroad. With all the constitutional independence of the BBC foreigners believed it to be an instrument of the Government even in peace.[12]

Having registered this view he said that the most important thing was to arrange matters so as to avoid overlap, waste and friction and he thought that the most hopeful solution would be for the Council to confine itself to specifically cultural activities, leaving the Ministry responsibility for all else. In particular the Ministry felt that five subjects should be left to them: lectures (except for a small and carefully controlled service to Anglophile societies), visual propaganda, sundry grants (' ... another way of suggesting that the Council should not receive a grant for special activities without prior agreement with the Ministry'), press (except *Britain Today*) and broadcasting. There were other activities where it should be possible to agree on a division of responsibility. These included books and periodicals ('You felt that this would be the end of Anglophil societies ... so on this issue we are unfortunately not at one'), entertainment (he suggested the Council should act as the Ministry's agent, receiving advances from the Ministry's vote but not being prevented from initiating proposals) and films (the Council to be responsible for the production, distribution and exhibition of purely cultural films only).

Reith concluded by saying that however comprehensive an agreement was reached, other points would arise from time to time and it would be well to arrange for some rather close and formal contact. 'I suggest that you might invite me, as Minister of Information, to nominate someone to serve on your Executive and Finance Committees.'[13]

To this Lloyd replied ten days later in a long letter in which the logic is so irreproachable and the willingness to compromise so small that it is both a landmark in the history of the British Council and a curiosity in the art of letter writing.

Beginning with two paragraphs of civilities of a significantly ominous kind, Lloyd explains in the second that he believes differences have arisen through a misconception of the nature of the Council's functions and consequent attempts to allot whole branches of activity *en bloc* to one body or another. In the third he said that the Council would be glad to receive a representative of the Ministry (Sir Walter Monckton had been suggested) on the Executive Committee. 'I do not think it will be necessary for him to be a member of the Finance and Agenda Committee as well; it would indeed be a waste of his time. The smaller Committee consists only of the Chairmen of Advisory Committees and a Foreign Office representative.'[14] Commenting, the Deputy Secretary of the Ministry of Information said: 'Even the proposal that the Minister should nominate a representative on the British Council would be of no avail, since Lord Lloyd politely puts aside the suggestion that our representative should be a member of the Finance and Agenda Committee, where alone (I suspect) it would be possible for him to exercise any decisive influence.'[15]

The last two paragraphs are also taken up with civilities. In between there are twenty-three others. In one of these Lloyd concedes that the Council has nothing to do with broadcasting and makes no claim under this head, and in another he says he is prepared to agree to further discussion on (his own) conditions to be agreed; but in general they are stylistically interesting, difficult to argue, patronisingly explanatory and completely unyielding. Parts of three paragraphs are given in illustration of the content and tone. In reply to Reith's point that it was impossible to say where political propaganda began and cultural left off, he wrote:

It is a fundamental paradox that the political effect of cultural propaganda increases in proportion to its detachment from political
propaganda, no matter how honestly and candidly the latter may be
conducted and however wide the evidence it may win. To ignore
this principle, which has been proved a thousand times in the experience of ourselves and of foreign propagandists, is to court failure.
The existence, or suspicion, of Government control does not affect
the issue: I am sure that you would not regard the existence of this
suspicion in regard to the B.B.C. as an argument for the submission
of the B.B.C. to Government, any more than it can be argued that,
because *The Times* is considered abroad as an official organ, therefore
it may as well become one.

In paragraph 8, headed 'Lectures', he said:

Unless the Council can send a fairly constant stream of lecturers to its
Anglophil Societies, the societies will die. It is largely by sustained
contact between us in this country and our societies abroad through
our lecturers that we are able to maintain their unflagging interest and
cohesion. That our cultural societies should be used as platforms for
speakers from a purely political organisation would, as I am sure you
will see, be fatal. It would simply mean that from being Anglophil
and cultural societies, spontaneously formed by inhabitants of the
country, they would unwittingly be used as centres for active political and contentious propaganda. This is exactly what they can never
be and yet continue to exist for the purpose for which they were
planned by their founders.

In paragraph 16:

You refer to the negotiations with the Export Credits Department
for a sum of £250,000 to stimulate the export of British books, but
I do not think that you can have clearly understood the exact nature
of the scheme. This money is not primarily intended for the supply
of books to the libraries of Universities and Anglophil Societies, but
is to guarantee British publishers against losses in respect of unsold
copies of books supplied by them to foreign booksellers. The negotiations have now reached the point at which the scheme is to be tried
out for six months. The idea originated here and, as its successful
prosecution is dependent upon the Council's co-operation in taking

over 50% of cost price copies of unsold books and in distributing them to the libraries of Anglophil Societies, Universities and other bodies, I think it would be most unwise if, at this stage, this responsibility were suddenly transferred to the Ministry.*[16]

The Ministry of Information expressed great disappointment with 'Lord Lloyd's long and argumentative letter', although 'perhaps we ought not to have expected anything better from him'.[17] It was suggested that the matter should be discussed direct with the Foreign Secretary, Lord Halifax. There is no record of this having been done, but there is evidence that Lloyd had already secured his support 'to resist any attempt to circumscribe or to absorb the functions at present carried out by the Council'.[18] And in any case, Lord Halifax seemed himself to be weary of discussion with Lloyd. In an unpublished manuscript, Anthony Haigh, who acted for Leeper on the British Council, says that it had been his task to sit in at a tussle between the Treasury and the Council about the size of the Council's grant. He had reported to Leeper who, convinced by the Treasury arguments, had sent him to the Finance and Agenda Committee to urge acceptance of their offer. 'I had done my best, but the Chairman, Lord Lloyd, had dug in his toes and insisted that the matter should be referred to the Foreign Secretary, Lord Halifax.'[19] Lord Halifax had asked for further exploration before he made up his mind and Haigh saw Lloyd 'and found him entirely stubborn and determined'.

During the next few days the matter was discussed at every level, before a compromise solution was achieved. At one stage I suggested to Lord Halifax that he should himself see Lord Lloyd. 'What's the use?' he asked. 'He'll only say to me what he has already said to you'.[20]

Once more Lloyd had his way, although only after securing a settlement from the Ministry of Information and with the imposition of certain conditions. The grant for 1940–1 was £480,673, an increase of almost £100,000 over the previous year, but it was agreed that the Council should ask for supplementary grants only in exceptional

---

* This scheme was devised by Sir Stanley Unwin to overcome the inability of British publishers to supply books on 'sale and return' and the difficulties caused by fluctuating exchange rates and the necessity to pay in sterling.

circumstances, should not divert funds from one country to another without consultation with the Treasury, and must seek Treasury sanction for all large projects, new services, new appointments of staff, and capital expenditure. These conditions were imposed permanently.

In May 1940 Neville Chamberlain resigned as Prime Minister and Winston Churchill succeeded him. Lloyd was offered and accepted the post of Secretary of State for the Colonies but he insisted on continuing as Chairman of the British Council and, with his indefatigable appetite for work, he seems to have given it hardly less attention than before. At the same time Anthony Eden succeeded Lord Halifax at the Foreign Office and Duff Cooper succeeded Sir John Reith at the Ministry of Information.

The last of these changes provided the occasion for a further attempt to take over the British Council. Circumstances had changed, since Duff Cooper and the Chairman were now colleagues in Government, and Duff Cooper professed friendship for Lloyd. In November of that year when Mr Waddell for the Director-General of the Ministry of Information circulated one more draft about the Ministry's relations with the British Council, he received a reply on behalf of the Deputy Director-General which commented as follows:

> D.D.G. asks me to say that he is entirely in agreement with the contents and conclusion of this paper. He knows, however, that Lord Lloyd is not prepared to consent to the British Council coming under this Ministry. The aim can only be achieved, therefore, if the Cabinet can be induced to overrule Lord Lloyd's objections.[21]

In November of that year a weary civil servant wrote a paper in which he said:

> The whole of the trouble has been caused by the Council taking a view of cultural activities which is peculiar to itself. As long as the Council is outside the Ministry we have some chance of contesting its incursions, but taking it over will not change its views and taking it over under a promise not to interfere with its cultural activities will merely prevent the Ministry opposing these views in the future. The Minister will have to foot the bill for anything the Council calls cultural or face a charge of bad faith.
>
> I have doubts about the tactics of a Cabinet Paper. Lord Lloyd and the British Council are persuasive in discussion. It is difficult to get a

Cabinet in wartime to study the detail which shows up how badly the Council behaves in practice ... There is a lot of Hitler diplomacy about the Council's methods. They make swaggering impossible claims and proposals in the hope that something will be conceded. Whenever we have disputed directly with the Council we have lost something in the settlement.

After saying that the Council's ambit was narrowing, he wound up:

Unless they can poach from us they have little to do, and sooner or later public opinion will recognise that their large and expensive organisation is not justified in this war.[22]

Reading the British Council papers of this date, one begins to understand why in 1931, faced with the impenetrable, if perfectly honourable, inability of the High Commissioner to Egypt to see any point of view but his own, the Foreign Office had thought the only solution was to get rid of him. Rather than exhaust themselves, both the Ministers of Information and the Chancellor of the Exchequer eventually abandoned the struggle with the British Council and Lloyd remained in command of almost the whole of the field which he wished to retain. On this occasion, however, his views were right at the right time, and the prophecy that the Council's ambit was narrowing as a result of the war proved entirely incorrect. British Missions in allied and neutral countries soon began to realise the value of the Council's presence in wartime and to make demands which, in spite of the necessity to withdraw from Germany and later from other countries, involved a great expansion of its activities abroad. At the same time the presence of an enormous alien population in Great Britain necessitated the formation of the Resident Foreigners Division, which later, with the arrival of so many members of the Commonwealth countries, came to be called the Home Division. Indeed it was the Council's great and obvious contribution to the war effort which finally ensured that, from the small beginnings in 1934, it grew in the space of five or six years into a national institution. The grant which was £330,249 in 1939–40, by 1945–6 had grown to £2,522,370 and continued to grow thereafter.*

In the autumn of 1940 Lloyd developed symptoms which, after

---

* In 1940/41 it was £433,099, in 1941/2 £611,728, in 1942/3 £966,705, in 1943/4 £1,573,958 and in 1944/5 £2,108,122.

several false diagnoses, were declared to be those of miloma, a disease
so rare that the only thing that was known with certainty about it was
that it almost invariably proved fatal. In February 1941 and at the
height of his career he died at the age of sixty-one. His death, much
mourned in the British Council, provided the occasion for one more
attempt by the Minister of Information to get control of the Council,
and this time he deployed very heavy armour.

Lloyd died on 4 February and on the 7th Duff Cooper wrote to the
Prime Minister, Winston Churchill. Having said that, owing to his
friendship with Lloyd, he had avoided bringing the matter of the
British Council to a head, he continued:

> The supposition is that the British Council exists only for cultural,
> and not for political propaganda, but this at the best of times was
> mere camouflage since no country would be justified in spending
> public money on cultural propaganda unless it had also a political or
> a commercial significance.[23]

Having given expression to this impeccably British sentiment, he
said that he thought the only way of preventing the British Council
from interfering and competing with the Ministry of Information was
to bring the two bodies under one control, and he suggested that in
future the Minister of Information should be *ex officio* Chairman of the
British Council. He did not think the extra work would be excessive,
it had been done by the Secretary of State for the Colonies, and 'in fact
some of the work of this department which has hitherto consisted of
disputes with the British Council would be avoided'.[24]

There is no record that the Prime Minister replied directly to this
letter but on 15 February he wrote to Sir Edward Bridges, Secretary of
the War Cabinet:

> I should like to see the arguments for maintaining the British Council
> set out shortly on one sheet of paper. I should have thought that with
> M.E.W. [Ministry of Economic Warfare] on one side and M. of I.
> on the other there was very little place for it ... I have no doubt they
> do their work extremely well, but I have to think of the public.
> What is the staff of the British Council, and how much does it cost
> in one way or another per annum.[25]

When suggestions were made for a new Chairman, a memorandum,

issued from the Prime Minister's office, said briefly: 'Let all parties concerned know that the British Council question and also the question of
a successor at its head will not be settled for another fortnight.'[26]

During the next few weeks suggested names for the post of Chairman included Earl Winterton, Mr Wedgwood Benn, and the Duke of
Devonshire. Writing to the Foreign Secretary, Anthony Eden, about
the last of these, the Prime Minister said:

> On personal grounds what you propose would be very agreeable to
> me. But the name of Malcolm Robertson has been brought to my
> notice. He is certainly a far abler and more experienced man; has
> great energy and is doing nothing; whereas the Duke of Devonshire
> is already employed.

He continued:

> There are however several important matters about the British
> Council which must be settled before we can make an appointment.
> First, is it to go on? Many people consider that now we are at war
> and have a Ministry of Information, it is redundant. It is certainly
> very expensive, and apart from junketings in South American states,
> there are very few countries open to it. There are no doubt a number
> of influential people who have ensconced themselves in this organisa-
> tion. Full justification will have to be shown to the Cabinet by defin-
> ing and explaining the reality of its work in the immediate future.
> On the whole I am inclined to think that its usefulness ended with
> the death of Lord Lloyd.[27]

Churchill went on to discuss the question of the dispute between the
Council and the Ministry of Information.

Once more Lord Lloyd's prescience in making sure the Council came
under the aegis of a senior Cabinet Minister stood it in good stead, and
once more the Foreign Secretary defended his own. On 20 May Eden
wrote to the Prime Minister:

> I attach great importance to the work of the British Council. I was
> responsible for the early development of its work when I was last
> Foreign Secretary. In my view it would be a grave error to close it
> down now after all the work that has been put into it.

Moreover, I could not agree to the transfer of its duties to the Ministry of Information, which I regard as a body quite unsuited for this type of work.

I attach my reasons for holding these views and hope that when you have read them you will not consider it necessary to refer the matter to the Cabinet.[28]

This virtually settled it, and in June Sir Malcolm Robertson was appointed to take over from the Acting Chairman, Lord Riverdale. Yet, although the end was in sight, even now it had not quite been reached. On June 21 with the circulation of a Minute to the War Cabinet, written in answer to the earlier request from the Prime Minister, the half-expected figure of Lord Beaverbrook appeared upon the scene. He dealt with the whole problem of Information and Propaganda and the British Council was let down surprisingly lightly. (Lord Beaverbrook had many fish to fry and the British Council was by no means his only target. In 1931 Duff Cooper fought and won the by-election at Westminster against the Empire Crusade Candidate backed by Lord Beaverbrook. In those days the *Daily Express* generally referred to him as Mr Cooper.) He said:

About the British Council, there are two choices: —
(a) It may pass under the Ministry of Information, or
(b) The Foreign Office should assist the Ministry of Information in the division of its functions, the British Council ... confining itself to cultural activities, entertainments, scholarships and systems of education.[29]

On 1 July a Meeting of Ministers considered the whole question and the next day a draft statement was circulated, the last paragraph of which was then re-drafted by Anthony Eden to read as follows:

Another agency is the British Council. By far the greater part of its activities are cultural, and to that extent we are not concerned here with its work. In so far, however, as it has also undertaken certain propaganda activities ... all such work at the British Council should be carried out with the prior approval of the Ministry of Information, who will appoint a special officer to keep in touch with the Council.

The educational and cultural activities of the Council will continue as at present. All the film work of the Council will be carried out in consultation with the Ministry of Information.[30]

Given the well-known difficulties of demarcation between the boundaries of cultural work and propaganda, this was virtually the recipe as before.

6

War in the Mediterranean

At the outbreak of war many of the British Council staff left to join the army, among them the Secretary-General, Colonel Bridge, who returned to his regiment and was sent as Military Attaché to Rome. He was succeeded by A. J. S. White, formerly a Deputy Secretary-General, and the author of the book so much quoted here. Colonel Bridge had won the liking of his staff because of his loyalty to them, but he was a difficult and hot-tempered man and unsuited to close co-operation with Lord Lloyd. White, on the other hand, very much admired Lloyd, and he describes with real if rather rueful affection the days when he was constantly summoned to the Colonial Office in the middle of an air raid, because 'Lord Lloyd was the sort of person who did not seem to notice bombs'.[1]

Soon however this relationship was also to be broken by Lord Lloyd's death, and in 1941 Sir Malcolm Robertson took over the Chairmanship. His appointment had much to recommend it. He had given distinguished service as one of Britain's Ambassadors and, above all, had shown himself predisposed to concern himself with cultural relations. As Ambassador to Buenos Aires, he had played an active part in the foundation of the first of the Latin-American Anglophile Societies. White says of him:

He believed most deeply in the British Council's mission: being devoted, to use his own words, to the idea of a peace of understanding by the peoples of the world in the achievement of which the British Council should have no mean share.[2]

White, however, went on to say:

He tried hard, perhaps too hard, to infect his Parliamentary colleagues with his enthusiasm: but he could not, or did not, spare enough time from the House of Commons to carry out the day-to-day direction of the Council's work and his constant failures to keep important appointments in Hanover Street led to difficulty.[3]

Standing by itself, this is rather a harsh view of Robertson's period as Chairman (although A. J. S. White is not a harsh man) because it will be seen that, working under appalling difficulties, he did manage to bring the Council through what was probably one of the most eventful periods of its history. However, he had one irredeemable fault – he was not Lord Lloyd. By his personal attributes, Lloyd had galvanised into being a body which, despite its recent small beginnings, already permeated the main seats of war, and which would quickly prove itself a diplomatic presence of the utmost importance to the armed forces in those areas. The great increase in the grant made annually to the Council during these years reflected an expansion in demand for its services which was in fact very much larger than the finance made available. This happened at a speed which quite outran any possibility of constructing an administrative structure to keep pace with it; and at a time when the requirements of the armed forces made almost insuperable the problems of recruiting staff of the qualities necessary for work which, designed to represent the British character, depended so much on personality and behaviour. Above all, the Treasury insisted on a fixed grant based on forward estimates, so that the Council was continally in a position of having to seize opportunities or satisfy demands from the diplomatic or military services for which no financial provision had been made.

Had Lloyd lived, it is just possible that his irresistible enthusiasm and unyielding persistence, combined with his detailed knowledge of the work and personnel of the British Council, might have altered the situation. He would have so badgered the Treasury that even that unimpressionable body might have responded a little, if only from a desire to get rid of him; but no lesser man, and particularly no one with other interests, as Robertson had, could have done much better than he did.

These factors had a long-term effect on the Council's reputation and standing. In the following pages it will be seen that it performed brilliantly in some countries, but because it was more open to inspection than government departments or the armed forces, its mistakes were remembered long after solid achievements were forgotten.

In the early months of the war the main function was one of reassurance. The special quality of German propaganda was that it was not only concerned with creating friendships; it had not failed if it produced feelings of antipathy, providing these were combined with fear. The following particularly graphic account of Germany's methods in Portugal was given by an anonymous writer in the Annual Report of 1940–1.

By every means in her power Germany attempted to win a position of supremacy in Portugal. Within six years the German community there was almost doubled. Merchants and tradesmen were sent out specially from Germany with the mission of making themselves agreeable to the Portuguese middle class and swaying their opinion to the German side. International conferences held in Portugal were attended by disproportionately large German delegations; aeroplanes, stuffed with learned Germans of the more obsequious kind, descended at the last moment to swamp the delegations of other countries. And finally the customary bands of tourists devoted themselves assiduously to sight-seeing in the slight leisure left by more assiduous propaganda.[4]

Caught between the menace of Germany and that of Russia, the countries of the free world looked anxiously to Britain. When in the early months of 1940, Russia invaded Finland and Germany occupied Norway, Denmark and, by the end of June, the whole of France, Britain became, however weak, the only hope they had. If one wishes to evaluate the presence of the British Council in Portugal, Spain and the Middle East, even in the years when Germany seemed all-conquering, one need only postulate a situation in which it was not there. The great strength of the British Council (insufficiently realised today as well as in the past) was that it penetrated foreign societies at many different levels often not reached by the more prestigious Diplomatic Service, while it offered through its contacts with universities, its English teaching, lectures, Council rooms and libraries, not merely actual benefits to the host population, but a means through which social and cultural intercourse could be established on a wide scale.

Following the fall of France, Italy entered the war. There were by now five British Council Institutions in Italy (apart from the original independent Institute in Florence) – Rome and Milan, started by Harold Goad but taken over by the British Council, Palermo, Naples and Genoa – and the staff of these as well as those of Rumania, Bulgaria and later Yugoslavia had to be withdrawn. It is not proposed here to deal with the Council's work before or early in the war in those countries which were later closed to it. In its time it has had a presence in 114 countries (see Appendix 2) and, although it has a reputation for staying to the end, it has often had to evacuate its premises in a hurry. Again, it would be merely repetitious to give the growth of students and members of the Institutes and so on in every country. It is enough to say here that the demand for books and periodicals, for lectures, exhibitions and performances and above all for English teaching steadily grew, while the limits imposed were seldom of demand, almost invariably those of finance, premises and staff. To give some idea of the scale, however, it may be useful to say that at the time the staff had to be withdrawn the Institute at Rome had 1,000 students, at Milan 450, Palermo 300, Genoa 250, Naples 200, while at Bucharest there were 3,500.

As had been foreseen, the countries bordering the Mediterranean were of the first importance to the war effort and by the end of 1942 (apart from Sweden and Iceland) Spain and Portugal were the only European countries accessible to the British. With one exception, all staff were safely withdrawn from the countries overrun by the enemy, as was the Sadler's Wells Ballet Company, which narrowly escaped capture in Holland and had to leave its costumes and scenery behind. In Portugal, where Professor West had played such an important part in the opening of the English Room at Coimbra, contributing at the same time to the pressures which culminated in the foundation of the British Council, an Institute was opened in Lisbon in 1938, a Casa da Inglaterra was inaugurated in Coimbra in July 1939, and an English Room in the University of Oporto in December 1940. (The English Rooms were integrated in the universities but supported by the Council.)

In 1941 Professor Ifor Evans, the Director of Education, visited Portugal and, reporting on this visit, made certain comments that were to become a regular feature of reports from all over the Middle East. 'Council officers overseas feel, during the war, that they are out of touch with England. Some question whether it is their duty to continue or to join the armed forces.' 'It is an uneconomical policy to keep a man who knows Portugal and the Portuguese as well as does Professor West, tied to a desk dealing with the work of a cashier.' 'Professor West should be given a secretary-accountant. As a general principle one may affirm that the more unsettled the situation, the more up-to-date should be the accounts.' 'The task of a British Council officer is harder than is generally imagined; it requires tact, social grace, tenacity, some ability as a lecturer or teacher, and a faith in Great Britain.' 'It is important that we acquire new premises in Lisbon. Professor West has, in the past, laid definite proposals before us. Our failure to acquire new premises is a dreary story in which the Council, the Foreign Office and the Office of Works are all involved.'[5]

As a result of this report, Professor West was made Representative in Portugal, and given extra staff and freedom from routine duties, so that he could visit Coimbra and Oporto and also other places where the development of British influence was desirable. In consequence of the demands for membership and tuition, the Institute at Lisbon twice outgrew its premises and in March 1942 the Council bought the Menino d'Ouro Palace, where the Institute can still be found.

Probably the most far-reaching of Professor Ifor Evans's recommendations was that the policy for Portugal must be separate from that for Spain. 'Our Portuguese policy can be linked with the Portuguese colonies and with Brazil; our Spanish policy with Spanish speaking states in South America.'[6] In fact it became the custom to send men to Spain and Portugal to train and perfect the language before going to South America.

The British Council established itself in Spain as a direct result of Lord Lloyd's friendship with Franco, whose cause he had consistently backed. In a report dated November 1939, Lloyd gave an account of an interview with Franco.

I described the world-wide activities of the British Council in some detail, and told him how anxious the Council was to obtain permission for the prosecution of the same activities in Spain now the Spanish war was over. He seemed already fairly well acquainted with the nature of that work, about which he had clearly made enquiries, and asked me questions about certain aspects of the Council's work in other countries. He said that he respected and admired British cultural standards more than those of any other country, and would unreservedly welcome the establishment of British Council activities in Spain in as full a measure as we cared to develop them ... He had already given instructions to the Minister for Foreign Affairs, under whom Spain's Cultural Department existed, that all facilities were to be given to the inception of our work.[7]

As a result of this interview (although after negotiations which took

longer than General Franco had suggested and in which stiffer terms
were imposed, the most important being that all Council staff should
be attached to the Embassy and should be Roman Catholic) Dr Walter
Starkie went to Madrid as Director of the British Institute.

His appointment was one of several which showed that, if the conditions of war made great difficulties in the recruitment of large numbers
of the general staff, they also made it possible sometimes to recruit men
of outstanding talent and distinction. Professor Starkie (a brother of
Dr Enid Starkie, to a later generation even better known) was an Irish
scholar and professor of romance languages, and he had earned fame by
wandering through Europe in search of gypsies and their music, earning his bread as he went by playing the violin. In Spain he had travelled
with a band of gypsies through La Mancha, the Don Quixote country,
and he wrote *Spanish Raggle Taggle*, which, published in 1933, had both
a critical and a popular success. He followed this with *Don Gypsy*,
published in 1936, also about wanderings in Spain.

Starkie was a short, fat man with a strong Irish brogue, but he spoke
perfect Spanish and had considerable charm. The strength of German
influence in Spain at this time was immense and probably no one but
he could have built up and maintained an Institute. Writing to Lloyd,
he said:

I have been doing my best to encourage the Falange Party to work
in with us but that of course puts some of our real friends among the
Traditionalists and the Monarchists in a difficulty. I am sure that
many of the officials who come to our receptions are more spies than
friends. At the same time it is best to ply them with soft words in the
hope of either converting them or else turning aside their ill-will.
Sometimes our greatest friends keep away from us for fear of falling
under the suspicion of the dreaded secret police.[8]

Starkie was not best fitted for the tasks of an administrator. Speaking
of him, R. A. Phillips said:

The most successful man the British Council has ever had in its service was Walter Starkie ... in Madrid ... He was also the biggest
rascal in the British Council. I remember he had committed some
terrible financial crime, and he had to come and see me about it (I
was Controller Finance at the time). I sat there (I knew him a bit) and
said 'Walter, you mustn't do this', and so on, and he said 'Terribly

sorry', and wrote it all down, what he had been supposed to do. Then out he went, and I could sort of metaphorically hear him tearing the bit of paper up as he went. He hadn't the slightest intention of taking any action but he wasn't going to contradict me. I knew it was useless, but I went through the motions and he listened politely. He did a wonderful job.[9]

Walter Starkie opened a school for young children, which still remains a feature of the Council's work unique to Madrid, and arranged classes at the Institute for beginners, commercial students, those taking diplomatic examinations and teachers of English. A story is told by one of his locally-engaged staff which may be apocryphal but is certainly illustrative. This man, who spoke English, went to ask for a job as a teacher at the Institute.

'Go in there,' Starkie is supposed to have said, pointing to the door of a room, 'and start now.'

By 1944 there were 1,574 students at the Institute, and 900 members, while the children's school had 146 pupils and a waiting list of eighty. Professor Starkie constantly gave lectures, and other guest lecturers included Professor Bodkin, Father d'Arcy, and Leslie Howard, the actor, who was killed by enemy action when his plane was shot down on his return from Portugal in 1943.

The Council several times arranged for the production of plays in Madrid, and brought over art exhibitions and soloists for concerts. In addition to the usual library of books and periodicals, there was a good music library. Probably the most influential of the public functions, however, were the Receptions referred to by Walter Starkie in his letter to Lloyd.

In Greece, where the British Council has always been welcome and often loved, its work was inhibited and finally overwhelmed by the course of the war. The Annual Report for 1940–1 gives a bland account of the usual rush of students when the autumn session began at the Institute of English Studies in Athens and of the disappointment of half of the 8,000 who applied, of new Institutes at Serres and Cavalla, of plans for others, and of the opening of a school for Maltese subjects in Athens. Nevertheless, all was conducted against a background of fear.

In 1939 Lord Lloyd had visited both General Metaxas, the Greek Prime Minister, and the King and had negotiated a cultural agreement which was signed on the entry of Greece into the war. At the same time he had reached a compromise with General Metaxas on the question of bursaries. The General had wished to control the nomination of students, to which the British Council could not agree, since bursaries were given on intellectual and not on political grounds. Professor H. V. Routh had been appointed to the Byron Chair of English Literature at Athens University in 1938. He also administered the Institute – which was purely English teaching – and was attached to the Embassy as Press Attaché responsible for British publicity.

This was an unusual arrangement and C. A. F. Dundas, the Representative for the Middle East, visiting Athens in October 1939, wrote to the Council in London.

The whole of my wanderings since the beginning of the war have confirmed that the usefulness of the British Council's work at the present time depends almost entirely on its institutions refraining from any kind of active political propaganda or connection with political activities. Even a suspicion that it is working on instructions from the Embassies and Legations concerned would rapidly undermine the confidence in the Council's integrity.[10]

Yet in illustration of the contradictions involved in purely cultural work one must quote a letter written only two months later by A. R. Burn, the Representative in Athens.

Perhaps my chief difficulty is that the British Council gets no credit whatever for its scrupulous refusal to take part in politics ... The strongest evidence of this is that our best friends, the most enthusiastic Anglophils among Greeks frequently reproach us of the Council for not 'making propaganda' as they put it ... Our friends also in general criticize us for the supineness of British propaganda, and seem to have difficulty in taking in any explanations offered.[11]

Burn had succeeded Professor Routh at the Institute early in 1940, when at the same time Lord Dunsany succeeded him in the Byron Chair.* Routh was described as 'very tactless and unpopular', and, in an example of his detailed knowledge of the work of the Council, Lloyd had written to Dundas in October 1939, suggesting that Routh should be moved to Cyprus. He said:

* Edward John Moreton Drax Plunkett, 18th Baron Dunsany (1878–1957), author and playwright.

My main object has been to get Routh out of Greece on to anybody's
back as quick as I can and relying full well on your illimitable powers
I think you will be able to deal with Routh, Pusey, Grant [not to be
confused with Michael Grant, the Representative in Turkey], and the
Government all at the same time![12]

Writing to Lloyd in June 1940 Burn said: 'Feeling in Greece remains,
as ever, staunchly and even pathetically pro-British, but recent events
spread feelings of despair and dismay.'[13]
He also wrote:

There is much nervousness, especially perhaps among our best men,
over the risk of reaching the ignominious safety of an Italian internment camp. If the Foreign Office could do something to assure us of
a diplomatic 'emergency exit' it would allay much anxiety, especially
in any man whom we may send to Corfu.[14]

Then on 30 September the Cairo Office reported: 'All reports from
British Council staff who have come through from the Balkans suggest
that the Council's work in Greece and neighbouring countries is
weakening.'[15]
In October the Italians invaded Greece to suffer heavy reverses at the
hands of the Greek Army. All foreign cultural organisations were
immediately closed and meetings of more than five people forbidden.
In March 1941 Churchill diverted 50,000 troops with tanks and equipment from North Africa to Greece and in April the Germans invaded,
driving the British to an evacuation comparable to Dunkirk. The staff
of the British Council continued until the last and at the Annual General
Meeting in June Lord Riverdale spoke of a message sent by General
Metaxas shortly before his death (January 1941) in which he said that
their work had contributed largely to the Anglophile spirit of the Greek
people.
    One of the most important areas was the island of Malta, neither
Europe nor yet the Middle East. Here the Institute at Valetta was constantly bombed. But a shelter was built and even at the height of the air
attacks the library was continually used. In December 1940, when the
bombing began, the programme included nine lectures, five concerts,
three film shows, three debates, seven play readings, four dances and a
chess competition. It needs little imagination to appreciate what all this
meant to a small island at war.

Assistance was given to St Edward's College, also bombed, and a grant made to Flores College. Mr Wickham, the Representative, received the first OBE awarded to a Council officer, and the Governor of Malta wrote:

The British Council may rightly claim a share in the influences that have helped the Maltese people to show the courage and steadfastness under repeated air attacks which have commanded the admiration of us all and the surprise of a very great number.[16]

C. A. F. Dundas (known as Flux) was appointed Middle East Representative in 1938. He has been described as a man of persuasive charm and considerable strength, who never failed to give a straightforward opinion to his superiors or to his staff. A first class British Council officer, he was responsible for the biggest single undertaking of its kind. The term Middle East covered Aden, Cyprus, Egypt, Ethiopia, Iran, Iraq, Palestine, Transjordan and Turkey. In each of these countries the British Council had to function in a different way, and, whereas in most European countries cultural equality with the host country could be assumed, this was not so in the Middle East. Secondly, each country had a special relationship with Britain. Thus Egypt, Ethiopia and Iraq had treaties, Aden and Cyprus were colonies, while in Palestine and Transjordan Britain was the Mandatory Power. Iraq refused to honour a commitment to allow military transit through her territories and Iran refused a request. Therefore in 1941 both countries were in effect occupied; Iraq by the British, Iran by the Russians and British. Turkey was independent and her neutrality vital to the allies.

In these areas the British Council had not merely to work for smooth relationships during the war but to prepare for a situation after the war when our influences could no longer be maintained by military power. In a report of a tour of the Middle East in 1942, Professor Ifor Evans (the Council's Education Director), wrote as follows:

British Council Institutes can alone give a meeting place for informal discussions and social contracts between the effective people in these countries and British officials and businessmen. By its activities in education, in technical services, in presenting British methods in agriculture, in sanitation and hygiene and by the supply of books, films and visual publicity the British Council can not only make Great Britain known but indicate that the whole of western civilisation can be known through British means and British personnel.[17]

To which one must add, as a generalisation, that, whereas in Europe the word culture could be defined in its narrower sense, and English teaching, books and newspapers, lectures, dramatic performances and exhibitions of art met the desire for international exchange, in the Middle East the need was (then as now) for education and science, medicine, engineering, agriculture and so on. The teaching of English was of primary importance and schools as well as Institutes were needed. Institutes had been opened in Cairo and Alexandria in 1938, and by 1943 there were many more in the Middle East area. It is not proposed to deal with these in any detail because, although the methods employed in them varied from country to country, the differences were not so significant as to need discussion. The more important Institutes were as follows: in Egypt, at Cairo, Alexandria, Port Said, Assiut, Mansura, Mehalla-el-Kobra, Minia, Tanta and Zagazig: in Iraq, at Baghdad and Mosul: in Cyprus, at Nicosia, Famagusta, Limassol, Larnaca and Kyrenia: in Palestine, Tel Aviv, Haifa, Jaffa, Nablus and Nazareth; and there were Institutes in Aden, Teheran and Addis Ababa. In Turkey an entirely different method was followed and this will be discussed separately.

In Egypt particularly, schools were even more important than the Institutes. Immediately before the war it was estimated that there was a Maltese and Cypriot population of 30,000 and a United Kingdom population, apart from the army, of about 7,000. Reporting, Dundas wrote:

> British parents are as a rule unwilling to send their children to Egyptian schools and therefore turn to the schools of the various foreign communities, French, Greek and, pre-war, German and Italian. As a result, the vast majority of British children were being brought up with little or no knowledge of English and no knowledge of the British Empire or British ways of life and thought.[18]

Dr Leslie Phillips, Director of the Institute in Alexandria from 1942 to 1946, said that from his observation the French method of setting up first-class educational settlements, staffed from the French educational system, was 'a good deal more likely to bring home the bacon'. He cites the case of a British girl who had been educated at the French Lycée and who was 'not only saturated in things French ... but she had at the same time learned to ignore, or even to despise, our own cultural achievements',[19] a fact which cannot be thought very surprising considering how little attention we had until recently paid to them ourselves. However, the Annual Report of the British Council for 1940–1 states that in the four big cities of Egypt – Cairo, Alexandria, Port Said and Suez – all United Kingdom, Maltese and Cypriot children could now obtain a British education whatever the means of their parents. This had been achieved either through scholarships, or, as in Alexandria, by financing and opening schools specially for Maltese and Cypriot children.

The best known school in the area was Victoria College at Alexandria, which had been run for forty years on the lines of an English public school and had attracted the sons of many of the leaders throughout the Middle East. When this was bombed in 1941, the Council subsidised its re-opening in Cairo and the majority of the boarders returned immediately. In August 1941, Ifor Evans, arguing that there should be a greater balance between the expenditure in the Middle East and that in South America, said: 'For instance, our contributions to Victoria College, Cairo, must be almost as great as all our contribution to schools in South America.'[20] Victoria College was given great importance because the Council looked for long-term results from the youth of the countries they worked in and it was normal to expect to find the leaders of tomorrow in the equivalent of the public school system. Yet criticisms of a bias in favour of the upper classes were not entirely justified. The Council owned three and supported eleven schools in Egypt alone.

In Iraq, in addition to the Institute at Baghdad, teachers of English were appointed to the Law College and Technical Schools, while English classes were arranged at the Staff College and Royal Military College.

In Cyprus there was the usual inability to accommodate all the students applying to the Institute until a large detached house was bought near the sea at Famagusta. Financial assistance was given to the agricultural Training School, for the improvement of the Moslem Lycée at Nicosia and to the English school; a teacher was sent to Platras for the benefit of the Polish refugees.

In Palestine the method adopted was to provide scholarships for the children of United Kingdom parents to attend schools approved by the Council, and financial assistance was given to these schools. At Tel Aviv the Council acquired control of an existing school of English.

The biggest regional organisation apart from Egypt was in Turkey and in November 1940 Michael Grant* was appointed Representative. Aged twenty-eight, Grant was a Fellow of Trinity, Cambridge. From the first he was outstandingly successful and Dundas and others who came into contact with him had the highest opinion of his ability. In Turkey the work could be carried on only through the Halkevleri (singular, Halkevi), institutes for social, educational and cultural purposes which had been founded by the People's Party in all important towns and villages throughout the country. There was also a considerable demand for English classes, while the Council advised the Turkish Government on the choice of Englishmen to fill a number of professorships at the University of Istanbul and English teachers were sent out to the schools.

The whole of the Middle East area was controlled and serviced by Dundas from Cairo, although as time went on Representatives were appointed to the different countries. Because of the difficulty of communication with London, he had an unusual degree of authority. Possibly for the same reason the written record of his administration is much fuller and more informative than is usual for this period.

He regarded his first task as the removal of the Council's work from direct Embassy control. There was little difficulty in this because the diplomatic staffs, except possibly at Ankara, where they were sometimes found obstructive, were aware of the value of the Council's work but only too anxious to get rid of the responsibility for it. Nevertheless, the difficulties were prodigious and not made easier by the rest of the local British population who, for reasons of race and of class, were apt to be hostile.

> For many years [Dundas reported to Ifor Evans] the Council's chief enemies are likely to be the local British communities. In the first place our contact with the local inhabitant is by most of the 'old brigade' considered to be lowering to British prestige. Secondly, in many cases our staff are liked and given privileges by the local inhabitant which are not extended to the 'old brigade'; this leads to jealousy.[21]

The greatest problems were the difficulties of finding staff of high quality and the constant shortage of finance. Dundas appointed and

* Later first Vice-Chancellor of the University of Khartoum (1956–8) and President and Vice-Chancellor of the Queen's University, Belfast (1959–66).

trained his own staff and he was unwilling to accept men who did not come up to the standard he thought necessary. His own standards were high and possibly arbitrary but he succeeded in the Middle East by the rigorous exclusion of men who might be undesirable. He was unwilling to receive members of the staff from Greece and the Balkans.

Writing to Lord Lloyd in 1940, he said that, although it might be unjust to condemn men on any basis but proven fact, a bad reputation, however slight the foundation, could not merely unfit them for certain posts but be transferred to their colleagues. He also said:

> I feel very strongly that some of the Council's Greek staff have gained (and a few deserved) a reputation for qualities which make their posi- tion untenable in the especially difficult and delicate circumstances of the present time. It is variously said that they are indiscreet, extrava- gant, lack any serious purpose, do not consider the public effects of their personal behaviour, or are irresponsible in financial matters. It is, too, repeatedly said, however slanderously, that they are 'pansies', 'longhaired' or 'soft'. This unsavoury reputation unhappily found its way both to Egypt and to Cyprus this summer, and we still have unwelcome repercussions of it from time to time.[22]

Two years later, in a confidential report, he said that a statement of the reputation earned by the Council in the Balkans ought to be made, adding that this could be vouched for 'by any of our staff working in this area and by Professor Ifor Evans himself who has come across several instances already'. He went on:

> Almost without exception English people evacuated from the Bal- kans to the Middle East have the same story to tell. Their criticisms fall under the following main headings: — 1) Maladministration. 2) Public immorality of staff. 3) No efforts made to conciliate British Communities. 4) Failure to limit minorities in our Institutes.* 5) Disloyalty of the staff to the Council. 6) Disloyalty of the staff to each other coupled with internecine quarrels. 7) Financial muddles.[23]

Dundas made these comments as part of an argument for appoint- ing a Representative in each country, saying that this degree of

---

* This refers to the fact that there was a temptation to compete for numbers by taking too many students from one section of the population or even those who were actually incapable of benefiting from the teaching.

maladministration could not have occurred under strong direction from the top. His view was obviously sound and it was quite soon acted upon, the method becoming part of the Council's permanent structure. His comments must be discussed, because there is no doubt that in the early years of its great expansion the Council acquired, at one and the same time, much sound and enduring appreciation of the value of its work and the kind of reputation (assiduously promoted by the Beaverbrook press) suggested by the terms 'longhaired', 'pansies', or 'soft'.

In the first place it has to be remembered that these words were apt to be used by members of the upper and aristocratic classes, as well as by officers of the regular army, about anyone with the faintest intellectual pretensions. The expression 'longhaired' did not necessarily suggest homosexual but was more often used as a term of contempt, as in P. G. Wodehouse, where intellectuals are invariably writers of slim volumes with titles such as 'Grey Myrtles'. (The word 'pansy' however was unequivocal.) One must therefore remember that the reputation of the Council staff, whether well-founded or not, was brought down to the Middle East by the rest of the British population evacuated from Greece and the Balkans, which included many members of what Dundas called the 'old brigade'. Nevertheless, these complaints were also made by members of the Council staff, and there seems no doubt that the unregulated intake of recruits to service the unexpected wartime demands did in some areas do the Council lasting harm, or that Dundas was right to refuse to receive staff *en bloc* from other areas.

He never hesitated to make criticisms of the Council's staff and work internally, but he was aware that nothing could prevent ill-founded rumour and gossip about an institution so widely spread, whose staff worked often in isolated areas and yet in the public gaze, and he instructed his staff to concentrate on its undoubted achievements.

'It is quite impossible in general', he wrote to one of them, 'to answer the adverse comments about the British Council but a few facts and figures might give you some ammunition.' He then went on:

1) No-one working in this area for the British Council has had more than a month's leave in any one year since before the outbreak of war. How does the idea get about that we get four months?
2) Directly through our classes in Egypt we are in touch with approximately 3,000 Egyptians anything from three to ten times a week. These Egyptians are drawn from the most educated classes and their influence is much greater than their numbers would suggest.

3) In addition to the people who attend our classes probably more than this number secure contact with our people or lecturers provided by the Army etc. and other British residents through our club activities. These people are representative of the most influential in Egypt. A glance at the membership of the Anglo-Egyptian Union will show what I mean and in the provinces the local Mudirs, Mamours, Hakimdars, Inspectors of Education, Headmasters etc. etc. are in the closest touch with our men.

4) We are always ready to replace our younger people by older men if we can get them but the conditions of pay and of the work are such that for the most part older men are unwilling to undertake it.[24]

And in relation to Turkey, he said:

i) The Minister of Education, Hassan Ali Yucel, leading member of the Turkish Cabinet, has specifically asked that British Council affairs should be dealt with direct between him and Grant rather than through the Embassy.

ii) Military Intelligence people are frequently trying to make use of our staff for purposes of their own.

iii) Military Intelligence have tried to pass people into Turkey with passports inscribed 'British Council'.*

iv) The Minister of Education invited our staff to the opening of the Book Exhibition but expressed a wish that none of the Embassy people should be asked.

v) When the British Ambassador wished to entertain some students the Minister of Foreign Affairs said that he would prefer that the Ambassador should not do so but that the Council could.

vi) The Secretary-General of the Party asks British Council personnel but no foreign diplomats of any nation, to Party ceremonies.

vii) The Acting Commander-in-Chief of the Turkish Air Force has asked Grant to dinner and pointed out that he would not have been allowed by the Marshal to do so if he had been in any way connected with our Embassy or the Services.[25]

---

* Many people believe that in the war years British Council staff were used for Intelligence work. There is absolutely no evidence for this and I have not met anyone working for the Council then or now who believes it. Since, if true, it would run counter to everything the Council stood for, it seems most unlikely, although it is clearly impossible to refute the suggestion that here and there some Council officer might have been persuaded or even inserted.

In all countries which wished to preserve their neutrality the Council was seen as less compromising than the Diplomatic or Armed Services. In this case, Michael Grant was also on very close terms with the Minister of Education, a fact which had the following fortunate consequence. Driving with him through Istanbul one day, Grant noticed a fine Byzantine building in a state of disrepair and suggested there was need for an expert on Byzantine art. This resulted in the transfer of Professor Steven Runciman from Palestine, where he was serving in the Ministry of Information, to become Professor of Byzantine History and Art at Istanbul University. In 1945 Professor Runciman went to Greece as British Council Representative, remaining there until 1947.

To find and keep staff who could meet the necessary standards was nevertheless a difficult matter. On 13 August 1940 Lord Lloyd wrote to Sir Miles Lampson, Ambassador to Cairo, and informed him that a definite ruling had been given by the Ministry of National Service exempting British Council staff at home and overseas from military service.[26] This does not, however, seem to have been final, and it remained a vexed and vexing question for the rest of the war. In the first place men over 41 (the limit at which conscription applied) were for a variety of reasons generally unsuitable for the work overseas, the most important being that all who were not actually too old were apt to have existing commitments they could not leave. The British Council staff were consequently often quite young and, while the Manpower Boards were never content to let the matter rest, many of the Council staff themselves were unhappy and restive in this equivocal and embarrassing position. The question was reviewed again and again. As late as 1943 Ernest Bevin, the Minister of Labour and National Service, in a letter to the Foreign Secretary, Anthony Eden, commented on the bad impression that was created throughout the Middle East by young men of obvious military fitness walking about in civilian dress, and went on to quote a report recently received from Egypt:

> The members of the Manpower Boards also disapproved of a paragraph in one of the earlier circulars dealing with persons engaged in education, which in effect granted automatic deferment to men on the staff of the British Council.[27]

He asked the Foreign Secretary to look at the question again.

In view of this protest the Foreign Secretary sent a telegram to Sir Miles Lampson stating that he had consented to release two members of the Foreign Office and there should be some pruning of the British Council staff. Lampson replied by sending an account of a meeting held the previous year in which it was shown that numerous of the Council's employees, both below and above the age of thirty, had been trying to join the forces but had been told it was their duty to stay. 'If even a few of the under-thirties were to be called up many others in the Middle East and elsewhere would resign and the Council's activities would be paralysed.'[28]

At the same time Lampson pointed out that twenty-one Council employees in Egypt had joined the forces as volunteers since the war, while the Council's present man-power shortage had been made acute through the requests of the Middle East War Council that it should provide teachers for the officers of the 120,000 allied troops in Africa. Commanders-in-Chief, Lampson wrote, were actually releasing teachers from the firing line and 'it would be absurd to conscript trained teachers while releasing trained officers for teaching work'.[29]

As a corollary to this correspondence, one must quote from a letter to Sir Malcolm Robertson sent only a month later by Sir Reeder Bullard, Ambassador to Teheran. In this he said that the Persians had tended to be pro-German but, now that they were beginning to be convinced that 'Germany is done for', they were also realising that they would have to accommodate themselves to a world in which the English-speaking peoples would have great weight. He continued:

Is is perhaps hard for you to realise how great your opportunity is. Bingley and Tett,* who have made a remarkable start in spite of the very limited resources at their disposal, estimate at 2,000 the number of Persians of the best and most useful type who could be enrolled tomorrow, if the facilities were ready. They have had to broadcast a statement that no more students can be accepted. This was after passing the 1,000 mark a fortnight after the Institute opened its doors and long before the date of its official inauguration could be fixed. The decision has naturally caused a great deal of disappointment, amounting in some cases to resentment.[30]

Then, having said that he hoped it would be possible to meet the

* J. S. Bingley went to Persia as the Council's first Representative in 1942. Norman N. Tett had gone to direct the new Anglo-Persian Institute in Teheran from Mosul, where he had been director of one of the Iraqi Institutes.

request of the Staff College for special classes in English for Persian Army Officers, he went on to give a list of ten other activities which had had to be shelved owing to a complete absence of staff. These included the admission of university students to the Institute's classes, a special class for teachers, a programme of social events, the provision of an Anglo-Persian periodical, cultural articles and photographs, English lessons on Teheran radio, the translation of books into Persian and special lessons for foreign missions, among whom the Turkish Ambassador, the Chinese Minister and the Afghan Chargé d'Affaires had already applied. Then he said:

> These are the problems of Tehran alone. But Tehran is not Persia … and if the Council is to do its work adequately, branch Institutes must sooner or later be opened at least in Isfahan and Shiraz.[31]

The personal difficulties of the staff were therefore very great. Always understaffed and overworked, watching opportunities slip by, it is not surprising that many of them would have preferred to join the army. A report on the British Council in the Middle East describes morale as 'uniformly low'.[32]

This was also because of the many anomalies over pay (older men had to be taken on at higher pay than those who had been with the Council some time, while alterations to basic salaries were sometimes made in special cases but in addition they were often isolated and sometimes responsible for the morale of others of the British population. Reporting in 1943, Professor Ifor Evans wrote:

> It is I think not always realised that work in the British Council is far more embarrassing than that in the Government Service. The duties are much less closely defined. The officer is left, particularly in provincial centres, in a position of far greater isolation. The task of being continually pleasant to Iraqis or Egyptians does seem to me to infect the personality: however admirable the motive, it has in it an element of insincerity. Above all the Council in London and the leaders of the Council in Cairo have never had sufficient expert knowledge and experience to be able closely to direct the work of new recruits who have been left frequently to discover their own devices in positions which should have been closely controlled.[33]

He also wrote:

The genuine problem lies in the fact that not a sufficient number of your officers have worked overseas, or even been much abroad. Take a census one day of where and for how long your senior officers have been out of England for the last four years.[34]

The greatest handicap of all, however, was as usual the Treasury, and here again one may quote Ifor Evans.

The British Council is being increasingly placed in a most embarrassing position in all the territories under survey. Those concerned with the development of British policy in these areas look to the Council to fulfil a prescribed purpose ... They take it for granted that to this end resources will be put at the disposal of the Council. When these requests go back to London they are received by the appropriate authorities in a manner which is frequently critical, as if the Council had committed some error in being invited to accept that share of the maintenance of British interests which all competent authorities wish to assign to it.[35]

He then cited the instances of the Council being asked by the Minister of State and the Service Chiefs to undertake duties for allied personnel in the area, and of a request from the Minister of State's office to consider cultural work in Cyrenaica, and he said:

On reference to London, funds were obtained only by the greatest difficulty and with at least the cryptic implication that the Council was consciously seeking some self-sought expansion ... In the Middle East the highest British authorities have faith in the Council and turn naturally to it for action. By the time their requests reach England the Council has by some strange transmutation been transfigured into a shabby suppliant whose motives are suspect.[36]

At the end of 1942 Dundas's health gave out. Professor Ifor Evans, then on tour in the Middle East, remained as acting Representative for the whole area until Professor T. S. R. Boase, a distinguished scholar and later President of Magdalen College, Oxford, was appointed to the post, reaching Cairo in November 1943. At this time R. W. G. Reed, who had been headmaster of Victoria College for twenty-five years and was extremely well-known in the country, was appointed Representative in Egypt. By then the fortunes of war were turning, and it is to Dundas that credit must go for the foundation and structure of the Council's work in the Middle East and for its survival and expansion during this most difficult period. His is one of the great names in the history of the British Council.

7

Latin America

At the outbreak of war A. J. S. White and Philip Guedalla were on a tour of South America, from where, in consultation with the local educational authorities, they were to make recommendations as to how the Council's work could best be developed. Guedalla, who was also to lecture on history and biography, cabled home offering his services to the new Ministry of Information but received a reply (from Lord Lloyd) telling him not to return. The South American countries were of vital importance to Britain for food supplies and for the oil of Venezuela. The two therefore together visited the Argentine, Brazil, Uruguay, Chile and Peru and A. J. S. White went on to Colombia and Venezuela. (Guedalla lagged slightly behind all the way because he refused to travel by air.) At the end of the tour they wrote a report making recommendations for the future, the majority of which were accepted. This report therefore gives a fairly complete picture of the Council's work in South America during the early years of the war.

A distinctive feature of the Latin American countries is that the Council did not need to establish Institutes there but supported the already existing Anglophile Societies (Asociaciones or Sociedades de Cultura Inglesa, known as the Culturas) and encouraged the development of others. The Culturas had aims exactly similar to those of British Institutes but were Latin American Institutions, controlled by boards of local nationals with local national Chairmen. The Council also supported British schools, many of which had been recently started, particularly in the Argentine and Chile. In Latin America, as elsewhere, the main effort was concentrated directly or indirectly on the teaching of English, although, as in other countries, lectures, performances of drama and music, film shows and the distribution of books and periodicals were all encouraged.

In an appendix to the report A. J. S. White makes some general observations. The South Americans, he says, were by nature more inclined to the French than to the British, and more to the British than the Germans. 'They admire our sporting qualities and our tradition for honest business, but they resent our aloofness and are ignorant of our culture.'[1] He continues:

> There is a feeling in the West and North of South America, which is common to all distant places I think, that those countries are not given the notice they deserve from Britain. It was a frequent remark that the British Council's work was welcomed because no-one else took an interest. It was also felt that more attention might be paid to the Diplomatic Representatives of these countries in London.[2]

White made some remarks which might be helpful to the British Council staff today, and, for that matter, are of general interest:

> I was also impressed by the harm that can be done in these countries by our failure to comply with small requests. Not only the British Council's efficiency, but also the efficiency of Britain itself is sometimes judged (and compared with that of other nations) by the response to minor requests ... I have seen too many instances of unacknowledged letters or delayed replies ... Much harm can be done to our reputation by this sort of thing.[3]

By November 1939 the Argentine Association of English Culture in Buenos Aires, which was well established and self-supporting and the prototype of most of the other Culturas, had 4,000 students and 670 members and had no difficulty in filling a large hall for lectures, films, lantern slides, etc. (In that part of the report which deals with Peru the authors say: 'There is great scope for placing British Newsreels. The documentary films hitherto sent have been very poor. It is not worth sending others unless they are first-class, as standards here are high.'[4] These remarks presumably applied equally to other countries.)

In Brazil the Society at Rio de Janeiro had about 500 members and 400 students, while that at Sao Paulo had over 1,000 students. There were two British schools in Rio and one in Sao Paulo. Uruguay had one Cultural Institute and Chile three, 'which fortunately draw their membership and support from different social and educational levels',[5] and also British schools. Peru had a Cultural Association with about 160 members and 120 students; in Colombia a British Institute was proposed in Bogota with branches at Medellin, Cali, and Barranquilla, while a Cultura was projected in Venezuela.

Guedalla and White recommended support for most of these enterprises, in many cases proposing capital grants to improve existing buildings or acquire new ones, and subsidies for the salaries of lecturers and
teachers in others. They also recommended an increase in the number
of bursaries and scholarships for Argentine and Brazilian scholars.

Throughout the whole course of the war cultural relationships with
the Latin American countries ranked only second to those with the
Middle East, and if the expenditure was not quite on the scale of the
Mediterranean Basin, this was partly because the Anglophile Societies
were so largely self-supporting. The difficulty of finding staff to cope
with the enormous expansion of the British Council's work was certainly no less, but the circumstances of war contributed here as elsewhere to an individuality in some of its leading personalities.

Pride of place must go to Sir Eugen Millington-Drake, who in the
long line of English eccentrics was a minor classic. Tall, handsome and
very rich, he had been educated at Eton where he achieved the unusual
feat of becoming Captain of the Oppidans, Captain of the Boats and
President of the Eton Society (Pop). According to a contemporary he
never got over this unusual hat trick.

Then early in the war he achieved a wider fame, because, as Minister
to Uruguay, he was credited with having had much influence on the
events which led to the sinking of the *Graf Spee* by persuading the
Uruguayan authorities to apply Article 17 of the Hague Convention,
which decrees that belligerents may not stay in neutral harbours longer
than is necessary to render them seaworthy. German as well as British
sources gave Millington-Drake much of the credit for this. The diary
of Commander F. W. Rasenack of the *Graf Spee* contains the following
good description of the man as well as of the events.

Mr Millington-Drake by clever propaganda and by his personal
activities has managed to gain the hearts of the Uruguay people for
the British cause. He made himself popular and they like him. He is
present on almost all sporting occasions, congratulates the winners ...
and gives trophies. He knows the minds of the people and how to
flatter them. This Englishman, who from the outset has all the
advantages on his side, is now the opponent of our Commander in
this diplomatic contest for the fate of the pocket battle-ship *Admiral
Graf Spee* ... The British Minister will therefore try to prevent by all
means in his power our Captain obtaining prolongation. Meanwhile
the Uruguayan Government sends us to the devil.[6]

Millington-Drake had also shown much interest in cultural propaganda and he was lavish in support of the Anglophil Society, which, following the pattern of Buenos Aires, he had founded in Montevideo. His energy and enthusiasm were notorious, but by the time he enters this story he had developed a *folie de grandeur* which gave him the manners and some of the attributes of minor Royalty. He was often the recipient of rebukes from the Foreign Office and in reply to a request to make his telegrams shorter since they wasted time and expense, he is reputed to have replied that time was not important and as to the expense he would pay it himself. He then sent as many telegrams and as long, but on his own account. He spoke Spanish well and was much addicted to lecturing and to poetry readings in that language as well as in English, and he was famous for a lecture he called *Joyas de la Poesia Inglesa*. 'Fabulous Millers,' a colleague wrote, 'with his handsome head and lion's mane spotlighted as he read – many, many times – the Spanish and English versions of "If"!'[7]

He was Minister at Montevideo from 1934 to 1941. Early in 1941 the Secretary-General of the British Council had begun to feel that it was essential to have a Representative in South America with headquarters in Buenos Aires. At approximately the same time, Lord Riverdale, Sir John Chancellor* and Sir Malcolm Robertson all received letters from Sir Alexander Cadogan (the Permanent Under-Secretary) in which he said that opinions in the Foreign Office tended 'to the view that, in spite of the great energy Millington-Drake has shown and in spite of the services he has rendered in Uruguay, the time was coming when it would be an advantage to our representation if a change could be made at Montevideo'.[8] He added that, although the very energy which had enabled Millington-Drake to do so much had led to his ceasing to be *persona grata* to certain members of the Uruguayan Government, the Secretary of State was both 'anxious to soften the blow to Millington-Drake and also to make use of his energy and of his knowledge of South America'. Was there any chance that the British Council would appoint him organiser or general representative in South America?

The suggestion was regarded with interest but also with caution. 'Millington-Drake might well be fitted for such a post', Sir John Chancellor replied. 'The only danger seems to be that his enthusiasm

---

* Sir John Chancellor, a member of the Executive Committee from 1940 to 1946, had served as Vice-Chairman 1940–1 to lighten the load on Lord Lloyd after he became Colonial Secretary.

sometimes runs away with his judgement.'[9] The Secretary-General expressed the view that Millington-Drake would be 'definitely unsuitable as our Representative unless we could attach to him a sort of Staff Officer with enough standing to keep a check on him and to keep the detail in his own hands'.[10] The British Missions in South American countries were then asked their opinion and these were mainly favourable to the idea, the only rider being received from Montevideo.

> Whatever may be the final decision regarding his headquarters, there is one point on which I would like to insist and that is that he should have a complete staff of his own and should do his own accounting. The burden on the staffs of H.M. Missions abroad is too heavy now-a-days to permit of their giving him clerical or secretarial assistance.

The writer added: 'In this connexion, I understand that Millington-Drake has an eye on Crombie, who is now on my staff. If so, I fear that I must disappoint him.'[11]

This then was the man who from the beginning of 1942 was Chief Representative in the Spanish American countries. H. H. Brissenden* was seconded by the Board of Education to become Deputy Chief Representative, in other words as 'a sort of Staff Officer to keep a check on him'.

Millington-Drake lectured and broadcast with enthusiasm and success in English and Spanish, and throughout the war managed to produce a team of other lecturers. He initiated prizes, made book presentations, arranged exhibitions, concerts, dramatic performances and film shows. He travelled extensively and extended his Empire wherever he went, maintaining good relations with the authorities in all the vast territories he visited.

To his own staff, Millington-Drake seems at best to have been an object of affectionate ridicule and at worst to have been heartily disliked. But E. E. R. Church, writing about him twenty-five years later said:

> It is certain that tens of thousands of Uruguayans saw El Draco off when he was finally recalled to England. And that he celebrated his

---

* Brissenden, who had spent some time working in Argentina, had earlier been approached by the Secretary-General as a possible Chief Representative himself, but had turned down the appointment because 'he finds it difficult to leave the important work ... which he is engaged upon at present and also he is disinclined to leave this country in war-time'.[12]

Council appointment by donating thirty thousand pounds for Council uses in Latin America ... It is almost certainly true that one of his secretaries once ran the length of the main platform at the Buenos Aires station while EMD wrote a last telegram on bits of a toilet-roll ... When in London he had the use of the Chairman's room which immediately looked like Victoria Station on a Bank Holiday.[13]

Slightly absurd, he nevertheless has an honourable place in British Council history. He created for the British Council a provincial empire that ran from the Atlantic coast to the Andes. By the end of 1944, in addition to the Cultura in Buenos Aires itself, there were eight provincial institutes; in Chile, 2,300 students and 2,000 members were enrolled at Santiago, Valparaiso and Concepcion; there were five Colombian-British Institutes, one in Paraguay, one in Peru, one in Venezuela, and five provincial branches in Uruguay, in addition to the Cultura in Montevideo. In Uruguay Millington-Drake was once loudly cheered on entrance to a football stadium because he had brought over a football coach with whose help the Uruguayans had beaten the Argentinians.[14]

From 1941 to 1943 E. E. R. Church, quoted above on Millington-Drake, was Representative in Brazil. A far less colourful person, he was nevertheless a first class British Council officer. Francis Toye, who was sent to succeed him as Director of the Rio Cultura when Church was appointed Representative and who later succeeded him in that post, has left this account of him;

Despite few external attributes of distinction he is, in his way, a very remarkable person: conscientious, competent, simple, and, above all, the only man I have ever known whose modesty is so innate, so genuine as to be a positive strength. Previously he had served in a rather humble teaching capacity, first at Bombay, later at St Paul's School in Sao Paulo, whence somebody had been discerning enough to remove him to the direction of the Rio Cultura recently founded by private initiative. Unlike many teachers of his professional status he suffered neither from vanity nor from an inferiority complex; he was content to remain cheerfully himself. When the British Council established connection with the Cultura they soon came to recognise his sterling qualities; indeed, they now intended to establish him as their Representative in Brazil with the specific object of founding new Council Institutes at various places.[15]

Toye goes on to say that, since Church had the defects of his virtues, and was socially timid, he was not necessarily a good choice as Representative, since even if shyness is a minor defect it did constitute a handicap 'in an official whose business it was to meet people, to make friends with them and enlist their support for the projects he had in view'.[16] He adds: 'I dwell on this only because it explains why to succeed Church as representative was comparatively easy, whereas to succeed him as director of the Cultura was very difficult indeed.'[17]

All of which brings us to Francis Toye himself, the most distinguished and the best remembered of all the British Council Representatives in South America. A music critic of some note, he wrote a biography of Verdi which has not been and is not likely to be superseded. In addition to this major claim to fame, he was for seven years Managing Director of the celebrated London *Restaurant Boulestin*. He succeeded Goad as Director of the British Institute at Florence and he was free to go to Brazil for the British Council only because, when Italy came into war and the Italian Institutes were closed, his offer to work for the Ministry of Information was refused. He resented this because, he said, 'I knew Italy and the Italians better than three-quarters of the diplomats and consuls lumped together, and work should have been found or made for me'.[18] It may well have been, however, that the very extent of this knowledge was held against him because, although he was inclined to deny excessive sympathy with the Fascist regime, he could hardly have stayed in Florence until the last minute if he had not in fact been *persona grata* with the regime.

Nevertheless, he was not merely a man of great distinction but in a different way almost as eccentric as Millington-Drake. Having, he tells us, appraised the Brazilians as liking a personality and being impressed by a stunt, he proceeded soon after his arrival to give them one. 'So far from compromising or apologising I would proclaim my background and openly glory in it.'[19] He therefore delivered soon after his arrival a lecture entitled 'Speaking Personally', which he afterwards learned was labelled egotistical, conceited, presumptuous, by the British, but was nevertheless a great success with a capacity audience of Brazilians. Emboldened by this success, he attended a performance of *Romeo and Juliet* at the Opera House, dressed in white tie and tails, and delivered a speech in Portuguese. This had been translated into simple language by the librarian of the Cultura, and learned by heart but it was confidently delivered. 'The fame of the exploit,' he wrote, 'resounded throughout Rio alike in social and academic circles.'[20]

His greatest fame, however, was for a lecture which he delivered in both English and Portuguese called 'The Old School Tie'. It might be an exaggeration to say that this was heard as often as the poem 'If' recited by Millington-Drake, but it was of frequent occurrence and earned him the name of The Old School Toye.[21]

He is more open in his book about the difficulties of staffing the British Council and the Cultura in time of war than are many of the official accounts, and, as Representative, he had to deal with alcoholics, a distinguished scholar with a double first but suffering from a disease which induced homicidal mania, and an exponent of the Direct Method of teaching English who was in the middle of a nervous breakdown. Of the difficulties of finding teachers he says this:

> We were at our wits' end to find adequate teachers to supplement our existing regular staff. I am far from sure, in fact, that we did so but, almost literally, I went out into the highways and byways to look for them. The result was as odd an assortment of bodies as can well be imagined. The outstanding success was a reformed drunkard recommended by the Anglican Bishop; among Brazilians there was an ex-Berlitz teacher with a perfect mastery of spoken English, whose spelling and writing of the language, however, left almost everything to be desired ... a highbrow pedant ... [with a] predilection for unknown idioms ... sometimes getting his phrases ... wrong as when, for instance, he remarked 'This afternoon I feel at the top of my shape'. At Niteroi we even condescended to an ex-trick-rider from a circus (English) who functioned efficiently enough until such time as he had to be got rid of for some misdeameanour.[22]

He tells us, however, that in spite of all this the hard fact was that the numbers at the Cultura increased at a prodigious rate from 700-odd in 1942 to 2,200 in 1944, with a further large increase despite raised fees in 1945, and he says also that the results were not too bad. 'We made a lot of money, costing the British tax-payer practically nothing.'[23]

When he became Representative, Toye's duties included liaison with the Culturas at Sao Paulo, Belo Horizonte, Santos and Chile which had to be visited at least twice a year. And since, unlike Church, he combined the direction of the Rio Cultura with the work for the British Council, his first step was to house the two under one roof. At the Cultura itself weekly lunches, debates, play-readings with semi-action became regular features of the curriculum, while Toye's most successfu

and most cherished venture was a choral society, 'unique of its kind in
Brazil, perhaps in South America'.[24] As well as British singers it included Brazilians, French, a Czech and a Pole, and he says of it:

> We never sang worthless music; our repertory ranged from carols
> and *The Mikado* madrigal to Stanford's delicious *Heraclitus*, and *The
> Blue Bird*, Elizabethans such as Gibbons and Morley, the Christmas
> choruses from *The Messiah* ... Of everything I accomplished in
> Brazil I look back with the greatest pride on that little Choral Society.
> Not till I returned to Florence and tried, with little success, to repeat
> the experiment, did I realize what a genuine feat it represented.[25]

When one adds that included among the British Council teachers in
Brazil was Frederick Fuller, a professional singer and a friend of the
national composer Heitor Villa-Lobos, whose songs he sang at many
concerts (later repeating his performance in London), one can reasonably say that, whether or not this was high art, it was cultural diplomacy
on a distinguished scale.

Two other things deserve mention, both as showing the scope of the
British Council's work and as reflecting the special tastes of the time.
The first was the six weeks' tour in 1941 by England's great plastic
surgeon, Sir Harold Gillies, who raised enormous interest by lecturing
and performing operations in Lima, Santiago, Buenos Aires, Montevideo, Rio de Janeiro and Sao Paulo. The second, even more successful,
was a small and comparatively unpretentious exhibition of British
children's painting, the work of pupils of elementary, secondary, public
and private schools shown in Rio de Janeiro, Sao Paulo and Belo Horizonte (two other collections were shown in Canada and at Savannah in
Georgia). No attempt was made to present these pictures as art, merely
as something new in education. It was a comparatively new discovery
that, before they develop logical processes of thought, children have a
natural instinct for symmetry, composition and colour harmonies, and
the paintings were exceptionally good of their kind. Press comments on
the exhibition included the following: 'The greatest proof of vitality
Great Britain could give to her friends in South America ... It is a
spectacle that moves us profoundly.' 'The individuality and sincerity of
all these pictures is a great educative lesson to our students ... They also
indicate the fundamentals of British education ... Personality above all.
Movements, initiative, personality, these are the secrets of British education. The science of order and balance without losing the originality,
this is what we must learn from them.'[26]

8

Home Division

Early in the war it became apparent that one of the most urgent problems the British had to face was the large influx of foreigners into England and that this lay well within the province of the British Council. To begin with this consisted chiefly of German, Austrian and Czech civilians who had sought refuge here to escape internment or death. Because of the Home Office regulations for immigrants, these people were largely unemployed and living on the charity of their hosts, or, however distinguished they were in their own countries, working in menial jobs, chiefly as domestic servants. In the autumn of 1939 they were joined by a considerable company of Poles.

As early as September of that year S. H. Wood, representing the Board of Education on the Executive Committee and later Chairman of the British Council Committee on Foreigners in Great Britain, suggested that something ought to be done for 'say 10,000 or 20,000' of these refugees,[1] and it was agreed that, together with W. Graham and Sir John Power he should submit definite proposals that could be put before the Treasury.

The preamble to these proposals made the point that the refugees were the legitimate business of the Council, since when the war was won they would return to their homes, carrying a good or bad impression of Britain with them. It was agreed that it would not be practicable for the Council to regard all refugees as within its province and that its activities should be limited to work on behalf of the most educated people, while it should not seek out those who were already enjoying a fair measure of social and cultural life at universities or among friends.

The original proposals were of a fairly limited kind – for receptions at which foreigners might be brought together with their own nationals and with British people willing to invite them to their houses, for a drive to secure free tickets for theatres, concerts and cinema houses, for the loan of musical instruments, artists' material and typewriters to those who depended on them, and for an attempt to find work, even of an unpaid kind, for some of the young.[2]

History would prove that probably the most important of S. H. Wood's proposals was that the Council should try to secure the services of Miss Parkinson, an officer of the National Union of Students, whose work for the Students' Committee of the Council was already well known. In the following weeks Miss Parkinson was approached and finally agreed to serve 'without emoluments provided she were able to have the services of her present personal assistant, Miss Lankester, whose salary of £4 a week would then be paid by the Council'.[3] From the beginning Nancy Parkinson therefore took charge of the section of the Council which, originally called the Resident Foreigners' Division, had its name changed to the Home Division when it became clear that its work would have to be extended to British subjects from all parts of the Empire.[4]

Nancy Parkinson is one of the great names in the history of the British Council, since she was so largely responsible for the work of the Home Division which soon became of the utmost importance to the national war effort. She had genuine creative ability and knowledge and experience which enabled her to get on easily with the officials of the various Ministries with whom she had to deal.

A compulsive worker, usually to be found at her desk in Hanover Street late into the night, she was often less popular with her own staff, who found her autocratic and rather bossy, qualities often attributed to women in a position of authority in those days when this was relatively so much more difficult for them to achieve. However, no one has ever denied her capacity, or argued the justice of her claim to responsibility for the organisation of this vastly and speedily expanding work.

The response to the initial appeals on behalf of the refugee population was immediate, and by March of the following year the Resident Foreigners' Committee was able to report several successful receptions; a carol concert at Sadler's Wells attended by over a thousand people, when carols of Britain, France, Austria, Czechoslovakia, Germany and Poland had been sung; a course of lectures on British Life and Institutions by lecturers who included W. Wedgwood Benn (The British Parliamentary System), Hugh Walpole (British Literature), Clive Bell (British Art), Ivor Brown (The British Theatre) and Harold Nicolson (The British People – Their Character and Way of Thought).[5] More than 3,000 complimentary tickets were received for theatres, art exhibitions and so on; and a scheme was initiated for the circulation of periodicals.

Then in the early part of 1940, with the invasion of Norway and the Low Countries and finally with the collapse of France, the refugee population already here were joined by thousands of people from Belgium, Holland, France and Norway, in most cases in a state of deep depression. To the collapse of their countries, separation from their homes and families, uncertainty about the future, increased aerial warfare over this country and, one supposes, growing doubts as to how long it would be before the enemy from whom they had escaped would overtake them, there had to be added the fact that the large majority could not speak English. Quite apart from the question of compassion, it was obvious that so many people in a state of near-despair might be a very great danger to this country and equally obvious that the first step towards restoring their morale was to teach them the language.

On 28 August 1940 an interdepartmental meeting was held at the Treasury attended by representatives of the Home Office, the Foreign Office, the Board of Education and the Service Departments. At this meeting it was agreed that the British Council should be directly responsible for the educational and cultural welfare of civilians and of the allied merchant seamen, and it received a supplementary grant of £17,000 from the Treasury for this work. It was also instructed to do similar work for members of the Armed Forces and internees, but only when asked by Service Departments and the Home Office to do so, when these departments would bear the cost.

S. H. Wood expressed himself as extremely pessimistic about the results of this arrangement:

> The Council is now engaged in, or on the brink of, such a substantial volume of work that it has had to ask the Treasury for larger sums than it has hitherto spent on foreigners in this country, but not larger than it has in the past spent abroad ...
>
> The conclusion of the conference, from which I dissented, was that when possible the cultural welfare for foreigners should be regarded as the responsibility of the government department concerned and that any money spent on cultural activities should be borne on the vote of that department. It is, of course, a pretty pattern. But what does it mean? It means that all requests from say Polish or Czech military units should be made to the War Office

17 and 18 Attracting children's attention: children's book exhibition at Sabadell, Catalonia, Spain (*above*), and in Athens (*below*)

19 Part of the queue to join the library in Hyderabad, India, when it opened in 1979

20 Kenyan university and technical college students at the issue desk of the British Council library in Nairobi

who would consider them and if they thought fit would ask the British Council to submit an estimate of cost, and the War Office might subsequently ask the Council to do the work.[6]

This might be reasonable, he said, if the Council were not already engaged directly in the work, if the government departments had machinery, leisure and the necessary experience to sort out and decide what were or were not practicable and desirable cultural activities, and if waste of time in passing estimates to and fro and ultimately to the Treasury were not involved. And he ended his letter:

It is of great political importance, but each separate government department sees its own little bit as a rather troublesome little problem of teaching the minimum of English to those whose welfare has been forced upon them. I have little doubt that the Treasury do not understand what it is all about; and are chiefly anxious to avoid the allocation of a largish sum to a body like the B.C. which is engaged on admittedly experimental work. The Treasury do not like experiments.[7]

This letter proved unduly pessimistic except in relation to the War Office. The Council was able to proceed with work among civilians and the allied merchant seamen (mainly Norwegians and Dutch but also considerable numbers of Belgian, Greek, French and Poles) from its own funds, and in addition both the Home Office and the Air Ministry immediately appreciated the seriousness of the problem and actively sought its aid.

Although the Council immediately submitted requests, many of which originated with allied governments, to the War Office, the latter refused at first 'to authorise cultural or educational work amongst the Allied armies on anything more than a trivial scale'.[8] This, according to the Secretary-General, A. J. S. White, caused resentment among the allied governments who could not understand why the Council, who were active among all other allied people, should be prevented from carrying out similar work among the allied soldiers.[9]

In April 1941 Nancy Parkinson reported a more satisfactory meeting at the War Office where it was agreed that, in consultation with British and Allied Welfare and Educational Officers, the Council should report on the needs of the various units. The War Office would then approach the Treasury for authorisation to spend the necessary funds.[10] These arrangements did not go forward without hitch but funds were eventually provided to enable recommended work to be carried out.

The Report of 1941–2 also announced that the work of the Council had been formally extended to British subjects who had come to this country from other parts of the Empire,[11] the immediate needs being for the most part those of the armed forces of the Dominions, and of men from the Colonies who were arriving in increasing numbers for other war purposes – seamen, technicians, lumbermen and so on.

Then in 1942 the Treasury sanctioned the expenditure of the Council's own funds on the armed forces of the United States while on service with their units, and both the War Office and the Air Ministry circulated a directive to all Command Education and Welfare Officers drawing attention to the various facilities offered by the Council.

That then was the scope of the problem. Before attempting to describe how the British Council set about its solution, it must be said that it would be a misconception to regard their work as in any sense charitable. To quote a writer in the 1941–2 Report of the British Council:

> It is well for the people of Britain to remember what they owe to the magnificent work of Norwegian, Dutch and Greek merchant seamen, without whom the Battle of the Atlantic could not have been won and to the Polish, Czechoslovak and Free French squadrons of the Royal Air Force. And it is not only in the Armies, in the Navy and Air Force that our allies are found, but in industry and agriculture.[12]

The same writer went on to say:

> Such organisation of the effort of the free peoples of Europe in exile has not been seen before. Were it to bring no material benefit to our allies or to ourselves, it would still stand as a social experiment of great fascination.

The work was organised on a regional basis, four officers being appointed – for London, East Anglia and the Home counties, for North England and North Wales, for South-West England and South Wales and for Scotland. The first thing was to teach English. Local and educational authorities co-operated in finding premises and providing teachers, the Council undertaking both things only when the local authority was unable to do so. The Council also worked in co-operation with the Allied and Neutral Seamen's Committee of the Ministry of Shipping and the Port Welfare Officers appointed by the Ministry of Labour.

Premises used for the teaching of English soon became miniature Institutes where books and periodicals could be distributed and cultural work carried on. Text-books for teaching, dictionaries and phrase-books were required in enormous numbers. The Institut Français received a grant from Parliament which was administered by the Council (and paid back at the end of the war). National hostels and club rooms for the seamen were provided in the majority of ports.

In July 1940 the first of a number of National Centres, the Polish Hearth, was opened in London and became the main focus of Polish cultural life. This was followed in January 1941 by the opening of the Czechoslovak Institute and by the Norwegian Seamen's Centre, both in London. The largest and best known, The Allied Centre, was opened in Liverpool, in April 1941. The premises were destroyed by bombing within a fortnight but the Centre had re-opened elsewhere by July. Ian Hay visited this Centre and left an account of it. (His visit seems to have been paid towards the end of the war and probably such a high degree of organisation was not instantly achieved.)

The centre and focus of inter-Allied activity in Liverpool is the Allied Centre in Basnett Street. It is also called the British Council House, because it came into existence through the initiative of that body, which furnished the original funds ...

It was originally an office building of several stories, and must be unique in the number and variety of schemes of interior decoration which it houses, for it provides a separate club-room for no less than seven of its principal nationals. Within these inviolate resorts they may foregather at will, segregated from the outside world, speaking their own language, and talking their own scandal; reading their own books and newspapers (so far as these are obtainable), and listening to their own national broadcasts, in addition to those furnished daily by the B.B.C. to each nation in its own tongue. The place is theirs and theirs only, and they cherish it like a corner of their own beloved soil.

Coming to furniture and decorations, the American room is certainly the most modernistic, but the Czech is by far the most distinguished ...

The decoration and colour scheme of their club lounge represents a triumph of improvisation. The room allotted to them was bare, drab, and dark, for it had no outside window – it merely looked into a dingy court – and an unsightly steam-pipe, running up the wall, disfigured one corner.

Today the doors and window frames are brightly painted, the furniture is Czech in style, and the walls are covered with gay murals, depicting legendary heroes and Czech peasants in their vividly coloured national costumes. Even the steam-pipe has been adapted to the general scheme: it is now painted to look like the chimney of a china stove, and for good measure a book-case disguised as a stove has been installed beneath it.[13]

Then, having said that there is a restaurant, a lounge, a lecture-theatre, a ball-room, a recreation hall, and a number of small rooms employed chiefly as classrooms for the study of English and other foreign languages (although on Fridays by a band of ladies of all nations who are there to mend socks and other garments), the author sets out on a round of the Club premises.

The big restaurant, like every similar establishment in Britain at this period, is packed ... The company is a complete League of Nations in itself. Here is a dusky West Indian in RAF uniform, beside him a Free French naval rating. Not far away sits a young officer in the uniform of the South African Air Force ... But the majority of the men present appear to be merchant seamen, of every rank and race, distinguishable by their heavy clothing and thick blue jerseys.

There are also some trousered young ladies with bandana handkerchiefs round their heads, mostly refugees working in Liverpool. This Polish girl is a student at the famous Liverpool School of Architecture, where some fifty young Poles of either sex are being trained. She is the youngest daughter of Marshal Pilsudski ... [There was also a medical school for Poles at Edinburgh under the direction of Professor Juracz. When the University of Edinburgh celebrated its 400th anniversary in July 1983, 40 former students turned up from 34 different countries to join the celebrations.] The principal centre of attraction in the Recreation Hall is the billiard-table, or rather tables. Their life is one of non-stop variety, for each nation plays its own game on them ... [14]

In the Centre films to suit the taste of individual nationalities were shown and from it outdoor sport was arranged, as well as external hospitality, of which Ian Hay wrote:

> The first acceptances, as usual, were cautious and diffident, but a typical Lancashire welcome soon abolished any suspicion of 'propaganda', and it became unnecessary to issue further invitations; for the guests now came and went of their own accord. One small household achieved a record by entertaining twenty-three Free French privates in a single afternoon.[15]

Allied Centres established with the help of the Council ranged from this one in Liverpool to the small Anglo-Belgian and Anglo-French Clubs at Brixham, the village in Devonshire to which the Belgian and later the French fishing fleets had sailed across the channel after Dunkirk. Here the fishermen and their families spent the war, their fleets, serviced by their own Governments, replacing those of the British fishermen who were sweeping mines or in the Merchant Navy.* With the help of the British Council the Belgian Government also opened centres in Cardiff, Penzance, Preston and Swansea and the French in Penzance and Warrington. Later centres were opened in London for the Belgians, the Greeks, the Yugoslavs, even a Turkish Halkevi, and the Polish and Czechoslovak Centres in London were duplicated in Edinburgh, where there were also Free French and American Centres and the Seven-Seas Club at Leith.

Like other war-time recruits, the Council's Regional Officer for Scotland, H. Harvey Wood, found that, having been seconded with all haste from Edinburgh University to work with the Polish Army in Scotland, he at first had nothing to do. Then he was asked to report on the educational and cultural needs of the Polish Army. In four days he visited practically all the units, covering 570 miles. He found that the needs of the troops were almost identical in all units, the first demand always being for the teaching of English. This had previously been carried on by volunteers from among local school teachers, whom Harvey Wood described as 'more than a little tired'. He reported 'a modest request' from Brigade Headquarters 'for about 300 small Polish dictionaries and 200 Minerva Dictionaries', for 'as many sets of our *British Life and Thought* pamphlets as can be spared, novels of a simple type, books on History, Economics etc. All books in Polish of English interest are urgently requested and of each of these they would

* There is a good description of this community also in *Peaceful Invasion* by Ian Hay, pp. 10–18.

like, if possible, about 150.'[16] The provision of films would depend on a mobile film unit, but lecturers, gramophones and records (of light music and Chopin) and musical instruments in quantity were asked for everywhere he went. A general experience all over the British Isles were requests for British and Allied flags, and portraits of the King and Queen, of the Prime Minister, and of Leaders of the Allied Governments.

Other requests were for materials for architects and draughtsmen, a travelling Exhibition of Art, small repertory companies presenting English and French plays, football, netball and basketball equipment and shoes for sprinting. Courses in agriculture and engineering were asked for and lectures on specialised subjects such as chemistry, architecture, wireless, agriculture, mechanics and so on.

In a broadcast delivered many years after it was all over, Harvey Wood left this account of his work.

The Polish Army in Scotland rapidly became a full-time responsibility for me, with regular visits to Bridge of Earn and to Polish units all over the country. Teachers had to be found in very considerable numbers, to teach English to Polish troops, to Polish airmen, and to the crews of Polish warships. Many of these teachers had never taught English as a foreign language before, and some of the best of them had never taught English *at all* before, but had been modern language teachers, and were therefore familiar with the problems associated with learning and teaching a new tongue. A few of them taught in the cities, but a great many had to live in close proximity to the units they were teaching, and these units were scattered all over Scotland from the Borders to the extreme north. Some did their teaching aboard destroyers and submarines, and occasionally went to sea with their pupils, in order that the continuity of their studies should not be interrupted. The Poles were wonderful pupils, and rapidly acquired a command of English which, if not always faithful to idiomatic usage, was more vivid and picturesque than the original.[17]

The conjunction of Harvey Wood and the Poles was a creative one, and many of the most interesting innovations of the war came out of Scotland. Most notable was the Exhibition of Allied Art organised in 1941 by the British Council in the National Gallery of Scotland at Edinburgh. This was predominantly by Polish artists, but there were contributions from Belgium, Czechoslovakia, Greece, Yugoslavia,

Holland and Norway. About 500 people attended the opening day, including representatives of the allied Governments. During the two months the exhibition was open, a concert was given in the National Gallery every Wednesday by musicians of one or other of the allied countries. Following its showing in Edinburgh, C.E.M.A.* toured the exhibition through Scotland and England. This show was followed by others of the work of artists of single nations.

The publications of the Council included *British Book News*, a monthly book list which still continues today and *Britain Today*, an illustrated monthly review published in English, French, Spanish and Portuguese, consisting of twenty-eight pages of text and eight illustrations and containing articles on a variety of topics including regular features on the theatre, art, films, architecture and music. Writers included Edmund Blunden, James Bridie, Ivor Brown, Clough Williams-Ellis, B. Ifor Evans, Jane and Maxwell Fry, Graham Greene, John Hayward, Edwin Muir, Janet Adam Smith and many other people equally distinguished at the time. In 1942 the British Publishers' Guild produced on the Council's behalf a set of twelve 'International Guild Books' in the languages of the various allied communities on such topics as the British Empire or the British System of Government (sold at 9d. to 1s.) and Longmans published a series called *British Life and Thought* on such subjects as British Trade Unions, and British Agricultural Research. *The Spirit of English History* by A. L. Rowse was published in Dutch and Norwegian at 1s. 6d. and *British Authors* by Richard Church at 2s. 6d.

English was taught at all allied boarding schools and books were presented to them, as also to the French Military Academy at Malvern, while a constant supply of lecturers, art exhibitions, musical performances and so on was arranged. Those who lectured for the British Council during the war included Thomas Bodkin, Father M. C. D'Arcy, T. S. Eliot, John Gielgud, W. G. Holford, Gilbert Murray, Dorothy Sayers, Stephen Spender, H. G. Wells and Rebecca West. Grants were made to students to take university or technical training (in 1941 alone 90 students of different nationalities and 100 Polish engineers received grants), and arrangements were made with the University of Cambridge Local Examinations Syndicate for special examinations for the Certificate of Proficiency in English and for a reduction of fees for allied servicemen on leave from the Canadian

* Council for Education, Music and the Arts. It is now known as the Arts Council.

and American Forces. The Council began, in collaboration with allied governments, to award scholarships for post-graduate and undergraduate study in order to train allied personnel for post-war reconstruction in their own countries.

One of the most enduring initiatives of the British Council was the Conference of Allied Ministers of Education which led in the long run to UNESCO. In October 1942, after discussion between Nancy Parkinson for the British Council, allied Ministers of Education, R. A. Butler, President of the Board of Education, and officials of the Board of Education and of the Foreign Office, Sir Malcolm Robertson proposed to the allied Governments 'periodical meetings when educational questions affecting the allied countries of Europe and the United Kingdom, both during the war period and in the post-war period, could be discussed'.[18]

The Conference of Allied Ministers of Education met regularly during the war, at first under the Chairmanship of R. A. Butler, later under Richard Law (the son of Bonar Law, later Lord Coleraine) and finally under Ellen Wilkinson. Richard Seymour, who wrote an account commissioned by the Council for Cultural Co-operation of the Council of Europe, said of these meetings: 'The first steps had been taken towards the formation of a World educational organisation.' He added: 'One firm hand presided over this work and at the same time guided the conference of Allied Ministers up to the establishment of Unesco, that of Dame Nancy Parkinson of the British Council.'[19]*

At its second meeting, the Conference of Allied Ministers set up a Commission to consider bi-lateral cultural agreements between allied Governments.† According to Richard Seymour the work of the Commission inspired the group of cultural conventions which the United Kingdom began to negotiate at the end of the war, while he also says: 'The signatories of the first bilateral agreements to accord with the recommendations of the Allied Ministers were also the signatories of the Treaty of Brussels', thus the Western European Union and the Cultural Experts Committee of the Council of Europe 'remained based

---

* In recognition of her services with the British Council Nancy Parkinson was made a DCMG in 1965.
† 'An intellectual [i.e. cultural] agreement is an instrument arranged between two or more states with a view to encouraging intellectual relations (artistic, literary, scientific, educational) between their peoples. It extends to one or several fields of intellectual life, without approaching that of political, economic or social relations, which are reserved to other negotiations.'[20]

on the foundations laid by the Allied Ministers'.[21]*

The Home Division, conceived for the benefit of the alien population in Great Britain during the war, nevertheless survived these
visitors' return to their own countries. The structure of regional offices
in the United Kingdom still exists, although altered to meet peacetime needs. In terms of the contribution made to the education, potential
abilities and happiness of vast numbers of people, it must be regarded
as one of the British Council's greatest achievements.

* It should be noted, however, that the first cultural agreement signed by Britain
was that with Greece, negotiated between Lord Lloyd and General Metaxas. It
remained unratified, owing to the outbreak of war.

9

Post-war Readjustment

In January 1943 Reginald Davies,* the Council's Finance Officer, newly appointed in an attempt to bring order into the confusion of the British Council's finances, wrote:

> In developing this multiplicity of activities to diverse types of people in so many countries, the policy has been one of opportunism and experiment. Wherever opportunity has offered, or need has been suggested, the Council has taken advantage of the one and has done its best to supply the other by whatever suitable means have presented themselves. In this way, during the short period of seven years, a great body of valuable experience has been accumulated; and results have been achieved of which the importance is widely recognised. It is therefore without any intention of criticising past policy that attention is drawn in this note to the financial effect of pursuing that policy, without modification, for any considerable further period.[1]

He went on to sketch a projection showing what the result would be if the Council continued 'to interpret its mission as widely as it has done in the past'.

The grant for 1943–4 had been raised from the 1942–3 figure of £966,705 to £1,573,958. The Council was working at that time in some thirty-six countries, of which more than a third were in South America and the West Indies, while a quarter were in the Middle East. Only three were on the continent of Europe. In five parts of the world only – Egypt, Portugal, Cyprus, Malta and Aden – was the work described as 'well-developed'; in five more – Turkey, Palestine, Iraq, Colombia and Uruguay – its activities were described as semi-

---

* A former officer of the Sudan Political Service, he had been Director of Publicity at the British Embassy, Cairo from 1939–42.

developed; for the rest they were in a stage at best initiatory and in many cases only embryonic.

What would be the annual cost, the Finance Officer asked, of fully-developed activities not merely in the countries where the Council worked at present but also, once the war was over, in countries such as the USA, the USSR, China, the Dominions and India, to say nothing of France, Germany, Japan and Italy? He added:

> On this hypothesis, it seems imperative to enquire whether the British Council's present policy does not interpret its mission in too wide a sense and whether there may not be some restrictive principle which should be applied in order to keep the Council's activities – and thereby the cost of them – within somewhat narrower bounds.[2]

In the following month Davies wrote to C. H. M. Wilcox at the Treasury Chambers, to raise a question of principle. He said that in the past the result of the annual discussion with the Foreign Office and the Treasury had been simply a figure for the grant-in-aid, in the light of which the Council had modified proposals contained in the estimates discussed. There had not been any question of Treasury approval of the final distribution of the budget. He went on to say that this year different proposals had been agreed and the Treasury was being asked to approve not merely a lump sum grant-in-aid but a forecast of a programme of expenditure set out in a certain manner:*

> You will see that we expect that the rate of our existing recurrent expenditure on 1st April, 1943, will be £614,000 per annum and that we are asking to be allowed to embark on new recurrent expenditure at the rate of £438,034 per annum, making a total of £1,052,034 per annum; and also to incur non-recurrent expenditure (in which category we have included such items as production of films, which, though generically recurrent in our programme, are not individually recurrent) to the amount of £782,243, making a grand total for the year 1943/44 of £1,834,277. We are also asking for a provision of unallocated funds under two heads – (1) a sum based on 5% of the net cost during the year of the programme analysed above, and (2) a further sum for expenditure on new services ... [3]

* For the 1943–4 estimates, the Council, at Davies's suggestion, had for the first time adopted the method of estimating used by the BBC.

Adding that it was important that the various items in the expenditure should severally receive Treasury approval, he wrote:

In the absence, for example, of any specific approval of a rate of annual expenditure on proposed new services, it is clearly possible for the Council to commit the Treasury by the end of the financial year to the whole new rate of recurrent expenditure of over a million pounds, by manipulation of a Grant-in-Aid very much smaller than that actually requested, since, by postponing the initiation of a new project until late in the financial year, cash expenditure on it during the year may entail a recurrent commitment of many times' its own amount.[4]

The Finance Officer of the British Council was clearly on good terms with Mr Wilcox of the Treasury and at a meeting later in the year he confided to him that he thought the Council had now reached such a size that it was no longer possible for the Chairman to supervise the details of the Council's work as Lord Lloyd had done, more especially a Chairman who did not give it his whole time. 'At the moment Sir Malcolm Robertson does try to control everything in some detail, with the inevitable result that he cannot do it properly.'[5] Davies also made the point that insufficient use was being made of the talent and experience of members of the Executive Committee, 'which is at present almost wholly a rubber stamp body'.[6] The Executive Committee were themselves becoming restive under this treatment, and Davies suggested that the Chairman and Executive Committee should concern themselves (the latter much more actively) with the formulation of the Council's policy and that the Secretary-General's post should be upgraded to one of Director-General responsible for the execution of that policy. He felt that it would be a waste of time putting up this suggestion to the Council as the Chairman and Secretary-General would inevitably oppose it, and again he thought one could not hope to get any support from the Foreign Office.

Davies had already embodied these views in a memorandum agreed with Sir Angus Gillan, Director of the Empire Division of the British Council, and he suggested that at some stage the Treasury might propose a strong Committee of Enquiry to look into the organisation of the Council to see whether it was really fitted to discharge the wider and extended functions which it was now undertaking.[7]

Unaware of any of this, the Foreign Secretary, Anthony Eden, had already written to Sir Kingsley Wood, Chancellor of the Exchequer, saying that he could see no alternative to applying for a supplementary grant-in-aid for the Council in July 1943. He explained that although the original grant-in-aid had included an unallocated reserve of £216,250, which had seemed at the time large enough to allow an adequate margin for expansion, this reserve had fallen two months after the start of the financial year to about £115,000, partly because the year opened with a deficit of £20,000 instead of an estimated balance of £20,000 and partly because numerous supplementary allocations had had to be made since the submission of estimates to the Treasury.

The Foreign Secretary explained the extreme difficulty of framing estimates in the autumn, for submission to the Foreign Office by the end of the year, which consequently covered a period of eighteen months after they were originally drawn up, 'especially in such abnormal times as the present, when it was impossible to foresee the course of the war and the opportunities which might occur as a result of the liberation of territories, the movements of populations and troops and the changes in the attitude of neutral countries'.

I am being pressed by our Representatives in China, Egypt, Iraq, Persia, Turkey (in fact in every country), as well as by the Minister of State in Egypt, and the Commanders-in-Chief in the Middle East and Persia/Iraq to do everything possible to help the British Council to expand their educational and general activities because the teaching of English, the provision of amenities such as books and films and the diffusion of information on Britain and British achievements are the best means of affecting the attitude of governments and peoples in areas vitally important to us, and of bolstering up the morale of Allied troops and of civilians who are refugees in this country or in the Middle East.[8]

Mr Eden added that he had not included any estimate of necessary expenditure in China, although a report from our Ambassador in Chungking on the need for scientific and cultural liaison was at present being studied. And he asked that the unallocated reserve, standing at about £115,000, should be increased to £400,000 and that the reserve against rising costs, then standing at £71,000, should be increased to £200,000. This would mean a supplementary of £415,000 but, as it had been decided that in future the Council should pay for the cost of the carriage of their material by Foreign Office and Ministry of

Information bags, provisional allocation should be made for this, 'say £30,000', which would bring the total amount required to £445,000.[9]

Mr Eden attached a memorandum showing the principal new projects the British Council were unable to carry out owing to lack of funds.

Commenting on this request, Mr Wilcox of the Treasury said that the fact that various items of expenditure totalling £40,000 only came to light after the estimates for 1943 were framed was 'one of the results of the Council's slipshod methods which Mr Davies, the new Finance officer, is doing his best to cure', and remarked that Sir Malcolm Robertson had come back from a tour of the Middle East 'imbued with the conviction' that, given sufficient funds, the Council could become 'the greatest single factor in the establishment of a lasting peace of understanding in the world of tomorrow'.[10]

In his reply to the Foreign Secretary, the Chancellor began by registering shock at being asked for more money so closely on agreeing to an increase of nearly £1,000,000, and said that he was not satisfied that the Council could not finance new projects by the pruning of old.

> One of the less satisfactory features of the Council is their lack of discrimination as to the comparative importance of their different activities and their anxiety to expand every side of their work without regard to the relative return.[11]

He complained that the Council increasingly asked for extra funds on the grounds that their activities were of immediate importance in influencing allies and neutrals. This raised the question of whether to concentrate on direct propaganda, which was the function of the Ministry of Information, or on the activities hitherto the concern of the British Council 'and if the latter whether the British Council is the most suitable body to undertake these wider activities as a matter of national short term policy'.[12]

This last was purely a debating point, suggested to the Chancellor by Mr Wilcox, but it was nevertheless threatening. The Chancellor refused to resolve the issue in the day or two necessary for a decision on the July supplementary grant and once more suggested the Council found the money from pruning current activities.

In reply, having expressed his disappointment, the Foreign Secretary said:

For the strengthening of our position and prestige the Council's activities are very necessary, especially in the Middle East, South America, and China, and we feel that any money spent there now will be returned a hundredfold. Expenditure in the areas which we regard as of less importance from the political point of view is negligible and thus no pruning is possible there ...

As regards the second question, viz. whether the Council should concern itself with short-term activities directed, in effect, to winning the war, the paramount consideration must surely be the winning of the war and the choice of the most appropriate weapons in any given area for the achievement of that aim. When the Minister of State, the Middle East War Council, the Commanders-in-Chief, His Majesty's Representatives and various Government Departments ask that the Council should undertake certain educational and cultural work for the purpose of influencing Allies and neutrals, there must be good reasons for this request.[13]

In reply the Chancellor said that he had examined again the list of new projects and he understood that some of the items were regarded by the Foreign Office itself as of doubtful value and others of no great urgency, while he thought that it might be suggested to the Canadian and American Army that, although the Council was willing to continue provision of films and books on a repayment basis, it had to work to an annual budget and could no longer provide them free. He admitted, however, that work in the Middle East and in Persia was of great importance and he agreed to a round sum addition of £100,000 instead of the £445,000 asked for.[14]

The questions that had been brought up by the Council's own Finance Officer and by the officials of the Treasury would clearly have to be answered, and, perhaps because he realised this, Sir Malcolm Robertson made a rather unexpected intervention. Writing to the Foreign Secretary in December 1943, he said that the British Council had come to stay, that its work was warmly welcomed, could not fail to have a beneficent effect, and could not now be arrested without grave effects on national prestige. The work developed year by year and the budget grew larger and larger. Then he said:

At present I am Chairman of the Executive Committee without any authority at all or any powers of decision. I have to refer practically everything either to the Foreign Office, the Treasury, the British

Council's Finance and Agenda Committee or the Council's Executive Committee, or all four. The result is that questions are dealt with piecemeal and decisions are interminably delayed. There is no real plan, no order of priority as between parts of the world or countries.[15]

Having said that he regarded the work of the British Council as an essential for the gradual bringing about of better understanding between the peoples of the world and vital to foreign policy, he continued:

In these circumstances I would urge you to consider whether the time has now come for the setting up of a special Cabinet Committee to consider the whole organisation and future of the Council and whether it should not become a Department of His Majesty's Government annexed to the Foreign Office like the Department of Overseas Trade. India, the Dominions and the Colonies are beginning either actually to make use of us or to wish to do so. I would, therefore, suggest for your consideration, that the Committee might consist of the Secretaries of State for India, the Dominions and the Colonies, the President of the Board of Education, the Chancellor of the Exchequer, and Dick Law, if, as I imagine, you would not have time yourself. Actually I feel that you should yourself preside![16]

Michael Palairet at the Foreign Office commented immediately on the surprising nature of this letter.

It runs contrary to what has hitherto been one of the guiding principles of the British Council — one that I have often heard strongly advocated by Sir Malcolm Robertson himself — namely, that the Council should on no account allow itself to be regarded as an official or governmental body because of the danger of its activities being dismissed as propagandist.[17]

Cadogan, Permanent Under-Secretary at the Foreign Office, suggested that the Foreign Secretary should ask whether this proposal was to be considered as an official one and whether it had the support of the President, and the three Vice-Presidents, without which he felt he would not be justified in proposing the setting up of a special Cabinet Committee on the subject.

Sir Malcolm immediately wrote withdrawing the suggestion of a

Government Department. 'The sentence was very badly worded!'[18]

No more was heard of this project for some time but in September 1944 Robertson wrote once more to Anthony Eden saying that he had heard indirectly that the Cabinet had decided to appoint someone to enquire into the Council's activities, and to make recommendations. 'I most sincerely hope that this is true.'[19]

Eden said that it was true it had been decided that a full inquiry into the future of the Council should be carried out forthwith 'under the auspices of the Foreign Secretary and the Chancellor of the Exchequer'.[20] Sir Findlater Stewart, who had served as Permanent Under-Secretary of State for India from 1930–42, had been asked to undertake the task and had accepted, and Robertson was at liberty to inform the staff and directing committees of the Council of this decision.

One other minute in the Foreign Office files is worth recording. Dated 26 November 1944, it is from the Prime Minister, Winston Churchill, to the Foreign Secretary:

I am quite ready to help the British Council in reasonable ways. I see they have overspent their large income this year by more than £50,000. A very unpleasant story about their sending out a party to teach the Spanish Dons how to stalk deer has obtained publicity in the newspapers. I think their expenditure and enterprises should be strictly scrutinized now. They are certainly one of the objects ripe for retrenchment when the war comes to an end. We must be very careful this does not grow upon us.[21]

The following story had appeared in the *Daily Express*:

The British Council has lent the services of the Scottish Deer Controller, Mr Frank Wallace, to General Franco. He is to advise the Spaniards on game preservation, and thereby develop 'closer cultural relations'.

The expense is not great, but the gesture is absurd ...

This kind of 'projection' of Britain is utterly misleading and most damaging.

Constant public scrutiny of the activities of the British Council will lead inevitably to the conclusion that it is unfitted to the great task of presenting Britain to the world.[22]

The truth of this matter was that a Mr Wallace, Deer Controller of

Scotland, had gone to Spain to advise the Spanish Tourist Agency about game preservation. Mr Wallace had been invited by the Spanish authorities but, as a result of repeated representations from H.M. Mission in Madrid, the Council had paid his fare. This action was approved by the Foreign Office.

The Findlater Stewart Report was not accepted by the Foreign Office and consequently will not be closely examined here. It is remarkable, nevertheless, because in so many matters – the need of the British Council for independence of any Government Department, the necessity for a five year budget to enable it to plan ahead, reform of the Executive Committee and emphasis on the conditions of service of staff and the need for personnel of the right calibre – its recommendations are startlingly similar to those in the Seebohm Report, the result of the most recent review of the Council, thirty-six years later.

But if the details of the Findlater Stewart Report are no longer of much importance, its history is sufficiently remarkable to relate. For many years it was the cause of much speculation and a deep sense of injury to those connected with the British Council, because, although the first suggestion for the need for an inquiry had been made by its own Chairman, neither he nor his Executive Committee were allowed to know the conclusions reached by Findlater Stewart, or to take part in the ensuing consultations between the various Government Departments. The Report, which was dated 8 February 1945, was circulated in confidence to other officials, but was kept secret from the Council despite repeated and increasingly angry requests from the Executive Committee for sight of it. There is still no copy of it to be found on Council files.

In a letter written to his Executive Council on 28 May 1945, Sir Malcolm Robertson said that he had been informed by Mr Eden that there was now no question of a decision being reached on the Findlater Stewart Report for several months, neither could the Foreign Secretary give any assurance that his own services would subsequently be required. In these circumstances, since he now believed the British Council should have a full-time Chairman, he had to choose between serving in that capacity, with no certainty that he would be asked to do so, and his future as an M.P. He therefore proposed to resign – a decision undoubtedly welcomed, if not actually contrived, by the Foreign Office.

In his letter Sir Malcolm gave a short history of the work of the British Council since he had taken over the Chair, in which he made the point (well understood by the Foreign Office) that by the terms of the Royal Charter 'the Government of the Council and the management of its affairs were vested in the Executive Committee and that they and only they could revoke, alter or add to its bye-laws'.[23]

He also said this:

As regards the Home Service [of the British Council], there is no security of tenure. Three months notice may be given on either side. The salaries, especially for the Senior Staff and the type of men and women that we need for it, are derisory. The pension scheme to which they themselves contribute, would not bear public examination ... The Permanent Overseas Service is somewhat better placed, but in their case also the salaries, notably in the case of our Representatives abroad who must be men of standing and known reputation, are inadequate to attract people of the requisite calibre. Their pensions are, in my opinion, unworthy of the services they are expected to render.[24]

In his letter, Sir Malcolm made a 'Confession of Faith' in which he expressed views on the long term benefits to peace on earth to be derived from the better understanding of the peoples of the world which were quite commonly held in those days, but which in the light of experience have acquired a melancholy ring.

Five years after these events a memorandum written in the Foreign Office recorded that, although the production of the Findlater Stewart Report was accompanied by a hail of newspaper articles, Parliamentary Questions and requests from Sir Malcolm Robertson that the findings should be made public or at least communicated to the Council, all of these were resisted 'ostensibly on the grounds that the Report was confidential and not for circulation, but actually because the findings were unacceptable to the Foreign Office'.[25] Although the officials of the Foreign Office were prepared to write fighting drafts for the Secretary of State in interdepartmental warfare with the Treasury, they were in fact extremely critical of the Council.

The inherent defect of Sir F. Stewart's Report [the 1950 document said] was that he confined himself mainly to questions of broad policy and did not examine in any detail the internal organization of the Council. His main finding was in brief that the Council ... should be given an even greater degree of freedom than it already enjoyed. [He recommended that the control by the Foreign and Dominions

Offices should normally be limited to broad strategic policy, subject to right of veto of specific projects which might be embarrassing to these Departments.][26] As the Foreign Office was profoundly dissatisfied, not so much with the work that was being done but with the extravagant manner in which the objects were being achieved, we were naturally disappointed that the question of internal organization had not been more thoroughly examined, and it meant, in effect, that the plans for the much needed overhaul were finally formulated in this Department.[27]

In April 1945, the grounds for Foreign Office dissatisfaction with the Report and proposals for the future of the British Council were embodied in an extremely critical document which, with appendices, ran to over forty pages. The writer, William Montagu-Pollock* said in a preamble that most of the shortcomings of the Council were probably due to the extreme difficulty which they had had in finding men of the necessary calibre for responsible posts at headquarters, and he also said that the Foreign Office had not been very helpful in this matter.

We have left the Council to build up a large and expanding organisation, without seconding to them any good men to run it, and they have had none of the advantages in the recruitment of personnel enjoyed by Government Departments in war time.[28]

He went on to say that many of the difficulties were the direct result of the unsatisfactory and ill-defined nature of the relations between the Foreign Office and the Council which would not be solved 'until those relations are put on more satisfactory basis'.[29]

There seem to have been two main criticisms of the Council. The first was directed to the question of sudden enormous growth. 'The Council has shown no tendency to restrict the limits of its work, nor has it protested to us against demands made on it by ourselves or others; rather have we had to restrain it from trying to "swallow all Whitehall".'[30] This had led to duplication and overlapping of work which was in fact more the responsibility of the Foreign Office or Ministry of Information.

By far the most serious criticisms were levelled at the Headquarters

* Later Sir William Montagu-Pollock, Ambassador to Peru (1953–8), Switzerland (1958–60) and Denmark (1960–2).

staff, and it was explicitly stated that these did not apply with equal force to the staff overseas. 'The impression gained by Mr Montagu-Pollock during his recent tour abroad was that it was remarkable how efficiently the Council was performing in the field considering how thin was the guidance and assistance from home.'[31] (Michael Grant however, testifies that he was well served by Headquarters, allowing for the war-time difficulties under which they worked and the demands he was obliged to make.)[32] The criticisms took two main forms, one of arrogance and the other of inefficiency. Having explained that the Secretary-General was assisted by a Deputy Secretary-General, on a level with whom came the Directors of seven Divisions, Regional and Functional, the writer said:

> These Directors sometimes meet in a kind of Soviet at which decisions appear to be taken, not as the result of any considered planning, so much as of an armistice reached at the end of a battle between competing regional and functional interests. For instance the Home Division, under the energetic direction of Miss Parkinson, is still continuing to expand and has recently purchased buildings at Newcastle, although we feel that work in the home field should be carried on in such a way that it can easily be reduced to minimum proportions when the war is over and when the majority of our allies leave these shores. This purchase was made without previous authority of any kind from the Foreign Office or Treasury, or from the Council's Finance and Agenda Committee.[33]

The most serious criticism was of inefficiency. This was supported by three Appendices written by members of the Council's own staff. One of these is sufficiently interesting and sufficiently impartial to be quoted at some length. The writer (anonymous) began by saying that in 1939 it was the policy of the then Chairman (Lord Lloyd) to expand the Council's work over the maximum area as soon as possible.

> It is difficult to see what else could have been done in the circumstances, but the staff assisting the Chairman were not themselves of very great experience or capacity ... The greatest trouble of all ... was that at a time when the better young men ... were seeking to get into the armed Forces, the Council was forced to recruit rapidly, and was not able to offer either attractive contracts or adequate salaries ... The Council have since then been to some extent handicapped in

their Overseas Service by men who were taken on at that time having risen by the normal process of promotion – a process much speeded up by the rapid expansion of the Council's Service, and by resignations, enlistments etc. etc. – to posts for which they would certainly never have been selected in the first place, and for which they would not normally be chosen now.[34]

These remarks, the writer said, applied to senior staff but had resulted in the appointment of juniors equally inadequate in calibre. He nevertheless pointed out that the Appointments Department had been in a difficult position because they were begged on all sides to produce extra staff.

The writer gave the opinion, as almost everyone connected with this inquiry would do, that the most essential step was the appointment of a new Chairman and the creation of a new post of Director-General or Controller-General. These, he said, must both be men of vision, with the power of inspiring the whole organisation, of toughness and integrity, and of the intelligence to see what had gone wrong and the capacity to put it right.[35]

Montagu-Pollock made two suggestions for solution of the difficulties besetting the Council. The first was that 'the headquarters organisation of the British Council, shorn of the Chairman, the Council, and Executive Committee', should be absorbed into the proposed Foreign Publicity Division of the Foreign Office, which would be under the direction of an Under-Secretary of State for Foreign Publicity.[36]

One gains the impression that the writer himself preferred this solution but at the same time had not much faith in its being accepted and he came a little unstuck when he explained exactly how this change should be made. Thus:

As regards work in the field, we propose that the Council should retain the façade of unofficial status. The feeling on this point of H.M.R.R. at such posts as Cairo and Angora, where the Council's work is most fully developed, is so definite that we think it would be inadvisable to override it by turning the Council's representatives at those posts into Cultural Attachés. We assume there will be no reason why members of the Council Service, even if they are in fact Civil Servants, and are working within the framework of the Foreign Publicity Division when they are employed at home, should not enjoy unofficial status when they are abroad.[37]

And to support this fiction he suggested the formation of a Limited Company, with nominal shareholders directed by the Foreign Office, to take over the properties and liabilities of the present Council, the offices used by the British Council Service in the field and at home to remain known as the British Council offices.

The suggestion that in order to forestall any public expression of anxiety that the Council might be caused to depart from its ideals and lose its strictly non-political nature, 'assurances should be given on this point when the proposed reforms are communicated to Parliament', again seems rather lame.[38]

The writer then went on to the alternative proposal for the re-organisation of the British Council. He said that the key to this would be the appointment of a Controller-General of first-rate ability assisted by a group of Heads of Divisions and he suggested that a Board of Governors would be an improvement on the existing Executive Council 'which is clearly useless'.[39] The suggestion was that the post of Secretary-General should be abolished and replaced by a Director- or Controller-General with full executive powers while the function of the Chairman of the Governing Board would be merely 'to raise the prestige of the Council, to defend its interests, and to give the Council the benefit of his wide experience'.[40]

'We feel bound to recommend,' the writer said, 'that whether the Chairman is to be whole or part-time, Sir Malcolm Robertson should be asked to vacate the post.'[41]

On 12 February 1946, at the request of the Cabinet, a Report on Government Information Services was produced by a committee of officials headed by Alan Barlow of the Treasury. This chiefly concerned the winding up of the Ministry of Information, but the future of the British Council was also considered. Like the Findlater Stewart Report, this document was not shown to the Council who, in this case, were kept in total ignorance of its existence. Montagu-Pollock's memorandum had clearly been studied and one of three plans put forward was to abolish the British Council altogether, its work to be taken over by the Overseas Departments, with the assistance of the proposed Central Government Information Office and His Majesty's Stationery Office. It was, however, pointed out that one of the main disadvantages of this plan was that the revocation of the Council's Charter would be opposed by the Council and 'might require legislation and *lead to political controversy*'.*

---

* My italics; Lord Lloyd could rest in peace.

At a Cabinet meeting called to consider the Report on 21 February 1946, the Labour Foreign Secretary Ernest Bevin, who at no time seems to have felt the admiration for the work of the Council so often recorded by his predecessor, said that he had at first been inclined to recommend that a new Government Department should replace the Council, but that he had decided on the compromise plan set out in paragraphs 32–34 of the Report of the Official Committee, provided the continuance of the Council was brought up for review after a period of five years. He believed that it might be possible for the Consular Service to take over many of the functions of the British Council which might then be abolished. Meanwhile, he must be kept fully informed in advance of the policy the Council were pursuing.[42]

The plan set out in the Report required that a closer scrutiny should be imposed on the Council's activities and that it should be required to show that its staffing was on sound lines; that it should no longer be its own production or procurement authority but should indent on the Government Information Office and HM Stationery Office; and that its sphere of work should be cut back to what is normally understood by 'educational and cultural'. It was admitted that there was a problem in definition here, but 'the task of the British Council may be broadly defined as long term education in the English Language, British arts and sciences and British institutions'.[43]

Cabinet agreement was reached on all these points, and in March the Foreign Secretary directed that suggestions should be made in regard to the appointment of a Chairman and Director-General. Several names were put forward for Chairman, including that of Lord Stansgate (who refused), Patrick Gordon Walker (who was disqualified by being an MP),* Harold Nicolson (if the Chairman had no Executive powers)† and Professor Boase (who had been Representative in Cairo, was first class academically but had returned as Director to the Courtauld Institute of Art at London University). Sir Richard Peck was proposed for the post of Director-General.

In May Ernest Bevin wrote to the Prime Minister that he had come to the conclusion that the best nominee was General Sir Ronald Adam,§

* The Attorney-General's opinion, obtained in May 1946, had been that although this was not strictly a matter of law, it was 'in the highest degree undesirable that any member of Parliament should accept the appointment if he wishes to retain his seat'.[44]

† We know from his diaries he was disappointed at not being asked.

§ Sir Ronald Adam had served as Adjutant-General to the Forces from 1941 to his retirement in 1946; he remained Commander of the Army Education Corps until 1950.

and Attlee minuted this document, 'I will approach him'. Sir Ronald Adam accepted the post of Chairman and was appointed by the Executive Committee on 5 June 1946.

After this appointment, the Foreign Secretary addressed himself to His Majesty's (Diplomatic Service) Representatives abroad in a Circular Letter covering a Definition Document outlining the agreements reached on the future of the British Council.[45] Much stress was laid in both the letter and the enclosure on co-operation between the Foreign Office and the British Council — not merely abroad, where HM Representatives were to keep themselves fully informed of the work and be ready to give guidance, while the staffs of both bodies were to regard themselves as constituting a single team serving a common interest, but also at home, where arrangements were being made for more general consultation. It was urged that there should be pooling of stocks of films, photographs, gramophone records, and, where possible, even of library facilities. In several paragraphs of the Definition Document the Foreign Secretary referred to the limits to be imposed on the Council's work which had been most economically defined earlier by the Council itself. It had been agreed that

> In strictly cultural subjects, which are defined as the English language, the British drama, Fine Arts, Literature and Music, the Council will undertake publicity and education directed towards any category of people and will use any medium for this purpose. In all other subjects the Council will undertake education rather than publicity and its operations will be directed not to the general public, but to certain defined groups.[46]

The Foreign Secretary stated that, although the British Council was to be reviewed after a period, it seemed likely that, even if it were then wound up, its activities and staff would be taken over by some other organisation. 'Our aim is therefore to create a British Council service with conditions of entry, salary and pension based as far as possible on those of the Foreign Service.'[47]

10

The Return to Europe

Although not informed of the findings of the Findlater Stewart Report or of the discussions which followed it, the Executive Committee and senior staff of the Council had a fair idea that their future was in jeopardy. In the year 1945–6 they estimated for a grant-in-aid of £4,673,000 and in March 1945 were informed by Richard Law (Parliamentary Under-Secretary of State for Foreign Affairs), in a letter which was noticeably unsympathetic in tone, that they would receive £3,500,000. He said:

> The salient facts are that Sir Findlater Stewart, having been appointed to carry out a special enquiry, has not yet laid his report before the Secretary of State and the Chancellor of the Exchequer; and that the Council has been subject to criticism by the Public Accounts Committee, on the floor of the House of Commons, and in the Press. Without subscribing to all these criticisms, the Chancellor considers, and his view is shared by the Foreign Office, that in these circumstances an increase in the grant-in-aid would be impolitic and difficult successfully to defend.[1]

To this Sir Malcolm Robertson replied in a long personal letter and more formally for the Executive Committee. He said that the criticisms of the Public Accounts Committee were made because a flaw in the financial arrangements subsequently put right, caused the grant for 1942–3 to be overspent; that he would like to be given chapter and verse for criticisms on the floor of the House as he had been present on all occasions when questions were asked and could recall none 'that were critical or intended to be critical'; and he asked, with some justice: 'Am I really to understand that two great Government Departments have paled before the scurrilities of the Beaverbrook Press? ... '[2]

Sir Malcolm pointed out that the Council has been pressed by HM

Representatives and the Foreign Office to develop work in all liberated countries and asked whether there was any possibility of obtaining extra funds by a supplementary estimate. And he wound up by saying:

> In conclusion I feel compelled to say that I have a fear that we are not receiving from the F.O. the whole-hearted support to which we are entitled when dealing with other Government Departments and notably the Treasury.[3]

In reply Sir Michael Palairet for the Foreign Office stated that the only case in which the Treasury would be willing to consider a supplementary grant would be one based on the need for increased activity in liberated Europe.[4]

This was a period of extreme difficulty for the London staff of the Council. From July 1945 to June 1946, when Sir Ronald Adam was appointed, they were left without a Chairman; the scheme they had put forward for grades and salary-scales for the Home Service staff had been held up by the Foreign Office ever since 1943, making recruitment of suitable staff extremely difficult; and, ironically, they were being pressed by Foreign Office missions all over the world to start or extend activities. We have already seen that work in the liberated countries of western Europe was given first priority, and, at almost exactly the moment when Montagu-Pollock in the Foreign Office was considering the abolition of the Council or the restriction of its activities, Sir Alexander Cadogan was writing to Sir Malcolm Robertson:

> Our opportunities for exercising direct political influence in most of the countries of Eastern Europe are likely to be limited. Indirect means of influence such as the long-term work of the British Council, will, therefore be very valuable. We should certainly wish the Council to operate in all the enemy countries of Europe, except Germany, as soon as opportunity offers ... As regards Italy, we have, as you know, already recommended that the Council should resume operations there as soon as the Embassy in Rome think fit ... We should like the Council to work in due course in Austria ... it seems likely that our Missions in Finland, Rumania and Bulgaria will wish to distribute moderate supplies of cultural books and other printed material in the remaining months of the current financial year. We are, therefore, now asking the Treasury whether they agree to the

Council operating in Bulgaria, Finland, Rumania, Hungary and Austria whenever operations become possible.[5]

The difficulties of engaging staff to work at home or overseas was to have a long-term effect on the Council's reputation. Speaking of this time, Miss McLeod (then head of the French Section of the European Division and later Representative in France) said:

> Those who had served in the armed forces were returning to their old jobs, those who had come into the Council as war service were also returning to their previous occupations and the only people who applied were school masters, not always very cultured and not at all at their ease in dealing with foreigners of all professions.[6]*

This impression was corroborated on various visits to several European countries by Miss McLeod in the late 1940s but, as these men were mostly on two-year contracts, they gradually disappeared. Miss McLeod added that better candidates gradually came forward; but she said, 'I did not feel sufficient confidence in the Council myself then to advise anyone to give up a good career for it.'[7]

The popular image of the Council Representatives is of a race of long-haired, effeminate and ineffectual men. This image, created gradually over twenty years, with perhaps some help initially from the 'schoolmasters', was the work of Lord Beaverbrook. From 1939, with a slight break during the war, the *Express* group of newspapers (in London the *Daily Express* and the *Evening Standard*) carried on a vendetta against the British Council. Week after week, year after year, these newspapers attacked without much finesse but with such an easy disregard of the truth that little trouble was taken to check the accuracy of the accounts they published. *Express* reporters, particularly overseas, had orders to send in stories, and newspapers in other groups often joined in the hunt, while the original articles were often copied in newspapers all over the world.

The campaign centred largely on two main themes. The first was the waste of money. Under the headline ARE THESE JOURNEYS REALLY NECESSARY?, a typical article began: 'Let us examine the bill we will

---

* These men must have been released from war-time occupation when others returned from the Forces. The shortage in the schools was too great for skilled young men to be available.

have to pay to tell the Persians, the Bulgarians, the Mexicans and the Germans how civilised we are ... '

And following some details of the Council grants:

What benefit do we get from our outlay?

The answer is in the intangible: we get the knowledge that in 66 countries a representative (or representatives) of the British Council is on hand to disseminate Culture ...

The Black Paper tells us that we must export goods worth at least £1,500,000 this year ... And faced with the expenditure of over two and a half millions of money which we could very well use at home, is it any consolation to know that the long arm of the British Council reaches to Pecs, Szeged, Cegled, Debrecen, Keckmet and Eger or that it has brought to these shores an ichthyologist from Brazil?[8]

Or, on a slightly different tack:

Here we taxpayers are paying 45 million Crowns a year for this institution which cannot work without possessing 14 cars and 10 chauffeurs in London, 20 in the Provinces and 40 abroad, so that its Staff need not on any account go on foot between its meetings and its premises. It is easy to understand why the machinery is so expensive, but difficult to conceive why these propaganda ladies and gentlemen are obliged to go by car, when the majority of business men in the frontline of the export battle, must, to be sure, fight on foot.[9]

As time went on the technique was to find institutions or causes in need of money and compare them to the happy state of the British Council. Presently the *Daily Express* would have the effrontery to take up the cause of the British Museum or of the collections of the Duke of Devonshire. Thus, after an article on the effects of shortages of cash at the British Museum:

Well, the Council can certainly afford luxuries. Its grant this year is a fat £2,600,000 − six times the sum allowed to the British Museum.

The sense of values at the Treasury must be upside down to allow such lavishness to the British Council while starving the British Museum.

The Council, by its inanities abroad, brings derision on Britain. Wind it up. And let the British Museum, an institution that confers real benefits on the nation, be the first to gain from the saving.[10]

Far more damaging in the long run was the second line of attack – to present the staff of the British Council as feeble, effeminate and effete. Once they had settled into their stride, the *Express* papers always referred to 'the long-haired lads and lasses of the British Council', or 'the Culture Boys'. Only a very few members of the British public have ever had any idea of what the British Council actually does or stands for, and, of those who have, large numbers have always believed it to be staffed almost entirely by long-haired aesthetes or third-rate poets – and this in spite of the fact that at the present day, for instance, the Council employs 4,166 people, including 2,555 locally engaged staff overseas.

To give an idea of the scope and spleen of the Beaverbrook attack one cannot do better than quote from an article published in the *Daily Express* in 1954. The staff of the British Council had published a pamphlet accusing the Beaverbrook papers of deliberately misleading the public and to illustrate this they gave fourteen examples of untrue reports. In its reply the *Express* said this.

Fourteen complaints – when it was possible to be wrong 260 times! For, in four years, the Beaverbrook newspapers have published 206 reports, apart from 54 leading articles in the *Daily Express*, showing up the futilities of the council.[11]

That is to say, approximately an article a week and more than a leader a month during the whole four-year period.

The staff of the British Council were, in the vernacular, on a hiding to nothing. *The Express* reporters were adept at writing stories which needed, if they were to be corrected, long-winded, often not entirely satisfactory replies. When the Information Officer of the British Council sent in a correction, the Editor of the paper concerned either ignored it or replied with a courteous letter of thanks saying he had been much interested. Occasionally they went too far, as when they complained bitterly of the tour of the Boyd Neel Orchestra in Australia and accused the Council of 'impertinence' in trying to 'sell' Britain to Australia. This drew replies from the Premier of Victoria, who said that in his budget he had provided funds to aid cultural activities in Victoria and looked forward to the co-operation of the British Council in developing them, and from the High Commissioner for Australia in the United Kingdom, who wrote:

It would be indeed unfortunate if any misapprehension over this matter should persist. The British people may be assured that Australia wants an ever-growing volume of cultural exchanges and very much hopes that the British Council will be able to maintain and, indeed, to expand its valuable work.[12]

But these letters were addressed to *The Times* and only a small percentage of *Express* readers would have seen them.

No wonder then that, as Richard Auty puts it, the Council grew gradually into a 'mood of self-justification, away from its previously unashamed projection of cultural achievements'.[13]

Nevertheless, in spite of the doubts about its future which so much concerned the Foreign Office, the lack of strength at its head and the difficulties of engaging staff, even in spite of Lord Beaverbrook, many of those Council officers who believe in the virtue of spreading the English language and culture remember this period as the halcyon days, a paradise lost. Here is a further quotation from Richard Auty.

The Council returned to Europe in the wake of the Allied armies, opening up in France and Italy in 1944 before the war was over. Interest everywhere in Britain was immense. She was the most popular of the Liberators and the most respected. She represented the continuity of Europe's cultural past which had been interrupted everywhere else by Fascism, war and occupation, a repository of civilised values. The reforms of the new Labour government were followed eagerly by peoples looking for models for their own social reconstruction ...

The Council's influence in Europe was immense, excepting only the Soviet Union where it was not allowed to operate. From Budapest and Ankara to Paris and Lisbon a network of offices and Institutes organised study visits and courses in the UK – and often locally too – for thousands of teachers, scholars and other specialists who had been starved of contact during the long years of the war. The Council exploited with great effectiveness Britain's greatest asset: her immense popularity. It was an excellent example of the principle of building on success. And it was done ... with impressive efficiency, flexibility and energy of a kind it would now be difficult to match.[14]

The first of many post-war Ambassadors to call for the services of the British Council was Rex Leeper, its founder, who had been appointed Ambassador to Athens as soon as the Papandreou Government was formed. He at once addressed the Foreign Secretary, asking for a resumption of Council work in Greece. And in the immediate post-war history of Greece can be found the answer to how the Council managed so often to work successfully when apparently so inadequately staffed. The law which in the war had ordained that the poor quality of some of the general staff should be compensated for by a few brilliant men whose services in peacetime would not have been obtainable still operated, and nowhere more brilliantly than in Athens.

The Council offices were re-opened in 1944 by Colonel K. R. Johnstone, who was still on active service in Athens. Colonel Johnstone, who, although he is the source of several quotations, has otherwise eluded these pages, deserves particular attention. He has been bracketed with Rex Leeper, Charles Bridge and Lord Lloyd as one of the Council's Founding Fathers. A King's Scholar at Eton and an Exhibitioner at Balliol where he obtained first class Honours in Literature and the Humanities, he entered the Diplomatic Service in 1928. The accident of his being in the News Department at the Foreign Office under Rex Leeper caused him to become liaison officer between the Foreign Office and the Council. In 1938 he was seconded full-time to the Council as one of two Deputy Secretaries-General. On the outbreak of war he resigned and joined the Welsh Guards. After a short period in Athens in 1944, he returned to the British Council as Controller of its European Division, later becoming Deputy Director-General. He was one of the most brilliant and imaginative officers and, although intellectually fastidious and shy in manner, he was very much loved. In his *Times* obituary, the writer made the presumably intentionally cryptic remark that 'but for the turn of Fortune's wheel, he would have made an informed, experienced and far-sighted Director-General of the Council'.[15] No one could have been better suited to re-open the Council's offices in Athens.

In October 1945, on his return to London, Johnstone was succeeded by Professor Steven Runciman as Representative. The Institute of English Studies was opened the same month to a scene of unparalleled enthusiasm.* In the square outside the Institute such a large crowd of

* An organisation called the Anglo-Greek Information Service had already started English-language schools in Athens and Salonica in former British Institute buildings. The Council took these over.

21 Students of engineering of King Abdul Aziz University, Saudi Arabia, study English in the language laboratory set up under a multi-million pound contract

22 Thai agricultural research students learn English at the Council's English Teaching Centre in Bangkok

23 Waiting to enrol for English classes at the British Council in Lisbon, 1978

students presented themselves for enrolment that the police had to be called out to deal with them. Immediately, 3,500 of them were enrolled.

Since there was a danger that too much time would in these circumstances be absorbed by the teaching of elementary English, it was decided that there should be a new Institute known as the British Institute of Higher Studies and to this Rex Warner was appointed Director. Quite soon he was joined by Major Patrick Leigh Fermor, already well-known in Greece for his war-time record in Crete, as Deputy Director. In late 1945 and early 1946 both Professor Runciman and Major Leigh Fermor lectured at the University and visiting lecturers included Harold Nicolson. In the first year the British Council sponsored a concert in which Royalton Kisch conducted the National State Orchestra and members of the State Opera Company in works by Constant Lambert, William Walton and Benjamin Britten, and an exhibition of British Graphic Art was held in Athens.

The record suggests that Messrs Runciman, Warner and Leigh Fermor may not have been by nature suited to the administration of the Council finances, but there is no doubt that they left behind them illustrious memories or that these endure to this day. In 1982 a leading Greek citizen, at one time Minister of Culture, said: 'The intellectual life of Athens after the war was formed by the British Council.'[16]

In Italy arrangements were immediately made for Francis Toye to return to the British Institute in Florence. Ronald Bottrall was appointed Representative in Rome in April 1945 and the Council moved into the Palazzo del Drago, Via delle Quattro Fontane, which housed both the Head Office for Italy and the Rome Institute. In the course of the year Council Institutes re-opened in Palermo, Milan and Turin. The presence of hundreds of thousands of British troops had aroused an interest in the English language, and by the time the peace treaty was signed there were 4,415 members enrolled in the Council Institutes.[17]

By the end of 1946 an exhibition of British books published during the war had been held in Rome, four concerts had taken place, while the first performance in Italy of Benjamin Britten's Peter Grimes had been given at La Scala, Milan. The Library in Rome had over 7,000 books and a music library had been formed; the Tate Gallery had held an exhibition in Rome and many contacts had been made in the scientific field.

A Council office was opened in Paris immediately after the liberation in 1944, in the premises which had belonged to the Travel Association, with Austin Gill as Acting Representative, while the British Institute returned to its pre-war building. The French welcomed the British as never before or since and, although all English teaching was done as previously by the British Institute, a series of exchanges was immediately arranged, some of Britain's most distinguished academics visiting France, including Professor L. P. Garrod who lectured on penicillin, while five French Professors of English and eleven French doctors visited Britain. By the end of 1945 there were staff in Paris competent to cover science, music, fine arts, and education; while offices had been opened in Grenoble, Toulouse and Nancy. There were the usual libraries and reading rooms, and books were sent to the University Library at Caen which had been destroyed. But the greatest successes were in the fields of art and drama, including ballet. In 1945 the Fine Arts Department organised an exhibition of the works of nine artists including Paul Nash, John Piper, Graham Sutherland and Henry Moore, and also an exhibition of these and other artists in the British section of the Unesco International Exhibition in 1946.

Henry Moore was fifty at the end of the war and his recognition by the international world had been slow. He has always been most generous in acknowledging the part played by the British Council in the event which was the turning point in his career, as well as the most memorable of all the Council's achievements in those years. In 1948 the International Exhibition at the Venice Biennale was resumed. (For those who have not seen it the Biennale takes place on the banks of the Grand Canal where it opens towards the sea and the works of many nations are shown in buildings which are their permanent property. The British Council's Fine Arts Department decided to send to Venice the works of Britain's greatest painter and her greatest modern master. Paintings by Turner were sent from the Tate Gallery accompanied by works by Henry Moore. In previous years the French had won many of the prizes and the French sculptor Henri Laurens was expected to win in 1948. When the International Sculptor Prize was awarded to Henry Moore, it was the beginning of a relationship between the artist and the British Council which has lasted over the years. The British Council has organised at least one major exhibition of his work every year ever since, including the monumental exhibition which went to Spain and Portugal in 1981, while because of its early and special relationship with him, it has been able to acquire a collection of his works. In 1982 these included four carvings, four bronzes, six bronze maquettes, seven drawings and 130 graphics. From these, the Fine Art

Department were able to organise two small travelling exhibitions of his works which they sent to fifty-one different countries.

No less enduring was another great post-war artistic event — the first Edinburgh Festival. Writing in 1952, Ian Hunter, one of the later directors of the Festival, said: 'A successful idea has many claimants, but it has been established beyond doubt that Rudolf Bing, when general manager of the Glyndebourne Opera, with the prestige and backing of that body, was the architect-in-chief.'[18] He went on to say, however: 'A war-time lunch in December 1944, at which Miss N. Parkinson, of the British Council, brought Mr Harvey Wood, Scottish Representative of the Council, and Mr Bing together, saw the seed take root.'

One should not make too much of this because the first Edinburgh Festival was supported in equal proportions by the Arts Council, the City of Edinburgh and private citizens. But there is no doubt that Harvey Wood demonstrated, not for the first or the last time, the great advantages the British Council enjoys by having permanent offices and a Representative on the spot. Sir Rudolf Bing himself paid tribute to Harvey Wood: 'He offered to gather a committee of Edinburgh notables and to set up a small committee at which I could explain the scheme ... The committee Harvey Wood formed was perfect for the purpose.'[19]

Harvey Wood was also Chairman of the Festival's Programme Committee until 1950, while the British Council brought over twenty visitors from fourteen countries including composers, conductors and critics, and organised the visits of forty students. The Council's Edinburgh International House (which replaced the war-time national centres) was much used by the overseas musicians and in association with the Arts Council the British Council arranged a series of lectures here. The Lord Provost of Edinburgh acknowledged the part played by the British Council when he asked that its name should be associated with that of the Festival Society.

Neither is it possible to write of the artistic events of those years without paying some tribute to the Sadler's Wells Ballet Company and the Old Vic Theatre Company, the latter led at this time by Laurence Olivier, Sybil Thorndike and Ralph Richardson. It is doubtful whether the British taxpayer is, or ever has been, aware of how much he owes these two companies in international renown. In the years immediately after the war, the Sadler's Wells Ballet Company visited Paris, Ghent, Brussels, Vienna, Prague, Warsaw, Poznan,

Malmo and Oslo.* The Old Vic Company went to Paris, Brussels, Australia and New Zealand.

Here is a verbatim account of the visit by the Sadler's Wells Ballet Company to Poland given by the British Council Representative, C. G. Bidwell, in evidence to the Select Committee on Estimates in 1947. He said:

> We have had during the last year several major activities, notably the Sadler's Wells Ballet ... the success of which is very, very difficult to explain. It was an enormous success with the Polish authorities and an enormous success with the Polish people. If our own Lord Chamberlain could have seen the theatres I think he would have resigned at once. They were absolutely packed to the doors and on the last night in Poznan people were standing on the front of the boxes and holding on to the vertical pillars. The Ballet themselves were extremely good ambassadors, and that was the first occasion on which we had had not only the promise of the Polish authorities to do things but their constant and active goodwill throughout, and tremendous co-operation. The Minister of Culture arranged with the Speaker of the House that the Sadler's Wells people should stay in Parliamentary accommodation, and things like that went on ... The Russian Counsellor went to our Chargé d'Affaires and expressed a great appreciation of that particular Ballet. In every way it was a tremendous success and we were convinced quite worth any cost that was involved.[20]

The British Council's entry into the Iron Curtain countries, which except in Poland and Yugoslavia (where work was undertaken on a significant scale only after President Tito's break with Russia in 1948, was to prove abortive, took place in response to pressure from the Foreign Office and in particular from the British Ambassadors. From Czechoslovakia and Hungary members of the diplomatic service expressed views which can be illustrated as follows:

> Owing to our inability at present to offer anything very concrete to Hungary in either the political or economic fields, I feel that it i

* By 1947 the British Council had opened or re-opened in the following European countries in addition to those already mentioned: Austria, Belgium, Bulgaria, Czechoslovakia, Denmark, Finland, Gibraltar, Hungary, Iceland, The Netherlands, Norway, Poland, Romania and Yugoslavia.

especially important that we should press on with our cultural
relations.[21]
The part which could be played by the British Council and the
Institute in cementing Anglo-Czech friendship can hardly be
exaggerated.[22]

And from Cavendish Bentinck, Ambassador to Poland:

The representative will find himself almost embarrassingly popular.
His problem will be to feed a starved and eager public. Since this
Embassy has been established, many people of all sorts have expressed
to us their desire for a speedy resumption of cultural relations with
the West.[23]

Then, a week later: 'The yearning for British cultural material here is
pathetic.'[24]
In the late 1940s after the Communist revolution it nevertheless
became evident that the governments of Hungary, Czechoslovakia and
Bulgaria meant to sever cultural relations. The first event of any
importance, however, took place in none of these countries but in
Poland. On 27 May 1949 C. G. Bidwell, the Representative there,
defected to the Russians (sadly that same Bidwell who had so eloquently
described the visit of the Sadler's Wells Ballet Company). Initially it
was believed that he had no particularly political motive, but that,
having gone through a form of divorce in Poland in order to marry a
Pole, he found this invalid in England, where he would have been
subject to a charge of bigamy. Even so, after his resignation he published a series of statements which were predictable in the circumstances
but very damaging and quite unexpected to those who had known
him. He alleged that the Council was controlled by agents of political
and economic imperialism and said:

I was convinced that the implementation of the programme which
the British Council's London Headquarters outlined for Poland was
incompatible with the interests of Poland and of the working class.[25]

This defection and more especially Bidwell's statements had a bad
effect on the morale of the staff in Poland, but not as it happened on
the future of the British Council there. Relations with the Polish

Government were not much disturbed and the Council has continued to work there without a break until this day.

In Czechoslovakia the defection of Dr Arna Rides, a British subject employed by the Council as medical officer in Prague, was a more serious matter. It became known that she had been in touch with the Communist Party for some time and she accused the Council of conducting a policy hostile to the Czech Government with the backing of the Foreign Office. 'The British Council follow the train of those who want to plunge humanity into the horrors of a new war.'[26] After her defection a sequence of public attacks was made on the Council, and its staff were severely harassed, while visitors to the Institutes were often intercepted by the police. At the same time political charges against the Council were also being made in Hungary. The policy of the Council was not to quit voluntarily since it was thought that this was what their enemies hoped for, but in the spring of 1950 the Governments first of Hungary and then of Czechoslovakia asked that they should be withdrawn. In June 1950 the Bulgarian Government followed suit.

The collapse of much of the programme for Eastern Europe was not more rapid, however, than the end of the post-war era of cultural expansion in Western Europe and many other parts of the world. In the autumn of 1947 the Council was informed that its grant would be cut by 10 per cent for the year 1948–9. This was not the result of animus on the part of the Foreign Office or Treasury but of a policy of cuts imposed by Ministers across the board, which ignored the difficulties of planning on a constantly changing financial basis. One Council officer complained that:

The Government thought that by fixing our ceiling we could quickly redistribute our finances – a lunatic mathematical outlook, which leaves out human nature, past commitments and the deplorable political effect on the aboriginals of Ruritania when the nice British Council which has been teaching them English free of charge for the past six years, walk out with their umbrellas and their English grammars.[27]

And, since the only way the Council could adjust to the cuts was by withdrawal from some countries and the closing of Institutes and provincial offices in others, they were in fact forced to walk out, not of some abstraction like Ruritania, but of Iceland, Switzerland, French North Africa, Bolivia, Ecuador and Peru, and to close Institutes in

Belgium, The Netherlands, Argentina, Colombia and Chile. In Switzerland the complaints this produced were so fierce that the Council's withdrawal was followed a year later by the rather ludicrous spectacle of a re-opening on a reduced scale. Neither was this the end of the matter. For some years cuts in the total budget were to some extent offset by additions for specific purposes from the Colonial Office, Colonial Development and Welfare Funds and the Commonwealth Relations Office but the Foreign Office grant was cut successively.

In 1949 the difficulties were added to by the devaluation of the pound, and by 1950 regional centres in France (Nancy and Lille) and the Institute at Rome had been closed, the Institutes at Palermo and Oporto handed over to the Anglophile societies and the centres at Valencia, Seville, Innsbruck and Graz reduced to a single teaching officer each. In Latin America Paraguay was added to the list of countries where complete closure took place. 'The first news I received of this axing exercise,' one of the Council's officers wrote, 'was a cable which informed me that Council support was being withdrawn from two anglophil societies in Colombia. They could not survive without our help. To watch them die was an extremely unpleasant experience.'[28]

Large cuts were made in Egypt in the expenditure on schools and some of the Institutes were closed, while further damage was done by the educational policy of Dr A. E. Morgan, who had followed Professor Ifor Evans as Director of Education. This policy consisted in discouraging the teaching of English in favour of discussion groups. On 3 August 1949, however, the Foreign Secretary wrote asking the Council to alter its policy and pointing out that His Majesty's Government 'regarded it as a primary task of the Council to further in any way they could the teaching of English and ... the spread of the British school system abroad'.[29]

In spite of the necessity to cut established offices in Europe, Latin America and the Middle East, the Council started new work in the Dominions and Colonies. It has been seen earlier that, because of alien cultural influences in the Middle East, the Council had worked in British colonies and dependencies there from its very beginning. Early in 1941, Lord Lloyd, at one and the same time Secretary of State for the Colonies and Chairman of the British Council, had approved a policy for the extension of the Council's work in the colonies on the grounds that there were a number of activities for which it was well-equipped and which might be more usefully carried out by a semi-official body than by the Government. Sir Angus Gillan had been appointed Controller of the Empire Division in 1941, and by 1945 the Council had Representatives in Nigeria, Gold Coast, Sierra Leone, Cyprus, Malta, Aden, Jamaica, Barbados, British Guiana, Palestine and Trinidad. In 1945 in a review of the Council's work in the colonies it was decided that this part of its activities should no longer be carried on the Foreign Office Vote but on that of the Colonial Office. This principle was soon after adopted by the India and Burma Office but not by the Dominions Office.

One other important principle was established at that time. The Secretary of State for the Colonies was answerable to Parliament for the welfare of the colonies and responsible for their cultural advancement. In consequence, the promotion of cultural relations as well as the spread of knowledge of the English language, life and literature rested with him and the Colonial Governments working under his direction. To meet this situation it was agreed that the British Council should in future operate in the colonies as his agents, receiving instructions as to the particular colonies in which its assistance was required, consulting with the Colonial Office on the general programme of its activities both at home and in the countries concerned, drawing up its estimates in accordance with the programme and estimates agreed. This principle – that the Council should act as agents for the responsible department – has generally been operated by Government Departments other than the Foreign Office and extended in later years to its relations with other bodies.

The scope of the British Council's work in the colonies was defined in 1948 as 'the carrying on of any activity in the cultural and educational sphere of which the chief purpose is the "projection" of the British way of life and the promotion of closer relations in cultural matters between the people of Great Britain and the people of the Colonies'.[30] An example of how this was to be interpreted seems both elaborate to describe and unlikely to be observed.

The Council might legitimately organize a visit to Britain by teachers from the Colonies to study British achievements in the field of education, and would not be debarred from doing so on the ground that the visit would also enable the teachers to improve their standard of work. They should not however bring them here to study educational methods or for training courses which would fall within the scope of Colonial Development and Welfare Acts.[31]

In 1949 a circular letter stated that the aims of the Colonial Office in promoting the work of the Council was twofold.

> In the long term we want to strengthen the links between Britain and the colonial peoples so that the latter, as they obtain greater control over their own affairs, will still value the British connection ...
>   We feel that the Council can do valuable positive work in countering Communist propaganda by showing that Britain and the Western tradition for which Britain stands has something better to offer than the Communist way of life.[32]

The Colonial Office were anxious that the Council should establish the principle of 'reciprocity' in the countries they worked in, make no ethnic distinctions and do everything to promote good race relations. They wished the work in the colonies to be largely technical and scientific while they had some fear that the Council was apt to be too 'aesthetic'. Writing to the High Commissioner in the Federation of Malaya about the newly-appointed Representative there, Sir Charles Jeffries of the Colonial Office assured him that 'The Council will brief him carefully that he should not devote too much attention to aesthetic matters'.[33]

The Colonial Office was also responsible for an important extension of the Council's work in Great Britain. In June 1948 £200,000 was allocated from Colonial Development and Welfare Funds to the British Council to enable it to take over the Colonial Office's student hostels and clubs in London, Edinburgh and Newcastle; to provide new student hostels and clubs at Glasgow, Manchester, Cardiff, Leeds, Dublin, Oxford and Cambridge; to meet the capital and running costs of these hostels and clubs; and to employ staff to run them. The housing and welfare of all Colonial students became the responsibility of the British Council, and in this way a large part of that organisation which had grown up during the war to deal with foreigners in England remained in being. Regional offices continued in Edinburgh, Cardiff, Manchester, Stratford-upon-Avon and Guildford.

Writing about this work in 1955, Sir Harold Nicolson said:

> In the old days overseas students, especially coloured students, used to suffer much on arrival from loneliness, homesickness, money troubles, cold, food, language difficulties and the problem of finding congenial accommodation. Those who came from remote and quiet

countries were often nervously affected by the speed and noise of
London traffic, by the reserved manners of the ordinary Briton,
and by our greater regard for punctuality and the employment of
time ... [34]

And speaking of the time at which he wrote:

Before they leave their own countries students are where possible
given 'introduction courses' in which they are instructed as to what
they may expect. No longer do they disembark lost and bewildered
at Liverpool or Tilbury, but are received on the quay-side by Council
representatives ... In the last five years some 14,000 Colonial
students have been met in this way on arrival.

In order to supervise this work and to find students accommodation,
fourteen area offices had been set up in England, three in Scotland, and
one each in Cardiff and Belfast. Speaking of the help and encouragement the students received Nicolson went on:

They are thus encouraged to return to their home countries, where
they will probably become prominent in their own politics or professions, with enhanced self-confidence and self-esteem, rather than
with dark memories of humiliation, loneliness or failure.[35]

The Council also began at this time to act as an agent to many international bodies in arranging programmes for short-term visitors. In
1952–3 it was responsible for the expenditure of £450,000 from sources
other than its own on organising courses and study tours and offering
advice and assistance to professional experts coming at their own or
their Government's expense.[36]

The working contacts with the Commonwealth Relations Office
which superseded the previous Dominions and India Offices in 1947
were less warm than with the Colonial Office. The former feared that
any attempt to project the life and culture of Britain might be regarded
as propaganda or come in conflict with the spirit of independence in
Dominion countries; and in fact Canada rejected suggestions that the
Council should open an office there until 1959, when a Representative
was appointed. Australia, as has already been seen, welcomed cultural
relations with some enthusiasm and the first Representative went to
Canberra in January 1947 at the invitation of the Australian Govern-

ment. A tour by the Boyd Neel Orchestra was a great success in 1947 and the Old Vic Theatre Company led by Laurence Olivier and Vivien Leigh made a tour of 4,600 miles from Perth to Brisbane and also visited New Zealand. The takings on this tour were more than £160,000 and there was a profit of about £40,000, although, as was the rule at the time, this went entirely to the Treasury.

The Boyd Neel Orchestra also visited New Zealand, where again a Representative was appointed in 1947. The Council followed many of its usual practices in these Dominions, although obviously the teaching of English was not one of them.

India inevitably bulks large, partly because today it receives the largest share of the Council's total budget of any country in the world, partly because of the political importance of the time, and partly because the negotiations which took place before a Representative was appointed illustrate so well the troubles the Council had at the time. In 1944 T. W. Morray (a Council officer) visited India and made a useful report in which he said:

> Indians still look instinctively to England: the extent to which we have anglicised the Indian public mind is often underrated and is one of the most extraordinary achievements of the British connection. But India is looking to other countries, notably America, and unless steps are taken in a systematic way to maintain the intellectual communion of the past, our best asset may be lost or cheapened.[37]

From the first it was clear that India would welcome only the best in the academic sphere. The Council had 'lost face', it was reported, by sending no more senior officer than Morray, and Sir Angus Gillan paid a further visit in 1947 after receiving an assurance that Pandit Jawaharlal Nehru would welcome this. Sir Angus, arriving in India after a long tour of South-East Asia, expected to be joined by Tunnard-Moore, the Council's desk officer for India. Reporting on his return, Sir Angus said:

> Before my departure from London I had been leaving most of the Indian detail to him [Tunnard-Moore]; I had been away since October, and I was consequently completely out of touch with the position. I must record that the fact that the Council could not afford his ticket created a very poor impression in the inner circle of our British friends and advisers in India.[38]

Tunnard-Moore himself had said:

> Everyone is agreed that the Council's Representative must be a
> high-ranking academician ... There is no hope whatsoever that the
> Council can recruit the kind of person needed at the sort of salaries
> we have been allowed to pay, even including all allowances and
> taxation advantages.[39]

During his visit Sir Angus Gillan received a formal invitation from
Pandit Nehru to start work. Partition, however, took place before
anything could be done. Following this Sir John Sargent, who had
recently resigned as Educational Adviser to the Government of India
and who fitted the role of high-ranking academician whose work was
known there, fortunately consented to undertake the preliminary work
of setting up an organisation. Before definite arrangements were made,
the Commonwealth Relations Office, by now grown wary, requested
an assurance from the Treasury that 'if a start is made with the Council's
work this year adequate funds will be forthcoming to continue it in the
next Financial year'.[40]

Finally W. R. L. Wickham was recalled from Brazil to become
India's first Representative; Owain Jones was sent to Pakistan. Premises
were opened in New Delhi and Karachi. In 1949, in the aftermath of
Independence, finding it impossible to acquire permanent headquarters
in Delhi, the Council moved to Agra where it remained until 1951,
when it returned to permanent headquarters in Delhi.

At this time the Indian Government was determined to substitute
Hindi for English as the common language, and there seemed some
danger that the knowledge of English would deteriorate. The Indian
Ministry of Education nevertheless welcomed the Council's assistance
and advice in introducing the most modern and effective methods of
teaching English as a foreign language. All these years later, one can
say without any doubt that the close relationship which has been
sustained between Indians of the upper and more educated classes and
ourselves has been much encouraged by the Indian love of English
literature.

The Council had begun investigating the possibility of work in
China as early as 1941, and in February 1943 a cultural scientific mission
headed by Dr Joseph Needham, Reader in Bio-Chemistry at Cambridge
was sent there. The influence of Dr Needham was overwhelmingly
directed to the supply of scientific information, and apparatus and

he believed that the warmth of the welcome he received from the Chinese was because 'it has been clear that we stood for the England of Newton and Darwin, of Rutherford and Fleming, and not for the classical learning of the squirearchy'.[41] P. M. Roxby, Professor of Geography at Liverpool University, reached China as the first Representative at the end of 1944, accompanied by his wife, who had been a Lecturer in History at Liverpool. Offices were opened in Shanghai, Peking, Nanking and Chungking. Much importance was attached not merely to the lecturers and supplies sent to China but also to the visits of Chinese students and professors to this country. To quote A. J. S. White: 'At the end of 1951 the Council centres were still having packed houses for their lectures, film shows, music recitals and exhibitions, and the libraries and reading rooms were more crowded than ever.'[42] But from the formation of the Chinese People's Republic in 1949 the Council's days were numbered, and when visas were refused to new or returning staff and the costs grew out of proportion to what could now be achieved, it was forced to close its centres and withdraw. Work had also begun in Burma in 1946 and the money saved in China enabled the Council to send a Representative to Japan in 1952, although with insufficient financial backing for him to do very much.

I I

Financial Stringency

In 1947 the constitution of the British Council was altered, the post of Secretary-General being abolished and the post of Director-General with responsibility for the administration of the Council being created. In the first instance this made little difference to the supreme authority because Sir Ronald Adam, while he continued to act as Chairman, also became the first Director-General. He was, however, supported by the creation of two new posts of Assistant-Director-General, one to supervise the regional work, the other the functional and financial. The first was filled by G. H. Shreeve, a civil servant from the War Office, the second by R. H. Davies, previously Finance Officer. Richard Seymour was appointed to a third new post, that of Secretary to the Council, while A. J. S. White, Secretary-General since 1940, became Controller of Overseas Division B.*

Sir Ronald Adam was an able administrator and a man who is remembered with much affection by his staff. R. A. Phillips gave the following description of him:

> Ronald Adam was a tremendous man, I think. He was a tremendously humane person. His father was Vice-Chancellor of Liverpool University ... and he was therefore familiar with what you might call the educational system which most regular officers are not. He had been in the top administrative job in the Army and was Adjutant-General at the War Office from 1941 to 1946. He had started the Army Educational Corps and a newspaper called *ABCA* ... which was sent round the troops to encourage discussion. Well these were

---

* There were three Overseas Divisions. Sir Angus Gillan was appointed Controller to Division A (the Colonies and Commonwealth), A. J. S. White to Division B (Latin America, the Middle East and the Far East), and K. R. Johnstone to Division C (Europe). Today these Divisions are no longer given letters but are known as the Africa and Middle East Division, the America, Pacific and South Asia Division, and the Europe and North Asia Division.

revolutionary things ... The Army has produced some good people
and Adam was one of these. He was wonderful with people.[1]

Adam had a quick and receptive mind and all the qualities of a leader.
He was extremely unlucky in the period in which he was Chairman
and later Director-General, since, during almost the whole of his time
discussions with the Foreign Office as to terms of employment and salary
scales dragged on, making recruitment impossible, cuts were imposed
almost annually, while one Committee of Inquiry after another sat to
consider the future of the British Council, no conclusion being reached.

In 1947–8 the Select Committee on Estimates, having heard witnesses
from the Council staff, the Foreign Office, the Colonial Office, the
Treasury and the Central Office of Information, had devoted its Third
Report to the British Council. Paragraph 7 reads as follows:

Notwithstanding criticism on specific points in the Council's organisation and activities which will appear in this Report, Your Committee have no doubts as to the value of the Council's work. They
consider it of special importance now, when international friction
and misunderstanding and misrepresentation of British policy abroad
are rife. The Council discharges a wide range of functions which in
other countries are carried out sometimes by direct Government
action and sometimes by a semi-official organisation with large
Government subsidies. Your Committee are convinced that there are
the greatest possible advantages to be obtained under the present
system whereby the work is done by a body corporate and not by a
Government Department. Where a diplomatic mission is accredited
to a foreign government, there are inevitably periods of strained
relations between the two. A body like the British Council is un-
affected by these, and its work can proceed unimpaired and without
interruption. The evidence indicated that the Council is regarded as
being outside politics and its work is not associated with propaganda,
or the political feeling of the day. Such a result could scarcely be
achieved under the auspices of a Government Department. Your
Committee strongly recommend, therefore, the continuance of the
existing system.[2]

In paragraph 40, having said that the criticism most commonly
levelled was that the Council's expenditure tends to be extravagant, the
Report continued:

Your Committee found no evidence of a general lack of control of expenditure. Indeed the finances of the Council seemed to them now to be well-managed and their economy to have been put on a proper basis.

And in paragraph 42, after saying that the Committee were nevertheless not satisfied that the figures for staff employed at home were as low as might reasonably be expected, the Report recommended that the size of staff employed in the United Kingdom be investigated by the Treasury Organisation and Methods Division.

This investigation duly took place and the Organisation and Methods Division's inquiry covered many fields besides that of the size of home staff, while they reported in much detail. Two paragraphs from the body of the Report and one from its Conclusions are particularly relevant. Paragraph 48 reads as follows:

When the Council has proposed to reduce its work or withdraw from any particular country, the Ambassador has, almost without exception, made strong representation for the decision to be reversed and in several instances the heads of overseas Governments have intervened personally to see that the balance of cultural relationships is maintained. Unless such impetus from overseas is to be ignored, some body (or bodies) for dealing with such matters is always likely to be needed, although the particular need and the nature of the service to be provided will vary by subject and by countries.[3]

Paragraph 49 continued:

Some of the most noticeable comments on the value of the influence of the Council's work come from statesmen and officials of other countries, and from Dominion Prime Ministers. In the recent past, the Council has in fact been expressly invited by the Prime Ministers, to operate in Australia, New Zealand, India and Pakistan. In the case of the latter two Dominions, it seems probable that the Council's activities will be particularly useful in helping to fill what might otherwise have been a vacuum when Great Britain withdrew from political and administrative control.

And on the matter on which an inquiry had been specifically suggested, the Report read (paragraph 87):

The review has been conducted against the background of similar O and M assignments in other parts of the Information field. With this and other experience in Government Departments as a basis for comparison the O and M team have in general found the Council to be operating economically with clear practical objectives and with a good standard of financial control.

This Report appeared in 1950 at a time when the Foreign Office had begun to prepare for the review of the work of the British Council scheduled to take place at the end of the five year period agreed to in 1946. Taken together with the Report of the Select Committee on Estimates, it appears to be very strong and impartial evidence that the Council's work was of sufficient importance for it to be allowed to continue and to receive a grant-in-aid sufficient to meet the most urgent demands being made upon it, even if safeguards were imposed to prevent unlimited growth and to ensure efficiency. This is not, however, how government works.

The inevitable period of austerity after the war had been prolonged by the need to re-arm to meet the emergency created by the Cold War. To pay for the cost of this rearmament the Treasury was looking for cuts in services which had already been progressively cut over the years. In a situation of this kind the Chancellor's eye is apt to land on the Government's Information Services because no definite or short term returns can be quoted, and because, in the case of autonomous bodies such as the BBC or British Council, no Government Department is directly involved. When cuts have to be imposed, the custom is for each Cabinet Minister to fight his own corner, without much regard to the overall national interest, and services not directly represented usually suffer most. Except when led by Lord Lloyd, or at times when Anthony Eden, who regarded the Council as having been conceived and inaugurated under his authority, was at the Foreign Office, the British Council has always suffered from a lack of direct representation or any powerful pressure group within the Government. In the estimates for 1951–2 (which according to custom, had to be submitted in the autumn of 1950) the Chancellor was looking for retrenchment in all directions and specifically for a cut of £2 million in the Overseas Information Services, that is, in the BBC External Services, the British Council, and the Information Services of the Overseas Departments (the Foreign Office, the Colonial Office and the Commonwealth Relations Office).

'Is it logical,' a writer in *The Economist* asked in 1951, 'to prune for rearmament purposes services which, if experience in the last war is anything to go by, are worth running as a weapon in themselves?'[4] Is it logical, one might equally ask, in re-arming for the Cold War, to press for cuts in the very services for which Ambassadors and High Commissioners are pleading so that they may combat Communist influence. These questions had a direct bearing on the seemingly endless series of inquiries into the Overseas Information Services which were a feature of the early 1950s. When it is impossible to satisfy the Chancellor without doing irreparable and unacceptable damage, while at the same time no one has sufficient power to refuse him, a Committee of Inquiry or an inter-Departmental Working Party can delay a decision.

These factors operated with particular force during the period of the Attlee Governments of 1945 to 1951 and, the record suggests, not merely because of the need for austerity and retrenchment referred to. There is a belief within the British Council that on the whole it has fared better under Labour Governments than under Conservative, but this is not borne out by the history of that time. Ernest Bevin, as Foreign Secretary, was sympathetic to the Council but not sufficiently enthusiastic to fight for it; Herbert Morrison, who succeeded him, sold the pass. As Chancellors, Hugh Dalton and Stafford Cripps pressed for cuts in the routine way, but their successor, the young Hugh Gaitskell, was obstinately determined to get them. Above all there is in the record the suggestion of a stoutly philistine attitude which allowed all three Chancellors to dispense with even the ordinary protestations of personal sympathy with cultural propaganda or regret at harsh necessity. Consequently, although nothing saved the Council from successive savage cuts, one Inquiry followed another in an attempt to delay or mitigate them, all coming roughly to the same conclusions, and culminating in the Drogheda Committee which reported in 1953.

It is habitual to regard the Drogheda Report as a watershed in the history of the British Council, and Lord Drogheda and his Committee as having, by their recommendations, changed the nature of its work, the area of its main targets, and the type of men and women it recruited. In fact, the Drogheda Committee merely confirmed the trend which had increasingly commended itself to officials in the Government Departments concerned, and which was probably first put on record in a letter dated 17 June 1950 from Sir Charles Jeffries of the Colonial Office to Sir William Strang of the Foreign Office. In his letter Sir Charles professed himself a great protagonist of the Council, which he said he believed was 'not only a possible instrument ... but perhaps the only possible instrument' with which to provide grounds of common interest in multi-racial communities, and he said:

> I can say with absolute certainty that if we could treble the Council's present activities in the more important Colonies it would have a really significant effect and would have a good chance of turning a tide which otherwise may well turn against us for all the excellence of our official administration.[5]

However, the purpose of Jeffries's letter was to argue that the present strategy of the Council was 'not right'. The Council began under the Foreign Office and, because of the war, expanded primarily as an instrument for attaching the sympathies of neutral and allied nations to our cause, while its activities in the Dominions and Colonies were an afterthought. An entirely different strategy was, he suggested, required today.

> In present world conditions, the first priority should be to consolidate the Commonwealth and in particular to strengthen the cultural links with those parts of the Commonwealth (i.e. India, Pakistan, Ceylon and most of the Colonies) where the link of blood-relationship with us is absent. The second priority should be to win over the 'emergent' nations outside the Commonwealth — China, Indonesia, Burma, Persia, Israel, the Arab States and so forth. Thirdly, I would put what can still be done on the fringe of the iron curtain — Poland, Yugoslavia, Germany, Austria, Greece, Turkey.
>   It is, I imagine, fair to say that one way of looking at the present world picture is as a struggle for the soul of the vast 'backward' populations of Africa and Southern Asia. In that struggle the Council can be a potent weapon; but only if its resources are concentrated and not dispersed.[6]

Proceeding on the assumption that no new money would be found for the Council and indeed that there would be further cuts, Sir Charles proposed that the money should be found for his first and second priorities by 'cutting out the major part of the Council's activities in respect of France, Netherlands, Belgium, Scandinavia, Spain, Italy and Latin America'.[7] And he said, speaking both of Latin America and of Western Europe, that he doubted whether the little the Council can do is really significant. He wrote:

When I hear of the wonderful work that is being done in such and such a centre, I question what it really amounts to. Certainly any corresponding activities by similar foreign bodies operating here do not make any significant impact upon the British public, and I suspect the same of our activities abroad. On their present scale they can at most touch only an infinitesimal fraction of the people.[8]

Later in this letter Jeffries said that an equally drastic reassessment of the Council's functional activities was required. 'We must just make up our minds that we cannot afford to send dramatic and ballet companies, musicians, picture exhibitions and so on to continental Europe, or even to the older Dominions, or to subsidise recordings of Bax and Walton. I say this with a pang, because I am all in favour of these activities ... ' (In researching into the history of the British Council it has been difficult to find anyone who is not personally in favour of the activities they are proposing to cut. One is forcibly reminded of the saying: 'When people speak of their honour, it is time to lock up the spoons.')

Sir Charles's views were not entirely accepted either then or at any other time and when, in a later letter, he said that his own interest in the matter was so great that he would, if desired, undertake the work of re-organising the British Council himself,[9] he drew from Sir John Troutbeck, of the Foreign Office, the comment: 'I very much doubt whether Sir Ronald Adam himself carries enough guns for the job, but I am quite certain Sir Charles would not.'[10] Nevertheless, he had succeeded in raising, however crudely, ideas that were in other men's minds. In the Foreign Office the point was made that if the work in Latin America was not as important politically as that in the Commonwealth and Colonies, it had great value commercially, and it was pointed out that, rather than allow the Council to abandon its activities in Venezuela, the Shell Company had undertaken to maintain its establishment at its own expense. While on the fundamental point that the Council reached 'only an infinitesimal fraction of the people', it was argued that the importance of the people touched might be out of all proportion to their numbers. 'In the by no means unlikely event of one of these [British Council] scholars becoming Minister of Finance, or some similar figure in his country, we should gain dividends far in excess of the money expended.'[11]

Nevertheless, with these provisos and on the understanding that there was certain work in Europe which must continue, particularly in Germany, Italy and Spain, there was from the start a good deal of

agreement with Jeffries's views. As regards Europe, the principle seems
to have been generally accepted that countries known to be friendly
were not in the first category of importance, while it was thought, for
instance, that 'in Spain there is a Government hostile to H.M. Government but not efficient enough to prevent the latter, through the Council, from cultivating a potentially friendly people.'[12] It was therefore
believed that the Council's activities 'ought to be maintained in
Spain until a friendly and acceptable Government supersedes the
present'.[13]

Nevertheless, although the question of a reorganisation of the British
Council's activities, both as to directions and as to functions, was to
have a profound effect upon its future, more immediate matters occupied the minds of the Departments concerned with it. In October 1950
Hugh Gaitskell succeeded Sir Stafford Cripps as Chancellor.* On
21 November Sir William Strang received a letter from Sir Edward
Bridges at the Treasury saying that, in a discussion between the Chancellor, the Parliamentary Under-Secretary for the Foreign Office and
the Secretaries of State for Commonwealth Relations and the Colonies
on Overseas Information expenditure, reference had been made 'to the
possibility of cuts in the British Council and it was suggested that this
should be discussed by an interdepartmental working party'.[14]

Following a discussion with the Cabinet Offices, it was agreed that
a Working Party on the British Council should be set up, composed of
representatives of the Foreign Office, Colonial Office, Commonwealth
Relations Office, Board of Trade and Treasury, and with an observer
from the Central Office of Information. It was also agreed that Sir John
Troutbeck should take the chair. Suggested terms of reference were to
review the British Council's activities and assess the value and establish
the priority of these with particular relation to overseas information in
other fields; to estimate the financial consequence of (a) abolishing the
British Council or (b) drastically cutting its expenditure; and to suggest
the geographic and functional fields in which economies could, if necessary, be made.[15]

In a minute to Sir William Strang on 2 December, however, Sir
John Troutbeck said that while the Colonial Office had agreed to the
proposals for a Working Party,

a new consideration has arisen. I understand that the Treasury have

* As Sir Stafford Cripps was a sick man, Gaitskell had in fact been responsible
for some of his work for several months. Now the budget would be his.

also suggested that a Working Party should be set up to inquire into the whole field of overseas information expenditure. If this is proceeded with, it seems really a waste of time to have a special Working Party to inquire into the British Council. This is particularly so because the ground in respect of the British Council has already been covered time and again, and there is really nothing that a working party could do but to reassemble in a new form the information that has been assembled already.[16]

And he reminded Sir William that after lengthy interdepartmental discussion, a draft Cabinet Paper on the question of the British Council had been prepared only a few weeks before, while the whole working of the British Council had been examined during the year by the Organisation and Methods Department. In spite of these objections the Working Party on the Future of the British Council met altogether nine times, representatives of all the Departments referred to being in attendance, and Sir Ronald Adam, G. H. Shreeve and Richard Seymour being called from the British Council to give evidence.

On 10 January 1951 the Secretaries of State for Foreign Affairs, the Colonies and Commonwealth Relations, the Chancellor of the Exchequer, President of the Board of Trade, Minister of Defence and the Financial Secretary to the Treasury (Douglas Jay) met senior civil servants from each Department to consider the Chancellor's request that the Overseas Information Estimates for 1951–2 should be reduced by £2 million to £8.5 million.[17]

The Foreign Secretary, Ernest Bevin, said that the question was what propaganda work the State wanted done and whether the barrage of hostile propaganda could be met more cheaply than at present. The Chancellor said all Departments would have to contribute to the economies. The proportionate cut on Home Information Services had been accepted and the Overseas Information Services would have to do the same. He himself believed the British Council's expenditure was much inflated. It incurred much criticism in the United Kingdom and was therefore rightly being examined again in a Working Party. (It was argued that the Chancellor had been reading the Beaverbrook Press. Among newspapers which had approved of the Council's work and opposed or regretted the cuts of the last few years were *The Times*, *Daily Telegraph*, *Manchester Guardian*, *News Chronicle*, *Observer*, *Sunday Times*, *The Economist*, *Spectator*, *Times Educational Supplement* and many provincial papers. Most Members of Parliament also supported it.) He said that he would like to aim at reducing the British Council by £1 million (roughly 30 per cent of its total grant-in-aid), and the rest of the Information Services by another million.

At the eighth meeting of the Working Party under Sir John Trout-beck (27 January 1951) the Chairman reported that a meeting had been arranged for 1 February between the Chancellor, the Ministers in charge of the three Overseas Departments, the Minister of Defence and the President of the Board of Trade and it was necessary that the views of the Working Party should be in their hands well before this date.[18] It was agreed that, since it would be best if Ministers had only one document to read, rather than submitting a Report, the Working Party should content themselves with sending a paragraph or paragraphs for insertion in the Report of the General Overseas Information Working Party now sitting under Sir James Crombie (at the Treasury). The Chairman suggested they should proceed on two assumptions (1) that the Council's activities were necessary (2) that the Council was the best instrument for carrying them out.

Sir John Troutbeck then wrote to the Parliamentary Under-Secretary for Foreign Affairs, Ernest Davies (in the absence of the Secretary of State) making, among other points, the following:

We are engaged today in a life struggle between two conflicting ideologies. The 'cold war' is in essence a battle for men's minds. The British Council is one of our chief agencies for fighting it. Far from cutting down its activities, we should today be thinking in terms of refurbishing its armour. To quote H.M. Ambassador in Rome, 'it is a very serious matter to cut down Information work in Italy at a time when we are straining every nerve to distract Italian attention from Russia and Communism and to attract it to Great Britain' ... it is sometimes suggested that Western Europe has so much civilisation of its own and is so 'like-minded' to ourselves that we can safely ignore it in the cultural sphere ... But this ignores a point made by other heads of mission in Europe that, e.g. Italians are particularly susceptible to the cultural approach, and that a similarity of outlook is actually the cause of an extraordinary thirst for information. It is surely unwise to take one's friends too much for granted. There are few European countries in which one can say that the cold war is won.[19]

And, having referred to the existence of cultural conventions with European countries:

> True, the existence of the British Council is not essential to the carrying out of cultural conventions. But it *is* the instrument we have chosen for doing so, and if we stopped its cultural activities in Europe, we should either have to transfer them to some other, and probably less efficient, body or ignore our obligations. We are already accused of not being serious about the European 'idea'. If we were to pull out of cultural activity in Europe, our critics would have an unanswerable case against us.[20]

And Troutbeck enclosed with this a memorandum explaining that, although the two Working Parties had been very active, they would both have to report that, 'in the time available before final estimates are due, they cannot present Ministers with a balanced scheme showing how £2 millions can be saved with the minimum damage'.[21] And he went on himself to argue very strongly against the proposed cuts.

The Working Party under Troutbeck elicited two written statements of sufficient interest to be referred to here. The first of these was a Memorandum put in by the staff of the British Council and signed by H. P. Croom-Johnson, Chairman, Staff Side, Joint Staff Committee, which commented on the increasingly widespread feeling of insecurity and uncertainty among staff, resulting from over-frequent changes in the direction of the Council's work, cuts in its grant-in-aid and establishment, and redeployment of staff in successive years; the adverse effect this was having on the Council's work and prospects of retaining or recruiting good men; and the need for a firm decision on the degree of importance the Government attached to the work of the Council and hence on the extent to which the Council could offer a career. It was pointed out that, since 1938 when Lord Lloyd accepted the Chairmanship, it had been accepted in principle that the Council should be regarded as a permanent body, forming an integral part of the country's organisation for National Defence, and the Council had been encouraged to hold out to existing and potential staff the prospect of a career in its service. 'On no other terms could it have secured, either before or after the war, staff of the requisite qualification or calibre.'[22] While some of its officers had nearly sixteen years service to their credit, discussions on conditions of entry, salary and pension (to be based as far as possible on those of the Foreign Service) had now been dragging on for the past five years, 'Civil Service salary scales are only now on the point of being introduced, while no decisions have been come to on any corresponding improvement of tenure or of pensions rights.'[23]

After dealing with the cuts in the grant-in-aid and in the establishment, the Memorandum refers to a 'profound sense of uncertainty and unsettlement among Council staff of all grades', and says:

> The Staff Side feel bound therefore to warn the Working Party that a further substantial cut in the grant-in-aid and major reorientation of the Council's work may put the Council in the position in which it is unable to retain its best staff or to recruit suitable replacements. The younger, abler or more ambitious of the serving officers are unlikely to continue in a profession in which they can see no continuity in their work or hope of settled conditions and professional advancement. The Universities have told the Council bluntly that they will not recommend their best graduates to enter its service as long as conditions of service remain so unstable.[24]

The Memorandum recommended that the Government should state exactly which of the Council's activities were in the long-term interests of the nation and could be guaranteed regular funds, and which would be supported only on a day to day basis. 'The Council will then know the extent to which it can recruit and train a permanent professional staff and the extent to which it must rely for additional activities on scratch recruitment.'[25] It also warned that work on an *ad hoc* basis with a scratch staff was unlikely to result in very effective results or the economical use of public funds.

The second was a letter from G. H. Shreeve, the Deputy Director-General of the Council, setting out the size of the cuts that would be necessary to meet the Treasury demand for a total Estimate of £2,500,000, which would involve a cut of half a million pounds on Estimates. At the end of this letter Shreeve said:

> The Council does not propose, either directly or through its officers, to explain these proposals, should they be adopted, to the Governments, educational institutions, or institutes, in the countries in which the reductions are to be made. It will expect this to be done by the Ambassador in foreign countries, and the High Commissioner in the Dominions, and that where the proposals conflict with obligations under cultural conventions the work which the Government decides

must be continued under those conventions will be undertaken by the missions.[26]

At a meeting of senior civil servants of the Foreign Office on 31 January 1951 it was agreed that only a small cut in Overseas Information Services could be offered the Chancellor and that if he refused it the matter ought to go to Cabinet for a decision.[27]

At the Foreign Office on the following morning it was decided that the Chancellor should be offered a cut of £750,000, of which the share of the British Council would be £250,000. This offer was immediately refused by the Chancellor, who expressed his intention of going straight to the Prime Minister to ascertain whether he preferred the matter to be settled in Cabinet or by a committee of senior Ministers.[28] A minute was therefore sent to the Prime Minister stating the Foreign Office case and saying that the Foreign Secretary, who was away, would wish to discuss it personally with the Prime Minister.[29] Minutes were then sent by the Commonwealth Relations Office and the Colonial Office. The former said that economies could be effected by reducing or eliminating certain cultural activities which 'though extremely valuable do not directly affect the cold war',[30] and consequently a fairly substantial reduction should be aimed at in the work of the British Council, while it was also prepared to agree if absolutely necessary to curtail 'the valuable work of the Council in India and Pakistan'. The Colonial Office document, on the other hand, emphasised the importance of the plans which had been worked out for the British Council in the Colonies:

> It is the only agency of this kind operating in the Colonies ... and Colonial Governments unite in praise of the value of its work, particularly in the promotion of good race relations ... I hope therefore that you will agree with my colleagues and myself that cuts of the kind and to the extent desired by the Chancellor of the Exchequer would be very regrettable.[31]

Mr Gaitskell immediately replied in a Cabinet paper. Of the British Council he said that, although he agreed that it had now discontinued a large proportion of its most 'rarefied' work and was concentrating primarily on education, he did not think it followed that all the present expenditure, still less the increased provision proposed for 1951–2, could be justified. He was not convinced that the Council's effort was concentrated sufficiently on the countries and people who mattered most. He pointed out that according to the 1950–1 estimates the Council spent more in Egypt than in any other single country (about £114,000 net) the next highest being Italy (£87,000) while for South America the estimate was £202,000. He said:

> The result [i.e. of cutting by 11%] would be to reduce very considerably the Council's cultural activities, to restrict the number of countries in which it operates from 63 to 48 and to limit its activities at home to 15 towns instead of the present 23. I consider that these reductions represent a reasonable measure of concentration on those countries and activities which are of most value to our national interest.[32]

Mr Attlee, replying to the Foreign Office Memorandum, said that the problem should be referred immediately to the Information Services Committee and if they could not reach agreement, to the Cabinet. And on 6 February he received a deputation from the British Council Executive Committee. Attlee had himself been a member of this committee and he was personally sympathetic, but he said that in present circumstances some cut might be found necessary.

In March 1951 Ernest Bevin gave up the post of Foreign Secretary owing to his state of health; he died on 14 April. His successor was Herbert Morrison. According to Lord Esher (Chairman of the Council's Drama Advisory Committee and a member of the Executive Committee), Morrison is reported to have described the Council as 'a racket'.[33] At a Cabinet meeting on 2 April, Morrison said that the Chancellor proposed a cut from £11.7 million to £10.15 million in the estimates for the Overseas Information Services, and the Ministers concerned had intended to urge the Cabinet to approve a cut of only £900,000.[34] However, since assuming office as Foreign Secretary he had 'discussed this matter further with the Secretaries of State for the Colonies and Commonwealth Relations, and had persuaded them to accept the lower figure proposed by the Chancellor' – thus giving away £650,000. At this meeting it was therefore agreed that provision should be made for an expenditure of £10.15 million on overseas information services in 1951–2.[35]

In 1951 the whole future of the British Council was also under review, the five years agreed to in 1946 being at an end. On 26 July the Secretaries of State for the three Departments involved reported that

the main conclusions which could be drawn from experience of the
Council's activities during the past five years were first that the Council
played an important part in the maintenance of British political and
trading influence and an increasingly important part in developing
good relations between Britain and the peoples of the colonies and
Commonwealth; that it was valuable as presenting a positive alternative to Communism; and that if the Council did not exist, some other
agency supported by public funds would be needed in its place;
secondly, that there were solid advantages in this work being done by
a non-official body and not by a governmental organisation.[36]

It was therefore recommended that the Council's existence 'should
be prolonged indefinitely, but that some form of review should take
place at the end of ten years,' and 'that the non-official status of the
Council should be preserved.' A third recommendation was that since
some form of stabilisation of its authorised expenditure was essential,
'the Overseas Departments should be instructed to work out, in consultation with the Treasury, a reasonable minimum figure below which,
subject to exceptional circumstances, the income of the Council should
not over a number of years be permitted to fall'. A fourth recommendation was that attention should be given to the possibility of
making further reductions in the size of the Council's headquarters.[37]
(Commenting, the Chancellor of the Exchequer said that he accepted
the second recommendation and strongly supported the fourth. He was
doubtful about the expediency of accepting a firm commitment to
enable the work of the Council to continue indefinitely at a given level
of activity, and he was certainly not prepared to guarantee an annual
income of the order contemplated.)

When these recommendations were communicated to Sir Ronald
Adam, he replied in a long letter of which the most important point
was probably the following: if 'the assured minimum income' exercise
was to help the Council to a stable budget over a period of years,
whereby it could plan more effectively and avoid waste, neither of
these purposes would be served if the assured minimum were much
below the actual income.

If in a given year we were operating on a grant of £x, we should not
be helped in the least by knowing that in the following year we
should not get less than £x minus £500,000, though we might hope
to get more: the disruptive effect of a potential cut of that size is too
great. It seems to us, therefore, that the assured minimum should be

a realistic figure intended to cover the work that the Council might be expected to do, and that if extra money were provided, it should be for extra work or rising costs.[38]

This letter was written on 11 October 1951. On 25 October there was a General Election and a change of Government.

On 10 March 1952 Philip Noel-Baker asked the Prime Minister in the House of Commons whether, in view of the strong views expressed in all quarters of the House, he would give instructions that the proposed cuts in the Foreign Service of the BBC and the British Council should be abandoned. Winston Churchill replied that the BBC's grant-in-aid was being maintained at the same level but: 'The British Council's expenditure should certainly be included in the economy measures to which many of our activities must be subject.'[39]

On 2 April Ernest Davies, Labour MP for Enfield, East, moved an amendment asking Her Majesty's Government to reconsider reductions in the provisions for the Government Information Services and began a debate in which it was shown that he was correct in saying that he had support for this amendment from all over the House.[40] To anyone not familiar with the British parliamentary system it might come as a surprise that the arguments against the cuts should be put by the very man who, being unable to prevent them while Parliamentary Under-Secretary at the Foreign Office, had so recently been forced to defend them. In this Debate most of the arguments were already well known but the protagonists deploying them had changed sides.

Anthony Nutting, who had replaced Davies at the Foreign Office, began by making some predictable remarks about the state of the nation's finances when his Government had taken over from its predecessor and by reminding the House that the Estimates had already been in preparation at the time of the last election. However, during the course of the Debate, he made an announcement which, although at first sight equally predictable, did turn out to have a new, and time would prove, important clause. He said that the Government proposed to hold an Inquiry into the Overseas Information Services. He went on:

Each successive year the Overseas Information Services have been subjected to the overriding requirements of finance. 'What can we afford?' has been the standard by which they have been judged, rather than 'How much is it politically essential we should do?' It is high time ... that an inquiry was made into the political aspects of this field. We have, therefore, already taken steps to invite the Departments concerned to consider the whole range of our Overseas Information Services from the political and strategic aspects.[41]

Later in the Debate in answer to a question by Patrick Gordon Walker, John Boyd-Carpenter said that this would not be 'an exactly similar Committee' to that which had sat under Sir John Troutbeck but a new body 'designed to carry on the particular review' for the reasons which had been given.[42]

Over the five years ending 31 March 1954 the total reduction in the Foreign Office Vote to the British Council was 42.4 per cent.* The principal effects of the cuts in the last two of these years were a reduction in staff on the establishment of 26 per cent (since 1946-7 of 43 per cent) and a reduction of 41 per cent or £85,000 in Latin America, as a result of which the Council's own offices were closed and all resources concentrated on support of the Latin-American-British Societies and Institutes. The Annual Report for 1952-3 stated that if the Latin-American-British Societies succeeded in maintaining their activities the Latin American contribution to cultural relations would exceed the British Council's by about 70 per cent.

In Europe all French provincial Centres were closed, Institutes were closed in Italy at Turin and Venice, and in Spain at Valencia and Bilbao. Expenditure in The Netherlands, Belgium, Norway, Sweden and Denmark was reduced by 47 per cent. There were substantial reductions in Egypt, mainly of staff administration and grants to schools. The Council having closed in the Sudan in 1950 in order to expand in Ethiopia, the Institute in Ethiopia was closed in 1951.† All supply

*	Year	FO Grant	% reduction
	1948–49	£2,570,000	11.8
	1949–50	£2,551,000	0.7
	1950–51	£2,226,000	12.7
	1951–52	£1,862,000	16.4
	1952–53	£1,682,000	9.7
	1953–54	£1,679,200	0.2

† 'The Emperor did not forgive the Council ... When the financial climate improved a few years later and we proposed reopening an office in Addis Ababa we were allowed to do so but without any favours like free premises which we had enjoyed before.'[43] The Centres at Shiraz, Meshed, Tabriz and Isfahan were also closed but this was as a result of a decision by the Persian Government to restrict foreign cultural work, not because of the cuts.

services were drastically reduced, notably on the arts, which, having never received more than 4 per cent of the total budget, were now reduced to 2.5 per cent. Also reduced were publications, lectures, books, periodicals and scholarships. From 1947 to 1952 the sums assigned for the purchase of books for Council libraries dropped from £81,000 to less than £20,000.[44] In the Colonies the Institute at Aden was closed and in the Commonwealth the offices in Melbourne and Canberra. Staff were reduced in New Zealand and in India, Pakistan and Ceylon. In the United Kingdom three offices and centres were closed and there was a general reduction in staff.

The melancholy and bitterness of that time still drifts down over the years. Writing of Latin America, in the early days so dear to us, A. J. S. White said:

Britain had courted these countries when it was desperate for friends during the war but had jilted them as soon as the war was over, and the bitterness caused by abandonment must have outweighed the goodwill earned for Britain during [the Council's] brief existence. It would have been better if the Council had never started work there at all but it had not occurred to anyone that a long-term body like the Council would be required to abandon a number of its projects after such a few years.[45]

And writing in 1982 Richard Auty said:

In France, the closest and most difficult of our European Allies whose continuing gratitude could by no means be relied upon, the entire network of provincial centres was closed and work continued from Paris with a reduced staff …

Not much was left. Our European friends and clients were astonished. Each closure brought protests. The whole of Europe had become almost everywhere Anglophile and in the worlds of education and culture it was difficult to understand this almost ostentatious turning of the shoulder. It is impossible to estimate now how much Britain lost politically and commercially through this strange error of judgement.[46]

The Drogheda Report

On 5 April 1952 Anthony Nutting, Under-Secretary of State at the Foreign Office, wrote to the Parliamentary Under-Secretaries at the Colonial Office, Commonwealth Relations Office and Ministry of Defence, to the Secretary for Overseas Trade at the Board of Trade, to the Director-General of the BBC and to the Chairman of the British Council, saying that the Foreign Secretary (Anthony Eden) hoped very much each of them would be willing to designate someone to serve on the inquiry he (Nutting) had spoken of on 2 April in reply to Ernest Davies's Amendment on the Information Services.[1] Sir Ronald Adam replied, nominating Richard Seymour to represent the British Council. Nutting said that J. W. Nicholls, Assistant Under-Secretary of State, would represent the Foreign Office and suggested that he should also act as Chairman.

In the Foreign Office it was agreed that no Committee composed of officials dealing with Information could produce a report that would satisfy the House of Commons; and, that since the crux of the matter was to find out what was the impact of the various Information Services on the people to whom they were directed, it would be necessary for some first hand inquiry to be made in a representative range of countries. 'Clearly only a small independent Committee would be suitable for this purpose.'[2] It was therefore agreed that the Committee of Officials should be 'led' to recommend the setting up of an *independent* Committee of Inquiry.

The Committee of officials reported early in July, coming to the general conclusion that 'the scale of present activities ought to be intensified'.[3] Nicholls had nevertheless failed to win unanimous agreement to the proposal to appoint a Committee of independent persons, and Eden had to intervene himself. He too failed to obtain agreement from the various Secretaries of State of Departments concerned and therefore took it to the Cabinet. At this Cabinet Meeting (29 July) he first secured agreement to the proposal that in future there should be no financial limit on the aggregated expenditure of all Overseas Information Services but that each Department responsible should justify its own estimate separately. Second, he secured agreement, although not unanimous, to the proposal for a further independent inquiry.[4]

When Anthony Nutting announced to the House of Commons the decision to appoint the independent Committee of Inquiry he said that in the meanwhile 'the present level of activity of the overseas services will be maintained'.[5] And in reply to a supplementary question, he appeared to agree that this meant the overseas services would be protected against any increase in cost.

First choice for the position of Chairman of the new Committee was the tenth Earl of Drogheda. He had entered the Foreign Office in 1907 and remained there until 1918, when he succeeded in his desire to see war service and joined the Irish Guards. After the war, although already over thirty, he decided to read for the Bar, to which he was called by the Inner Temple in 1935. He practised mainly in the Divorce Court and took a prominent part in the reform of the divorce laws in the House of Lords. In the Second World War he entered the Ministry of Economic Warfare, and Hugh Dalton, the political head, made him joint director in charge of operations. In 1942 he was promoted to Director-General. In 1946 he became Lord Chairman of Committees in the House of Lords and he also served as Chairman of the Cinematograph Films Council from 1944 to 1954 and Chairman of the Films Selection Board from 1946 to 1954. He was an immensely charming man, of a most kindly nature but, in Hugh Dalton's words, 'a live wire and a war wager'. He was joined on the Committee by Victor Feather, representing the TUC, J. L. Heyworth, a director of Lever Brothers, Gervase Huxley, a specialist on Colonial Affairs, D. H. McLachlan, foreign editor of The Economist, J. W. Platt, the managing director of Shell, and Mary Stocks, an educationalist and broadcaster and in those days often the 'statutory woman' on such committees. Sir Robert Bruce Lockhart was forced to resign early owing to illness. Robert Marett of the Foreign Office was appointed Secretary.

The Drogheda Committee started work in the autumn of 1952 and presented a report to the Government in July 1953. After holding meetings twice a week (sixty-seven in all) in London to take evidence, the Committee broke up and its members travelled in different directions to look at the Overseas Information Services on the ground. McLachlan went to Germany, Victor Feather and Mary Stocks to Yugoslavia, Greece and Turkey; Platt went round Africa, Heyworth to the United States and Latin America, and Lord Drogheda, with Robert Marett, spent six weeks on a trip which took in the Lebanon, Syria, Pakistan, Ceylon, Malaya and Singapore and, coming home, Calcutta, Delhi, Cairo and Rome.

There is in existence a file of extracts from the British Council Representatives' comments on the visits of the members of the Committee.[6] From this one learns that Lord Drogheda was gradually converted both to the value of the Council's work and to a belief in the efficiency with which it was carried out. In Pakistan the High Commissioner reported him as saying that he 'had been pleasantly surprised to find that Council officers were not long-haired aesthetes, but ordinary, normal, decent chaps'; in Sarawak he said 'he found his present job the most fascinating he had ever had'; in Malaya that 'he was greatly impressed by the work being done by the Council and thinks it essential that it should be maintained and given every opportunity to expand'; in Egypt that he was 'delighted to have had an opportunity of doing it [his tour] and that practically without exception he had been most impressed by the personnel that he met and by the work that they were doing'. From Egypt the Representative wrote:

> There was very little left for me to do, as he had been considerably impressed by the centres he had already visited, and I could do no more than try to confirm this good impression. He seemed to be more interested in extension than in survival. He has, I think, a little prejudice against cultural work. Educational work would have his entire support.[7]

And from Rome it was reported that Lord Drogheda had left England with 'grave doubts on the Council's value, but had been steadily converted during his tour'.

The accounts of the various Representatives were borne out by the Drogheda Committee themselves. In an introductory section of their Report they said that they had reached four main conclusions:

> First. – The Overseas Information Services play an important and indeed essential role in support of our Foreign, Commonwealth and Colonial policies.
> Second. – This work should be done well, continuously and on an adequate scale.

Third. — If all these requirements are to be met more money must be spent on the Overseas Information Services.

Fourth. — Changes are required in the pattern of the work in order to bring it into line with our political, strategic and commercial needs.[8]

And the Report goes on to say that, although the Committee were at first inclined to be sceptical of the value of activities still comparatively new and the subject of much criticism, these conclusions had been forced upon them by sheer weight of evidence.[9]

The Drogheda Report shows a real appreciation of the reasons, not always obvious, for the success of the Council's work and the demands for it both in foreign countries and in the Commonwealth. There is an admirable description of the essentially 'inter-locking' nature of its various activities, a feature already well developed and still of the utmost importance to the success of its vast undertakings today. The first step was to increase the knowledge of the English language — by direct teaching, the appointment of Professors of English to local universities or by assisting the improvement of teaching in local schools. The Report continues:

A knowledge of English gives rise in its turn to a desire to read English books, talk to British people and learn about British life or some particular aspect of it. Indeed a knowledge of English is almost essential today for the study of many branches of science and technology as also, of course, for the study of English literature, history and British institutions. Foreigners who have taken the trouble to learn English are therefore usually glad to belong to a British Institute or Anglophil Society which will provide them with a good library of English books and periodicals (which would in many countries otherwise be unobtainable). But to be successful the Institute or Angophil Society requires also to develop the atmosphere of a club in the life of which lectures, films, musical recitals, play-readings and other 'cultural' activities all play their part …

The Institute also forms the headquarters from which the British Council Representative and his assistants systematically set out to make contact with and cultivate the educational, scientific and cultural leaders in the universities, in Government, and in learned societies and other institutions throughout the country. Films, lecturers, books, periodicals etc. are sent out from the Institute to these bodies on request and in this way the range of influence of the Council is spread over a wide area ...

As a result of all these contacts both inside and outside the Institute the British Council representative will receive many requests from people – some of them already eminent in their professions, others post-graduate students – who wish to visit the United Kingdom, usually in order to study some subject. From such applicants are chosen the distinguished visitors ... whom it is considered worth while to assist, as well as British Council scholars and bursars. Accordingly an organisation is maintained by the Council in the United Kingdom to look after all those various categories of visitors, many of whom pay their own expenses and merely require facilities.[10]

Although this list of activities is by no means exhaustive, the Report goes on, it does give an idea of how goodwill and understanding of this country are built up, not merely among the existing leaders in the educational and cultural world, but among those who may reach a position of influence in the future.

Thus, although the method all through is strictly non-political, at the end of the process a considerable political or commercial benefit is likely to be received. But this will come only after a period of years. It is for this reason that British Council work must be regarded as essentially a long-term investment.[11]*

The Drogheda Committee believed that, although the operations of the Council should be closely integrated with those of other information services, there was a sound case for its retention as a separate organisation in the United Kingdom and in most other countries, and they reported examples of situations in which the Council had been able to continue work in spite of much political tension. They had no doubt that in London the existing structure of the British Council was much more suitable for the type of work which had to be done than would be a Government Department.

Of the Cultural Conventions, the Committee had this to say: 'Either

---

* Reading this account and comparing the Report with the 1977 Report of the Central Policy Review Staff one cannot avoid melancholy reflection on how much the use of English in England has deteriorated in the meantime.

these Conventions must be regarded as being pure humbug, or it must be accepted that the United Kingdom by virtue of signing them has assumed certain obligations.'[12] And, after referring to other specific obligations such as the Colombo Plan Scholarships, it goes on: 'There is thus an irreducible minimum of cultural relations work, the precise scale of which only Her Majesty's Government is in a position to determine, which must be done as a matter of obligation quite irrespective of any political or commercial advantages to be gained.'[13]*

So far, so good. There was, however, or so many people have thought, a sting in the tail. The fourth and last of the Drogheda Committee's recommendations was that changes were required in the pattern of work of the Overseas Information Services in order to bring it into line with political, strategic and commercial needs. Elsewhere the Report recommends 'a fundamental re-orientation of the work of the Council – a change of emphasis from cultural to educational work and from the more developed to the less developed parts of the world.'[14]

The Report goes in great detail into what is meant by this extraordinarily succinct sentence, which, in as much as its recommendations were to a large extent adopted, while offending against no principle in the Council's Charter, introduced a new and utilitarian philosophy – 'a change of emphasis' – quite remote from the intentions of its founders or the ideals of many of its staff.

The Committee believed that the value of the Council's work in any country rested on the following factors:

1 The nature and extent of British political and commercial interests.
2 The attitude towards the United Kingdom of the educated classes.
3 The extent to which the educational and cultural leaders and university graduates were likely to have political influence.

---

* The Colombo Plan resulted from a meeting in January 1950 of the Foreign Ministers of eight Commonwealth countries (Australia, Canada, Ceylon, India, New Zealand, Pakistan, South Africa and the United Kingdom) and was designed to promote economic and social development and political stability in South and South-East Asia. £8million sterling was provided over three years from 1 July 1950 to be spent on
   a. training personnel from countries in the area.
   b. sending experts and advisory missions to help with planning and reconstruction.
   c. the provision of equipment for training or use by technical experts.
The British Council administered scholarships for incoming trainees on behalf of the Commonwealth Relations Office.

4 The extent of the danger of Communism, especially in universities and among intellectuals and the degree to which the work of the Council was likely to lessen this danger;

5 The demand for cultural and educational contacts with the United Kingdom (including the desire to learn English): and the extent to which this demand could be filled by private enterprise or required official assistance.

In the light of these criteria, the Committee believed it to be urgently necessary to build up the organisation in the Indian sub-continent and to increase its range so that it would be in touch with all the principal university towns. Second, they envisaged small increases in Burma, Indonesia and Thailand and endorsed the proposal of the Foreign Office to initiate English teaching in Indo-China.

In the Middle East, in spite of the tense political situation, the work of the Council should be maintained in existing centres and extended to the Sudan, Libya and Kuwait. Importance was attached to restoring the school subsidies in Egypt and Iraq.

High priority should be given to the British Colonies. English teaching was the function of the Colonial Governments and the Council's main task would be in the sphere of adult education in the broadest sense, and to assist in the development of social and cultural life by encouraging societies for the study of local problems and working through these. 'By bringing different racial elements together in activities which have nothing to do with politics the Council can do a great deal to break down racial prejudices.'[15] A further main task was to look after Colonial students in London.

In view of the importance of the work in the Colonies the Committee had no hesitation in endorsing the proposals which had been put to them by the British Council for a modest strengthening of offices in a number of Colonies and for opening new centres in Malaya, Tanganyika and Hong Kong.

In Latin America the work was mainly done by Anglophile Societies most of which were self-supporting. Since they would soon deteriorate into little more than language teaching schools if the British Council did not subsidise them to the extent of sending out London-based senior staff, and 'since relatively we get a lot for our money out of them', the Committee recommended that the existing level of expenditure should be maintained to keep in being Anglophile societies in Argentina, Brazil, Chile, Colombia, Mexico, Peru and Uruguay. Also recommended was an increased number of scholarships and bursaries to engineering students from these countries.

It was when they turned to Europe that the Committee made plain what they meant by a 'change of emphasis from the more developed to the less developed parts of the world'.

The Drogheda Committee believed that the method taken to renew cultural ties after the years of Nazi occupation was ill-chosen, since the traditional centres built round libraries 'with all the usual accompaniment of cultural activities' were not only expensive to maintain but part of a long-term method, although the problem to be solved was 'a short-term one arising out of the special conditions of the war'. European countries shared with us a common cultural heritage, had a high standard of education and literacy, were geographically close to us and economically relatively well-off.

And now, except in a few countries, conditions in Europe on this side of the Iron Curtain have virtually returned to normal. The number of British visitors to Europe is increasing and plenty of Europeans are now visiting the United Kingdom. Moreover, most of the European countries are now firmly committeed to a policy of the closest co-operation – political, economic and military – with us in N.A.T.O.[16]

In relation to Communism, the Report states:

We do not believe that a knowledge of the English language, a taste for British books, admiration for British medical science or modern sculpture are likely to make the slightest difference to the outlook of the average educated European on the subject of Communism.[17]

Finally: 'It seems to us that most of the European countries can well pay for anything that is done for them in these fields and that if we can provide services which they really want they would willingly do so.'[18]

The Committee therefore recommended that all existing British Council teaching Institutes, libraries, Anglophile societies, etc., in Europe should be made self-supporting within three years or closed down. 'At the very most, after the three-year period has elapsed, any subsidy ... should be limited to paying the salary of the Director ... and the supply of books and other services.'[19]

Visits to the United Kingdom by European post-graduate students, scientists, educational and cultural leaders, etc., should be encouraged, but, except in exceptional circumstances, they should be expected to pay their own way; while major exhibitions of British paintings and sculpture or European tours by British theatrical companies and orchestras should also pay their own way. At the very most they should be guaranteed against loss, and even then only when commercial prospects were considered favourable.

Finally, over the next three years British Council offices in Europe should be closed down and Cultural Attachés appointed to form part of the staff of the Embassy and to deal with inquiries, widen the range of contacts of the Mission, maintain liaison with Institutes and societies which became self-supporting and to 'stimulate and assist, although not as a rule financially, cultural and educational exchanges'.

In Portugal and France Institutes might survive on a semi-paying basis; changes should be gradual in Italy, Greece and Austria, owing to the unstable political conditions; while in Spain the status of the British Council Representative should remain unchanged 'so long as the Franco regime endures'.[20]

Turning to the Dominions, the Committee recommended that, since in Australia and New Zealand the work was essentially that of liaison, British Council centres should be closed and Cultural Attachés appointed, while they advised against the Council starting work in Canada.

Speaking of services provided from London the Report said it was imperative that the supply of books, periodicals and display material for libraries and reading rooms should be restored; and also films, lecturers, musical recordings and exhibitions, although they recommended a more careful selection 'as regards quality of lecturer and the suitability of his or her subject'.[21] Speaking of the Arts they said: 'We are unable to make any recommendation for an increase in the allocation for the arts; on the other hand we do not think that it can be reduced.'[22]

They said it was desirable that companies like the Old Vic should make occasional visits to the Commonwealth but suggested that some exploration might be made into the possibility of finding some other means of underwriting these ventures to avoid the unrealistic method of finance whereby the Council had to make provision within its annual budget for the gross expenditure involved 'without being able to take credit for any receipts which may be received'.[23]

The Report recommended an increase in the number of bursaries and scholarships for under-developed countries and for the more distant parts of the world such as Latin America.

The number of scholarships granted by the British Council is very small when compared with those given by other countries. For instance, the United States give about 4,000 scholarships compared with 1,200 given by the French and 243 scholarships and 163 bursaries given by the British Council. At the moment the British Council can only offer 7 scholarships each year for a vast country like India, 4 for Pakistan and one each for Indo-China and the Sudan.[24]

Finally on the question of staff, the Committee recommended a long-term programme for work overseas and a permanent service on the lines of the Foreign Office: pensions (estimated to cost an additional £86,800 a year); that allowances in the Colonies should be based on those received by members of the Administrative Branch of the Colonial Service; and an expansion of the establishment to make due provision for leave, sickness and training.

Nearly two years later, on publication of a summary of the Drogheda Report, a writer in the Annual Report of the British Council for 1953–4 welcomed many of its findings and then made the following comment:

There is, in fact, an element of disinterestedness in the Council's work which is nowhere acknowledged in the Committee's Report but which ought nevertheless to find some recognition in any general account of the Council as an institution. The Council has a certain representative aspect. Just as universities and museums exist (and are subsidised) not solely as centres of public instruction or recreation but also out of respect for art or learning in themselves, so the Council exists as a body which helps to interpret overseas the permanent features of our national life and to make available to the rest of the world the British contribution to the knowledge, welfare or enjoyment of mankind.[25]

However, these words were not written until April 1954, although the Drogheda Committee reported to Ministers in the previous July. In the intervening months everything in Whitehall continued as before.

There was no disagreement in the Foreign Office or anywhere else with the recommendation that the emphasis of the Council's work should be changed from cultural to educational work and from the developed to the under-developed part of the world. The rub was that the net effect of the proposals would be to increase expenditure on the Overseas Information Services as a whole by about £2½ million, although the full amount would not be incurred immediately because the programme of expansion would have to be phased.*

The Foreign Office was pessimistic from the start. 'The experience of the last three years may have darkened my judgement,' one official wrote to another, 'but I simply cannot believe Ministers will adopt the Drogheda Report or anything like it.'[26] Neither did this view prove unnecessarily gloomy. On 21 October another official wrote:

> The Chancellor [R. A. Butler] is disappointed since he had hoped that the Committee 'would show us ways in which we could make substantial withdrawals in certain fields in order to concentrate resources more effectively on tasks of first priority'. The Board of Trade ... have said much the same thing. Neither Mr. Butler nor Mr. Amory are apparently in the least impressed by the fact that an independent body of tax-paying citizens (including two big business men), after a fairly exhaustive examination of all the evidence, have been forced to the conclusion that, far from cutting down the information services, a very considerable expansion is needed.[27]

He went on to say that the sting of the letter from the Chancellor was in the tail, which suggested that the economies recommended by the Drogheda Committee should be accepted and the money saved used for increased efforts elsewhere.

> The dangerous implication here is that this would be enough to enable H.M.G. to say that they had accepted the Report 'in principle' and made a start in applying the recommendations.[28]

In the circumstances the Foreign, Colonial and Commonwealth Relations Offices began by proposing that the Cabinet should agree in principle to the expansion programme 'but spreading it over five years instead of three; and to agree now to carry out next year ... some of the most urgently needed improvements and increases, at a net cost of under £600,000'.[29]

In reply, the Chancellor put in a paper to the Cabinet saying that he

* It is impossible to isolate here that part of the Drogheda Report which refers only to the British Council or to show the separate effect each general proposal would have. The reference is to the Overseas Services as a whole unless otherwise stated

could not recommend any increase in the financial provision for the coming year, but that if the Overseas Departments would carry out the Drogheda recommendations for reductions in certain activities (e.g. the BBC and the British Council in Europe) he would be ready to agree that the saving could be used in the coming year for increased effort in other directions. (It was estimated that, as far as the Council was concerned, rising costs would be more than double the total amount of any saving that could be effected in Europe.)

Faced with this conflict of opinion, the Cabinet set up a sub-Committee of 'neutral' Ministers, consisting of the Home Secretary, the Lord Privy Seal and the Minister of Labour, to consider the matter. This sub-Committee after three meetings reported that, although impressed by the arguments for expansion of Overseas Information Services, they thought the need for limiting Government expenditure in the interests of national economy to be of greater importance. They could not therefore recommend any overall expansion of these services in 1954–5. Neither could they recommend the use of savings to finance rising costs 'as it would be difficult to defend publicly a policy of acceptance of the recommendations which involved savings with the rejection of those involving increased expenditure'.[30] They added that they proposed to continue to study the Drogheda Report.

At the Cabinet which considered the recommendation for 1954–5, deadlock was reached between the Foreign Secretary and the Colonial Secretary on the one hand and the Chancellor on the other. An effort was then made to break this by means of informal consultation between Ministers outside the Cabinet. The Foreign Office produced a succession of plans for a small programme of expansion in 1954–5, each more modest than the last; the first to cost an additional £460,000, the second an additional £300,000, the third only £150,000 (plus rising costs in each case). Still no agreement was reached.

So matters stood at the end of January 1954. Then the Chancellor called a meeting to discuss the possibility of breaking the deadlock. He did this on his own initiative but it was suggested that he may have taken action 'as a result of a telegram sent to him from Berlin by the Foreign Secretary, urging that he should take a more positive line'.[31]

Anthony Eden's telegram no longer exists but it signalled the end of the long years of cuts. The question of the estimates for 1954–5 was settled by the Chancellor offering some additional money, although the larger part of it was needed to offset risen costs. In the upshot the Council received an increase over the previous year of £93,000 and were allowed to retain savings (in Europe and elsewhere) estimated at £60,000, although at the request of the Financial Secretary to the Treasury no account of the settlement was given to the House of Commons.

Agreement was, however, no nearer on the Drogheda Report, and in March 1954 it became known that the neutral Cabinet Committee chaired by the Home Secretary would resume its considerations. In April a summary of the Drogheda Report was made public. The full text was withheld. Nutting wrote to Eden on 25 March 1954: 'It has been drafted on the assumption, which I am sure you will approve, that nothing in the Drogheda Report ought to be suppressed except passages to which there are security objections, passages which would give offence to foreign countries and passages which describe Information techniques in too revealing a way. Nothing is being omitted merely on the ground that it is critical of the Information Services or that it would be embarrassing to this or preceding Government (or to the Treasury!).'[32] The summary was generally welcomed by the press: 'Organized official propagation abroad of the British point of view is a new thing [The Times leader remarked] ... The committee, however holds, rightly, that it has come to stay, and since it is to be done it is true economy to do it well.'[33] And a writer in The Spectator said: 'Whatever it is precisely that is worrying the Government, it is to be hoped that when Mr. Eden announces the official decision later in the year, timidity will not prevail.'[34]

At this time the end appeared to be in sight. On 13 May Anthony Nutting reported to Eden a 'not unsatisfactory' meeting with the Home Secretary's Committee at which he had put forward the proposal that the entire Drogheda programme of additional expenditure should be adhered to but spread over seven years instead of five. 'May I tell the Home Secretary that you agree?'[35] Eden replied in the affirmative and added the interesting comment: 'I am more than ever sure we will have to do more — but this cannot be decided in present regime.'[36]

On 1 June Nutting reported a further conversation with the Home Secretary who had told him that he had just seen the British Council deputation, which had made a forceful case. The Home Secretary had said that 'the way now seemed clear for him to make a recommendation to the Cabinet on the lines agreed ... namely to spread over seven years the requirements originally scheduled for five and to grant for the Financial Year 1955-6 the requirements listed as first priority by the Overseas Departments.'[37]

At this point a strange intervention was made by Lord Swinton. Although by now a man of seventy, the former Philip Cunliffe-Lister (created Viscount Swinton in 1935) was still a powerful Minister, one with a long and distinguished past. A member of the Cabinet for the first time in 1922, he did great service to the country when he was made Minister of State for Air in 1935. He was responsible not only for a three-fold expansion of the Air Force in as many years but also for the decision to order the Spitfire and Hurricane fighters straight off the drawing board.

In 1954, in addition to being Secretary of State for the Commonwealth, he was Chairman of the Committee on Civil Expenditure and it was in the latter role that he intervened. He wished to make a reduction in the expenditure on Information from £10.2 million to £9.5 million and in order to do this, he proposed, among other things, that all British Council activities should be cut except 'in India and Pakistan and other under-developed territories, which are particularly important to the United Kingdom, provided the Government are satisfied that this work is being conducted by the British Council efficiently and on the right lines'.[38] (A Foreign Office official commented: 'There is in any case some confusion in his argument on this point since, after speaking of a reduction in Information expenditure from the existing figure of £10.2 million to £9.5 million (and the first figure is the cost of *overseas* Information at present), he goes on to suggest that the lower figure could probably only be attained by cutting certain *home* activities as well as overseas activities.')[39]

Lord Swinton also wrote to the Home Secretary asking him to reconvene his neutral Committee in order to work out a plan for effecting economies in Information expenditure. (Anthony Nutting for the Foreign Office pointed out that having held three Inquiries this would be tantamount to holding a fourth.)[40] The Home Secretary replied to Lord Swinton saying that his Committee had already reported (to the Cabinet) and was not qualified to undertake the task now proposed for it.

Lord Swinton continued to give much trouble because, although at the time he was travelling abroad, he insisted that no decisions should be taken in his absence, a difficult matter because Eden was also away for long periods at this time.

However, the end was in sight. Lord Swinton managed to delay matters for several months, but his chief claim to be remembered in this context is that, while overseas, he arbitrarily shut down the British

Council offices in Australia, New Zealand and Ceylon. In the first and third of these the Representative remained as Cultural Attaché but there was no further Council presence in New Zealand until 1960.

Both Parliament and the press were getting restive. On 6 July Ernest Davies initiated a debate on the Overseas Information Services and, for want of anything more positive to say, Anthony Nutting was forced to dwell on the Opposition's record while in Government. Afterwards he wrote to the Foreign Secretary: 'I just got away with a debating speech ... because the Opposition over-stated their case. But I don't expect such luck again.'[41] And, although it would be five months before an announcement was made, the Foreign Secretary continued to use his influence to block Lord Swinton's proposals. In October he circulated a memorandum to the Cabinet in which he said that it was his clear understanding from a discussion which had taken place before the summer recess that the Overseas Information Services should be exempted from the economies which Lord Swinton's Committee was making.[42] Sir Norman Brook, Secretary to the Cabinet, wrote at the same time to the Chancellor supporting this view. Brook said that he had deliberately refrained from recording that Churchill 'had virtually promised that the Overseas Information Services should not suffer at any rate the full cut ... which the Swinton Committee had proposed ... lest it stiffen other Civil Departments in their resistance.'[43]

Finally on 8 November the Foreign Secretary said in reply to a question by Ernest Davies that the Government accepted the broad principles of the Drogheda Report, although what expansion could be undertaken next year 'will have to depend to some extent upon how far we can avoid rising costs'.[44] In fact the Chancellor had agreed a figure of £300,000 additional money for the Overseas Information Services, of which £100,000 would go to the British Council, £73,000 to cover rising costs and £27,000 to re-open its office in Persia. (In the margin of a progress report to the Foreign Secretary written at the time, there is a note in Eden's handwriting: 'Lord Swinton has consistently criticised Drogheda and opposed me. No need for CRO [Commonwealth Relations Office] to get a penny.'[45]

In a debate in the House of Lords on 8 December, Lord Reading, Minister of State for Foreign Affairs, said that the recommendations of the Drogheda Committee would add £2.5 million to the existing expenditure and the Government had been forced reluctantly to conclude that this further large sum should not be spent and a more modest programme should be arrived at. And he said it was proposed 'to streamline our existing services and gradually to expand them in what are judged to be the key areas'.[46]

This was the end of the matter. The British Council received an additional £100,000 in 1955–6 and rather more than that in the following year. In any case the years of austerity were coming to an end.

For eighteen months Cabinet Minister, Ministers of State and leading civil servants had spent much of their time in arguments about sums of money which according to one of the latter were comparable, in the case of the annual additions recommended for the Foreign Office Information Service, to one day's subsidy to the Egg Marketing Board, and as far as the total bill for the Information Services was concerned, to rather less than the cost of two bombers.[47] Neither was there anywhere any conflict of opinion over the suggested 'change of emphasis' in the work of the British Council.

The Drogheda Report merely gave form and substance to the prevailing ideas of the time. The British proved once more that, unlike the French, the Germans and the Italians, they will not pay for something they understand and regard as little as the projection of their own national culture. The Council could hardly have survived much longer in the idealistic form envisaged by Rex Leeper and Lord Lloyd. Indeed the whole history of the Drogheda period suggests that, without the presence of the most powerful Foreign Secretary of the twentieth century (at this time Heir Apparent to the Prime Minister) cuts would have continued to emasculate it until it was fit only to be taken over by some Government Department. Those people (and there are many) who regret the passing of the earlier phase might reflect that in the United Kingdom half a loaf is better than no bread. The recommendations which have led to the Council's development as a world-wide educational force also ensured that a small percentage of a very large budget would continue to be spent on presenting British art and culture to other countries.

PART TWO
1954-84

13

Sir Paul Sinker: The Hill Report

From 1946 to 1954 Sir Ronald Adam held the post of Director-General to the British Council as well as that of Chairman of the Executive Committee. A. P. Sinker was appointed Director-General in February 1954, being knighted when he took up the position. Sir Ronald Adam remained as Chairman until 1955; he was succeeded by Sir David Kelly, who had previously served as British Ambassador to Argentina, to Turkey and to the Soviet Union, and who on his retirement in 1951, became Deputy Chairman of the Central and East European Commission and later Chairman of the Britain in Europe Committee.

Asked for a third name to join those of Sir Reginald Leeper and Lord Lloyd as of the first importance in the history of the British Council, few of those qualified to say would hesitate to name Sir Paul Sinker. Born in 1905, Sinker became a Fellow of Jesus College, Cambridge and a University lecturer in Classics. During the war he was one of a number of hand-picked dons who, on leave of absence from a university, served in the Admiralty. He distinguished himself by his tremendous drive and ability and after the war he went to the Treasury for five years. In 1950 he was loaned to the Government of Egypt as adviser on Civil Service questions and on his return was appointed First Civil Service Commissioner, concerned with the recruitment and regulation of entries. From there he was seconded to the British Council.

In a farewell speech made fourteen years later, summing up Sinker's career in the British Council, R. A. Phillips, at that time Deputy Director-General, said: 'To the British Council Paul Sinker brought many Roman gifts ... He brought law, straight roads and a great Empire. Analyse any of Paul Sinker's achievements in the British Council and they can be fitted under those heads.'[1] He also said this:

The Director-General has given us, I would say, three particular things. Drive, a sense of direction, and professionalism. Drive, enormous drive, sometimes back-breaking drive, with a foot flat out on the accelerator. A sense of direction; he knew exactly where he was going and wanted to go, and was obstinate about it and rightly so, and as a professional his professionalism was complete ...

His final achievement, I think I would simply state in this way: that he understood what the Council could do and he was able to explain this to Whitehall and to the world in terms and language which were comprehensible to them, so they too came to understand us and to appreciate what we could do, so that their confidence in us grew. We were no longer a bunch of long-haired, crackpot intellectuals, concerned with deer-stalking or Morris dancing, but a body of trained and professional people – a new service, of immense importance for the future of this country, expanding as our imperial role decreases, a new service dedicated to the purposes of tomorrow.[2]

Sinker's mandate in 1954 was to develop the Council as a practically effective organisation on the lines laid down in the Drogheda Report and he recognised that, in order to be able to attract good recruits and to restore the morale so badly damaged in recent years, the first necessity was to get proper terms of service for his staff. He is quoted as saying, 'The real problems are always establishment problems.'[3] James Livingstone, who was Director of Personnel Department, 1956–62, and Controller of Establishments Division, 1962–9, wrote: 'I greatly enjoyed working to him. He was the first senior officer of the Council, in my experience, who really understood problems of staff structure and management. He took in at once points I had been trying to get across for years.'[4] He added that a lot of Sinker's method rubbed off on to those who worked for him and through them on to other people.

In the British Council Sinker was known, according to E. E. R. Church, as 'the Headmaster', but he nevertheless inspired great affection in many of his staff. If others, while recognising his great ability and the services he rendered the Council, felt for him rather less warmth, this was because he was regarded by some as slightly philistine. British Council staff were (and still are) divided between those who regarded the reorganisations and reforms which followed the Drogheda Report as an unavoidable necessity, and those who actually welcomed them. No one (either then or now) has believed it a practical proposition to try to increase substantially the proportion of the budget devoted to the arts, but some people join the Council because of an interest in them, and are both adroit at using such money as there is to the best advantage and concerned to defend the arts departments against encroachment. Others are primarily interested in education or administration.

In the same way, some people still mourn the passing of the old eccentrics, among whom many were very talented, while others regard it as an excellent thing. There is a continuing rift among British Council staff in regard to these matters not always related to their personal taste. Sinker, for instance, was a very cultivated man and in his private life interested in books, furniture and pictures. He is sometimes defended against the charge of philistinism on the grounds that in the circumstances of the day he felt it necessary to stress the need for a change of emphasis and to pose as less interested in the arts than he actually was. A better defence might be that during his reign there occurred the most glorious period for the arts in all British Council history. But this was because Lilian Somerville was in charge of the Fine Arts Department and Sir Paul, far too astute not to recognise talent when he found it, let her have her head.

But these things are after all a matter of instinct and feeling and reveal themselves spontaneously. Sinker expressed himself easily and well and there are large collections of his speeches and newsletters to Representatives. One can go a very long way without coming across anything but the most cursory reference to the arts. When he had been five years in the Council, he contributed an article to the Annual Report for 1958-9 entitled 'The Main Tasks'. This has an introductory section and is then divided into four parts, Educational Work, Personal Contacts, The Printed Word, and Other Tasks and Future Development. British drama, music and the visual arts are dealt with in one paragraph under the last of these.

Sinker's preferences showed themselves in other ways. He chose people for their administrative ability or for their scientific or technical qualifications or for their qualifications as teachers. James Livingstone said: 'Sir Paul has given the service a strong sense of direction. He has trained the older staff and brought in and inspired an important nucleus of the younger staff.'[5] Sinker had therefore a long-term influence on the type of person attracted to join the Council. He turned a small, unexpectedly successful but often amateurish institution into a great empire and a vast educational force. But there must be some significance in the fact that, in his valedictory speech, R. A. Phillips referred to the old British Council in terms invented by Lord Beaverbrook.

Finally it has to be said that Sinker had all the luck. Where Ronald Adam, who was scarcely less able, sustained years of disproportionate cuts, when it was impossible to recruit and difficult to retain staff of the necessary calibre, when morale was appallingly damaged and there was uncertainty both about the future of the work and the value attached to it, Sinker took over as the terms of trade turned in Britain's favour, the long years of austerity were almost over and that short period of 'You never had it so good' was only just around the corner. Then in 1956 the fiasco at Suez so altered Britain's position in the world that the Government was forced to turn to its neglected Information Services in an attempt to restore some of its lost prestige.

Sinker cannot be given the whole of the credit for the creation within the Council of an integrated global service with established pay scales and a pension scheme, because there had been discussion with the Treasury on these matters since 1945. After the 1946 decision on the Council's future, it had been agreed that it should have an Established Service which would give a proportion of its staff permanency and a reasonable tenure. The two services – Home and Overseas – had previously received grades and scales of pay which were quite different. In July 1950 it was agreed that both should receive rates of pay related to those of the Information Class of the Civil Service. When Sinker joined there was a Home Pension Scheme and an Overseas Pension Scheme, differing slightly but both contributory, with the pension being dependent on the total amount contributed during service. There was no scheme for officers who were over forty-five when they joined, although of the 159 officers too old to join existing schemes, 125 were able to complete ten years' service before their sixty-fifth birthday.

Sinker entered the struggle for improved conditions with determination and zest. Recruitment of staff had stopped altogether in 1949, and the new requirements of the Drogheda recommendations made it imperative that it should begin again. Because of this gap and because of the subsequent heavy recruitment which followed in 1956, there was a block in the promotion prospects of the more junior staff in the late 1970s and early 1980s. It is said that Sinker refused to begin recruitment until he was given an assurance of being able to offer a permanent career. Certainly, as a result of a Government decision, the Foreign Secretary wrote to the Vice-Chancellors of universities saying that it had been brought to his attention that universities had for some time been chary of recommending British Council service to undergraduates seeking appointments because of the insecurity of tenure and unsatisfactory pension arrangements. In the current financial year, he said, £445,000 was being added to the Council's grant-in-aid, bringing it to over £2,000,000. He continued:

> This money can only be put to work if new recruits are enrolled. I should therefore be most grateful if your authorities concerned with appointments would in due course bring to the attention of potential candidates the importance which Her Majesty's Government attach to recruits of good quality coming forward to enable the Council to fulfil its responsibilities. The Council has now existed for twenty-one years, during which time it has served a most useful purpose, and it is the hope and intention of Her Majesty's Government that the Council shall remain a permanent feature of the British overseas services.[6]

Sinker also secured many improvements to the overseas service, concessions for children's education and children at posts, grants for transfer and installation, car depreciation, allowances for lower grades and so on.

He correctly identified the main task of the Council and the methods of presentation most likely to appeal to Whitehall. He understood immediately the tremendous importance of the teaching of English and he stimulated the Minister of Education into appointing an interdepartmental Committee of officials representing the Foreign, Scottish, Commonwealth Relations and Colonial Offices, the Board of Trade and the Ministry of Education, to examine and report to the Cabinet on the teaching of English overseas. This report is one of the most important and influential in the history of cultural relations; underlying the findings of the Hill Report and the future direction of British Council work, it was the precursor of educational aid.

The authors of the Teaching of English Overseas (TEO) Report begin by predicting that 'within a generation English could be a world language', a second language where it was not already the native or primary tongue. Nevertheless, unless present opportunities were seized and the spread of English reinforced by more co-ordinated effort and more generous financial support, it might be supplanted as a lingua franca, either by regional languages such as Hindi or Arabic, or by some other European language. Again, it might be efficiently taught but used for politically biased purposes, as in Communist countries.

Having referred to the almost limitless demand for the English language in the western world, the Report continues:

> In both the Middle and Far East the United Kingdom has the strongest reasons, military, political and economic, for extending the use of English and for making available as many teachers and technicians as possible. She ought not to stand by ... while Libya is offered a German professor of English for her new university and Egypt exports Egyptian teachers of English and other subjects to Kuwait.[7]

The summary to this part of the Report is as follows:

> English is a commodity in great demand all over the world; it is wanted not only for reasons of friendship and trade with the English-speaking countries but also for other reasons not necessarily connected with any desire to imitate British ways or to understand British history and culture. We are, therefore, looking at the language mainly as a valuable and coveted export which many nations are prepared to pay for, if it can be supplied in the right quantities, and which some others would be glad to have on subsidised terms if they cannot pay the full price. English is, moreover, an export which is very likely to attract other exports – British advisers and technicians, British technological or university education, British plant and equipment and British capital investment. There are clear commercial advantages to be gained from increasing the number of potential customers who can read technical and trade publicity material written in English.[8]

In the second section the authors say that, because the responsibilities of the Education Ministers in England, Scotland and Wales are limited to their own three countries, like manufacturers who 'have covenanted not to sell their goods abroad', the main effort is made by the British Council. After some description of the Council's work, they continue:

> The Council has assured us that, given a supply of suitable candidates for posts abroad and satisfactory terms of employment, it could multiply by many times the number of teachers it placed abroad, both for teaching English and for teaching other subjects through the medium of English.[9]

The burden of this part of the Report is that, whether one looks at the present interchange of teachers with non-English speaking countries, at recruitment of teachers from the UK, the supply of expatriate teacher-trainers, or lecturers in education with special reference to the teaching of English as a foreign language, the answer is invariably the same: the supply does not meet the demand.

The position was much the same with the United Kingdom. London was the only University in England which had a department concerned with the teaching of English as a foreign language. In Wales, because English had long been taught as a second language, research had been carried out at Bangor and Aberystwyth, and Welsh teacher training colleges trained students to teach English as a second language, but there was no comparable work in Scotland.

There were a great number of private establishments teaching English but 'the teaching ... varies enormously in competence'. In the conclusion to this part of the Report the authors say:

This haphazard expansion of the teaching of English overseas is in marked contrast with the careful and sustained efforts of the French authorities to further the teaching of their language overseas. For many years past the French Government has regarded French cultural work, both in foreign countries and in French dependencies, as an important part of its foreign policy. This cultural work is essentially based on the teaching of French. To this effort, which still continues, France has owed and owes much of her prestige.[10]

In speaking of the United States, the Report makes the interesting comment that, as a country which has to deal with very many immigrants, America had devoted much research to the rapid instruction of large numbers in elementary English and had made many advances in technical method but its main teaching overseas agency, the United States Information Agency, had given little prominence to extensive English teaching until it compared notes with the British Council. Having said that there was a preference overseas for the Queen's English as opposed to American English, the Report goes on:

Broadly speaking, United States methods are more immediately and widely successful in teaching English rapidly to large numbers, whereas the British effort is perhaps more successful in the careful tuition of selected pupils up to a higher standard ... It is amply clear to both that the demand for English is greater than either of them is ever likely to be able to meet and that there is, therefore, scope for the maximum effort by both sides, though it needs co-ordination.[11]

Detailed consideration is given to the methods necessary to increase the 'extremely small number of United Kingdom teachers overseas'. Among the most important are means of safeguarding superannuation rights and raising the salaries and standards of living overseas, positive measures to help returning teachers to find suitable posts and proper contracts ensuring satisfactory conditions while abroad. Having commented that outside the Colonies, 'the salaries offered to expatriate teachers tend to be derisory in relation to the cost of living', the Report recommends an extension of the method used by the British Council of paying subsidies to schools or to the holders of individual posts (although they recognise objections to the payment of subsidies), and on the question of unsatisfactory contracts it says:

The best solution to these difficulties would be for the teacher going overseas to have a contract with the British Council, which would be responsible for filling the post on behalf of the oversea authority. Except for appointments in Colonial territories, where it is unnecessary, we recommend this arrangement, wherever it is practicable.[12]

The Report makes proposals for increasing the supply of teachers from overseas through scholarships for training in the UK and, in a most important section, deals with training.

It is the need for special training in fresh techniques which distinguishes the problems of teaching English as a foreign language from those of oversea teaching generally. At present very few United Kingdom teachers overseas have had any special training in teaching English as a foreign language, and the standard of English teaching by native teachers overseas is low, often deplorably so.[13]

It is later added that 'it would be desirable to distinguish between foreign teachers who will return to their own countries to teach English as a foreign language and teachers from Colonial territories who will be teaching English as a second mother tongue.'[14]

Reference is made to a new development envisaged by Edinburgh University (at the instance of the British Council and with the backing of the Overseas Departments) for a one-year course for training men and women, for both the UK and overseas, who will be responsible for training teachers in their own countries; and it is proposed there should be courses below university level for the same purpose.

Proposals are made for the supply of text-books and — at the instance of the British Council — on how to meet requests from overseas Governments or education authorities for advice on drawing up a syllabus and the writing of text-books. There is a paragraph on teaching aids and one on research.

In January 1957 Dr Charles Hill was appointed Chancellor of the Duchy of Lancaster, with a seat in the Cabinet and responsibility for the co-ordination of official Information Services at home and abroad. He describes himself as having been 'washed into the Cabinet by the turbulent waters of Suez' and he explains that it was on the overseas side of the work that he could exercise authority, 'for the simple reason that I advised overseas ministers on the distribution of the available money between departments'.[15]

Once the total sum for the year's expenditure had been determined — I took a lively part in bargaining as to its size with the Chancellor of the Exchequer — the sharing out of the cash between the three main spenders, the overseas departments, the BBC and the British Council, was largely left to me. I did not exactly pay the piper but to some extent, I could call the tune.[16]

Accompanied by Harold Evans, Dr Hill toured extensively overseas trying to discover the strengths and weaknesses of the information services and the effectiveness of the work of the BBC and the British Council. Of the British Council he says this:

At the start of the job I knew no more about the British Council than I had learnt from the Press, and that was more derisory than informative. Before I left the job, I had come to regard the work of the British Council as unquestionably the most effective single thing which our country was doing to present itself overseas. Once convinced of this, I made up my mind to support it and to strengthen it. When I began, its money allocation was about three million pounds; when I finished it was well over six million [1961]. Today it is over ten million [1964].[17]

Following some description of the work of the British Council, his account continues: 'The more I saw of the Council the more I admired its work.'[18]

During the course of Dr Hill's inquiries the British Council submitted two papers. The first covered the developments since the Drogheda Report, including those foreseen for the next year or two, the second was a five-year plan. From the first we learn that in the meantime the Council's grants had risen by about £760,000 but that only about £130,000 was due to the execution of the Drogheda Committee's recommendations (some of which were not carried out). The balance was for rising costs (about £282,000); for particular salaries, which, being based on Civil Service scales, had been affected by recent pay increases; for capital expenditure on buildings; and for extra work requested by the Government but not covered by the Committee's recommendations (re-entry into Iran £27,000; expansion of welfare work for overseas students in the United Kingdom, £80,000; Soviet Relations Committee, £30,000). We also learn that drama, music and the fine arts accounted only for about 2 per cent of the Council's expenditure, the remainder falling under the broad heads of education, the sciences (pure and applied) and professions, and English language and literature.[19]

The Council was then asked to submit its five-year plan and, reporting to a meeting at the British Council, Sir Paul Sinker said that he had gained the impression that Dr Hill was likely to base his recommendations firmly on those of the Drogheda Committee and to support the recommendations made in the Report on the Teaching of English Overseas. He said he thought it would be wise for the British Council's plan to follow the same lines.[20] It therefore referred immediately to the two main Drogheda recommendations and said that this reorientation had already taken place:

The proposed five-year programme is aimed in the same general direction. The emphasis of the programme is mainly on educational work, e.g. the work proposed in the TEO Report, and on the under-developed countries especially of the Arab world and Asia. We also propose to place special emphasis on our work in the scientific field.[21]

Speaking of the TEO Report, doubt is expressed as to whether the rate of suggested expansion is practicable or desirable. 'Our programme envisages expansion at about half the rate suggested ... '[22]

The comment is made that, since Drogheda did not recommend an increase in the allocation for the arts, this side of the work had proportionately diminished. 'This country is therefore lagging behind other nations in that respect and is failing to make use of a powerful influence on public opinion abroad. It is therefore proposed that an extra £55,000 should be allocated, for tours and exhibitions abroad.'

In July 1957 the Secretaries of State for the Overseas Departments, the President of the Board of Trade, the Chancellor of the Duchy of Lancaster and the Financial Secretary to the Treasury presented a White Paper to Parliament (Cmnd 225) on Overseas Information Services. This has become known as the Hill Report. It differed from previous Reports in that it contained not recommendations but decisions already taken by the Cabinet. Quite short, it is absolutely explicit.

On the British Council it says that the Government has decided that certain extensions are urgently necessary, first in the Council's overseas posts, and second, in the teaching of English. There is to be expansion in Burma, Indonesia, Iran, Iraq, the Persian Gulf, South America, the Sudan, Thailand, Turkey and Yugoslavia; in the Commonwealth, in South Africa, Ceylon, India and Pakistan; in the Colonies, in Hong Kong, Nigeria and Uganda. Having explained the importance of the English language and having repeated in essence the findings of the TEO Report, the Hill Report continues:

Scholarships will be established – 50 in the first year rising to 100 in the fourth year – to enable additional key students from overseas to come to this country for training in teaching English as a foreign language. Provision will be made for the training of teachers in English as a foreign language within the public teachers training scheme. Steps will be taken to strengthen the existing arrangements for the training of overseas teachers in their own countries ...

The Government have decided on other forms of expansion in the British Council's central services. They include the necessary staff increases at headquarters and in the regions, an improved staff pension scheme, more British Council books and periodicals for libraries, and the extension of the British Council's programme for the care of visitors, including courses, studentships and bursaries, chiefly from the Commonwealth and the Middle East. Increased grants will be made for the inter-university exchange scheme, for student welfare services and for a modest expansion of the arts programme to be concentrated on drama.[23]

In effect, the only one of the proposals put forward by the British Council which had not been agreed was that for an increase of £55,000 for the arts.

The middle 1950s were dominated to an unusual degree by international incidents. For the British Council the period began quietly and perhaps inauspiciously with a resumption of relations with the Soviet Union. The Soviet Relations Committee was set up in May 1955 at Government request and was kept fully occupied in arranging visits between groups of professionals, academics, scientists and so on. *Hamlet* was played in Russia by a British company and a British orchestra toured there. Then in early 1956 the USSR suppressed a revolt in Hungary with a show of military force and as a result arrangements, including a visit to Covent Garden by the Bolshoi Ballet and a return visit by Sadler's Wells, were cancelled.

From the first the British Council played a large and worthy part in the reception of Hungarian refugees in Austria. Then, in November 1956, the Warden of St Antony's College, Oxford, William Deakin, arrived in Vienna to select Hungarian students to fill 150 places offered at British universities by the Committee of Vice-Chancellors and Principals and he sought the Council's help. Candidates from the refugee camps all over Austria had to be found and interviewed, and those selected sent on as quickly as possible to London. Here the Council was again responsible for their accommodation and food. Council officers also started English language courses for these students in Leeds (which were subsequently taken over by the University), Birmingham and Oxford and also found teachers and material for courses not under their own management.

After the deportation from Cyprus of Archbishop Makarios in March 1956, although the Council continued to operate on a reduced scale in Cyprus itself, it was advised by the Greek Government that they could not be responsible for the safety of people using the British Institute in Athens and this, as later the Institute at Salonika, was closed. The Council's offices in Athens, Salonika and Corfu nevertheless continued to function.

Most serious of all from the British point of view was the adventure at Suez. Following it, Council premises at Cairo and Alexandria were sequestrated, as also many of the British Schools with which it had been associated. The Council organised the return of British teachers and assisted them in finding employment. Work in Syria was suspended and, temporarily, work in Jordan, but in the United Kingdom, out of 360 Egyptian students studying here at the time, about 300 chose to remain.

In Europe the effect of the Drogheda recommendations was not less than might have been expected. There was no real reason why, in order to strengthen the Council's work in the Colonies and Commonwealth, the work in Europe should have been so devastated, or why the minute contribution to the arts should not have been increased. Richard Auty writes:

Our European friends and clients were astonished. Each closure brought protests. The whole of Europe had become almost everywhere Anglophile and in the worlds of education and culture it was difficult to understand this almost ostentatious turning of the shoulder ... Fortunately this [the Drogheda Report] advice was not wholly followed and a Council presence was maintained in most countries. Though the presence was often minimal its inadequacy was compensated by the ingenuity and imagination of a committed corps of Council staff who were able for long years to achieve important results through their cultivation of personal contacts at all levels in the cultural and educational worlds. They thus had an influence out of all proportion to the resources at their command. HMG thus got a great deal more out of the Council for Britain than it really deserved ... This almost missionary conviction of the importance of their work characterised the Council staff of that day but it has never been adequately recognised elsewhere ... This again is an unsung period of Council heroism where Britain was served quite unknowingly by people whose judgments proved to be sounder and more durable than those of the politicians who judged our cultural efforts abroad (in almost total ignorance of them) or, indeed, of our sponsors themselves, who should have known better.[24]

Reporting in the Annual Review 1955-6, on a visit to Europe, the Chairman, Sir David Kelly, wrote:

The shattering reductions of a few years ago have created the freely expressed impression that we are no longer interested in preserving, let alone improving, our relations with our traditional friends. That the Council's work has not fallen below the minimum line of usefulness is due to the eager help offered by the local authorities. Thus in Norway the Secondary School Teachers Union have themselves

defrayed the cost of visits by Council officers to 117 schools outside
Oslo; in Oslo and Stockholm the Council's English libraries have
been saved from dispersion by being taken over as units, by the City
Library in Oslo and an adult education organisation in Stockholm.
In Brussels an Anglo-Belgian Society has taken over the Council's
premises and provided accommodation there for the Council's
solitary representative. In one capital, at an Embassy dinner attended
by a cross-section of the academic world, and the Press, theatre and
the arts, an experienced member of the government in an impromptu
speech referred with surprising bitterness to the reduction almost to
nullity of the Council's local work.[25]

An exception to the European rule was made for West Germany.
As soon as a British Ambassador had been appointed to the German
Federal Republic, the Embassy in Bonn took over the cultural and
educational work from the Control Commission. The Council had
given some help, principally in the form of scholarships and the
appointment of lecturers to German universities, but had not been
otherwise concerned. Then in the autumn of 1957 the British Government invited it to take over the work from the Embassy.

The take-over was fixed for the autumn of 1959, but in the spring of
1958 a British Council officer, James McDonaugh, was appointed
Deputy Counsellor 'Cultural' to the Embassy with a view to carrying
through the transfer. Writing of this time McDonaugh says:

It was vital to continue as much as possible the good work being
done and it was equally vital to establish the British Council's
identity as different from and separate from the CRD [the Embassy's
Cultural Relations Department]. The reason is, of course, obvious.
The work of the CRD derives from the occupation; it began with
the re-indoctrination of the German people with the ideas and concepts of democratic government, and at every turn it was still in
1958 instinct with a sense of political mission. The name under which
its institutes worked, 'Die Brücke' – the Bridge – meant precisely
this to most of the Germans. Over the years these institutes had added
other purposes and connotations – but it was a label which the
British Council had to avoid. At the same time 'Die Brücke' had
generated everywhere a fund of goodwill and this had to be preserved. It must never be underestimated – because it is a source of
strength on which all the British Council's work since, and political

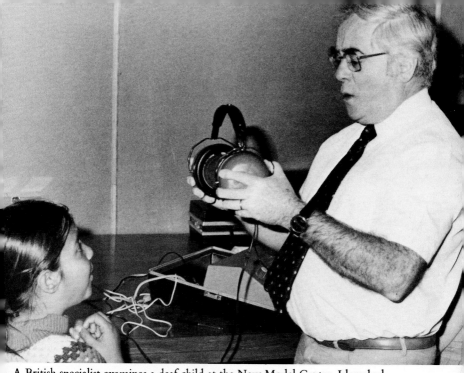

A British specialist examines a deaf child at the New Model Centre, Islamabad, Pakistan; his visit was paid for by the British Aid Programme

A doctor from The Netherlands on a British Council course in nuclear medicine

26 Overseas students on a Fruit Science and Technology course at East Malling, Kent

27 A British Council scholar from Greece visits the Shelley Museum in Bournemouth

relations also, have relied. By 1957 nevertheless the political basis
for cultural work was an anachronism. The Cultural Convention
recognised this by implication.[26]*

McDonaugh goes on to say that the existing system was vast (having
been a charge on the German economy through Reparation Costs or
other sources) and had to be slimmed down, while the Institute form of
organisation (with libraries, English classes, films, lectures and so on)
had outlived its usefulness. About the Brücken he nevertheless says:

> The extraordinary local value of most of them was proved by the
> zeal with which town authorities, adult education societies and
> charitable organisations rushed to take them over, guaranteeing their
> costs, if in return we promised (as British Council) to supply and
> maintain the library. It was an astonishing gesture of affection and
> trust on the part of the German towns. Many of them still exist, and
> I think it ought to be recorded.[27]

The British Council kept – not as Institutes in the old sense but as
Regional Offices – the premises at Cologne, Hamburg, Frankfurt,
Munich, Stuttgart and Berlin. Headquarters was put into 'Die Brücke'
at Cologne because the town council bought the premises on condition
that the British Council took it over. Here the name 'Die Brücke'
remained, subtitled the British Council.

Speaking of the Cultural Relations Department, from whom the
British Council took over, McDonaugh says, 'The great principle
which we developed from them – and developed ceaselessly – is that
the best cultural relations work is done when your host as a friend
helps you to do it.'[28] By the time Richard Seymour arrived as Representative to open the British Council doors in October 1959 relations
had been established with German institutions and authorities too
numerous to list.

One of the most distinguished works of the British Council in the
late 1950s was the initiative of Eve Denison, creator and Director of the
Council's Department of Recorded Sound, a part of the little-regarded
Arts Division. This was the commission to the Marlowe Society, under
its famous director, George Rylands, for readings of the entire works

* A Cultural Convention had been signed with the Federal German Republic on
18 April 1958 and ratified on 17 March 1959.

of Shakespeare on records. These recordings, at first anonymous, were spoken by amateur actors trained at Cambridge by Rylands himself, and by some professionals, many of whom had studied under him in the past and returned out of respect for their first director. Writing of some of the earliest recordings, J. C. Trewin said:

> What struck me ... was the freedom, the flexibility of the anony-mous Marlowe speakers; there was no hampering preconceived idea of X or Y's performance. The plays came through in the music of a set of voices, subtly orchestrated, that spoke lucidly and simply in the very spirit of Shakespeare. We expect that quality of speech, that directness of treatment, from the Marlowe Society, under George Rylands. It has long been honoured for its unforced com-mand. Here the artists — with some professionals among the amateurs — offer renderings of *As You Like it*, *Troilus and Cressida* and *Othello* that are properly timeless: performances to prove, as Bernard Shaw said, that the ear is the clue to Shakespeare.[29]

Trewin said that the records were not intended to replace major theatrical productions:

> But it is hard to imagine anything better for a listener prepared to listen to uninterrupted, luminous speech. It is obvious what treasure the records must be to a school, or to people who come to Shake-speare for the first time, and especially to those overseas students with whom the Council is mainly concerned.[30]*

In March 1959 Sir David Kelly died and in July Lord Bridges suc-ceeded him as Chairman. Lord Bridges, who was the son of the Poet Laureate, was at the end of a career of quite unusual distinction. A Fellow of All Souls, he won the MC in the First World War and in 1919 entered the Treasury, where he remained until 1938. From 1938 to 1946 he served as Secretary to the Cabinet and to the War Cabinet. He was in charge of the civilian side of the secretariat and was in this respect the Prime Minister's right hand man. From 1945 until his retirement in 1956 he was Permanent Secretary to the Treasury. He

---

* In conversation with the author George Rylands said that he regarded these recordings as the greatest educational achievement of his whole life. They are now being re-issued on cassettes.

was a Fellow of the Royal Society. Bridges worked closely with Sinker and the partnership is considered the most influential in the whole history of the British Council.

This partnership had an auspicious start, because, in the year of Lord Bridges's appointment, the Government Departments which in 1957 had presented to Parliament the White Paper known as the Hill Report (Cmnd 225) now followed it with a further White Paper (Cmnd 685). The main part of the section on the British Council reads as follows:

The Government are satisfied that the demand overseas for help by the British Council in education fully justifies yet further expansion of the Council's services. More money will, therefore, be provided to subsidise teaching posts, to encourage exchanges of University teachers, to provide for more scholarships in this country and to provide special British Council Officers to advise on English teaching problems. These facilities will be available to certain countries which wish for assistance in the teaching of the English language. There will be some further expansion of other British Council activities.

In Addis Ababa, the Council's centre is to be re-opened, a new centre and office are planned for Mogadishu and a new centre for Hargeisa. More teachers of English will shortly reinforce the four who went to Somalia in the autumn of 1958. Facilities for learning English will be offered by the Council in Cambodia, Lagos, Libya, Morocco, Tunisia and Vietnam. The Council's work in Nigeria will be strengthened. Funds are being provided to make possible exchanges of visits and other activities in the educational and cultural fields with Czechoslovakia and Hungary.

The Government grant to the British Council which stood at £3½ million at the beginning of 1957 and £4 million after the White Paper of July 1957 will be raised to about £5 million to enable these expansions to take place and to provide for the additions to the British Council library services.[31]

14

Sir Paul Sinker: Educational Aid

As the countries of the British Commonwealth attained independence, the demand for English language teaching proved insatiable. In both African and Asian countries the relevant constitutions provided that at a fairly early date English should be replaced by one or more of the vernacular languages, but in multi-lingual countries English remained the most convenient lingua franca. As one observer put it, in Uganda Swahili merely added one more to the fifteen recognisable languages spoken. A similar point might have been made about Hindi. English was historically the most usual common language of the educated classes in the tropical countries and in addition the language of the United States, of international commerce and of technology. (Even the Russians, recognising its importance, tended to write their propaganda to India in English.) The driving force was the need for education. Because of the absence of text-books in the local languages or the limitations of the languages themselves, English was the key to education, itself the key to personal or national advancement.

By the 1960s new generations were growing up in developing countries who learned English not from Englishmen, but from Africans and Asians who had once been taught by Englishmen. There was therefore an interest in common between the United Kingdom and the other countries who were concerned to improve the standards of English teaching.

From the earliest years of the British Council there had always been a certain amount of prating about the reciprocal nature of cultural relations. (Recently the word 'mutuality' has been added to 'reciprocity' to cover two slightly different shades of meaning, neither of which will by this means be made clear to the uninitiated reader.) In the teaching of English overseas, as in the rest of the aid programme, the advantages to the United Kingdom need no stressing. Yet there was a genuine element of disinterestedness in the work of the British Council to which the Commonwealth nations responded in their effort to solve their individual problems on a co-operative and reciprocal basis.

In August 1959 the first Commonwealth Education Conference took place at Oxford as a result of a decision of the Commonwealth Ministers at the Trade and Economic Conference held at Montreal in 1958, which had also proposed a plan for Commonwealth Scholarships and Fellowships. At its opening session the Conference on Education set up four main Committees to study and make recommendations on (i) the Commonwealth Scholarships Plan (ii) the training of teachers (iii) the supply of teachers for service in the countries of the Commonwealth other than their own and (iv) technical education.

At Montreal it had been decided that the Scholarship and Fellowship Plan should cover some thousand Commonwealth scholars and fellows, of which total the United Kingdom agreed to be responsible for half and Canada for a quarter. At Oxford Australia undertook responsibility for a further hundred and India the same. It was agreed that the majority of the awards should normally be to graduates in the academic field but that other persons who played an important role in the life of their community should not be excluded; while a limited number of awards should be made to senior scholars of established reputation. It was emphasised that much of the success of the Plan would depend on satisfactory arrangements for the reception and welfare of scholars.[1]

Much stress was placed on the need to increase the number of teachers available and in particular the teaching of English as a second language received much attention. One of the most important recommendations of the Conference at Oxford was as follows:

The teaching of English as a second language is still a relatively unexplored field. We suggest that the situation should be reviewed and the problems considered at a meeting within the next year or two of twenty or thirty persons of outstanding experience drawn from the whole Commonwealth. Such a conference should be held preferably in Asia or Africa.[2]

As a result of the Commonwealth Conference a further Conference on the Teaching of English as a Second Language was held at Makerere College, Uganda, in January 1961. The Conference was chaired by Professor Michael Grant, now President and Vice-Chancellor of the Queen's University, Belfast, and attended by distinguished educationalists from the Commonwealth countries, and also by observers from other countries. including the United States.

The Report emphasised first the need for more adequately trained teachers at all levels, and stressed that, while the aim was to provide qualified teachers who were indigenous to the country in which they taught, expatriate teachers from the English-speaking countries would be needed for many years to come. The need for increased teaching and new criteria for the training of teachers were suggested, the inter-relationship between language and literature emphasised, as also the importance of modern linguistics and psychology. Consideration was given to the need for new thinking on tests, examinations and sylla-buses; and for the first time we hear of courses in English to meet the special needs of those entering technical, scientific or medical occupa-tions.[3] This was a conference of experts whose findings were for the consumption of experts, but it was a landmark in the history of the British Council, the importance of which need hardly be stressed.

The second Commonwealth Education Conference, held in Delhi in January 1962, was important for its acceptance of a proposal made by the British for a career service in teaching English in Commonwealth countries. This resulted in the Aid to Commonwealth English Scheme (ACE) which was administered by the British Council and under which graduates were given several years training in teaching, both academic and practical, as a preliminary to a guaranteed career. It was originally agreed that thirty additional teachers should be recruited to the Coun-cil's permanent service over the three years 1962 to 1964 inclusive.[4] So many requests were made for these 'ACEs', however, that in 1962 the number was increased to sixty to be appointed over the eight years to 1970.

In 1959 in an article, 'The Main Tasks', Sir Paul Sinker had singled out two which he regarded as of pre-eminent importance. These were educational work, especially but not exclusively in the field of English language teaching,* and the fostering of personal contacts between the British and people overseas, especially between opposite numbers in the fields of education, science and culture and in the professions.

Towards the first of his objectives, the Council offered studentships to fifteen selected graduates at a time to take a year's course of training in the teaching of English as a second language (twelve at the Univer-sity of London Institute of Education and three at the University of

---

* The proportion of teachers administered by the British Council who are teach-ing English naturally varies, but over the years a figure of about 70 to 75 per cent English and 25 to 30 per cent Education, Science, Technology and Social Sciences seems to be about average.

Leeds). In an imaginative undertaking in Madrid arrangements were made, with the assistance of the Spanish authorities and in connection with the Council's own Institute and School, to provide trainees with teaching practice under realistic conditions. Advice and short training courses were provided for newly recruited teachers going overseas to teach English or other subjects in English and the development of research and training facilities in British universities was actively encouraged. Overseas teachers were able to attend courses in the United Kingdom and by 1960–1 the number attending was 850. Some fifty courses were also held overseas, these being particularly in demand in India, Pakistan and Malaya. In 1960 over fifty lecturers from universities, training and technical or commercial colleges were sent to Commonwealth countries.

The Council also became involved in large-scale programmes of research into material and methods overseas. Council staff worked with Indian staff in the Central Institute of English at Hyderabad (financed by the Indian Government and the Ford Foundation) which provided courses for the staff of Indian training colleges. They were also on the staff of the Language Teaching Institute at Allahabad; and in Madras they were working on a scheme to re-train secondary-school teachers and equip them to teach primary-school teachers. In Pakistan Council-recruited staff, partly financed by the Ford Foundation, worked on research into and preparation of teaching materials at the Language Unit of the Punjab in Lahore, while in Karachi, Dacca and Peshawar, Council Education Officers were involved in plans adopted by the National Education Commission for the general reform of English teaching.

Other activities included the support of schools; the conduct of examinations overseas; and the organisation of advisory tours in education and other subjects. The Council's staff handled an immense volume of day-to-day inquiries on educational matters of all kinds.

Something must be said about one of the most influential and colourful personalities of the 1960s, Dr A. H. King, the Council's Controller of Education Division. He is described as a very powerful character, very stubborn, with single-minded ideas. Sir Paul Sinker liked and admired him and was much influenced by his views in the educational field. Dr King was responsible for a change of emphasis in educational policy which, although to some extent necessary, was again thought by many people to have been carried to damaging extremes, and which had a long-lasting effect. Largely through him, the old system of the British Council Institute and the direct teaching of English as a preliminary to knowledge of the British culture and people fell out of favour, and although some Institutes remained, some were closed and none for the time being was opened. Dr King was convinced that the British Council must identify itself with English language teaching, but that this must be done by co-operative work within the academic institutions of the receiving countries. Secondly, he believed, as one of his colleagues put it, that 'it was a mistake to carry the luggage of literature' into the sphere of language teaching. He recognised correctly that not everybody wants to learn literature and that it is not necessarily the best methodological approach to what has become known as English for Special Purposes (ESP). If, for instance, what is required is the ability to write minutes or give orders, this is not easily acquired by studying a Shakespeare play. Yet Dr King made insufficient allowance for the fact that if what you want to learn is the structure of language for any purpose which is not purely technical – the moment the elements of discourse or expressiveness enter in – the background becomes social and cultural and must include literature.

In an open letter to Dr King in the Council's magazine *Home and Abroad*, a colleague quoted the Council's Charter to the effect that the teaching of English was for 'the purpose of promoting a wider knowledge of our United Kingdom of Great Britain and Northern Ireland ... and developing closer relations ... with other countries' and then went on: 'Yet wedges have been placed between the knowledge and the language and between the language and the cultural relations, and these wedges are being hammered steadily in by the Council's 160 or so [May 1971] language specialists.'[5]

In reply Dr King defended himself as follows: 'What I tried to do during my years on the subject was to bring reality into it by refusing to admit literary targets where literary targets were not possible because linguistic targets had not been fulfilled.'[6] He also said:

Official cultural work is a chimaera. It is always undervalued and devalued because it is official. Persons willing to undertake it are not likely to have the true seeds of the matter in them, and if they have, the seeds will not be allowed to grow. The official hand is a dead hand; everything turns grey under it; even the printed matter looks wrong. This is not a question of aesthetics; it is a matter of morality, of sincerity of intention.[7]

Finally he must be quoted as saying:

> I do not think that the Council can set any goals or carry out any
> policies independent of the personal quality of the people it places in
> the field. Aid-expenditure in education and the Council's efforts in
> education overseas will prove in the long run to have had value only
> in terms of the opportunity that has been given for British people of
> goodwill, culture and expertise to make friends in the countries to
> which they have been sent ... and to convey something of value in
> British culture through these channels of friendship.[8]

Dr King's ideas are always interesting and, as far as it goes, his logic
unanswerable, but in practice his policies proved arid. By discouraging
the method of the British Council Institute and the direct teaching of
English as an introduction to the culture of the country and replacing
this method by one more 'realistic' – that is, utilitarian – he not only
gravely restricted the opportunities of 'the man placed in the field', but
diminished the purely British aspects of the culture to which the
language opened the door.

There is, therefore, some entertainment to be derived from the
knowledge that, when he left the British Council in 1971, having by
then become a Mormon, he went to teach English literature at the
University of Utah.

Sinker's second task, the fostering of personal relationships, acquired
momentum through the phenomenal demand of countries reaching
independence for assistance in their own countries and training and
education in Britain. Immediately after the war it was estimated that
there were about two or three thousand foreign students in Britain. By
1950 there were 10,000; by 1956, 30,000; by 1961 there were over
55,000, of which approximately 36,000 were from the Commonwealth.
The majority paid their own way or were financed by industry or their
families or by local communities, only relatively few receiving grants
of one kind or another. The Council has never been able to assume total
responsibility for all the overseas students who came to Britain; but
however they arrived here and whatever their educational requirements, the Council, through its Home Division, was responsible for
assisting with the accommodation and welfare of many of them.

Faced with this influx, the Government provided £3 million to increase the accommodation for students. The target was some 5,000

extra places in hostels and an expansion of the welfare service to meet this. The Council was to administer this sum, co-ordinating the programme as a whole and stimulating action where the need was greatest. In addition, a new centre for Overseas Students in London was opened in Portland Place.

Mention must be made, too, of the Council's Medical Department. Writing at this time, E. A. Carmichael of the National Institute for Medical Research and Chairman of the Council's Medical Advisory Committee, said:

The experience of the Medical Department of the British Council is unique. The department is able to obtain the very necessary unbiassed information upon which to base advice or action, through the representatives of the Council stationed in almost all the countries of the world. It has already for a long time been concerned with arrangements for exchange of scientific medical staff as well as visits by prominent members of the medical profession, and for the provision of medical books etc. This has only been possible by the good will built up between the Medical Department and members of the medical profession, university departments and scientific institutions.[9]

In the same way an increasing proportion of the Council's work lay in the scientific field, both in the pure science of academic study and in applied sciences such as engineering and agriculture. About 56 per cent of its own postgraduate scholarships went to scientists, but its main work, here as in other fields, was that of intermediary. In an increasing number of countries there was at least one scientifically qualified member of the staff who was in day-to-day touch with local scientists; and in Britain the Council was in contact with both individual scientists and such organisations as the Royal Society, the universities, professional associations, Government departments, laboratories and industry and also with the British Library. The task was not merely to make information on British science available in a general way, but to help the overseas scientist find his way through the maze of material to that which was of particular significance to him. To do this the Council provided libraries stocked with current British books and periodicals and increasingly also retrieval services, which sought first to identify the precise requirements of overseas scientists and then to meet them. In the other direction the Council could do much to smooth the arrangements for British scientists travelling abroad.

Finally it acted as agent for H.M. Government in supervising the fellowships schemes of many international bodies under which students of science came to the United Kingdom.

In science and medicine there was real scope for 'mutuality', since it was not only a matter of first class importance to Britain that her status in the worlds of science and medicine should be recognised, but, if she were not to withdraw into the narrow confines of a small island, fundamental that the facilities, climatic conditions and materials of overseas countries should remain available to her research workers. The field of tropical medicine is a most obvious but by no means unusual example of what is meant.

In language teaching the Education Division in London gave advice on methods, syllabuses, text books and material, while the recently established English Teaching Information Centre gave a service of abstracts of information on existing books and current research in the teaching of English. The uses of television for language teaching were being investigated and research was being done on other audio-visual aids such as language-practice booths (where individual students could repeat sentences they heard on tape until they were satisfied with their own pronunciation) and the combined use of film-strips and tape-recording. The Council had for two or three years produced programmes of direct English teaching by television in Teheran and was about to assist TV-ELT on a schools programme in Delhi. *English Language Teaching*, a quarterly review on the teaching of English as a foreign language, had been published by the Council since 1946. In 1961 it was taken over as a commercial enterprise by the Oxford University Press, who published it in association with the Council.

A task of almost equal importance was given the title of The Printed Word. By 1961 the Council was running 125 of its own libraries in about 60 countries and supplying material to about another 55, of which 30 had recently been opened in African and Asian countries. Most of these were used for reference and study purposes and also for lending. The issues in India alone totalled 812,000 in 1961. In response to a suggestion made by Dr Hill, special multiple-copy collections of text books were sent to India and Pakistan so that students could keep them during the period of study.

The Council's librarians increasingly began to assist in the planning of libraries for schools, and university and national library services in countries where they were often the only people with relevant training and experience, while some part of the funds for books and periodicals were used for presentations of books and also for subscriptions to specialised journals.

From all of which it can be seen that, when in March 1961 the Prime Minister, Harold Macmillan, announced the Government's intention of setting up a new Department to be called the Department of Technical Co-operation, under the charge of a Minister with rank equivalent to that of Minister of State, for the purpose of 'co-ordinating, promoting and carrying out arrangements for furnishing countries outside the United Kingdom with technical assistance in the field of economic development, administration and social services',[10] the British Council was already thick upon the ground.

The British Council had been informed of the proposal to set up a new Department and had shown immediate concern. Reporting a visit from Sinker and Lord Birdges to discuss the possible effect on the British Council, an official of the Commonwealth Relations Office wrote:

> It is clear that what is worrying them is the impression they have derived ... that the new Department will seek to continue after independence the functions of the Colonial Office Education Adviser, and the bodies associated with him, over the whole field of educational development. This suggests to them that the educational functions the Council at present performs in, for example, India and Pakistan will either be closed to them in Commonwealth countries becoming independent in the future, or (what they clearly dislike) that they will be shared between the Council and the Colonial Adviser and the associated bodies.[11]

Later the writer argued that nothing should be said to embarrass the Council or prejudice in advance the outcome of discussions on the functions of the new Department. 'It would not be helpful to have anything said which would bring the British Council and its Executive Committee prematurely about our heads.'[12]

The Council's fears were not without some basis, since, although there was no intention to disturb its functions, there was the obvious possibility of some overlap between its work and that of the new Department. At the same time, however anxious they were to reassure the Council, the Government were unwilling to make commitments which would restrict their ability to distribute duties in future. 'It cannot be axiomatic that nothing which the Council does now should ever in any circumstances be done by someone else.'[13] Neither was sympathy with the Council's aims unanimous. In a letter written early in February 1961 (although not one to which the Council was privy) an official of the Colonial Office said that he thought what was worrying the British Council was not that the new Department would usurp functions the Council already possessed but that it might prevent it from expanding:

> The Council appear to consider, with what precise justification I do not know, that they are the Government's chosen instrument for educational liaison with independent countries, whether Commonwealth or not; and they seem to want to be assured that that position will be reserved for them in respect not only of already independent countries but of those which may become independent in the future. Only on this reading of their views can one understand their apparent anxiety lest the new Department shall in respect of independent countries be able to furnish the kind of advice and help which Colonial Office advisers and departments have been able to supply to dependent territories.
>
> But if the position were sustained that the Council ought to monopolise the furnishing of United Kingdom aid and advice in respect of education, then I think we should clearly lose one of the strong reasons for having a new Department at all. It is precisely in order to enable independent as well as dependent countries to have the kind of advice, if they want it, hitherto available only to dependent countries, that the transfer of these advisory functions, and some part of the related administrative machinery, to the new Department is contemplated.[14]

On which a Foreign Office official minuted: 'This seems to me to beat the old anti-Council drum as the CO always do.'[15] And he said that there were many reasons for forming the new Department other than that of furnishing aid and advice in respect of education. Yet he felt the beating of the drum was a matter for uneasiness, because the Colonial Office also had an axe to grind. It was by now public knowledge that the new Department would be staffed by about 1,050 people of whom 1,000 would be 'job-perpetuating ex-Colonial personnel'. 'If they get a statutory green light ... to embark on education', one Foreign Office minute read, 'they will surely inevitably duplicate with the British Council and cause rancour and confusion.'[16]

When in March the Prime Minister made the announcement to set up the new Department, the Council's fears increased. The immediate cause for concern was the inclusion of the words 'social services' in the description of the new Department's responsibilities, since these were normally used to include education. As Sir Paul Sinker put it in a letter to Sir Patrick Reilly of the Foreign Office: 'This appears to us prima facie to cover the greater part of the Council's activities.'[17] In the same letter he said:

It is of course for HMG to decide from time to time how to allocate such responsibilities and we would not have sought an amendment to the Bill even if we had been given time to do so but we do ask to be told what HMG's intentions now are. We think also that these intentions ought to be put in black and white because, as the Chairman points out, there is always the risk that statutory authority may at a later stage be held to prevail over present intentions unless the latter are clearly expressed at the outset.

And in pursuance of clarity on this matter five questions were sent to the Permanent Under-Secretary of State at the Commonwealth Relations Office:

1 Will the Council remain under the direct sponsorship of the three Overseas Departments of State whose representatives sit on its Governing Body?
2 Will the Council retain its world-wide (outside Colonial territories) responsibility for English language teaching activities as envisaged in its Charter?
3 Will the Council retain its present responsibilities for looking after overseas students in the UK? ...
4 Will educational work on behalf of HMG in foreign under-developed countries and in India, Pakistan and Ceylon be carried out by the British Council as at present or will it be taken over by Embassies and High Commissions?
5 As to educational work in the ex-Colonial countries of Africa, i.e. in countries where educational work has hitherto been the responsibility of the Colonial Office, the Council recognises that the position may be different from that in the countries under 4 above. Can the Council be assured that it will be brought into consultation

especially in regard to the future functions of Council staff now serving in Nigeria, Ghana, Sierra Leone etc.[18]*

To this in the course of time the Permanent Under-Secretary replied:

> The British Council can rest assured that it is not intended to disturb the existing relationship between the Council and the overseas departments, which will continue to be represented as at present on the Executive Committee. The Secretary of State for Foreign Affairs will continue to speak for the Council in Parliament on all the Council's activities other than those directly related to the Commonwealth. Similarly, it is not intended to alter the responsibility given to the Council in the Charter for promoting a wider knowledge of the English language abroad.
>
> Arrangements for the welfare of overseas students in the United Kingdom will continue to be one of the Council's main responsibilities. It is the intention that the present educational responsibilities of the Council in foreign under-developed countries and in India, Pakistan and Ceylon should, in general, remain undisturbed.
>
> These for your reassurance, are the lines of our present thinking. But, of course, the Minister of the new Department may well feel moved to consider these matters in so far as they seem to border on his concern. In particular, assistance to the newly independent Commonwealth countries in Africa in the field of education, in the light of pre-independence arrangements, and the facilities which the new Department of Technical Co-operation will be in a position to offer in respect of these countries will be for further consideration. I am sure the Council will be consulted before decisions are taken, affecting the scope of its responsibilities.[19]

In the House of Commons, speaking on the Department of Technical Co-operation Bill, the Financial Secretary to the Treasury said:

> So far as I know, there is no reason why there need be any major change in the situation of the British Council under the new relationship. Given good will and co-operation, I am sure that no serious problems need arise here.[20]

* All countries which had recently achieved or were approaching independence in which under existing arrangements the Council had staff working.

The British Council was not entirely happy with these assurances but Lord Bridges took heart when he found that the Foreign Office were 'on his side' and were prepared to draft a fresh statement of the relationship between the British Council and the new Department which would then be put to the Treasury. On 1 June he spoke on the Second Reading of the Department of Technical Co-operation Bill in the House of Lords. After confessing to an interest in some aspects of the work of the new Department, and having referred to the need to make sure that countries given aid had sufficient people with the right training and educational standards to carry out efficiently the projects for which aid is given, he said that the British Council had staff stationed overseas in no fewer than 75 countries, the greater part of whose work was directed to educational ends. Then he went on:

> It would be a mistake to think of this educational work solely in terms of the teaching of English overseas. Important as this is, the work of the Council covers a much wider field of education in foreign countries and in independent countries within the Commonwealth.[21]

He hoped, he said, that it would not be thought that his remarks were made 'from the point of view of a landowner looking out over his property to make sure the boundary fences are in good order and not in danger of being broken down' since this was not the point of view from which he spoke and 'indeed the Council have received assurances that they will be consulted on these borderline questions'. He believed that the Council's experience could be of great value to the new Department and he wanted to make clear that any help which the Council might give was at their service both now and in the future.

In fact, the British Council was in a very strong position. In the first place, the responsibilities of the new Department were limited to countires receiving aid and its terms of reference gave it no interest or position in the developed world. In the second, there was no intention that, apart from a few technical officers, it should establish an overseas service. The Council, on the other hand, had a headquarters staff, trained representatives working all over the world, much hard-won experience, and, in addition, the offices and staff of the Home Division. Much of its work could not be taken over by the new Department and there could therefore be no purpose in diminishing or duplicating its organisation in certain limited spheres.

In the third place the newly independent countries were showing themselves understandably touchy lest they prolong the colonial position by accepting aid from a British Government Department,* and the autonomous position of the British Council enabled it to allay these fears, while, since it also worked in foreign and developed countries, the element of patronage was eliminated.

In the fourth place, largely as a result of the increase in propaganda from Communist countries, the demand for British Council representation or expansion was making itself felt on all sides. (Western broadcasting which in 1948 had been three times that of the Communist countries was now three-quarters.)

Nevertheless, the Financial Secretary to the Treasury had been right in drawing attention to the need for goodwill and co-operation, a need which would remain constant over the years. According to some opinions, Sir Andrew Cohen, the first Permanent Secretary of State to the new Department, was, like Sir Paul Sinker, an empire builder. Yet he approached the British Council with the same courtesy and good sense that Lord Bridges had shown in the House of Lords Debate, although the analogy of the landlord who looks to his fences in reality fitted them both. When one considers how a similar matter might have been handled in the fields of sport or the arts, one must reflect on the suitability of our governors to govern.

Sir Paul Sinker showed similar good sense. While it is recorded that he and Sir Andrew Cohen were in some ways too alike in temperament not to have preliminary difficulties, they both learned over the first six months to respect not merely the cards in the other's hand but also the capacity each had for rational decision.

Presumably, it was also a matter for satisfaction that Dennis Vosper, the Minister appointed to the new Department, combined his duties with those of Minister Co-ordinating the Overseas Information Services. In this capacity he decided to conduct a comprehensive Review of the Overseas Information Services and in 1962 he produced a Report. This Report, unlike the Hill Report, was not published as a White Paper setting out agreements already reached by the Cabinet, and unlike the Drogheda Report, was not even published in summary. Its findings were never disclosed and, because it was a Cabinet Paper, are not available for quotation or comment today. At the time senior

---

* At this time the newly independent Nigeria was showing itself reluctant to receive aid from Great Britain.

officials of the British Council did not labour under the disadvantages of preceding generations, however, because, although the final Report was withheld from them, they were at least shown and even consulted upon the later drafts. They must have learned therefore that as a result of the opinions expressed by HM Missions all over the world, the Minister for Technical Co-operation had received a very favourable view of the activities of the British Council.

The British Council put in four Notes. The first and longest of these was a description of those of its activities it hoped to have strengthened under the headings English Language Teaching and related educational work, and Visits both 'inward' and 'outward'. It also asked for an increase in the finance allocated to the improvement of Council premises overseas. The Note concentrated on the developing areas and 'for the sake of brevity' omitted reference to Cultural Conventions, Anglophile Societies, and the export of British drama, music and the arts.[22]

In June 1962, the views of Ambassadors and High Commissioners expressed in answer to the questionnaire having become known, the Council was encouraged to submit a second Note providing further details and widening their recommendations for extension to their work. This time they gave estimates of the cost of the proposed expansion, showing that the total recurrent cost of their proposals would be £975,000 – the work to be initiated in the financial year 1963-4.

From a third Note put in by the British Council in July, it is plain that Dennis Vosper had taken fright at the size of these estimates and had requested the Council to submit proposals for phasing their programme into immediate and less immediate priorities. It was understood that he himself attached the greatest importance to increased ELT scholarships, visits and libraries, and Sir Paul Sinker therefore gave priority to these things and put the strong recommendations received from Ambassadors and High Commissioners for new or increased representation into the second category. This was unacceptable to the Foreign Office and, as one official put it, meant that their proposals would either never be carried out or at best carried out only in 1964-5. (New British Council representations had been asked for from Bolivia, Syria, Afghanistan, Algeria, Indonesia, and additions to existing representations from the Sudan, Iran and South Africa, while an expansion of educational and cultural exchanges with Russia, the Satellites, Poland, China and Japan was also urgently required.) In a fourth Note the British Council abandoned the system of priorities but proposed that the suggested expansion should be carried out over two years instead of one.

The financial requirement for the complete expansion proposed for the British Council was estimated to be just over £1 million — £220,000 for English Language Teaching and education, £100,000 for English Language Teaching by Television, £222,000 for inward and outward visitors, £317,000 for establishment or reinforcement of Council representation, principally in Asia and Africa and behind the Iron Curtain, £100,000 for starting or strengthening libraries in some Commonwealth and foreign countries, and for the development through the Council of public library systems in some dependencies and newly independent Commonwealth countries, and a further £50,000 for Council premises.

In fact the Vosper proposals were not immediately or entirely agreed to and in 1963 the Vosper Review continued through a Second Phase to co-ordinate the unfinished items. In 1963 General de Gaulle vetoed British proposals for entry into the Common Market and in the papers concerning the Second Phase we find for the first time for many years suggestions for an expansion in Europe.

In 1962–3, the year of the Vosper Review, the total of the British Council's grant-in-aid was £6,664,392, in 1963–4 it was £7,838,156 and 1964–5 it was £9,702,881. It continued to rise, in some years owing to increase in grants from departments other than the Foreign Office, and in others owing to Foreign Office increases.

15

A Spate of Reports

The 1960s, particularly the late 1960s, were remarkable for a proliferation of reports. Of these, the Beeley and the Duncan Reports were reviews of the Overseas Services of a traditional kind, but the Hedley-Miller and the three British Council/Department of Technical Co-operation (DTC) Reports were intended to define and rationalise the relationship between the Department of Technical Co-operation and the British Council. These Reports must be taken chronologically because they bear upon each other, but the four which concern relations with the new Ministry are of a highly technical nature. They are, nevertheless, important to this history because these agreements led directly to the fact that in 1984 the British Council budget is £173.5 million, 55 per cent of which is provided by the Overseas Development Administration.* The Hedley-Miller Report has an interest of its own, since it is a glorious example of the financial arrangements which may be arrived at when a Committee is headed by a Treasury official.

In order to avoid overlapping and dissension Dennis Vosper and Sir Andrew Cohen had initiated talks with officials of the British Council when they first assumed their duties. Under Dennis Vosper's regime, but at the initiative of the Council, the first of three Working Parties was set up at Under-Secretary level in 1964, 'to examine the working of the recruitment machinery of the DTC and the British Council in the educational field, and to advise whether closer co-ordination or revised demarcation of their work would promise significant improvements in the provision of teachers for overseas service and, in particular,

---

* In 1964, when the first of Harold Wilson's Labour Governments came to power, the name of the Department of Technical Co-operation (DTC) was changed to Overseas Development Ministry (ODM), and in 1970, when under Mr Heath it became a department of the Foreign Office, it was re-named Overseas Development Administration (ODA). It reverted to the status of an independent Ministry in March 1974 under Mrs Hart, but was incorporated into the Foreign and Commonwealth Office again as ODA in May 1979.

to consider whether in the interests of greater speed, efficiency and simplicity of operation it would be desirable to establish for an experimental period a closer working association between the appropriate departments of the DTC and the British Council and, if so, to recommend what form this should take.'[1]

This Working Party was headed by Norman Leach for the Department of Technical Co-operation and R. A. Phillips for the British Council and its Report has become known as the Leach/Phillips.

The Leach/Phillips Report was concerned exclusively with recruitment to teaching posts below university level (university recruitment to Colonial countries being undertaken by the Committee for University Secondment and the Inter-University Council, on both of which the DTC and the British Council were represented). Note was taken of the fact that well over 50 per cent of the posts filled by the British Council were in the field of English language teaching, whereas the DTC appointments were spread fairly evenly over the whole range of subjects.

The main recommendation of the report was that there should be a geographical division of responsibility between the British Council and DTC corresponding largely to the pattern that had developed historically. Broadly speaking this confirmed DTC's responsibility for Africa south of the Sahara, the Caribbean and those countries in South East Asia where the Council did no recruitment. The British Council was confirmed in India, Pakistan, all developing foreign (i.e. not Commonwealth) countries other than those allocated to ODM and all developed countries. This meant in practice, Africa north of the Sahara, the Middle East, Thailand, Japan, Australia, Canada, New Zealand and Europe. Areas of potential overlap were identified as Latin America, Ceylon, India, Pakistan, Malaysia, Burma, Thailand, Iran, Syria, Libya and Sudan.

Having noted the areas of overlap, the Working Party attempted to identify points at which the two recruitment departments might be closer or more efficient. They expressed themselves as impressed by the amount which had already been achieved and recommended that personal liaison with opposite numbers should be extended, and all relevant material exchanged; a small working group should devise a common application form to meet the needs of both departments; where appropriate each organisation should send a representative to take part in the selection of candidates for posts in which they both had an interest; each organisation should keep the other informed of all arrangements for training and briefing for teaching overseas, so that teachers recruited by the other organisation could be included where desirable. Recommendation 10, described by the British Council's Controller Recruitment Division as 'a very important and open ended commitment on our side',[2] stated: 'Wherever possible the services of the British Council overseas staff should be available to DTC on request, for such matters as obtaining information about posts, and helping with the welfare of teachers at post.'[3]

The Leach/Phillips Working Party was a valuable advance in the establishment of personal relationships, and its Report laid down the methods to be adopted in the future to avoid misunderstanding.

A meeting was held at the Treasury in December 1964 to discuss a proposal (made apparently by the British Council) that the Ministry of Overseas Development might assume financial responsibility for the educational work of the British Council and that the appropriate part of the Council's funds might be provided from the Votes of the Ministry instead of from those of the Overseas Departments.

Two differing views were expressed. Sir Andrew Cohen on behalf of the Ministry welcomed the proposal and said that the work of the Council and the Ministry in the training and provision of teachers for developing countries had become so similar that the divided administration could no longer be defended. He thought there would be a good deal of detail to be worked out but the transfer would be right and timely. The Foreign Office view, however, was that it was untrue that the Council activities were indistinguishable from those of the ODM. The Council's teaching of the English language, established for many years, sprang from their prime function as a cultural arm of foreign policy and differed from the usual concept of aid in that it was directed to our own national interest. The Foreign Office would prefer matters to remain as they were.[4]

Sir Paul Sinker said that the British Council recognised the difference of views. It felt that its policy directives should come from the Government as a whole and it would like to see machinery for consultation provided, perhaps at Under-Secretary level, to keep the policies of Departments, in relation to the Council, in accord. He also said that the Council thought that the general expansion of educational aid would be more effectively administered if its staff overseas were brought fully into play. For this reason it favoured a larger measure of control by the Ministry of Overseas Development. It felt it right, however, that the Foreign Secretary should remain the Minister with responsibility for the Council as a whole.[5]

As a result of this discussion it was decided that the question of the proportion of costs that would need to be transferred should be explored before the major questions were decided. It was also agreed that a small Working Party should be set up at Assistant Secretary level, the Treasury to find a Chairman.

This Working Party was set up immediately under the Chairmanship of Mrs Hedley-Miller of the Treasury, and included representatives from the Foreign Office, Commonwealth Relations Office and Ministry of Overseas Development and from the British Council. The Colonial Office was not represented because the Council's educational work in the colonies was 'minimal'. The Working Party reported in May of the following year, 1965.

Paragraph 3 of the Hedley-Miller Report, headed 'A definition of "educational work" ', says:

> The Working Party found that it could not distinguish with precision between the Council's educational work, often associated with English Language Teaching, which primarily fulfils purposes similar to those of the ODM's activity in this field; and its other activities which are designed primarily to promote a wider knowledge of Britain abroad. (In this Report the latter will be referred to simply as 'information' work.) At one extreme is work already done on behalf of the ODM. At the other are activities concerned with drama, music and the visual arts. But the provision of libraries, or welfare work among overseas students in the United Kingdom do not fall neatly into either category, and the Council carries out a wide variety of activity in, or in connection with, developing countries, which are of broadly educational character but are not necessarily to be regarded as falling within the ambit of the ODM.[6]

The Report goes on to explain that against this background the Working Party had examined each subhead in the 1965–6 Estimates relating to expenditure by the British Council and had arrived at an appropriate division of cost. It was remarked that in many cases this determination was necessarily based on judgment rather than precise calculation:

> The cost of common services – travel, accommodation, buildings, hospitality etc – was in most cases apportioned on a basis related to

the apportionment of the cost of the relevant staff. Allowance was made for the Council's educational work in developed countries (where the ODM does not operate) which was treated as 'Information activity'.[7]*

Paragraph 5 of the Report reads as follows:

The proportions adopted for the various subheads are set out in the attached Appendix. The following overall division emerged from the total of the individual items:

	Percentage	
Foreign Office	41	⎫
ODM	36	⎬ Estimated
CRO	20	⎭
	—	
	97	
Colonial Office	3	Actual
	—	
	100	

The Report recommended that this division of costs should be accepted as a basis for decisions and that acceptance would necessitate the establishment of suitable machinery in the form of a standing Committee for joint consultation between the Overseas Departments and the ODM and the Council in respect of priorities, finance etc. Part of the final paragraph says:

We were not asked to make a recommendation about the procedure for the future, but the Committee may find it helpful to be aware of the view taken by the Working Party which is that, since, as this Report makes clear, the percentages reflect a series of judgments rather than precise calculations, they should continue to be used until there should emerge so substantial a redistribution of the Council's activities as to cast serious doubt on their validity.[8]

* The countries in which the ODM had no involvement had previously been identified as (Foreign Office) Europe excluding Turkey, Japan, USA, Israel and South Africa, and (Commonwealth Relations Office) Australia, Canada, New Zealand, Malta and Cyprus.

As a result of the recommendations of the Working Party it was agreed:

1 That the ODM should take over financial responsibility for the educational activity of the Council and
2 That the Foreign Office should still retain overall responsibility for the Council's work and account for the grant-in-aid of the Council.

The system of percentages was agreed to and first took effect in the financial year 1966–7. It had one particular flaw of such an obvious nature that to the lay mind it is incredible that the eminent body which designed it could have overlooked it. This was underlined in the 1967 Beeley Report:*

A curious result of the decision to classify 36 per cent of all British Council expenditure as aid is that no additional overseas information function can be given to the Council without increasing the aid budget, and *vice versa* … It would not be possible for the Ministry of Overseas Development to transfer any of its educational activities to the British Council, however strong the case for so doing might be in terms of logic and efficiency, because to do so would automatically transfer 64 per cent of the cost to overseas information.[9]

This problem exercised some of the best brains in the Council and the various Departments for some years but no solution could be found which, while satisfying the Treasury's financial systems, also served the interests of the Foreign Office and ODM.†

The second of the Working Parties to examine collaboration between the Ministry of Overseas Development and the British Council was set up in 1966. R. A. Phillips once more headed the British Council team and A. R. Thomas the ODM. The Report of this Working Party has become known as the Phillips/Thomas. From it we learn that an Inter-Departmental Committee, on which the British Council was

---

* See pages 237–9 ff.
† Late in 1963 an agreement was reached to exclude from the percentage calculations the money paid by ODM to the Council for administering certain aid schemes — an agreement which the Controller of Finance of the British Council described as 'no more than a palliative', but which meant that it became possible to estimate for such projects, although it did not solve the problem of purely general increases arising from ODM work of a different kind.

represented, had been set up at Under-Secretary level to consider broad outlines of policy and settle any disagreements between the Departments sponsoring the Council.★

The Phillips/Thomas Working Party came into being as a result of discussions between Sir Andrew Cohen and Sir Paul Sinker, with the following terms of reference:

> To examine collaboration between the ODM and the British Council, both in Britain and overseas, particularly in such matters as recruitment, training and the use of Council staff overseas in the administration of educational assistance, with a view to achieving maximum efficiency and economy; and to make recommendations.[10]

The Working Party met thirteen times and exchanged briefs of two kinds: one, geographical, where the work in a number of representative countries was undertaken; and two, subject, which covered recruitment, volunteers, training, books, advisory tours, English language teaching (ELT) and technical aid agreements.

It endorsed both the geographical division of responsibility described in the Leach/Phillips Report and also the recommendation that the services of the British Council overseas staff should be available to ODM on request.

With regard to non-university posts it recommended that recruitment in the specialist ELT field should be primarily a British Council responsibility without prejudice to the source of funds, subject to continuous and close consultation with ODM.

Over university posts it took note of the present arrangements by which these were chiefly the responsibility of the ODM-financed Inter-University Council (IUC), but said that it might be necessary to re-examine the present position should there be any question of reorganising IUC; while if this happened, consideration should be given to the use of British Council overseas staff — a recommendation which might be said to cast a shadow before it.

Much time was spent on the means by which consultation should take place on the future of advisory tours, volunteers, training and technical assistance.

★ This Committee, which was set up under the Chairmanship of Sir John Nicholls, appears to have met only once in October 1965. Its terms of reference were to keep major questions affecting the Council's work under review.

The Working Party agreed that the papers prepared by the various departments were both informative and educative and provided a valuable contribution to deeper understanding in each body of the work of the other. In conclusion it quoted a paragraph from the Foreign Office Circular No. 013 of 21 March 1966 in which the Foreign Secretary announced to HM Representatives that ODM would henceforward become a major shareholder in the Council:

It follows from these new arrangements that henceforward the ODM will have a formal and constitutional interest in the overseas activities of the British Council. The Council's staff, both overseas and in Britain, already assist with much educational work which is the responsibility, financially and otherwise, of the ODM. The Council is concerned with the schemes for Voluntary Service Overseas; with the refresher courses for local teachers which are held annually in developing countries with tutors provided from Britain; with various scholarship and traineeship schemes; and in many other ways. This collaboration is obviously desirable and it is hoped that the Council's services will be used for educational work at overseas posts whenever such utilisation is efficient and economic. The contribution of the ODM to the Council's budget is, at present, strictly in respect of the Council's existing activities. But the Ministry will, in the future, have a claim on the Council's services, and in the course of time this may require reconsideration of the distribution and functions of the Council's manpower overseas.[11]

The year proved to be once more one of economic stress. Cuts were made in the grants to the Overseas Information Services for the first time for several years. The Council was fairly lightly affected but had to reduce its recurrent expenditure by some £500,000.* In August Eirene White, Minister of State at the Foreign Office, announced her intention of holding a comprehensive review of the Overseas Information Services on the lines of the Drogheda Report, in consequence of which no further cuts were imposed on the Council for the following year. In January 1967, she asked Sir Harold Beeley to conduct the Inquiry and he agreed to do so.

* Representation was withdrawn from Jamaica, Trinidad and Barbados, Fiji, Burma and the Congo, while some services in Britain for visitors and students were cut.

Sir Harold Beeley, who had had a career partly outside the Foreign Office as a University lecturer, had been Ambassador to the Union of Arab Republics from 1961 to 1964. In 1967 he was Ambassador and Alternate Delegate to the British Disarmament Delegation in Geneva, a post from which he was temporarily detached. He was given a staff of three but conducted virtually a one-man inquiry. In the space of two months he visited France, Germany and Poland; Canada, the United States and Brazil; India, Pakistan and the Lebanon; Nigeria and Senegal; J. S. Ellis, of the Foreign Office News Department, who travelled with him, went to Kenya. Sir Harold visited the headquarters of the British Council, BBC and Central Office of Information in London.

The terms of the Beeley Inquiry were to examine and review the activities of the Overseas Information Services and agencies in relation to other instruments of policy at the disposal of HM Government and to make recommendations with specific reference to their targets, general effectiveness and flexibility, and to their comparative efficiency in relation to the need to contain expenditure.

Sir Harold Beeley reported in May 1967. No decision was taken on his findings until early 1968. In February of that year the British Council was informed that the Report would not be published in full or in part, and that, although copies would be made available to the Executive Committee at its next meeting, it would not be possible for members to have copies to take away as it was a classified document.

In his Report Sir Harold expressed the view that the Council should not be concerned solely with British aid but should be enabled to fulfil its role as an instrument of cultural exchange; and that the presentation abroad of British drama, painting and sculpture, of ballet and music were activities which should be expanded rather than reduced. (At that time these activities accounted for less than $2\frac{1}{2}$ per cent of the Council's expenditure.) He quoted an Argentine music critic, who, after a visit of the New Philharmonia Orchestra, suggested that more account should be taken by 'governments of highly civilised countries ... of how the presence of such tokens of their spiritual life influences the public image which is held of them'.

Sir Harold said that advantage should be taken of the opportunity which appeared to be presenting itself as a result of the more liberal attitude developing in the Eastern countries of Europe, and, having referred to the fact that five Council offices had been closed in France at the time of the Drogheda Report, he expressed the view that this

measure should be reversed at least to the extent of creating a post in
Marseilles. (In 1967 General de Gaulle vetoed Britain's entry into the
Common Market for the second time. Sir Harold quoted Max Beloff
as follows: 'The relative neglect of cultural contacts with Europe over
the last decade has presumably not been without its effect in supporting
the view that Britain is reluctant to consider herself fully a member of
the European family.')

Beeley recommended that cuts in entertainment allowance should be
restored and that a sum of £380,000 should be provided so that the
Council could expand its work in Eastern Europe; return to Indonesia
(where English had supplanted Dutch in the schools); open an English
Language Teaching Institute in Saudi Arabia; and restore some of the
services cut in the previous year, in particular those in scholarships and
entertaining.

His most important recommendation was that the level of expenditure on overseas information should be stabilised for the four-year
period ending in 1971–2.

At the meeting at which the Executive Committee of the British
Council were allowed their view of this Report (classified for some
reason not obvious in view of the nature of its contents), the Director-
General said that it was very satisfactory that the Government regarded
the Council's work as sufficiently valuable to justify full provision for
the risen costs of the present scale of activities (including additional
costs arising from devaluation) and also for most of the recommendations made in the Beeley Report for additional activities. He also said
that he had been informed that there would be a four-year standstill of
expenditure on overseas information, reckoned at constant prices, a
decision which had the advantage of giving some degree of assurance
of financial stability but meant that new opportunities could only be
taken by redeployment.

The Review Committee under Sir Val Duncan differed from those
previously discussed in that it had not merely to examine and make
recommendations on the working of the Overseas Information Services
but on Overseas Representation as a whole. It was urgently required to
review the functions and scale of the British representational effort 'in
the light of the decisions on foreign and defence policy announced by
Her Majesty's Government on 16 January 1968, the balance of payments, and the changing international role which these imply for the
United Kingdom'.[12] (On 16 January the Government had announced
a determination 'to cut down our demands and ambitions at home and

abroad within the limits of what we can currently earn'[13] – a determination which had resulted among other things in the decision to withdraw our armed forces east of Suez by the end of 1971.) The Duncan Committee was to make recommendations on the furtherance of British commercial and economic interests overseas; to consider the value of the work done and information submitted by overseas posts in the political field; to have regard to the functions and scale of representation by other major Western European countries; and 'to bear in mind, in the light of the current need for the strictest economy, the importance for obtaining the maximum value for all British Government expenditure and the consequent desirability of providing British overseas representation at lesser cost ... '[14]

This Committee began work in September 1968 and reported in July 1969. It made many very far-reaching proposals for readjustment of the Diplomatic Service in the light of modern conditions, only a few of which are relevant to this book. Working within a system of two categories of its own devising – the first referred to as the 'Area of Concentration', which consisted of the advanced industrial countries 'with which we are likely to be increasingly involved to the point where none of us will be able to conduct our domestic policies efficiently without constant reference to each other' – i.e. about a dozen or so countries in Western Europe, plus North America and a few others such as Australia and Japan; and the second to comprise the whole of the rest of the world – it made recommendations estimated to effect a saving in total expenditure of the order of 5 per cent by the mid-1970s.

The Duncan Report is of an importance in the history of the British Council almost as great as that of the Drogheda. It made a number of detailed recommendations but the main weight of its thrust is contained in two paragraphs. The first is as follows:

In view of the importance of Western Europe in British foreign policy, especially during a period when Britain hopes to establish itself as a member of the European Economic Community, we consider that there is now a strong case for shifting the balance of British Council activities towards Western Europe; in this area, in our opinion, the maxim 'les absents ont toujours tort' will apply in the cultural just as much as in the political or economic field. We recognise that it might be necessary to increase the British Council's budget in order to give effect to this conclusion.[15]

The second recommendation of major importance was a natural corollary of the first:

> The Council's task is to display British culture in a manner which will be impressive and interesting to overseas citizens ... It is clear that the resources devoted to communicating the content of British culture, in the form of music, drama and the visual arts are rather small by comparison with expenditure on the instrument of communication, the English language itself. We should like to see the balance shifted in favour of the arts. It is in our view important that weight should also be given to Britain's scientific and technological achievements and thought.[16]

The Report had earlier made it plain that it did not envisage any diminution of the Council's activities in the Commonwealth countries. In the section on Cultural Representation it states:

> We are in no doubt that the British Council will become an increasingly important medium through which Britain will project her interests and her new approach to international relations ... As Britain turns from politico-military relations towards other ways of making her presence known to other countries, especially outside Western Europe and the North Atlantic area, it will be necessary to develop more fully the other forms of contact with governments and peoples. In our view, the British Council, like the BBC's external services, will be in the forefront of this approach. It will be well placed to use the special status of the English language to secure the wider objective of creating an audience which will be interested in future British aims and aspirations, as well as in her history and culture. It also has the important advantage of concentrating most of its effort upon the educated classes who are likely to form the most influential levels of societies overseas ... [17]

There is an interesting passage in support of the recommendation that the balance should be shifted in favour of the arts:

> We conclude that broad policy considerations suggest that the importance of effective cultural representation per se is such that it would be highly undesirable to subject the British Council to further reductions in their expenditure. We have found it useful to note the

size of the German and (especially) French equivalents of British Council activities. There are difficulties in establishing true comparisons between these countries. Neither France nor Germany has followed the British pattern of giving responsibility for cultural matters to a grant-aided Government body with operational autonomy. The French cultural programme, moreover, is very closely linked with the aims and conduct of French diplomacy, and their cultural officers are members of the staff of overseas Missions. Nevertheless, the Foreign and Commonwealth Office have been able to identify, for illustrative purposes, the following broad comparison of annual expenditure on cultural matters. France spends between £40 million and £50 million, Germany around £20 million, compared with our £12 million. Although it is impossible to make precise comparisons in this field, the available evidence has served to confirm our view that the present scale of British Council expenditure is not extravagant in relation to other Western European countries' expenditure on cultural work.[18]

The Report makes recommendations in relation to libraries, education and English teaching (there is one of the first suggestions that English language teaching might be a valuable source of funds), visits and exchanges of persons, inspection, superannuation, training, career structure and aid. In relation to the restrictions in career structure caused by the small size of this self-contained service and the consequent difficulty of attracting staff of the highest academic and cultural distinction, short-term contracts are proposed. In the chapter on aid, the Report has this to say:

We have the impression that there is some duplication between British Council activities and those of Missions in the aid field and we recommend that consideration should be given to allotting more of this work to the British Council.[19]

The British Council gave a general welcome to the Duncan Report but seems not to have been as elated as in view of its comments on their work and its recommendations for their future they might have been expected to be. In the first place, as one official put it, what was the Duncan Report? Not a set of agreed recommendations to be put into practice but a guideline for further discussion in which the Treasury would undoubtedly take part. An Interdepartmental Steering Party

28 British Council consultants have a contract with the Sri Lankan Government to help to train 37,000 craftsmen: work on a building site

29 Anglo-Indian co-operation tackles traffic congestion in Calcutta, with British experts funded by the British Aid Programme

30 Concentrated reading at the British Institute, Madrid, in the 1940s

31 A delegation of Chinese academics, responsible for developing the use of computers in Chinese universities, on a tour of British companies

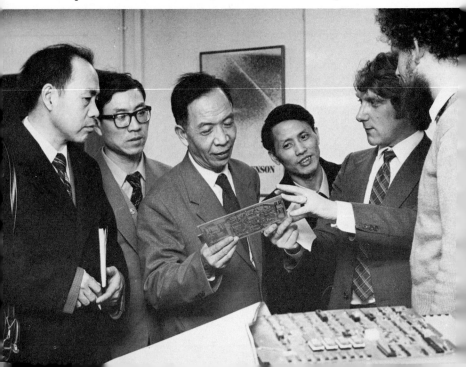

was immediately set up to consider it, representatives of many departments, the Cabinet Office, the BBC and the British Council taking
part. This Committee quickly decided that draft sections of a Report
on the Duncan Report should be prepared by Working Parties on the
different subjects. Working Party 'C', one of three set up to consider
Chapter VIII, Information and Cultural Work, was to consider the
recommendations for the British Council.

In the second place, there was a contradiction in the Duncan recommendations, since they envisaged at one and the same time a shift
towards Western Europe and more of the work of educational aid
being allotted to the British Council – this at a time when a four-year
standstill on expenditure on overseas information had recently been
announced. In the third place, the recommendation for increased activity
in Western Europe ran straight into the noose prepared by the Hedley-
Miller system of percentages, in that as matters stood ODM would
have to bear part of the cost of increased activities in Europe and could
do so only by restricting some of its own.

Finally the Council was determined not to make plans for any major
redeployment of resources until it was clear what its function would
be outside Western Europe, and what money it would have for its
new work.

Nevertheless, there was some cause for elation. From the start it was
plain that at least the Council would not share in the cuts. Then the
favourable comments made by the Duncan Committee were echoed
on all sides. In a debate on the Report in the House of Lords on 19
November 1969 several speakers referred to it in terms of approval and
Lord Shackleton for the Government said this:

> On the British Council I should have liked to pay a much fuller
> tribute than I am able to do, had I the time. We are considering what
> steps should be taken to expand the Council's activities in Europe
> while not losing sight of the important role which the Council must
> continue to play in the rest of the world.[20]

Most important of all in relation to the work of the Council, it was
clear that, as with the Drogheda Report, the Duncan Report did not
so much anticipate Government policy as promulgate it. As early as
September 1969 the Steering Committee on the Duncan Report
circulated an interim Report on Information and Cultural Work,
prepared by the Official Committee on Overseas Information, which

contained the following paragraph:

> The Committee consider that the Duncan Committee's major
> recommendation that there should be a shift in the balance of the
> British Council's activities towards Western Europe is fully in line
> with HM Government's general policy towards Western European
> integration and should be made progressively as soon as possible.[21]

This paper went on to say that the contradictions apparent in the
Duncan recommendations required further study but that the need for
an increase in cultural manifestations was recognised by the FCO.*

The Report of Working Party 'C' recognised that the Council's
budget might have to be increased and drew attention to the need to
review the method of estimating the Ministry of Overseas Development's share of the Council's budget. It here drew attention to a British
Council/ODM Working Party (with FCO participation) set up to
re-examine co-operation between the Council and the Ministry in the
field of education.

These deliberations continued into June 1970 when the Chairman of
the Steering Committee reported to the Foreign Secretary. On the
British Council he had this to say:

> Studies of the implications of an increase in the British Council's
> activities to Western Europe and of the Duncan Report's recom-
> mendations for increasing cultural manifestations abroad have been
> undertaken. Proposals for increased activity in Western Europe have
> been prepared which, if fully implemented, would cost some
> £500,000 annually. In view of the increased British Council com-
> mitments in the aid field and in areas outside Europe compensatory
> savings would be difficult to find elsewhere. The Departments
> concerned are agreed that cultural manifestations should be increased
> but, except for the Treasury whose position is reserved, that this
> should not be done at the expense of other Council activities.[22]

The British Council/ODM Working Party, to which Working

---

* An apology is due to the authors of the Berrill Report. In the Introduction to
this book I referred to their use of the term 'cultural manifestations' with some
derision, because in my then state of ignorance I believed it originated with them.
I have since found out that it was probably invented in the Foreign Office and is
constantly used both there and in the British Council.

Party 'C' of the Steering Committee had drawn attention, started work in 1969 and therefore had the opportunity to study and quote from the Duncan Report. This was the third of the Working Parties set up to secure closer collaboration between the two bodies, R. A. Phillips appearing once more for the British Council and James Mark for ODM.

Although progress towards co-operation had been made by the Leach/Phillips and Phillips/Thomas recommendations, the British Council still complained that the aims and working methods of the two organisations overlapped to a degree which presented serious problems; that there was a lack of co-ordination in the planning and execution of educational work both at home and overseas; that the Council's experience and resources were not being fully used; and that, because in the spheres of English language teaching and books, overseas governments wanted more than, with its limited funds, the Council could provide, ODM was gradually encroaching on fields hitherto regarded as essentially its own. The recommendation of the Duncan Report that more aid management work in education should be allotted to the Council provided timely confirmation that a fundamental review of the operations of the two organisations was desirable.

The Mark/Phillips Report is historically of the first importance. After the most detailed examination of the areas of overlap between the two organisations, policies were agreed with a view to achieving the most effective and economical educational aid in face of the gradual demise of the old Colonial educational service. It marked a watershed in the affairs of the Council and was probably the most important set of recommendations of the twenty years 1960–80.

None of this was easy to achieve. The British Council had honourable grounds for concern, but the ODM was largely staffed by members of the ex-Colonial Office, about half of whom, it has been estimated, had special knowledge of the countries where the areas of overlap mainly occurred. That the Working Party achieved so much has been credited by a witness present at the time to the wisdom and impartiality of James Mark. R. A. Phillips was by now well-known and respected in the ODM and he might be described as a bonny fighter, but James Mark was a man who could be convinced by reason.[23] The most important of the Mark/Phillips recommendations were:

(i) ODM should initiate regular and systematic discussion on the whole programme of aid to education in developing countries, and the Council should take part in these discussions which would be not merely for the exchange of information but for the formulation of a coherent policy;

(ii) where there were British Council Representatives in the developing countries they should be used to the greatest possible extent in the administration of educational aid;

(iii) the British Council should continue to be regarded as ODM's professional advisers on ELT, and ODM should refer all ELT projects to it for evaluation and advice;

(iv) that there should be unification of terms of service for all ELT specialist personnel, who would thus form a single body of career staff employed by the Council, whether financed by it or by ODM, and that this should be achieved by setting up an Aid to Foreign English Scheme on the lines of the existing Aid to Commonwealth English scheme;

(v) that there should be a review of the Commonwealth Bursary Scheme involving consideration of the appropriate administrative arrangements in the United Kingdom and their distribution between ODM and the Council; and that as soon as this review had been completed the respective responsibilities of ODM and the Council in the administration of technical assistance trainees should be re-examined;

(vi) in view of ODM's desire to increase the scale of its activities on books and the Council's extensive operations and wide experience in this field a small group should be set up to consider the scale, direction and management of increased aid in books.[24]

The Mark/Phillips Report was endorsed by the Council's Executive Committee and despatched to Missions under the signature of the Minister of Overseas Development (by now Judith Hart). A further consequence of the agreement arrived at was that Stewart Smith, one of the ablest of the Council's younger officers was seconded to ODM as Principal in Schools and Teacher Training Department, ostensibly to work on educational schemes in liaison with the Council. He had in addition the task of improving relations between the two organisations.

All these deliberations were overtaken in June 1970 by the General Election which brought Edward Heath to power. One Committee still continued to sit, however. For the first time since 1947–8 the British Council was the sole subject of a House of Commons Select Committee, the Report of Sub-Committee E of the Estimates Committee, published in April 1971, being concerned solely with its affairs. It is not proposed to discuss in detail the inquiries or findings of this Committee but to refer to them where they relate to matters of sufficient importance in the history of the Council. All that is necessary to say here is that, like so many other Committees, this one expressed itself as in no doubt about the Council's actual or potential contribution to international relations and to educational development overseas; recommended that the Government should take all possible steps to ensure that it was not forced for financial reasons to withdraw existing representations; and that it should be afforded some guarantee that its budget would not fall below a certain level during the period of the standstill.

16

Problems of
Administration

In the meantime much of importance had happened in the Council itself. In 1967 Lord Bridges resigned the Chairmanship after one of the most successful terms of office in the Council's history. Sinker wrote of him:

> As Chairman he became our big gun; and a big gun should be seldom used and then only when a successful result is virtually certain and when the ground has been carefully prepared. That at least was my view, and Edward agreed. During his nine years of office, on the few occasions on which he went into action with Ministers – chiefly on major financial matters and on staff conditions – his interventions were extremely effective.[1]

And if there is something unexpectedly grudging in this valediction, one can feel certain that this was inadvertent.

In January 1968 Lord Fulton was appointed to succeed Lord Bridges. For twenty years a Fellow of Balliol, although seconded to the Civil Service for the Second World War when he worked in the Ministry of Fuel and Power, he became Principal of University College Swansea (1947–59) and in 1959–67 the first Vice-Chancellor of the new University of Sussex. He had been Chairman of a great many bodies, including the Inter-University Council on High Education Overseas, and he was Chairman of the Committee on the Civil Service which reported in 1968.

Also in 1968 Sir John Henniker-Major* succeeded Paul Sinker as Director-General. Educated at Stowe School and Trinity, Cambridge, Sir John served in the Rifle Brigade in the Second World War and was wounded during Rommel's offensive in the Western Desert. In 1943 he

* Almost invariably known at that time as Sir John Henniker; later 8th Baron Henniker.

joined Sir Fitzroy Maclean's mission to General Tito, was twice para-
chuted into Yugoslavia and awarded the Military Cross. He re-opened
the British Diplomatic Mission to Belgrade during the closing months
of the war. In 1946 he became Assistant Private Secretary to the Foreign
Secretary, Ernest Bevin. In 1953 he was Head of the Personnel Department at the Foreign Office and played a part in putting into practice the
post-war reforms. He was British Ambassador in Jordan 1960–2 and in
Denmark 1962–6. Immediately before joining the Council he was
Assistant Under-Secretary at the Foreign Office, supervising the African
departments.*

Sir John Henniker assumed office as Director-General of the British
Council in unpropitious circumstances. In order to understand this, it is
necessary to return in time to the appointment of Sir Paul Sinker in
1954.

Sir Paul was seconded from the Civil Service to take up a five-year
appointment. At a meeting of the Joint Staff Committee on 23 February
1954, Sir Ronald Adam described the arrangements which had been
made for the appointment of his successor, and said: 'The appointment
has been limited to the term of five years because it is hoped at the end
of that term to select a successor from the Council's serving staff.'[2]

It has come to be widely believed in the British Council that this
public statement covered a more specific private undertaking to K. R.
Johnstone (then Deputy Director-General), whose personal distinction
and service to the Council would have made him an obvious choice if
the Director-General were to be appointed from among the serving
staff, but it seems likely that Johnstone was spoken to in general terms
and persuaded that he was of an age to give way for a limited period,
after which his claims to promotion would be most seriously considered.

In any case, in October 1958 the then Chairman, Sir David Kelly,
wrote to the Chairman of the Staff Association, reminding him of the
1954 promise to the staff, and said:

> It seems to me desirable, therefore, that I should tell you that we
> have been taking into full account the hope expressed by Sir Ronald
> Adam in his 1954 statement, and the Executive Committee will be
> reminded of it at the appropriate time.[3]

---

* In October 1968, following a merger, the Foreign Office became the Foreign
and Commonwealth Office. Here, as is customary, it is sometimes referred to as
the Foreign Office.

A month later Kelly wrote again to the Staff Association to tell them that it had been decided that Sir Paul Sinker should continue to serve as Director-General and that acceptance of this invitation would mean 'his ceasing to be a member of the Civil Service on secondment and his complete identification with the Council and its fortunes as a member of the Council's permanent staff'.[4]

In reply, the Chairman of the Staff Association said that his members were deeply impressed by Sir Paul Sinker's very important contribution to the development of the British Council and 'particularly grateful for what he has achieved towards the establishment of the Council's service on a more secure footing'.[5] He said that the Staff Association were confident that it spoke for the staff in assuring Sinker of their continued loyalty. He referred, however, to the statement that, before the Committee came to its decision, it had considered the claims of all Council serving staff in Grades A and B, and went on to say that the Committee of the Staff Association hoped 'the staff may assume that this will continue to be the practice on all parallel subsequent occasions.'[6]

In 1967, when the question of Sir Paul Sinker's successor arose, the Controller of Establishments Division (James Livingstone), who was also Chairman of the Joint Staff Committee, lost no time in making known to the Chairman of the British Council the views of staff on a large number of issues affecting the appointment. Those most relevant were as follows:

> Council senior staff fear that owing to various factors such as the proliferation of posts for Vice-Chancellors in the new Universities there is likely to be a dearth of candidates. They think that it would be undesirable in principle that a former diplomat should be appointed since they believe that as a matter of policy the unofficial aspect of the Council should be stressed overseas. They are likely in practice to look with critical and it may well be with exceedingly well-informed eyes at any candidate from the Diplomatic Service. They think that most people in public service are likely to regard the next three years or so in the British Council as likely to be years of standstill and would therefore suspect that the best candidates would hold back. They would fear a Diplomatic Service candidate at this moment would be one not regarded by himself or his superiors to be in the running for the highest Diplomatic Service posts now or later ... Nearly all consulted think that an appointment from the Diplomatic Service (whether of foreign or commonwealth provenance) is to

be avoided. The experience of the diplomat inculcates a different attitude, the more difficult to shake off in that both act in the same geographical scene ... [7]

Livingstone goes to much trouble to describe what the staff believe are the qualities needed in a Director-General, although he adds that 'it is extremely unlikely that such a paragon can be found'. Then he says:

Most and perhaps all senior staff would consider that the claims of outside and inside candidates should be looked at simultaneously. At least some of them would lean to the view that unless an outside candidate can be found who is outstanding and seen to be outstanding the Council's interests at this juncture and for the next five years might be best served by the appointment of a serving officer ... Owing to pessimism about the chances of getting an ideal man certain Controllers would hope that the Committee would look very hard at the practicalities of the Council's present position before coming to a final decision and take full account at that stage of the possible advantages of a serving staff appointment – compared to those advantages seen in outside candidates.[8]

In the circumstances in which he wrote the spokesman for the Joint Staff Committee could hardly have expressed their views more strongly.

On receipt of this letter the Chairman wrote to E. E. R. (Dick) Church,* lately retired, telling him that the Executive Committee would very much like to co-opt him to the Appointments Sub-Committee as an assessor or adviser. He said: 'You have no rival in knowledge of the Council and of its staff; you are deeply trusted by your old colleagues and your retirement gives you an independence of position. We should greatly value your advice.'[9] Mr Church subsequently agreed.

After carrying out what the Chairman described as 'an extensive trawl', the Sub-Committee drew up two lists of names suggested by members of the Executive Committee, the most promising and the rest.[10] At this stage the people mentioned were mostly unaware that they were being considered. However, R. A. Phillips (of the British Council/DTC Reports and Deputy Director-General) appeared on List A, the most promising names.

This list was gradually reduced to a short list, all of whom were sufficiently interested to attend for an interview, and R. A. Phillips's

* See pp. 108–9.

name was once more included. The Chairman then asked for 'first choices' and the name of Sir John Henniker headed the list. The same name figured in the 'first three' of the members who had not made it their first choice, E. E. R. Church dissenting. In their choice of candidate, the Chairman and Executive Committee had completely ignored the two most urgently stated views of the Staff Association.

In March 1968, when Sir John's name was announced, the press were almost unanimous in praise of the appointment, only the *Guardian* remarking that he was a career diplomat 'and on the face of it this does not augur too well'.[11] In April 1970, however, giving evidence to the Select Committee on Estimates, Lord Fulton had to answer questions on the method by which the Director-General was chosen. On this matter the Committee's Chairman said: 'Part of the worry we have is that you neither select from inside nor do you advertise. You seem to be involved in a sort of closed shop.'[12] And Mr Roebuck, having had the method described to him said: 'This was not a trawl; it was a message through the grapevine to certain selected people.'[13] When the Report of the Expenditure Committee was published, paragraph 30 read:

> The Committee stress once more that they are making no adverse comment about the present appointment when they describe the process of selection as highly unsatisfactory. They cannot regard a system which relies so much on unspecified consultations between interested parties as the most satisfactory method of ensuring a fair decision. They consider that the appointment of a Director-General ought properly to be an internal matter for the Council itself, and they do not understand why it should require the approval of the Foreign Secretary. They agree with the Staff Association that, while appointments from outside need not be excluded, it would normally be right for the post to be held by an existing member of the permanent staff; and that where this was not possible, public advertisement would be infinitely more desirable than a series of private discussions. They accept the view of the Staff Association that, if the Director-General were to rise from the ranks, it would be appropriate for the Chairman of the Executive Committee to bring to the Council 'the prestige of a national figure' ... as Lord Fulton clearly did during his term of office. The Committee recommend that the process of selection for the post of Director-General be reviewed and revised, to ensure that the permanent career staff are afforded at least an opportunity of succeeding to this post.[14]

These proceedings were reported in the press but on this occasion without causing much comment. They were probably not lost, however, on the senior staff of the British Council.

In any event it is an open secret, at least among people concerned in any way with the Council, that Sir John Henniker failed to get that degree of loyalty and support from his staff which was necessary if he were to make a success of his appointment. In the papers of the time references can often be found to 'the C. P. Snow atmosphere at the top'.

In August 1971 *The Times* reported that Sir John Henniker had regretfully decided to resign his position:

The manner of his announcement leaves no doubt that Sir John is sorry to go, and indeed he let it be known when his appointment was first announced in March 1968, that he was particularly looking forward to 'the satisfying continuity of work in the same job until he is 60'. When he goes, he will still be only 55.[15]

In the previous year Lord Fulton had said that he did not wish to extend the period of three years for which he had been appointed and in consequence he also resigned as Chairman at about this time. He was succeeded by Sir Leslie Rowan in July 1971. Sir Leslie had been a member of the Civil Service, Principal Private Secretary to the Prime Minister during the war and later Head of Overseas Finance at the Treasury, afterwards leaving to become Managing Director and Chairman of Vickers. The Parliamentary Opposition and the press, who had missed the opportunity to comment adversely on the method by which the Director-General was appointed, proceeded with a singular lack of consequence to make up for lost time on the appointment of Sir Leslie. If it is required that the Chairman, who has none of the involvement with staff of the Director-General, should be a 'big gun', it is highly unlikely that such a one would answer an advertisement. Nevertheless, in the House of Commons Maurice Edelman asked the Foreign Secretary what names were submitted for his approval other than that of Sir Leslie Rowan; whether the appointment was advertised for public competition; and what were the entertainment and travelling expenses of the previous Chairman in his last year of office. William Hamilton complained that the appointment had been made 'on the principle of the old boy net', and Denis Healey said:

Many of us know Sir Leslie Rowan and his work as a Treasury Knight and head of Vickers, but we feel that there must be some other person better qualified to promote British civilization and culture overseas. It should not have been dealt with in this hole and corner way.[16]

Although Sir John Henniker's resignation was announced in August 1971, it did not take effect for a full year. It may be accounted generous that, during his term of office, he particularly addressed himself to the question of staff structure and to an attempt to improve career prospects. This question was complicated by the fact that there were three distinct groups: General Duties officers, who accepted complete transferability between home and abroad and who filled most of the senior posts; Specialists, mainly English language teachers, scientists and librarians; and Home Serving officers who had no commitment to serve abroad and limited prospects of advancement. The wastage at higher grades was estimated at about 30 per cent, and, answering a question put to him at the Select Committee of Estimates as to what this might be attributed to, a witness replied that there were two main causes:

The first important one is the lack of delegation. You come from a university and you do not think you are given sufficient responsibility to get on with a worth while job, so you go. The second important one is lack of prospects ... There is the fact that in the public service the level to which a reasonably efficient man can aspire is assistant secretary or counsellor in the diplomatic service. That is equivalent to our Grade B. In the Council the most he can get is Grade D, so you are two steps behind your contemporary in the public service.[17]

At a meeting with Sir William Armstrong, Permanent Under-Secretary at the Civil Service Department, Sir John Henniker, who was accompanied by his Acting Chairman, Lady Albemarle, said that he was convinced that many overseas posts were undergraded for their responsibilities in comparison with the Diplomatic Service – the only other service working in comparable conditions. Representatives overseas had highly important representational functions, and they had to deal with leaders of intellectual life. For this men of high calibre were required. He gave examples of Representatives at comparatively low grades who had to deal with vast areas or with problems of great difficulty.

Though Council Representatives were not expected to move in the same circles as the Diplomatic Service, and though it might be desirable for them to live rather more informally and modestly and become more integrated into local life, the volume of representation was certainly no less. Moreover, their job was often more difficult; they did not move automatically into the established fabric and contacts of a Diplomatic Mission, but had to make their impact, with a more undefined status, by personal qualities. The Council's independence threw greater responsibilities on them. Unlike their diplomatic counterparts they did not work under the direct supervision of the Head of Mission. Though they would naturally seek his help and guidance in any serious crisis, their day-to-day judgments and actions were taken independently.[18]

Even more important than the target grades (i.e. the grade which the average General Service officer could expect to reach by certain stages of his career) was the question of the top or A Grade. The three top posts were all at home (of the present holders one had never been abroad and another not since the war). This was a wrong balance in an essentially overseas service and imposed an unhealthy rigidity on the proper use and development of talent. If the staff were to be given every opportunity of producing their own Director-General, this could be done only by increasing the number and range of posts from which he could be chosen, which would mean creating a number of Grade A posts overseas.

Sir William Armstrong was sympathetic to the case that was made and in the event two more Grade A posts were created, one in India and the other proposed initially either for Nigeria (then the second biggest representation) or Germany.* With regard to the raising of the target grades it was felt that as the Civil Service were investigating, at the Council's own request, its management and structure, nothing useful could be done until the results of this examination were known, while it was hoped that the report would contain some recommendations about upgrading.

When the Civil Service Department Report (known, from the names

* In fact, it was eventually allocated to France.

of its authors, as the Moore/McCosh Report) appeared it had this comment to make:

> We have been conscious that morale amongst Council staff in Head-quarters is not as high as it might be. This, we believe, is partly attributable to clashes of personality at top levels during the past four years in an organisation where, because of the informal methods of working and diffused decision-making, the influence of individuals is great. The Council seems to have lost its identity and self-confidence ...
>
> In combating this morale problem we believe that a lead from the top is of prime importance. The Council's general aims and specific objectives for the 1970s require to be clearly stated and widely pub-licized among Council staff. But this needs to be supported by a deter-mined devolution of decision-making to improve job satisfaction.
>
> We also believe there should be a reappraisal of public relations policy with the aim of presenting a more positive and outgoing image.[19]

This Report was critical of the staff at the headquarters of the British Council. It also had this to say:

> The career expectation of a good General Service recruit is that he will reach Grade D at about 40, although a significant number will subsequently attain higher grading. Admittedly this compares un-favourably at present with Diplomatic Service but we are not satis-fied that there should be a comparison on level terms. The criteria for selection and the jobs themselves are different. Furthermore, if one makes comparison with the academic world as another possible alternative career for those who choose to join the Council, it is difficult to assert the inadequacy of a career which offers virtual certainty by the age of 40 of a salary scale with a maximum of £4,500 [about £16,656 in 1984] and which provides other material as well as intellectual satisfactions.[20]

The most important criticism was that senior officers in the Council seemed reluctant to devolve work. 'The creation of senior posts would aggravate the situation by sucking minor matters up to senior levels.'[21] The relevant recommendation was:

> That the present total complement of 27 A, B and C posts in Head-

quarters should be regarded as a ceiling for at least five years. We make no recommendations about the number of posts at these levels overseas but we have already commented that we believe the balance between senior home and overseas posts should move in favour of the latter ... [22]

These were years of generally rather low morale in the British Council. The stimulating period of the post-war years when Britain led Europe in so many fields was over. 'We must recognise that the Council has only Britain to sell and our effectiveness and morale inevitably reflects to a considerable degree that of Britain as a whole ... '[23]

There was some depression, too (as it turned out, unnecessary), because of the five-year standstill on finance. After a period of fast growth the need had been for sufficient money to consolidate. In particular there was much to complain of in the standard of the Council buildings. Answering questions at the Select Committee on Estimates, R. A. Phillips said:

The standard of building we require overseas is obviously dictated by the country concerned. I do not think that the British Council must always have prestige buildings on prestige sites. On the other hand I do not think our buildings should be a discredit to this country, and many of them are. We have a capital programme for re-housing ourselves overseas which is based on a five-year plan. In the context of buildings for the British Council, which are sometimes relatively big buildings because they house libraries, this five-year programme is based on an average annual expenditure of about £400,000. There are some 150 British Council offices and centres to be charged, so to speak, against this sum as well as any private domestic housing which we may consider it in our interests to buy for our overseas staff. A sum of £400,000 for five years sounds a lot but in the context of this programme it is not enough and it will not bring our buildings up to a respectable standard within five years, and by the end of this five years I have no doubt that certain other of our buildings will have deteriorated.[24]

Asked whether the trouble was the design or the size or the general condition of the buildings which were not satisfactory, he answered, 'All of those things. Sometimes it is the size, and some are pretty squalid.'[25]

In 1972 Dr F. J. Llewellyn was appointed Director-General, the appointment to take effect from 1 July. On this occasion the post had been advertised, and great trouble had been taken over the selection procedure. Eighteen applicants had been seen, including three staff, the interviews which had taken place at the Royal Society had been conducted in alphabetica' ,rder, and Sir John Wolfenden had taken full part as an external member. James McDonaugh, the staff assessor, had been present the whole time. 'The selection committee had been fully aware of the desirability of selecting a serving officer for the appointment, but after very careful consideration they had decided that they could not include a staff name in the final list.'[26]

From 1946 to 1966 Dr Llewellyn had served in New Zealand, holding successively the appointments of Professor of Chemistry and Director of Laboratories at the University of Auckland, Vice-Chancellor and Rector of the University of Canterbury, Chairman of the University Grants Committee, and of the New Zealand Broadcasting Corporation. Returning to England he was appointed Vice-Chancellor of Exeter University in 1966 and served as Council Member of the Association of Commonwealth Universities and as a member of the executive of the Inter-University Council for Higher Education Overseas.

Before this appointment was announced Sir Leslie Rowan sent for R. A. Phillips, the Deputy Director-General, to tell him about it. Phillips thanked him and returned to his room where he wrote a letter of resignation, giving fifteen months notice to take effect on his sixtieth birthday.

In April 1972, only nine months after his appointment as Chairman, Sir Leslie Rowan died suddenly. The Vice-Chairman, Lady Albemarle, took over as Acting Chairman, as she had done on previous occasions (from March to July 1959 and from January to June 1971). In October Lord Ballantrae was appointed. Ballantrae was better known as Sir Bernard Fergusson under which name he had had a distinguished career as soldier, author and poet. Born in 1911 and educated at Eton and Sandhurst, he joined the Black Watch in 1931 and served as ADC to Wavell, the subject of his book, *Wavell: Portrait of a Soldier*. From 1962 to 1967 he served as Governor-General and Commander-in-Chief to New Zealand. He was made a Life Peer in 1972, and took up his appointment with the British Council in November of that year.

17

The Common Market

In retrospect the reasons for low morale in the early 1970s were less than they appeared to be. The British Council was now fully established as an arm of British diplomacy as well as a recognised organ of educational aid. In a debate on the Report of the Select Committee on Expenditure in Session 1970–1 and the related Report on the British Council, speeches from all sides of the House of Commons made it plain that its value and potentialities were widely understood. In the negotiations for entry into the Common Market it was an essential part of Government strategy.

In deference to the fact that most of the countries of Europe gave more importance to culture and cultural relations than was the habit of the British, a Working Party was set up to conduct an inter-Departmental study of Anglo-French Cultural Relations, and the scope for more intensive collaboration in this sphere.

Even after the withdrawal of de Gaulle, the French remained the chief obstacle to British membership of the community. The difficulties of reassuring them were, however, two-fold and to some extent contradictory. In the first place French scepticism as to the true attachment of Great Britain to Europe had been reinforced by the cultural withdrawal of the 1950s and 1960s. On the other hand, cultural competition was potentially a source of Anglo-French conflict.

Owing to the growing predominance of the English language, French fears of 'cultural extinction' were a major psychological obstacle to improvement in their relations with Britain. Early in 1971 it was reported in the French press that thirty-five distinguished literary personalities had signed a letter to President Pompidou, expressing their anxiety about the possible repercussions on the use of the French language of Britain's accession to the Common Market; and it was public knowledge that President Pompidou himself was extremely concerned about the enlargement of the community to include, not merely the United Kingdom, but also three other countries whose second language was English. Everything had to be done to reassure him in this respect as in others.

The essential cynicism of the British recourse to re-entry on to the abandoned cultural scene was less remarked because in the first place it was part of a much larger readjustment of policy, and in the second it was natural to design festivities to mark the expected culmination of our negotiations. In addition, some real grace was given to the attempt to improve cultural relations by the genuine enthusiasms of the Prime Minister, Edward Heath, and the British Ambassador, Christopher Soames. Although not a career diplomat, Christopher Soames, a High Tory and the son-in-law of Sir Winston Churchill, had been appointed in an act of exceptional prescience by the former Labour Prime Minister, Harold Wilson. By the vigour of his personality and the grandeur of his ideas, he added a degree of panache to the belated resumption of our cultural presence to suit our political needs.

From the first he understood the possibilities of the British Council but he believed, as he put it in a letter to Sir John Henniker, that 'to realise its full potential, the work of the British Council needs a substantial change — a change not in degree but of kind'.[1] He went on to say that he agreed with E. W. F. Tomlin, the Council Representative, that the premises of the Council were entirely inadequate for the job. Here he quoted an expert as saying: 'The offices and Library are situated on seven floors of a building whose utter unsuitability for its purpose needs no amplification here', and he said that he nevertheless understood that 'there was no provision for Paris in the Council's capital programme for the five-year period 1970/71 to 1974/75'. He urged Sir John that this should not be the last word on the subject, saying that he saw no difficulty in convincing the French that an increase in our activities did not represent a threat to French culture but was rather a means of supporting and enhancing it because we knew it was worthwhile.

Following this intervention the British Council submitted a note to the Cabinet Interdepartmental Study on Anglo-French Cultural Relations on the project: to build or buy in Paris a Franco-British Centre to house (a) the British Institute (b) the British Council. (The British Council did not and does not teach English in Paris because the British Institute was there before it, but it gives a subsidy to the Institute — at that time £9,500 a year. The British Institute is a Franco-British institution connected both with the University of Paris and the University of London, concerned with teaching English to French students, but also assisting French departments of British universities by providing courses in French, and British education authorities with vacation courses for British teachers of French.) In a preamble to the British Council paper it was stated:

The British Institute has a down-at-heel building with insufficient space for its work ... They compare very unfavourably with the Cultural Centres of many other countries including Germany, Canada, Japan, the US and even Denmark. The British cultural effort in France is also very small in relation to the level of similar French activity here – where there are three Institutes, a Lycée and 80 Alliance Françaises.[2]

As a result of the Ambassador's letter the British Institute and the British Council discussed together the possibility of sharing a new building on the Left Bank of the Seine and, although it was considered impossible to do more than guess at the cost, it was presumed this might be in the order of £850,000, less the value of the two buildings at present in use.

The difficulty of finding money for a new building in Paris within the Council's capital programme was all the greater because this coincided with heavy expenditure over two or three years on the Council's own new Headquarters building in London. The Council, having outgrown the premises in Davies Street which it had occupied since 1950, when it moved there from Hanover Square, and having overflowed into different offices all over London, had leased a site in Carlton House Terrace, where number 10 Spring Gardens, the office building it has since inhabited, was in process of building. In addition, it had certain undertakings, not precisely defined, towards building a new centre in Delhi.

Sir Christopher Soames remained persistent, however.

With the imminent prospect of Britain becoming a member of the European Economic Community [he wrote to the Foreign Secretary] the threadbare nature of the Council's presence in Paris will become increasingly evident. It is simply not equipped to make the impression it should. Given Paris' position as the cultural centre not only of France but to some degree of the whole of continental Europe, the British Council should be active here on a corresponding scale. The first requirement is for the Council to be housed in appropriate premises which will enable it to undertake cultural activities which it is not able to at present, and to house the largest Council library in Europe.[3]

The Executive Council and officers of the British Council watched the activity on the cultural front with experienced eyes. They understood by now that Reports are important when they mirror Government policy rather than propose it, and they were unconcerned about the seeming contradictions in the Duncan Report – that they should play an increased role in educational aid and at the same time shift the emphasis of their work towards Western Europe. A British Council witness to the Estimates Sub-Committee (R. A. Phillips) said:

If the British Council is asked to play an increased role in Europe, we are willing to do that; I would go so far as to say that we are anxious to do that but not, and I repeat emphatically not, at the cost of what we are doing in the developing world.[4]

And in a later exchange with the Chairman:

Q: Duncan wanted the best of both worlds without suggesting how it could be financed?
A: It was not the Duncan Committee's business to suggest how it could be financed and no one has suggested how it can be financed. All I am saying categorically is that I sincerely believe, as an old Council hand, that if HM Government [have] decided to have a closer relationship with Europe we shall play our part in that but not at the expense of what we are doing in the developing countries.[5]

This confidence was justified because there were certain obvious and immediate ways in which cultural relations with France could be expanded. The French had for some years pressed for financial help in increasing the number of youth exchanges between the two countries.* The British Council had allotted £4,000 a year partially to subsidise exchanges, but this compared with £50,000 a year which it spent on exchanges with West Germany (allocations to Germany were apt to be

---

* Youth exchanges are reciprocal visits by members of youth organisations between the ages of fourteen and thirty. Not intended for school-to-school exchanges or those which form part of a curriculum, they are for the purpose of giving young people an insight into the life of contemporaries in other countries and to help break down prejudices and misunderstanding. Almost every country in Europe

large because the work was a legacy from the Control Commission), and with £2,000,000 which the two Governments each spent annually on Franco-German youth exchanges. Including additional staff and administrative costs and a small sum for subsidising regional and municipal links in the two countries, which in the case of Germany were one of the main sources stimulating and providing sums for youth exchanges, it was estimated that it would cost £70,000 a year to raise the Franco-British scheme to parity with the British-German scheme.

The British Council also suggested a new scheme of senior scholarships and fellowships tenable in British universities and comparable to the Commonwealth Scholarships scheme.

In 1970 Mr Heath paid a historic visit to Paris where he had most successful talks with President Pompidou. Following this Maurice Schumann visited London in November 1971 on the invitation of Sir Alec Douglas-Home. He had discussions with Geoffrey Rippon, Chancellor of the Duchy of Lancaster, and the Minister with responsibility for European affairs, as well as with the Foreign Secretary, and later he called on the Prime Minister. Following discussions a Joint Anglo-French Declaration was issued, in which the two countries referred to their long and deep-rooted friendship and their hope that this historical friendship would flourish in a new and yet closer relationship as fellow members of this European community. Ministers had approved a series of measures – the Declaration went on – designed to build on this foundation and to foster in both countries a greater knowledge of each other's language and culture. Those relevant to the British Council included an expanded exchange programme of British and French teachers, youth exchanges and the forging of stronger links between British and French towns.[6]

As a result of the agreement with the French, the British Council received an extra £100,000 annually. This has come to be known as the Heath/Pompidou money and was to be used for an increase in youth exchanges, civic links and a senior scholarship scheme for British post-graduates in France. It was agreed that the British Council

---

takes part in the scheme and visits are for at least seven days, ten in the case of the Soviet Union.

Civic Links, better known as Town Twinning, provide for the exchange of local government officers and representatives of every kind from architects to police and firemen, as well as for Trade Fairs and social and cultural activities. It is not an élite activity but involves masses of people, small towns and villages showing the highest proportion involved.

should provide a secretariat for the Joint Twinning Committee, which retained an outside Chairman and acted not as an Advisory Committee to the Council but as a central clearing house for the maintenance of existing links and the creation of new ones.

The significance of the Heath/Pompidou money was that it was the first increase to the Council for work in Europe for twenty-three years. It was, however, only a beginning, and was purely for work in France. At about this time Geoffrey Rippon wrote to the Prime Minister saying that, because the terms of reference of the Working Party of officials related only to Anglo-French relations, it did not go as far 'as we would like' in exploiting the opportunity provided by our entry into the Communities to increase both our influence in Europe and the under-standing of Europe in this country. He suggested that a new study should be undertaken to cover all those types of cultural co-operation which flourished within the Community to see how we could raise the level of our activities to match theirs. He believed a new allocation of funds, 'perhaps up to £2 million' annually, might be needed and he sought the Prime Minister's approval to ask officials to undertake a broad study on these lines.

On 27 March 1972 the Director-General of the British Council, in a Newsletter to Representatives, described first the course of Anglo-French agreement leading to the allocation of the Heath/Pompidou money and then went on to say that, together with J. D. B. Fowells, he had represented the Council on the Interdepartmental Committee which considered the Rippon proposal. He said that the arguments for the new work being assigned to the Council were that it had the organisation to handle the work, that it could therefore put it into effect more quickly than any other body, and that it was well accus-tomed to working with other people and to subsidising their activities. He wrote:

Out of £6 million of new money which has been allocated by HMG over four years for the development of educational and cultural rela-tions [in Europe] the bulk – about £3½ million – has been allocated to the Council ... Ministers have, however, made it clear that they will keep a close eye on the development of our programmes particu-larly in the field of youth exchanges which they regard as crucial, and in the field of arts and books in which the Paymaster-General (the minister with responsibility for the arts) is particularly interested.[7]

Broadly, emphasis was laid on expansion of youth exchanges, both in an increase of them and to make them more effective. (The Council did not normally arrange the programmes but provided money for local authorities and voluntary professional bodies to operate the exchanges, and advice and assistance through its offices at home and overseas.) The Civic and Regional Exchange programme between Britain and Germany inherited from the Control Commission was to be the model for a Regional and Civic Links programme with other countries, and money was to be provided for the strengthening of the Joint Twinning Committee for which the British Council would provide the Secretariat. A European Unit of the Council's English-Teaching Information Centre – a repository for information about all aspects of English teaching overseas – was to be added to the existing Commonwealth Unit. More money was to be provided for the arts to assist British participation in European Festivals. Libraries were to be strengthened, as also book promotion. Exploratory visits between specialists in the medical, scientific and legal fields were planned to identify opportunities for co-operation.

In addition both London and overseas staffs had to be strengthened, and new posts included Science Officers for Paris and Brussels, an Arts Officer for Paris, and an English Language Adviser to direct the language training programme in the European Commission. For the first time a major English language teaching programme was set up in France to co-operate with the Ministry of Education. Work in Holland and Belgium, long neglected, was increased, as also in Italy, and, since Geoffrey Rippon had insisted that the money should not be spent only in EEC countries, the new exchange schemes were extended to Spain and Portugal, Greece, Turkey and Yugoslavia.

With the intention of marking Great Britain's entry into the European Economic Community, the Festival of Europalia 1973 was devoted to British arts. (Europalia is a non-profit-making institution in Belgium which each year organises a festival devoted to the arts of a single EEC country.) The Council was responsible in some degree in 1973 for the majority of the exhibitions, of which three were the Queen's drawings, a National Trust exhibition of treasures from country houses, and a collection of modern paintings from the Tate Gallery entitled Henry Moore to Gilbert and George. (The music programme included five major British orchestras, five ensembles, many soloists and the English Opera Group's production of 'Death in Venice'. Three major drama companies and the Royal Ballet were also there.)

Sir Christopher Soames got his new British Cultural Centre in two adjoining Second Empire buildings in the Rue de Constantine facing across the Esplanade des Invalides. Behind the façades, these were altered to accommodate the British Council and the British Institute together. He also got an exhibition of British Romantic Painting in 1972, which he described as 'the outstanding event of the Year' and about which he said:

The mounting of such a major display of British art posed both a challenge to the Council's ingenuity and an unprecedented strain on the resources of their fine arts department. The extraordinary success of the exhibition, which drew over 150,000 visitors and made a stunning impact on the art-loving public, even among the smug cognoscenti who thought they knew all the answers about this kind of painting, is testimony to the drive of the organising committee under the direction of Lord Clark and the imagination, zeal and dedication of those who were charged with the hanging of the pictures.[8]

No Head of Mission since Sir Percy Loraine has deserved so well of the British Council as Sir Christopher Soames.

18

New Sources of Income

In 1974, after he had been two years in office as Director-General, Sir John Llewellyn initiated an exercise to which he gave the name 'Forward Plan'. Explaining this to Representatives he said:

> We need to widen our outlook and consider the whole span of work which we should be doing. I want to take to the Executive Committee and to HM Government a strong refutation of any suggestion that our existing resources are adequate for the job which is entrusted to us, and to accompany this with a carefully prepared estimate of the resources which will be required for the future ...
>
> In Britain's current situation we cannot hope for additional funds in the immediate future; indeed our situation may deteriorate further before it begins to get better. However, levels of public expenditure for 4 or 5 years ahead are laid down annually by the Public Expenditure Survey Committee, and if we hope to benefit from a renewal of Britain's prosperity towards the end of the decade we should have our case prepared for the PESC deliberations early next year.[1]

Sir John Llewellyn then asked each Representative to make without delay a realistic and fundamental appraisal of the optimum pattern of activity in his country, assuming a 5-year period during which the Council's resources might be adjusted from their present level to an optimum. The proposals would then be collated and married to the ideas of the specialists at Headquarters. He said that the Forward Plan would not of itself produce additional funds, certainly not in the short term and possibly not at all, but nevertheless it was not merely an academic exercise.

> I intend that the results shall be taken seriously and used. It amounts to a fundamental assessment of the desirable scope and direction of

the Council's work in the next decade which will give us an indicator of the size and structure of the organisation we would need to undertake that work satisfactorily.[2]

The Director-General's initiative seems to have been welcomed, if not always with enthusiasm at least without protest, and to have been generally accepted as a useful exercise. Proposals were sent in not merely by Representatives, but by the Legal Adviser, Adviser on Education, the Headquarters Divisions, and so on. The early stages of the inquiry produced a brisk exchange between one Representative and his Ambassador on a matter of perennial concern. The Council officer preferred long-term personal contacts to what he referred to as 'circuses', the Ambassador placed his faith in what he (regrettably) called 'manifestations'. His concern, he explained, was less to make and keep contacts with large numbers of individuals at a professional level than to make an impact on the public as a whole. In an ideal world one could profitably pursue both courses, but, with limited resources, major events should take priority over minor. The Ambassador believed that, far from manifestations hindering day-by-day contacts, they were likely to bring these in their train. But he explained that when he spoke of manifestations, he meant the really big affairs (he mentioned the Royal Ballet and the Tate Gallery) and here he gave the game away. The Royal Ballet, exhibitions from the Tate Gallery, the National Theatre Company and the Opera Companies make an unsurpassable impact wherever they go, but the extent to which they can be travelled is very limited, their cost is enormous and they appeal almost equally to Ambassadors all over the world. The British Council must undertake the more difficult task of promoting cultural relations by long-term measures and by the conspicuous excellence of numbers of small exhibitions and performing groups.

The Forward Plan did not fulfil the hopes of its author. It was based on the false premise that better times would come again. Perhaps for this reason, while adding up to a body of analysis and opinion which was to prove useful in a different context, it produced very little that was new. As one commentator put it, ideas and innovatory programmes were conspicuous by their absence, while the compilers seem to have been 'inhibited by the inclemency of the present economic climate in this country and it is understandable that it should be so'.[3] There was disappointment nevertheless that, at least from Europe, there were not more recommendations on how to develop civic links and youth exchanges. Someone at about this time remarked that, as with women's clothes, the date of any Council policy statement could be determined by its fashions. Civic links and youth exchanges were very much the fashion in the early 1970s.

. The brave words of the preliminary statements of the Forward Plan were considerably weakened in the summary to the Final Report which explained that 'this re-assessment does not aim to set out specific plans for the future because it is not possible to say at this stage when year one of the development period might be'.[4] Nor in the actual economic climate could one expect very much from the estimate that the level at which the Council 'could usefully be working at the end of five years is about twice the present level, and this implies an increase of about 60% or 70% in the Council's mixed money funds'.[5]

Council staff themselves appear to have felt reservations on this score. 'I know that you wanted this sum total in your mind for bargaining purposes', the Assistant Director-General, Ellis Gummer, wrote to Sir John Llewellyn. 'Some years ago Ministers are alleged to have said that the Council's level of expenditure was "about right", and you will now be able to say that at least the workers in the field dissent by a large margin. However I am not sure that this argument is persuasive in itself and you may well not have intended to raise a claim for all the margin as it stands.'[6]

In the Foreign and Commonwealth Office it seems to have been received with some consternation. Commenting on it, one official said he could only underline that it was quite impossible to see when such a development might start, while the sums of money envisaged were not merely unobtainable from the Treasury at the moment, but might remain so for some time:

I should like to know what plans you have for releasing the Paper and obtaining publicity for it. Any such plans should in my view, be very carefully considered, since there might be a danger that publicity in present circumstances might lead to criticism.[7]

Criticism and embarrassment were avoided because of the announcement that Overseas Information Services would be the subject of another Government study – the Programme and Analysis Review (PAR). The PAR exercise had the double advantage that, by colliding with the end of the Forward Plan, it made it inopportune for that to be published, while providing an outlet for the evidence which had been accumulated and which was ready for presentation to the new Committee.

The Forward Plan was, as it happened, conceived at a singularly inopportune moment, since its completion coincided with the necessity for the British Government to seek a loan from the International Monetary Fund and to accept the terms imposed as a condition of receiving it.* Cuts were and would remain the order of the day.

Long before this the Council had run into difficulties in securing finance to fulfil the demands made upon it. In parenthesis, it may be remarked that, although year by year the grant-in-aid showed an increase, this was due partly to rising costs and partly to extra demands made upon the Council by Government Departments. The actual money was never enough. All too often encouragement, even instructions, were given for an extension of some operation without any long-term security that the new activities would not sooner or later be at the expense of the old. Thus the Rippon money, so welcome for a re-entry into Europe, was given only for a period of four years with no certainty that it would be renewed – neither (after a change of Government) was it renewed.

One of the greatest difficulties was the method by which the Council was funded. The Hedley-Miller system of percentages was still in force and, in spite of refinements to it, still operated in an extraordinarily clumsy way. The reader may like to be reminded that, because certain elements of the Council's organisation, such as the Representative himself, his office and its staff, as well as the general overheads of the London offices, might be said to have both 'an Information and an Aid content', these were shared between the two departments according to fixed percentages agreed after elaborate estimates had been made. Initially this was in the ratio of 36 per cent ODA† and 64 per cent Foreign and Commonwealth and Colonial offices. This ratio was revised in 1968 following Sir Harold Beeley's Review and, by October 1970, had become 31 per cent (ODA) to 69 per cent (FCO).[8] The difficulty remained that ODA could not raise its contribution unless the Foreign and Commonwealth Office could do the same and *vice versa*.

---

* The IMF loan of $5,300 million was made in June 1976 but it occasioned a Mini-Budget in the previous December after it had been agreed in principle. The Annual White Paper on public expenditure of 19 February 1976 postulated a reduction of £3,400 million.

† See note on page 230.

In 1970 the Public Expenditure Survey Committee forecast a decline in money available to the FCO on the information vote but a substantial increase in the money available to ODA for aid, while early in 1971 it was agreed that, on the basis of the actual pattern of work done, the Foreign and Commonwealth Office was probably contributing £500,000 too much and ODA £500,000 too little.[9] According to the Foreign and Commonwealth Office, the simple solution would have been for ODA to contribute that much more and the FCO that much less.[10] This would have left £500,000 under the overseas information limit for additional deployment. The danger was that the Treasury would certainly try to treat that as a 'fallen cost', that is, to claw it back from information funds, leaving the position as far as the British Council was concerned exactly as before. (Correspondence with the Treasury suggesting that ODA should take over responsibility for the Council's public library development scheme had brought evidence that these fears were not unreal.)

There were certain other nuisances to which this situation might be thought to contribute. Although in consequence of the Mark/Phillips Report it had become accepted that the British Council should act as educational adviser to the Heads of Missions, and while it was increasingly seen as the co-ordinator of educational work overseas, no similar development had occurred at home. Three bodies, the Inter-University Council (IUC), the Council for Technical Education and Training Overseas (TETOC) and the Centre for Educational Development (CEDO), were all working more or less in the same field as the British Council. All three were funded by ODA and were continually given increased funds and new or extended responsibility. These bodies made some demands on the Council's overseas staff, but without any serious attempt at co-ordination in London.

As early as 1970 a paper to the British Council Executive Committee said, 'The ODM [Overseas Development Ministry] has money for growth and expansion and is using this to establish or strengthen bodies whose work may overlap with the Council's while the FCO has no extra money.'[11]

In these circumstances a Working Party was established to examine arrangements for funding the British Council and this held its first meeting in December 1970. It met through 1971 but there is nothing in the record to suggest it was successful in finding any radical solution to the problem. This was not merely because of the need to present the case in such a way as to forestall the Treasury's predictable reactions, but also because of the very real difficulty of finding a satisfactory solution.

The immediate short term problem of altering the ratio of existing percentages without simply losing the money back to the Treasury seems to have been overcome by the straightforward method of an open explanation of the difficulty. This was made possible by the expressed wish of Ministers for an expansion of British Council activities in the area of the Persian Gulf following the withdrawal of the British military presence, and by the need to step up activities in the developed countries of the old Commonwealth (Canada, Australia and New Zealand), because of the impact on those countries of our intended accession to the Common Market. Money for these things would have to be provided by some means.

At a meeting of the Executive Committee on 5 October 1971, the following statement was made:

The FCO and ODA have agreed that this position ought to be corrected. The ODA is willing to provide its increased share, and the FCO has indicated that, if as a result, corresponding funds are thereby released on its side (under the so-called 'Information ceiling') it wishes to allocate them almost wholly to the Council. Since the Council is unable to accept additional FCO funds, because of the percentage formula, unless they are matched by additional ODA funds in the agreed ratio, this would mean that ODA would have to back any such increased FCO provision by a further ODA grant at the rate of 35%; and it has very generously agreed to do so.

These revisions require Treasury approval. This has been sought with the request that the FCO should deploy to the Council £420,000 of the funds so released while the ODA would add a further £230,000 (making the total additional charge on ODA approximately £760,000). The net result would be to increase the Council's budget by £650,000.[12]

Treasury permission was given in a letter written on 1 November 1971.[13] There was a slight hitch to these arrangements because, for reasons of interest only to students of the side-effects of Treasury rules, James Mark, acting for the ODM, found himself with less money than he had thought he had. This difficulty was also overcome.

The system of the Hedley-Miller percentages had, however, shown itself too inflexible to remain and the attempt to find some better means of deciding the proportion of 'mixed money' due from each of the two departments was continued right into the middle 1970s. In 1975 an alteration to the formula was proposed and eventually accepted. It was called 'Banding' and was based on the same system of percentages, the difference being that the work of deciding how much is developmental and how much purely informational was examined in each country separately, this being done by the Representative in the country in the first place. The results were afterwards aggregated to produce a total. Ratios were re-examined every year to ensure that they kept pace with actuality. In the first year the results showed a total for ODA slightly in excess of the previous figure. The Foreign and Commonwealth Office agreed to match this excess to avoid reduction in its share of the budget and the net gain to the British Council in a most difficult year was approximately £1 million.

These were some of the problems of the British Council in the mid-1970s. The fashions – the two major initiatives of Sir John Llewellyn's reign – both of which had long-term bearing on Council policy and organisation, were DTE (Direct Teaching of English) and PES (Paid Educational Services).

It may be remembered that during Dr Arthur King's period as Controller, Education Division, 1959–69, the old system of British Institutes, where students were taught the language as an introduction to libraries, lectures and so on, had given way to a policy which concentrated scarce resources on 'multiplier' systems – that is the training of teachers, preparation of books and curricula, co-operation with universities and so on, while at the same time much more emphasis was placed on science, medicine and engineering. Dozens of small Institutes and Council-subsidised Anglophile Societies were closed in Europe and the Middle East and only a few of the larger Institutes remained.

This was the situation in 1975 when Sir John Llewellyn visited Spain and found that the two Institutes at Madrid and Barcelona were expected to earn a surplus through English teaching in the current year of £100,000. On his return to England, he ordered an immediate investigation into the revenue-earning potential of the direct teaching of English.

The warmth of welcome given by the Controllers of the Overseas Divisions to this project suggests that the Institute system had, in addition to the stimulus provided by Spanish surpluses, a natural appeal. As one of them put it, although it had been fashionable since the later 1950s to regard the Institutes as not central to the Council's interests, they were in fact 'crucial to its image overseas in providing a public presence and in preserving its cultural nature'. He maintained that, without them, the Council 'tended to become no more than an exchange service which could be administered perfectly adequately from the back rooms of Embassies'.[14] It was recognised, however, that Institutes were not appropriate everywhere.

In Europe the Institutes and the direct teaching of English were by now confined to the Latin/Mediterranean fringe but they still flourished in Lisbon, Oporto, Madrid, Barcelona, Naples and Athens. There were now no Institutes in Northern Europe and, although surpluses were being made in Spain, it was not certain what was the case elsewhere. It was therefore proposed that a Study Mission led by Finance Division but supported by English Language Officers (among whom was to be John Mallon from Barcelona) should visit all the Institutes in Southern Europe with the object of establishing proper accounting criteria for profit and loss, market and fee-bearing potentials, and to try to discover whether there were purely local reasons to account for the success in Spain.

The Study Group visited thirteen centres in Southern Europe and the Middle East, and they established that the possibilities of increasing revenue were probably great. While almost certainly providing better services than most of its competitors, the Council charged lower fees; there was much under-use of resources, with equipment and classrooms often remaining unused for half the day and relatively expensive staff, who should have been engaged on management, staff co-ordination and the development of extensions to English classes, too often involved in classroom teaching.

Following this Report, Representatives, not merely in Europe but in many countries of the Middle East, were asked to formulate detailed plans for a maximum increase in direct teaching of English. The Study Group, who had by now developed so much enthusiasm for their task that they were nicknamed 'the Apostles', were able to provide small sums of money to expand or renew equipment as well as to give advice.

The direct teaching of English almost immediately became a central part of British Council activities in Southern Europe and in the Middle East. In Iran, by the time of the revolution, earnings had reached £1 million a year, and in the six years from 1976–7 to 1982–3 overall income from teaching rose from £4.5 million to £15.5 million, considerably more than the rate of inflation for the period.

However, although surpluses were made in many places, these could

32 The John Alldis Choir in China gives an impromptu performance at the
request of the kitchen staff of the Pavilion for Listening to Oriols at the
Summer Palace

33 The British Pro Cantione Antiqua singers, performing at a festival at Wratislava,
Poland, with Council support

34 Sir Peter Hall's production of *The Oresteia* at Epidauros, 1982

often not be moved from one country to another because of currency restrictions, and in some countries the operation ran into difficulties. In Germany the Representative reported from the first that, owing to the size and effectiveness of the provision of English teaching throughout the educational system, and because of a network of institutions giving part-time tuition to adults, there was no room for a Council undertaking. 'Our conclusion is,' he wrote, 'that DTE would not be a rewarding operation in this Representation.'[15]

The 'Apostles' were not easily persuaded, however, and in spite of this advice English teaching centres were capitalised at far too high a level in Hamburg and Munich. Competition with a private sector school of English in Munich was resolved by an agreement to 'share' the market, the private school catering for the general and elementary language learner who wanted English for personal reasons, and the Council reserving to itself the specialist end of the market and providing classes in English for the specific needs of business executives, law firms, etc. It was, however, from the generalist rather than the specialist end of the market that the profit was to be made, and the Munich centre, like the Frankfurt one, ran at a loss from the outset. But the experiment of catering on a commercial basis for the specialist needs of business organisations proved so valuable to the Council that the Munich centre, unlike the Frankfurt one, was not closed down. The German experience was repeated in Holland where British Institutes at Amsterdam and The Hague continue to need subsidy.

Certain principles were laid down. All operations were to be of the best, teaching must be spread throughout the day and classrooms used for ten or twelve hours, while under-cutting of commercial competitors must be avoided. This last was an early source of concern, because some schools were inclined to view the advent of British Council teaching operations as a possible danger to themselves. Partly because the desire to learn English is insatiable, but also because the Council charged high fees and took the upper – that is the more educated – end of the market, these fears have largely been allayed.

In October 1974 the first paragraph of a paper circulated by ODM contained the following recommendation:

The technical assistance programmes to the oil-rich states should be paid for by the governments concerned as soon as practicable, beginning with the large programme for Iran; but this phasing out should not be pressed to the detriment of our general relations with these states.[16]

Behind this statement lay the transformation which had taken place as a result of the massive increase in oil prices. Through this some of the least developed countries of the world had become some of the richest, by means which had done tremendous damage to the economy of many of the donor states.

The newly-rich countries were quite willing to pay for aid. Their wealth was derived from a limited and wasting asset and they felt great urgency to use it for lasting development. Nor was there any really new principle involved in the idea of Paid Educational Services (known at ODA as Paid Technical Assistance or Pay-TA), because the British Council had been handling the training of students for other donor countries and for multinational organisations for many years. What was new was the possible size of the undertakings which was the subject of inflated expectations, not merely in the Council offices but in the departments concerned in Whitehall. At this time the opportunities for earning revenue from technical aid were believed to be much greater than in the end they were, and many unreal aspirations were held. Initially it was visualised that large contracts for complete undertakings would go to one country or organisation, whereas in the event the Arabs preferred to retain control and spread their risks by parcelling out the contracts themselves — one firm being employed to build, another to provide the equipment, a third the educational services.

The claims of the British Council were obvious. No other organisation had its network of contacts overseas or at home, or so much experience, not merely in education but in identifying the needs of developing countries. It could send out consultants to decide what was necessary in the way of laboratories, classrooms and equipment, and in this way to determine the kind of building necessary to cover these. To quote a Council officer: 'You actually tell the Government what they need.' Neither the building nor the equipment would be the concern of the Council but, once they had secured their part of the contract, they were in a position to influence the choice of building contractor and of the suppliers of equipment.

The difficulty was to get started. The USA, France and Germany were already in the field so there was some urgency. Thought was given in the British Council itself to the possible dangers and disadvantages of bidding for these big contracts. Would services paid for by a foreign government lead to some distortion of the Council's character, putting it into a master-servant relationship which was inappropriate to a quasi-official body sponsored by the British Government? A more serious possibility was that finance to capitalise the new venture and, more particularly, resources in very short supply might be diverted from the poorer countries to those able and willing to pay.

The more immediate difficulty was how to find the finance for the first initiatives. The Treasury, alone among Government Departments, remained unimpressed by the obvious opportunities involved or by such arguments as the need for 'a sprat to catch a mackerel'. However, a start was made and an inter-Departmental Committee was set up under the chairmanship of ODM to plan the method of approach. Since the work chiefly consisted in estimating for very complicated educational services at full cost and top speed, this body was too cumbersome and too slow to produce much result. Here the British Council took the initiative by asking to be allowed actually to bid for the contract for a new University at Riyadh. Receiving permission, they scraped up a little money and put together a mission which, led by Eric Ashby, put in estimates to the Saudi Arabian Government. A consortium of American universities won this contract but the British Council got a most valuable experience and proved that this was the only way to enter the field. Impressed by this performance, the inter-Departmental Committee decided to offer the Council the opportunity to 'assemble educational packages for export'.

In 1975 the Council signed a contract with the Saudi Arabian Government for services in connection with the English Language Centre at the King Abdul Aziz University at Jeddah. Spread over eight years in 1–2 year contracts (the terms of Council participation changing with the changing needs), it was connected with a large-scale programme to provide a special English Language course for first-year engineering and medical students. This required the provision of a senior Council officer as Director of Studies, the recruitment and payment of a team of language teachers and the technical and office staff; responsibility for procuring the equipment including language laboratories, TV, recording, photographics, classroom equipment; and the provision of English language consultants to advise on and evaluate the courses. The Council's services were to be scaled down in the later contracts, but by 1981–4 it still had responsibility for providing the Centre's Director, for the overall design and consultancy service of the

English Language programme and for disbursing the Centre's budget for staff and equipment (valued in 1983 at £5 million).

As things turned out this was the largest contract the Council would ever get, but, coming when it did, it was the basis of all future Paid Educational Services undertakings. The Saudi-Arabian Government paid in advance and these huge payments – over the eight years the turnover has been £13.7 million and the net management income £610,000 plus £1 million interest on advance payments – financed other undertakings and through the investment income enabled the Council to build up reserves. (A completely separate department – the Educational Contracts Department – administers the sale of educational services at full cost to the client. Contracts are so devised that there is no hidden subsidy, estimates taking account of all overheads and making allowance for estimates which are unsuccessful. With that guarantee, the Treasury allows revenue to be banked in a special account and carried forward.)

None of the initial fears seems to have been realised. On the contrary, PES has been extended to countries other than the oil-producing, and, in developing countries, is often financed by the World Bank or some other international agency. In these cases, the Council does not seek to identify the needs of the country concerned but bids for a contract designed and controlled by the Bank lending the money.

A typical contract is one for computer studies in Singapore – to train 200 students every year at Higher National Diploma level. British International Computers Limited provides the hardware and the British Council is responsible for the recruitment, training and consultancy services for the new teaching centre. A more unexpected contract is for a Construction Industry Training Project in Sri Lanka. Here the targets include training for 9,600 experienced construction workers to upgrade existing skills; training for about 1,800 mechanical equipment operators and mechanics in operation and maintenance; training for 900 work supervisors who have little or no site experience; and training for 80 or more experienced senior managers in improved work planning. The specialist appointments include training advisers as well as operators for mechanical equipment and training advisers for masonry, carpentry and plumbing.

One event of the late 1970s was the establishment of the Visiting Arts Unit. This was a direct result of the Helsinki Conference on Security and Co-operation in Europe, and in answer to complaints of the immense imbalance in 'cultural imports' which existed between

countries of the Eastern bloc and Great Britain – that is in translations
of books and periodicals, knowledge of writers and poets, and relative
ability to put on exhibitions. The Visiting Arts Unit was established in
London in 1977 with financial support from the Foreign and Commonwealth Office, the British Council, Arts Council and the Gulbenkian
Foundation. It is administered by the British Council and provides
advice and help in placing cultural events in suitable galleries, museums
or theatres and some financial support.

It appears to fill a long-felt need. By 1981 the Chairman, Sir Hugh
Willett, reported that individual artists, craftsmen and performers from
abroad, as well as organisations ranging from national Arts Foundations
to commercial galleries, call upon its services, 'with or without introduction by correspondence, telephone or personal calls'; while it had
also given financial support to 145 events in the performing or visual
arts, imported from 49 countries and taking place at a great many
places in Britain. Its services have not been restricted to the Eastern bloc
of Europe, but extended to countries all over the world.

Finally we come to PAR (the Programme and Analysis Review), an
administrative procedure for evaluating selected areas of national
policy. PAR together with PESC (the Public Expenditure Survey
Committee), the system whereby governmental departments make a
rolling forward estimate of their expenditure plans for four or five
years, had been developed over several years but was particularly
beloved by the Heath Government. Peter Jay began an article in *The
Times* in 1972 with the following ditty:

> PAR AND PESC, PAR AND PESC,
> Are new games which the Treasury play.
> Their heads are in clouds and their feet on the desk,
> With a double excuse for delay.[17]

And, although he quickly denied that he personally held such a naive
or cynical view, his thoughts had strayed sufficiently from a more
respectful path for him to have invented it.

PAR, like everything else which is applied to different areas of
national policy, must vary in quality. The British Council, the BBC
External Services, and the Overseas Information Services had by now
been examined and reported on so often that it would have taken an
extremely original mind to find anything new to say about them. The
proposal to hold a Programme and Analysis Review on the Overseas

Information Services is first mentioned in British Council papers in 1971. The Report, called 'Projection of Britain Overseas', appeared in early 1976.

The British Council must have enjoyed one exercise in which they were asked to take part. This is described in the Report as follows:

> Illustrative possibilities for Radical Change.
> To enable us to focus on the implications of any major re-deploy-
> ment of effort and resource allocation, we invited the Agencies to
> rehearse the consequences in operational terms of an increase or
> reduction in their individual allocation of funds by a hypothetical
> 20 percent.[18]

The Council were in a spendid position to fulfil the first part of this request because they had just completed a similar exercise for Sir John Llewellyn's Forward Plan. They entered into the second part with considerable zest, postulating the need to close or reduce representa-tions all over Europe, including Eastern Europe and the Soviet Union, with lesser reductions in Israel and South Africa; to cease for all practical purposes activity in twenty-three of the countries funded for both Information and Aid, with smaller reductions in eight others; and to make corresponding reductions in scholarships, courses, books and arts and in staff, both London-appointed and locally-engaged.

Speaking of the British Council, the Report of the Programme and Analysis Review stated:

> Subject (and institutional) priorities vary from country to country
> and from time to time. The main targets are in spheres where the
> Council has its own special expertise – English-language teaching,
> education generally, science, medicine and technology, the printed
> word, and the arts – but there are no subjects, other than politics,
> pure commerce, journalism and military science, which the Council
> cannot cover with the assistance of outside experts across the whole
> spectrum of British life today from taxation to the control of air and
> water pollution ...[19]
> As with the BBC, the Council serves the national interest: it is
> effective in achieving widespread recognition and respect for our
> social, educational and artistic achievements which remain unaffected
> by our general domestic performance and yield opportunities, increas-
> ingly exploited, for cultural and educational interchange which can

lead to contacts useful to the export industries. The Council's own paid educational services are not a negligible factor in its capacity to contribute directly to exports.[20]

The recommendations included that the validity of the Council's existing geographical priorities should continue to be re-examined at regular intervals; that it should seek to establish new representations in the Philippines, Syria and Zaire, if necessary at the expense of posts elsewhere; and that it should consider 'diplomatisation' of certain of its posts.

On publication of the Report Sir John Llewellyn received a letter from the Foreign and Commonwealth Office, thanking him for the 'help, understanding and forbearance' shown by himself and his colleagues in the course of PAR. This letter went on:

It was a wearisome business, and a time consuming one, for all who were involved in it; and at times also a disheartening one for those who have laboured in the information and cultural vineyard and then find the ensuing vintages subjected to the sort of wine tasting imposed by an exercise of this sort. I only hope that the results, in the long-term, will justify the work which was put in, if only by securing a better understanding of what 'information' and 'culture' is all about; and then, let us hope, by getting the right conclusions drawn.[21]

19

The Berrill Report

The first indication that the Central Policy Review Staff (the Think Tank) had been asked to carry out a major review of all the Overseas Services was contained in a highly sensational and inaccurate front page story in the *Daily Mail* of 29 December 1975. On 14 January 1976 James Callaghan, the Foreign Secretary, made a statement to the House of Commons. He said that, with the agreement of the Prime Minister and those of his colleagues concerned, he had asked Sir Kenneth Berrill, Head of the Central Policy Review Staff, to review the entire range of foreign policy requirements, both at home and overseas, and to consider what the future pattern of our overseas representation should be, the terms of reference to be as follows:

> To review the nature and extent of our overseas interests and requirements and in the light of that review to make recommendations on the most suitable, effective and economic means of representing and promoting those interests both at home and overseas. The review will embrace all aspects of the work of overseas representation, including political, economic, commercial, consular and immigration work, defence matters, overseas aid and cultural and information activities, whether these tasks are performed by members of the Diplomatic Service, by members of the Home Civil Service, by members of the Armed Forces or by other agencies financially supported by the Government.[1]

Later in the Debate which followed this statement James Callaghan, apparently explaining the leak to the *Daily Mail*, said:

> The CPRS started to make inquiries on its own initiative, it has made no report. A certain amount of gossip resulted and was leaked to the newspapers. If there is to be complete co-operation on this matter, I have asked Sir Kenneth Berrill that all concerned with the review at

any time should maintain the normal requirements expected when they undertake these jobs.[2]

Speaking of the Overseas Services he said: 'The work they do has been done well, and often outstandingly well, but the purpose of this review is to examine whether the tasks themselves may require to be changed.'

In replying to James Callaghan, Edward Heath agreed that, following our entry into Europe, the review was a timely matter, but he went on:

Is the Foreign Secretary convinced that the CPRS is the best means of carrying out such a review? The terms of reference are indeed very broad, perhaps rightly so. The task of considering the functions of British diplomacy in all its aspects is an enormous one. The CPRS – I set it up – was not founded for such a purpose nor do I believe that its staff is properly equipped for such a purpose. While I would welcome a review of this kind, I must take leave to doubt whether the head of the CPRS and his staff are properly and adequately equipped and are suitable for this task, especially if they are to carry out the other activities for which the CPRS was formed.[3]

James Callaghan said that he had asked Sir Kenneth Berrill to consult the widest range of outside interests on this matter and to associate them with his work.

Doubts about the suitability of the Think Tank for this particular task nevertheless persisted. Sir Kenneth Berrill was an economist and in the course of time it became known that his team would consist of three middle-rank civil servants from the departments concerned (the Foreign Office, Ministry of Defence and Overseas Development Ministry), two young economists and one sociologist. There were other aspects of the affair which invited comment. Not only had James Callaghan agreed to the suggestion that Sir Kenneth and his team should carry out this massive task for which they had no obvious qualifications, but he had asked that it should be done quickly. The team in fact reported in eighteen months. Finally, when Sir Kenneth was asked whether the team would be travelling abroad to look at operations on the ground and consult consumers/users, etc., he replied that it might be difficult for them to do much travelling as they would be able to devote only about 25 per cent of their time to this review.

Sir Kenneth wrote immediately to Sir John Llewellyn, asking him to submit information on the British Council and specifically to send the paper submitted to the Programme Analysis Review, 'Planning Ahead' (the Forward Plan). In reply to this request, the British Council put in a memorandum describing its history, organisation and activities. A suggestion by Sir John Llewellyn that the Council might be represented on the Interdepartmental Group, set up to co-ordinate the requests made by the CPRS for basic information and to provide a forum for discussion of the main issues, was refused on the grounds that this was confined to Government Departments. Sir Kenneth agreed however that the British Council should receive papers relevant to its work and be invited to be present when the group discussed issues with which it was concerned.

The members of the CPRS Review Committee conducted their inquiry in a novel manner right from the start. In place of the normal courtesies, they asked blunt, sometimes hostile, questions, receiving the answers in a deadpan silence or stating openly their disagreement with the views expressed, all the time taking up what appeared to be a deliberately philistine stance. Whatever their qualifications for their task, they showed no lack of belief in their capacity to carry it out. After their first encounter with the Council, Sir John Llewellyn reported that his team had been rather shaken by what they regarded as the apparent naiveté of the visitors. The Council had prepared for the session the day before with the Director-General acting as devil's advocate, and in the event they had been surprised how few key questions had been asked. They were not, for instance, asked about the relationship between the British Council and the Diplomatic Missions, while Dr Blackstone (the sociologist on the team) had observed that, although she travelled a certain amount in Europe, she had never found it necessary to call on the Council and was not quite sure what its importance was. In a minute referring to this meeting, the Assistant Director-General, J. D. B. Fowells, said: 'We were a little worried that they seemed likely to complete Stage 1 dealing with policy – and presumably emphasis – not only with a minimum knowledge of what goes on overseas but with no real impression of what the customer wants.'[4]

But the first recorded hint of real trouble is in a letter from the Foreign Office representative on the CPRS team, M. I. Goulding. He said:

The CPRS does not question the proposition that cultural and educational exchanges are a desirable objective in their own right,

whether or not they can also be shown to serve this country's material interest. What we are not yet convinced of is that the British
Council's effort in promoting these exchanges with developed countries adds enough to what would anyway take place to justify the
manpower and money involved ...

It has been put to us that without the Council's financial and
administrative support, exhibitions of British painters and sculptors
and tours by British stage companies simply would not take place.
This too is a difficult question to assess, because the promoters of
exhibitions and tours have an obvious incentive in saying that, without the Council's help, they would not go. But we should be interested in anything further you can tell us about this, with examples of
activities which only took place because the Council helped and of
others which did not take place because the Council withheld
support.[5]

Later, in reply to a question from the Representative in Brazil on
whether he did not accept that winning friends and influencing people
was a legitimate part of foreign policy, M. I. Goulding replied: 'In a
limited way. Relations of the kind you speak of are based on self-
interest, nothing more. But our views are so different that it's hardly
worth arguing about this.'[6]

There are in existence many accounts from Representatives of the
visits of members of the CPRS to their offices. These make it plain that
the team, like many economists, were inclined to see life entirely in
terms of their own discipline. Dr Blackstone asked: 'What proportion
of those projects [art exhibitions and music and drama companies] supported by guarantees against loss, in fact make a loss? When companies
make a loss are they supported again?'[7] (The answer to the first question
is almost all. When considering later the recommendations of the
CPRS, the reader should be clear that the arts are subsidised in Britain
by the Arts Council and overseas by the British Council. Few companies or even small orchestras could travel or indeed perform in
Britain without some subsidy.)

The philistine approach did have the value of forcing staff interrogated
to give thought to things they had for long taken for granted and to
find concrete and simple terms to express concepts too easily accepted
as abstract or unquantifiable. Representatives seem to have been warned
in advance what to expect. Almost every report begins with the
statement that the team had not been as 'abrasive' as had been expected.

Indeed, in the case of Dr Blackstone, she had been most pleasant and relaxed. She is described as 'taking copious notes in an enviably clear longhand like a reporter in the Court of Law'.[8]

Everywhere they were in a rush. Raymond Adlam, English Language Officer in Germany, began his account as follows:

> They were entirely courteous and friendly throughout, displaying neither the abrasiveness we had been warned about, nor the intelligent questioning that I had hoped to encounter. I would have welcomed a more lively approach, but no doubt they were tired at the end of a wide-ranging week. They began by apologising that their visit was so short, explaining that their request for a full day (which they seemed to think would have been enough) had not been approved by the Embassy. When I said that a whole day would scarcely suffice to survey only the ELT element in the German operation let alone the whole picture they moved into their cross-examination.[9]

From Paris the report was much the same:

> Dr Blackstone visited the office between 11.00 and 12.00 on 12 October ... and she eventually appeared again in the office at about 17.40. She stayed on until 19.45, talking briefly to the Assistant Representative (Arts), Science Officer, Exchanges Officer, English Language Officer and Deputy Representative. She should have seen the Librarian but ran so behind time that she abandoned the attempt.[10]

From the developing countries the reports were more encouraging. Thus from Teheran:

> The questioning – mainly Dr Blackstone but supplemented by Mig Goulding and Sir Kenneth – was incisive and to the point. They had read their briefing carefully, asked specific questions and sought precise answers. They were at times rigorous but never abrasive. In all we found them stimulating interlocutors. On individual issues their method was to probe to (presumably) satisfaction but to express few opinions of their own.[11]

And from Saudi Arabia:

There was no sign of belligerence in their approach and our description of the logic of our position over PES and the work we were doing seemed to meet with understanding and approval. They did not ask any questions about cultural manifestations or the Council's activities in other parts of the world but stuck to the situation here.[12]

However the Representative from France (Richard Auty) reported that the Ambassador had said one should not be taken in by optimistic accounts. He had seen similar accounts, particularly from Washington, which were quite contradicted when he talked to Berrill himself. He believed the Council should start mobilising its forces just as he was trying to get the FCO to do. It was no use sitting back to see what would emerge. The report continued:

As far as France is concerned he had told Berrill that it was essential that the British Council should remain as it is. It would be particularly ridiculous to cut it down at a time when we had embarked on the new venture of the Cultural Centre. It was clear to him, however, that Berrill considered that the British Council need only work on a 'care and maintenance basis', the French being asked to pay for exchanges which interested them in the Arts or the academic world from their own resources. We should not be taken in by the agreeable Tessa Blackstone who he thought was likely to be particularly unyielding and he felt that the Berrill group were only concerned to find evidence to confirm their existing prejudices which were based, he said, on a 'class-war attitude' – referring no doubt to the presumed political attitude of Berrill and Tessa Blackstone.[13]

M. I. Goulding and Dr Blackstone also visited the Regional Office at Leeds. Here they really grilled the Representative with many detailed and intelligent questions, Dr Blackstone nevertheless scoring once more with her undoubted charm.

The final paragraph of this Report reads:

Their departure at 17.10 was hurried as Goulding was aiming to catch the 17.30 ... They maintained their independence throughout refusing all offers to help them get back to their hotel for their luggage and to catch the train. Our impression is that they will be concentrating on our 'Rolls Royce service' for Visitors and

SRS's* and that we do too much for them. When we said they had a lot to absorb in just a day, Goulding said: 'I did the Embassy in Washington in $4\frac{1}{2}$ days.'[14]

On 1 January 1977, in the middle of the CPRS inquiries, Lord Ballantrae resigned the Chairmanship of the British Council and was succeeded by Charles Troughton. (He was knighted in June 1977 and will be referred to as Sir Charles.) His appointment was initially for a term of three years, but he was reappointed for a further three in 1980, and then agreed to serve for a further twelve months until December 1984. He served for a total of eight years.

Previously Chairman of W. H. Smith Limited he had served on the Board† of the British Council since 1974. He was educated at Haileybury and Trinity, Cambridge, and he won the Military Cross in France in 1940. Taken prisoner at Dunkirk, he treated this experience as an opportunity to study law, and he took a First in the Bar Finals before he was released. After the war he joined W. H. Smith. His term as Chairman of the British Council has not yet become part of history, but it can already be said that, by his enormous zest and enthusiasm, as well as through his business instinct and experience, he has given invaluable services to the Council. His travels have taken him almost all over the world and wherever they went not only he but also Lady Troughton have invariably contributed to the morale of British Council officers and of their wives. Since 1980 when Sir Charles was joined by John Burgh as Director-General, there has been general agreement that this was the best team since Lord Bridges and Sir Paul Sinker.

Sir Charles was a little unlucky in the year of his appointment because on 4 April 1977 the worst fears that had been building up about the CPRS inquiry were confirmed. Writing to Sir John Llewellyn, Sir Kenneth Berrill sent him what he describes as a brief paper setting out 'in very summary form our conclusions about objectives, priorities, methods, requirements and what seem to us the shortcomings in the present system'.[15] He said the second half of the paper described the

---

* Special Responsibility Students: the students who come to Britain on Council or Government-funded schemes for whom the Council assumes a special responsibility, as opposed to the many foreign students who come to this country on their own initiative and at their own expense.

† In 1976, in recognition of the fact that the Council's Executive Committee had long ago ceased to exercise any executive function, its title had been changed to 'the British Council Board'.

three options which seemed to flow from the conclusions about objectives, etc.

The paper of 1977 is different from the final Report both in structure and in language and indeed is merely a summary of points for discussion. However, it includes an outline of three options to meet the requirements of 'the functions that need to be performed in the UK and overseas',[16] and these do not differ in essence from those proposed in the final Report. Sir John replied to it in a short, rather inadequate paper, which took the matter no further. But the British Council had by now gone into a state of collective shock.

The Berrill Report, which was published in August 1977, is a massive document dealing with an enormous range of Government services. Only that part which concerns the British Council is considered here, but it should be understood that the pessimism concerning Britain's future and the radical nihilism of the recommendations about the Council were characteristic of the whole Report. In an introductory section signed by Sir Kenneth Berrill, the following passage occurs:

> This review has taken place after a period of decline in the UK's power and influence. This is because our economic performance since the last War has failed to match that of other industrialized countries … In today's world a country's power and influence are basically determined by its economic performance. Inevitably therefore the UK's ability to influence events in the world has declined and there is very little that diplomatic activity and international public relations can do to disguise the fact.[17]

All the recommendations of the Review are based on this conclusion.

Chapter 12 is devoted to Educational and Cultural Work and deals not only with the British Council but also with the work of the Technical Education and Training Organisation for Overseas Countries (TETOC), the Inter-University Council (IUC) and the Central Bureau for Educational Visits and Exchanges (CBEVE), stating that only the Council has staff overseas.

Under the heading Resources, the organisation and resources of all four bodies are set out in much detail and, under the heading Analogues, two paragraphs are devoted to similar work in other countries, chiefly in France, Germany and Italy; sixteen paragraphs are given to the methods of the British Council and three to its organisation and staffing. These paragraphs show the members of the Think Tank to have been considerably more receptive than the reports of some Representatives might lead one to believe.

To some extent the activities of which the CPRS approved are implied as a residue from those of which they disapproved. There is one key sentence:

> The advocates of cultural diplomacy argue that a country's interests can be served by making other countries aware of its values in general, and more specifically of its literature, music, painting, scientific, medical and technological research and its contribution to the humanities and the social sciences. We are sceptical of this argument.[18]

What chiefly emerges is that, while accepting the arguments for the provision of educational aid in poor and intermediate developing countries, and for educational co-operation with countries of the Soviet bloc, they do not take the same view of educational co-operation with what they classify as Group E countries, that is non-Communist developed countries. They say:

> We do not deny that the Council's activities in these countries, particularly in Western Europe, generate educational exchanges and other activities which would not take place without the Council's involvement. Equally, however, existing links between educational institutions in such countries and those in the UK are already strong and varied. We were not persuaded that the additional activity generated by the Council was of sufficient value to justify the considerable resources that go into it. We believe, accordingly, that educational co-operation with Group E countries should be given low priority and the Government's role should mainly be a responsive one of providing help and support for those who have difficulty in making the contacts they need. This should especially be so in English-speaking developed countries.[19]

Speaking of the provision of the arts and culture, they say:

> It should be given low priority in developing countries, especially the poorest, because it is of doubtful relevance to their needs and because resources spent on other activities would normally bring greater benefit to them. In Group D countries (the Soviet bloc), on the other hand, this should be a high priority objective because it contributes

to our objective of breaking down barriers between East and West and because little of it can normally take place without Government support. The people of Group E countries (non-Communist developed countries) have easy access to British culture, especially in the white Commonwealth and the United States. The Council's activities generate cultural exchanges which would not otherwise take place; but unless one believes (which we do not) that these produce political or economic benefits for the UK, there is little case for financing them from public funds. Audiences in such countries should pay the full cost.[20]

Paragraph 12.49 reads as follows:

We are conscious that the Council has established itself in the national life and that it is highly regarded in many quarters overseas. But we are confident that if Ministers were starting from scratch to devise means of carrying out the functions implied by our conclusions about objectives and methods, they would not invent the British Council and the other quasi-independent bodies.[21]

The Report then considers two options: A: Abolition of the British Council; and B: Retention of the British Council but abolition of its separate representations overseas. The authors speak with great impartiality of the disadvantages of option A (which on any grounds must be regarded as fairly considerable), and say that in the light of these considerations they have outlined the less radical option B. They summarise their recommendations as follows:

We conclude that present arrangements for the Government's overseas educational and cultural activities should be radically re-examined, and we put forward two options, of which we think there is much to be said for the first.
The main features of option A are:
(a) the abolition of the British Council and the other smaller agencies (IUC, TETOC, CBEVE);
(b) establishment of a new recruitment and placement agency in the UK to do the recruitment and placement work of the Council, IUC, TETOC, CBEVE, the ODM and some of that of the Crown Agents;
(c) the establishment of an overseas capability in the DES, including

an educational exports unit, and the transfer of the small amount
of remaining cultural work to the Arts Council;

(d) all responsibility for educational aid administration overseas to be
transferred to the ODM; in the UK the new agency would act as
its agent;

(e) educational and cultural work overseas to be performed by
diplomatic posts and Development Divisions, with resident
educational experts from the DES and the ODM as appropriate.

The main features of option B are:

(a) the retention of a separate British Council in the UK, incorporating
TETOC and the IUC and undertaking all *educational* recruitment
and placement for ODM and the Crown Agents;

(b) the retention of a separate CBEVE in the UK;

(c) the incorporation of British Council representations overseas into
diplomatic posts except in a few special cases;

(d) considerable reductions in the numbers of educational and
cultural staff overseas and in London to take into account our
recommendations about priorities and about standards in the
administration of educational aid. [A general complaint running
through the whole report is of too lavish standards.][22]

In hindsight it is popular to believe that no one spoke up for the
CPRS Review, particularly not for that part affecting the British
Council. This is not entirely true. The *Evening Standard* liked it, so did
the *Morning Sun*; *Punch* indulged in a poor imitation of the kind of
comment at which Lord Beaverbrook's papers had so excelled; more
important, a leader in the *Observer* said that the Report 'is, in fact a
thorough, refreshingly frank and intelligent piece of work' although it
swiftly added that 'some of its conclusions are muddled and its proposals too mechanistic'.[23] Anthony Howard in the *New Statesman* said,
'One thing to be said strongly in favour of the CPRS team who produced this report is that they do not suffer from any form of *pietas*.'[24]
But, when speaking of a photograph of the seven members of the
review team, he added a comment which had much bearing on the
degree of shock the CPRS had inspired and continued to inspire in
the recipients of its attentions:

When it first struck my eye, I thought it was an election poster summing up Dr David Owen's vision of the New Britain: everyone, as it
were, youthful, informal, bright-eyed and ready to cut out the cant.[25]

On the death of the Foreign Secretary, Anthony Crosland, Dr Owen had been appointed to succeed him. Dr Owen, who was then thirty-eight years of age, appointed, as one of his first acts, the almost equally young Peter Jay, a man with a distinguished university career, obvious intellectual attainments and much standing as a political commentator but no experience of the Diplomatic Service, as Ambassador to the United States of America. Dr Owen had justified this appointment on the grounds that in Washington a change of style was necessary so that the Embassy should be more in tune with President Carter's new administration. Not only this, there was something about Dr Owen's own style which suggested to many people that his approach to the problems of overseas representation might have much in common with that of the 'informal, bright-eyed' CPRS team. This factor ensured that the recommendations of the Report would not slip by as a result of inattention.

With very few exceptions, most of which have been listed, the CPRS Report was received on all sides with expressions of outrage and dismay. The largest part of all comment was not about the British Council but about the Diplomatic Service. The Report recommended that 55 Embassies, High Commissions or Consulates should be closed, the Diplomatic Service merged with the Home Civil Service to make way for a new Foreign Office group, that the number of Rolls Royces should be cut, as also the BBC external services. These things excited much anger or derision. Here the comment quoted will concern the British Council.

A *Times* article began as follows:

Cries of anguish have come from almost all parts of the globe in response to the Think Tank's proposal to abolish or reduce the British Council and to cut and re-orient Britain's overseas broadcasting. Even allowing for the grinding of personal axes, the number of letters to this newspaper has been remarkable and we have been able to print only a small proportion of those received. Even more remarkable is that such a large correspondence has been almost wholly unanimous. Scarcely a single letter has come to the defence of the Think Tank's report. Can this be because the report was so blatantly and obviously wrong in this area of its investigations? ...

Britain's values have been formed by centuries of international traffic in culture and information. If Britain ceases to attach high importance to continuing participation in this traffic, loses faith in the contribution she makes to it, and fails to respond to the demand which her excellence generates abroad, her own cultural bloodstream will become that much poorer, her self-respect that much lower, and in the long run her international influence that much smaller. You cannot stop doing something you are good at without impoverishing yourself as well as others. Fortunately the Think Tank seems almost alone in failing to see this.[26]

An unusually large number of letters were actually published by *The Times*, and although many of these were from English writers, publishers, Members of Parliament, University Professors and so on, others came in protest from distinguished people from all over the world. The British Council received dozens more, mainly from overseas countries. One or two points were made again and again in letters, articles and in speeches in the House of Lords. The quotations given here are chosen for the distinction of the writer or of the prose or for economy in the statement.

Among the letters to *The Times*, three were from the Chairman or Managing Director of a publishing firm, and one from the Chairman of the National Book League (Michael Holroyd). All these wrote to point out the services to publishers performed in the export field by the British Council. The Managing Director of the Heinemann Group of publishers, Alan Hill, began a long letter in which he described the debt owed to the British Council by publishers with a substantial overseas business in the following way:

In reading the Think Tank's comments on the British Council, I find myself in the position of one arguing with an intelligent lunatic, just because the system of delusions is so perfect.

And he closed his letter as follows:

The British Council has a directly commercial role to play. This role cannot be performed by any other agency since it involves the conjunction of culturally and commercially minded staff in the same organization.[27]

The Chairman of Mills and Boon wrote to the *Bookseller* to refute the 'bizarre' proposals of the Review and went on:

I say 'bizarre' expressly because to normal people it seems odd that a report which stresses the importance of exports should at the same time propose the abolition of an organisation which is the book trade's major ally in achieving sales overseas of some £170 million in 1976.[28]

This sense of the bizarre was one that found expression from many people. Sir Charles Curran began a talk on Radio 3:

Every so often in the development of public policy, intelligent and informed people make the most howling blunders. If the British traveller abroad were to tell his hosts that British traditions and culture were a spent force, and of no further use as an illustration to the world of what can be done in a civilised and tolerant society, he would be regarded by his hearers as having taken leave of his senses. Yet that is precisely the effect which the Berrill report will have had on those people overseas who may have had the misfortune to read it. Everywhere I have been since the publication of the report – and I have visited many countries – I have been asked, in tones of sheer disbelief, whether the British Government is at all likely to accept the recommendations. With such faith as I could muster, I have said that I think it highly unlikely.[29]

An article in *The Economist* entitled 'Excellence is Bad', spoke of the 'Leveller and killjoy at work in this report' and said:

When excellence against the odds is in such rare supply in British public life, it is curious to see the thinktank's young turks, fresh from healthy attacks on Britain's decrepit car and power generating industry, turning to criticise it. A Tory Government might usefully turn them on to criticising the treasury instead.[30]

The most extreme charge against the CPRS team was made by Max Beloff (a right-wing writer) who said:

What purports to be a study of a particular aspect of public administration ends up as a political document. Looked at in this light, the arrogance which allows the authors of the Report to present views on matters in which they have no professional competence without even troubling to argue the case becomes more understandable.

There is all the difference in the world between a serious report and a manifesto.[31]

In *The Times* Iris Murdoch spoke of the shock to those who knew the work of the British Council:

> Its offices abroad are full of people coming and going in an easy informal manner, eagerly seeking every kind of information about our life and culture: seeking books, seeking access to the best language and literature in the world. Satisfying these customers are a small, devoted, and I should have thought comparatively inexpensive, staff who seem to exercise great influence in their regions.[32]

Sir Angus Wilson also wrote to the same effect, while another correspondent said that one had only to stand at opening time outside a reading room in Enugu, Blantyre or Madras 'at some risk to life and limb' to be convinced of the service that the British Council provides.[33]

On 23 November Lord Ballantrae initiated a debate in the House of Lords. One of the most important speeches came from Lord Thomson of Monifieth, until recently one of Britain's Commissioners to the EEC. He said he thought the report's proposals were inconsistent with the view that the Community of Europe was now the centrepiece of our possibility of influencing world events. 'I believe, along with other noble Lords who have spoken, that they have made a fundamental mistake by over-identifying power with influence. As power passes influence lingers.'[34]

Probably the most distinguished speech was that of Lord Goodman, Deputy Chairman of the British Council. He said:

> The gentleman who has prepared this report, with the assistance of some very bright fledglings ... is an economist. One of the disagreeable features of the report ... is the anti-humanistic bias with which it is totally informed. That, of course, explains the appearance in the report of what is now a notorious sentence:
>
> > The authors of this report are sceptical about the value of cultural influences in international relations.
>
> That could have been put in several ways – in very different ways. It could have been put in less positive ways. I do not believe it would have been put that way by anyone who had a more general concern

for the matters under review and did not bring a highly specialist approach to it.

It was unfair to the authors of this report not to give them more precise terms of reference. To set them loose on a matter as vast as this, involving so many implications and such a wealth of knowledge and experience, was totally unfair ... I venture to think that where a question of public support for the arts and the dissemination of culture arises, my own qualifications in this respect are not notably inferior to those of Sir Kenneth Berrill and those who have written the report. In the report I find one or two passages which pack into them such an amount of egregious nonsense that it is difficult to see how they could have been published by those who had given serious consideration to the matter and who had reflected and acquired knowledge about them.

One of the matters to which the authors refer is what they call – and it is not a very attractive phrase – 'cultural manifestations'. They say that over £2 million is expended on cultural manifestations. By that, they mean the dispatch of theatrical and operatic companies, orchestras and all the other things we send out to persuade people that this is a civilised country – because that is what it boils down to – and to persuade people that intercourse with this country is desirable and can be valuable on every score, not least the commercial one. They make the recommendation that that £2 million should be cut by half. This is a wholly unscientific recommendation. If the amount involved had been £4 million they would still have said: 'Cut it by half'. If it had been £1 million they would still have said 'Cut it by half', because it is the simplest thing to say and the simplest thing to recommend.[35]

And dealing with the suggestion that the British Council libraries were unnecessary in every developed country except Russia, he said:

Now what will the Russians think if the only country to whom we were addressing our propaganda was Russia? Could the authors have given any serious thought to this proposal? If anything would start a world war, it is the discovery by the Russians that we are concentrating all our propaganda effort on them.[36]

Baroness Elliot of Harwood referred to the difficulty of reading the report. 'If one wants to read the report one must refer to page 371 at least at every other paragraph one reads. There are three pages of what are called acronyms.'[37]

Lord Evans of Hungershall spoke of the 'numerous verbal banalities which border on the unintelligible', and quoted:

> On balance we think that the disadvantages of a powerful institu-tional ethos outweigh the advantages; this creates an additional general argument in favour of change.[38]

Lord Kilmarnock said:

> In the period 1945 to 1970 ... very largely as a result of initiatives by British Council in sending shows of *avant garde* experimental British art to such events as the Venice and Sao Paulo biennials and as far afield as Japan, the reputation of London as an art centre rose until it was the top of the world league. I am not setting out to make a strictly economic argument but anyone interested should ask dealers what this meant in terms of their trade ...
>
> In the performing arts which have not been mentioned either, it must be stressed that no country does or can send its cultural ambas-sadors abroad without some support ... Wherever the curtain goes up, there is no doubt of the tremendous esteem in which the British Theatre is held.[39]

Although many speakers allowed there was some good in the Report, only Lord Balogh was generally in favour of it.

20

Aftermath of the Berrill Report

It was a full year before the Berrill Report was finally disposed of. Towards the end of August 1977 it became known that a Ministerial Committee chaired by the Prime Minister and including the Chancellor of the Exchequer, the Secretary of State for Education and Science, the Minister for Overseas Development and Sir Kenneth Berrill would be considering the major recommendations of the Report and that a Steering Committee of officials would guide them. Both the Foreign Office and the ODM were asked to circulate papers and the British Council put in a Memorandum dealing with all relevant paragraphs of the Report.

In the Council despondency reigned. One of the first consequences of the publication of the Berrill Report was the cancellation by the Iraqi Government of one contract for English courses and the suspension of negotiations for another. The probable loss was put at between £4,000 and £6,000. The cable announcing this said that other contracts were also at risk but 'we are working to assure the Iraqi Government that the abolition of the British Council is neither imminent nor a foregone conclusion'.[1]

Few reactions were as strong as the Iraqis' but Representatives reported feelings of isolation and concern. At Headquarters (sometimes regarded as unduly sensitive) two recurring fears were brought to the surface. The first was that the Foreign Office would welcome an opportunity to take over the British Council. This anxiety was voiced by Sir John Llewellyn in a conversation with a Foreign Office official early in the year. The second was that ODM would seize any chance to do the same. The extent to which these fears were neurotic or justified emerges fairly clearly in the course of the events subsequent to the Review.

There was much lobbying. Lord Mountbatten wrote to the Prime Minister saying that, as President of the International Council of United World Colleges, he had personally visited 41 countries himself:

In every single case my main and most helpful contact has been the British Council Representatives. I have found them invariably to be excellent dedicated representatives of our country and our language and our culture.

I was at first surprised, but now have grown used to, the fantastic reputation they have in the country they work in. Incredibly they have almost always been invited by the National Committee to join them as full members, in spite of their being the only 'foreigners' to be accepted.[2]

And he asked the Prime Minister, in token of his friendship to him, to see Sir Charles Troughton, the Chairman of the British Council, personally.

This letter caused much consultation. *Problem:* how to reply to Lord Mountbatten's letter of 6 August to the Prime Minister? In the long run the request was refused on the grounds that there were no official reasons for giving extra consideration to the British Council beyond what would be given to other bodies equally affected. Apart from being wrong in principle, it could lead to further requests of the same sort. The Foreign Secretary, Dr David Owen, felt that he was the right person to see the Chairman and Director-General and said he was willing to do so. He also saw representatives of the British Council Staff Side and later he visited Spring Gardens. He was at all times courteous and interested and, while critical at some points, on the whole appreciative of the work of the Council. He told the Staff Side that the problem was that there was a lot of good in the Berrill Report but the dislocation of argument from recommendation was a feature of the whole of it. He said he had no doubt of the value of cultural diplomacy and did not agree with the tone of the Report in this regard. At a meeting with Sir John Llewellyn, the Director-General, he said that the onus of proof was on those in favour of abolishing the British Council and, in his view, the case for option A had not been made. As regards option B, he was not sure the CPRS had worked out its implications. If the British Council existed it must have representatives abroad and these must have appropriate experience. He was less convinced that the size of the organisation was right and he asked questions about the balance of the core of the British Council and the superstructure of secondments.[3]

The British Council Board's Memorandum to the Foreign Secretary stated that, of the 27 detailed recommendations of the Report, one related to redundancy and would therefore be invalid if options A and

B were rejected. Of the remaining 26, 9 were accepted Council policy, 5 would be given further study and 12 were, in the view of the Board, not consistent with Britain's best interests.[4]

Matters dragged on. It became known that the Ministerial Committee were unlikely to publish conclusions until they had been able to study the report of the Select Committee on Expenditure (Defence and External Affairs Sub-Committee), at that time taking evidence. A question was asked in the House of Commons as to the cost of the Berrill Report and the answer was £140,000. If, in addition, the time spent by Ministers, Department of State, Members of Parliament and outside bodies had been properly costed, an impressive figure would have been reached.

However, very little further space need be given the Berrill Report. There are volumes of papers concerned with the consideration given it by Ministers and their officials, but no one seriously believed its more radical proposals were likely to be adopted. When the Defence and External Affairs Sub-Committee reported, paragraph 141 of their conclusions read as follows:

We find the Chapter on Educational and Cultural Work one of the least satisfactory in the whole Review. Our rejection of the main CPRS comments and recommendations springs in no sense from an exaggerated caution or unwillingness to contemplate change. It rests on the simple proposition that, if damaging uncertainty and upheaval is to be avoided, the onus must be on those advocating sweeping reforms to make out a convincing case; something which, in our view, the CPRS have signally failed to do. This is all the more true in the case of a body, such as the British Council, which is held in high esteem in many parts of the world, as even the CPRS admit, and which can fairly claim to have stood the test of time. The Council is extremely fortunate, in our view, to enjoy the services of such an obviously dedicated staff, whose career structure is not as attractive as that of the Diplomatic or Home Civil Service. We are not sure that prospects could be substantially improved without changes in the character and size of the Council of the sort which we have rejected on other grounds, although we hope that the Government and the Council will examine the matter. We are convinced, however, that to adopt the main CPRS proposals would place an intolerable strain on the loyalty of the Council's Staff, for no obvious gain and with the prospect of real and lasting damage.[5]

Then in August 1978 the Government White Paper on the United Kingdom's Overseas Representation was published. Paragraphs 55 to 59 deal with Educational and Cultural Work. Paragraph 55 states that the Government believes that, although it cannot be quantified, this work plays a 'distinctive and valuable role in projecting Britain abroad, in furthering relationships with other countries and in stimulating the use of the English language', and that, while comparative figures were hard to obtain, it was clear that France and Germany spent more than the United Kingdom in this field.[6]

The most important statements are as follows in paragraph 56:

The British Council is one of the instruments through which Britain's longer-term national interests are, and will continue to be, promoted. The Government do not accept the CPRS recommendation for the abolition of the Council. But they consider that closer co-ordination is required with the Foreign and Commonwealth Office, and also with the Ministry of Overseas Development and the Education Departments. It is particularly important that the Council's valuable contribution in the field of educational aid should be implemented fully within the scope of aid policies determined by Ministers.[7]

Paragraph 57 states that a country-by-country examination of how far separate British Council offices abroad should be merged with missions is being conducted 'on the presumption that mergers, particularly of administrative support, should be effected unless there are good reasons for the retention of separate establishments. Considerations will vary from country to country.'[8]

Paragraph 58 announces that a Management Review of the British Council's structure and administration is to be undertaken. 'In advance of this Review, and as a basis for it, Ministers after consulting the British Council, will formulate a clear and considered view of what they believe the Council's role and areas of activity should be.'[9]

And paragraph 59 states that the Government see a continuing role for the British Council and the Inter-University Council (IUC) but that they are considering the rationalisation of the activities of these bodies and of the Technical Education and Training Organisation for Overseas Countries (TETOC) and of their relationship to the Education Departments and the Ministry of Overseas Development.

Each of these paragraphs was potentially a greater threat than the main recommendations of the Berrill Report because they bore a relation to the realities of the situation. Paragraph 59 can be quickly disposed of because, although the overlap of activities between TETOC, IUC and the Council had been a bone of contention before the CPRS review, no solution would at this time be reached.

Paragraph 57 – on the country-to-country examination of the possibility of mergers with Missions – was again on a subject recurrently under discussion. There might be varying degrees of integration and examples of different kinds already existed. The Governments of countries such as China or Hungary made it a condition of the British Council presence that the Representative should be Cultural Attaché and under the authority of the Ambassador; in a number of other countries the Representative was also Cultural Attaché but had completely separate Council premises; in the majority of countries he had no formal relationship with the Mission, although he was usually adviser to the Head of Mission on cultural and educational matters.

In 1978 letters were sent to Posts where the British Council Representative already had diplomatic or consular status and their offices were to some extent integrated with the Mission, and also to others where this was not the case; opinions were asked on the possibility of greater integration. Summaries of the replies make it clear that under the impetus of regular Diplomatic and other inspections, particularly those which followed the Duncan Report, a considerable measure of rationalisation had already been achieved. The vast majority of Posts favoured the *status quo* whatever it happened to be. The main reasons given for this were that mergers would create no savings in staff; that the Mission lacked expertise; that it would be undesirable either because the receiving country would not accept it or because it would undermine the value of the work done by a body seen at present to be independent. No post favoured total absorption of all the work of the Council, and in the vast majority of cases 'co-location' would have been excessively expensive or impossible because of insufficient accommodation. There was some scope for economies on a small scale, such as a pooling of stationery orders and local transport, but even here the physical separation of offices often made these impracticable. Mission staff were themselves taking staff cuts and many explained they could in no case take on extra work. The inquiry also produced an unexpected number of unsolicited appreciations of the work of the Council.

Far more serious was paragraph 56, where the sting was in the tail.

'It is particularly important that the Council's contributions in the field of educational aid should be implemented fully within the scope of aid policies determined by Ministers.'

Earlier in the year some consideration had been given to a proposal – emanating from ODM and said to be of interest to the Minister of State, Judith Hart – that educational aid and the staff dealing with it should be hived off from the British Council and carried out by a unit acting as an agency for ODM. This proposal was opposed by the Foreign Office where it was thought both that the cost of setting up a separate unit would be great and that cultural and educational activities were interlocked and the British Council well qualified to carry out all aspects of such work.

Writing to Sir John Llewellyn on 10 February 1978, however, P. A. I. Tahourdin, Deputy Director-General of the British Council, informed him that the Ministerial Committee considering the Berrill Report had rejected the two options for the future of the British Council put forward in it, and also the suggestion that educational aid might be removed and given to an agency acting for ODM. He said: 'At the meeting of Gen 89 [the Ministerial Committee] on 8 February Options A and B were thrown out and also Judith Hart's take-over bid.'[10]

This did not, nevertheless, end the matter. The White Paper on the Berrill Report had specifically stated that before a Management Review and as a basis for it, 'Ministers, after consulting the British Council, will formulate a clear and considered view of what they believe the Council's role and areas of activity should be'.

There was much room here for misunderstanding. The Management Review had been suggested in the first place by Sir John Llewellyn on the grounds that it was six years since the last Civil Service Department Review (the Moore/McCosh), and that there was need for a new review which would take account of the Council's increasing involvement in ODM's New Aid Strategy, the development of Paid Educational Services and the marked up-turn in Council revenue-earning activities. The difficulty was that, while Sir John and his Board were proposing an internal review to be conducted by the British Council, Ministers wished for an external review, directed by themselves for purposes which they would determine only after formulation of a clear and considered view of what they believed the role of the Council should be.

There was a genuine difficulty in defining this. ODM quite reasonably sought complete control in the aid field because in aid matters the Council acted as its agent. In cultural matters it was not the agent of FCO, but, under its Royal Charter, an autonomous body with a large degree of independence which the FCO had never sought to curtail.

The Foreign Office was asked to prepare a paper on the future role of the British Council and, as the representative of the Central Policy Review Staff, Dr Tessa Blackstone was asked to do the same.

The Foreign Office Paper, known as the Function-by-Function Paper was, perhaps deliberately, rather anodyne. The CPRS Paper spoke of over-administration of exchange work and proposed both an overall reduction of this activity, especially in Western Europe, and increased direction by the Department of Education and Science; a reduction of the home-based staff, both regional and at headquarters; a reduction in expenditure on the arts and a shift from Western Europe towards the Soviet bloc.

The Foreign Office Paper was throught not to provide a basis for discussion. The Chancellor, Denis Healey, scenting cuts, asked that the CPRS Paper be discussed. There seems no doubt that Ministers, who may not have completely understood the independence given the Council by its Royal Charter, wished for greater responsibility for its broad lines of policy.

A meeting was called in December 1978 but this had to be postponed. This was the 'winter of discontent' and Ministers had much on their minds. Dr Owen expressed himself in no hurry to proceed with the matter and as not wishing to be personally involved. In March 1979 the Chancellor brought the subject up again, asking that the meeting should be re-convened at an early date. But on 3 May there was a General Election.

During the period of these protracted negotiations the Director-General of the British Council, tired of waiting for some conclusion, gave instructions for an internal review of the Council's organisation to be carried out, with a view to examining the existing structure of relationships between Divisions and Departments, including that between Headquarters and Representatives; to examining the recommendations of major reports since 1972 and identifying the reasons why some of these had not been implemented; and recommending any organisational changes 'as seen in the light of the above'.

A paper called the Report of the Organisation Evaluation Project was produced. Apart from a general wish for better organisation and more power to the overseas arm, the authors seem to have had little that was definite to say and they expressed what they did say in language which would make George Orwell turn in his grave. Among the steps they proposed was the following:

> The rectification of the imbalance which has grown up between the roles of the various components of the Headquarters structure by re-establishing the leading role of the Overseas Division as the Representatives' representative in the marshalling of Headquarters' services and resources to ensure the implementation of the Representatives' agreed objectives.[11]

An organisation so largely concerned with the teaching of English should surely write it better than that.

During the same period a memorandum of much greater interest was produced by the Assistant Director-General, R. A. F. Sherwood. In it he said:

> We are about to embark upon a History of the British Council during its first 50 years. If this reveals nothing else, it will I am sure demonstrate the lack of seriousness, the ambivalence, the uncertainties and the contradictions with which successive British Governments have viewed the whole business of cultural diplomacy in the modern world. This has inevitably forced the Council on the defensive, from the earliest days, through the Beaverbrook campaign, to the recently concluded CPRS Review of Overseas Representation. Our information work has consistently come under pressure of one kind or another, and we have consistently had to justify it, especially in the developed world, not just in terms of cost-effectiveness (which would be reasonable) but in terms of the underlying philosophy. Even now, post-CPRS, we are told that Council work in Western Europe carries little conviction with Ministers and we may be asked to look at ways in which public expenditure on this can be cut back. It is always our information work that is under threat, never our aid work. Over the years this has led us to identify ourselves more and more with the aid camp. From the early days of DTC [Department of Technical Co-operation] we have striven harder and harder to get the educational share of the aid cake. There were good administrative reasons for this, which at the time I fully supported, and there can be no disputing that in countless ways the Council has

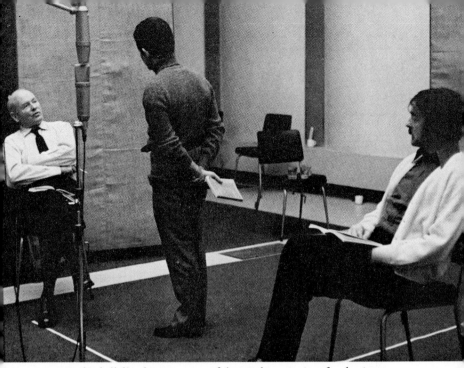

35 George Rylands (*left*) rehearses actors of the Marlowe Society for the Argo recording of *Othello*

36 Sewing silk screens for a backdrop for Bernard Shaw's *Candida*, which toured India with actors from the National Theatre

37 Actors from a production of
Twelfth Night by the Council's own
company, the London Shakespeare
Group, which toured 23 countries

38 Sculpture by Barry Flanagan
displayed in the British Pavilion at
the Venice Biennale, 1982

39 One of Henry Moore's giant sculptures being installed in the Museum of
Contemporary Arts, Caracas, for a Council exhibition of his work

benefited thereby. The whole of the Council's position however rested on our ability to work alongside ODM as a partner (albeit a junior one) without loss of independence. This was acknowledged in the Hedley–Miller formula, which explicitly recognised that since much of our information work in the developing world had an aid spin-off ODM should make a corresponding contribution to our budget. The vital point was that this contribution was in token of what we were already doing, and not in payment for specific ODM work. For all its imperfections the Hedley–Miller formula never deviated from the fundamental principle that everywhere our work was basically informational, and that the Foreign Office would remain our major shareholder. If it were otherwise, if there were no distinction between ODM and the Council in function and motivation in educational work in developing countries, one would have to ask the question, why should the Council exist as a separate organisation? The CPRS asked it, and to our consternation and dismay came up with the only logical answer. We need to remind ourselves that, as ODM itself clearly and correctly pointed out to the House of Commons Expenditure Committee in 1970, there is a basic difference of approach between itself and the Council, stemming from different objectives ... What Hedley–Miller failed to do was to provide us with additional funds. Hence we invented Banding. Banding has been described as merely a technical device to secure more money. In this it has undoubtedly been successful. But we have had to pay a price. Banding changed not only the FCO/ODM funding ratio, but the principle on which the Hedley–Miller formula rested. It does not require much stretching of the imagination to see that where ODM is paying 90% of the cost of the Council operation in a given country, they will inevitably (and from their point of view understandably) want to be concerned in detail with how that money is spent. Extending this to all countries where there is an aid element, it means that in effect nearly 36% of our mixed money activities are passing slowly into the hands of ODM and away from the control of the Board. Add to that aid administration and agency work where ODM already calls the tune, ODM effectively has control of more than half of what we do. One can understand that Mrs Hart should wish to see this formally recognised in the outcome of the consultations on the issues raised in the White Paper, or that ODM should wish to see these consultations pushed forward to a conclusion, while the Foreign Office is counselling caution and delay.[12]

Sherwood then asks the question what should be done and answers it as follows:

We should pay much more attention to our information effort and to its justification. This means being less defensive about it, less anxious to dress it up in more fashionable guises, more ready to proclaim our faith in the primary purpose and more willing to stand up to ODM on fundamental issues (our hand may be stronger than we think: it is at least arguable that by now we have become virtually indispensable to ODM).[13]

Sherwood thought the Council should push ahead with revenue-earning activities – Paid Educational Services and Direct Teaching of English – and look again at the whole question of the funding of the British Council. His memorandum ended:

Following the CPRS Report the Council enjoys a wider degree of public support than ever before. There is therefore much to be said for taking the initiative and establishing a clear position. The Board will be both our spearhead and our defence in this, and as a preliminary to this we ought also perhaps to look more closely at the role and composition of the Board. Finally, despite Government assurance on the continued existence of the Council given in the White Paper I believe that Council staff are still worried and anxious and seek a clear lead; if given it I have no doubt they will respond.[14]

21

The 1979 Cuts

If there was any disposition at the British Council to sigh with relief at the change of Government on 3 May 1979, it must have been short-lived. The exercise by outgoing Ministers to decide the future of the British Council envisaged more control of its policies and some savings. The advent of the Conservative Government marked a change in political philosophy greater than any that had occurred since 1945. Where, during the intervening years, the emphasis had been on what was necessary to meet the needs of the population, the new Government was determined to operate on the basis of what they believed the country could afford. So fervent was the belief in the imperative need to reduce public spending that cuts were to be made 'across the board', almost without regard to the consequential effects. The recommendations of the Berrill Report had in general been regarded as too bizarre to pose a very serious threat, and it is therefore not an exaggeration to say that the years 1979 and 1980 were the most threatening to the Council in the whole of its history.

The Council was early identified as a 'fringe body' and as such was subject to the process of financial examination and expenditure cutting ordered by Ministers for Government Departments. The immediate effect of this was that it was required to meet in full the call for a saving of 3 per cent on salaries for 1979–80 and its 'non-Salary expenditure was subject to the same limitations as applied to the public Service as a whole' – in other words subject to cuts.

The Government's determination to cut expenditure was carried out with a crusading spirit that soon made it plain that to show anything less than the maximum willingness to meet it might be counter-productive. The Council agreed without protest to the 3 per cent pay cuts, which it was hoped could be achieved by reducing recruitment together with normal wastage. Then, in common with Government Departments, it was asked to provide illustrative details of the impact on its operations of cuts of $7\frac{1}{2}$ per cent in 1980–1, rising to

$12\frac{1}{2}$ per cent in 1981–2 and to $17\frac{1}{2}$ per cent in 1982–3.

In August 1979 the Foreign Secretary, Lord Carrington, wrote to the Chairman of the British Council telling him that the Government had decided that the British Council must be asked to find savings of £3 million from the FCO grant-in-aid for the financial year 1980–1. He said that this figure had been agreed subject to the proviso that a full-scale interdepartmental review should be mounted of the activities of the British Council which were funded by the FCO (both aid and information).[1]

Replying, the Chairman said that the new Review was not un-expected, although it would be an exaggeration to say that it was entirely welcome, and in this letter he made the point that, while it was understood that the figure of £3 million related to the FCO's informa-tion money in the core budget, he hoped that any reduction in the ODA's contribution would not, at worst, exceed the corresponding figure implied by the present ratio of funding. 'In plain terms and in rough figures anything more than about $1\frac{1}{2}$ million reduction in ODA's contribution … would be extremely damaging.'[2] In a later letter he asked for 'observer' status on the inter-Departmental review, a request to which the Foreign Secretary agreed, with the proviso that the Council representative should not be present when the conclusions were being formulated.[3]

Unknown to the Council, there then followed a long wrangle with the Treasury, who wished for far larger cuts in the ODA contribution, but this was in the end settled at the figure of £1.6 million with a further £1 million cut in the aid administration money, making a total cut for 1980–1 of £5.6 million.

At the beginning of October 1979 the Chairman of the inter-departmental review (who had been appointed from the Foreign Office) wrote a paper in which he said that to a certain extent the deliberations of the Review Committee were shadow-boxing, because the Treasury were asking for swingeing cuts – £7 million in 1981–2 and a further £5 million in 1982–3. In the Foreign Office the further comment was made that fundamentally what Ministers had to decide was whether or not they intended to use the public expenditure exercise as a way of transforming the whole nature of the British Council.

The Council were asked for a great many papers showing suggestions where cuts might be made and costings of their various activities. At the end of October they submitted four papers to the Review Com-mittee. The figures in these papers and those in this account relate to the 1979 level of grant, which was £46 million, and they are in terms, not of what the proposed cut would be, but of what would be left over after the cut had been made. The first paper, known to the review as the £39 million paper, made suggestions for slimming both in functional and in geographical terms. The other papers costed drastic options such as closing all the Council's regional offices in the UK; withdrawing from Australia, New Zealand, Canada and the USA; abandoning support for the arts. In the report of the meeting which considered these papers, the Chairman of the inter-Departmental committee said that the cuts the Treasury were asking for were out of all proportion to the cuts demanded from the FCO or the BBC external services, and if applied would put the Council out of business. It was therefore decided that the FCO team should state firmly that they were prepared to accept, subject to some modification, the savings of the £39 million option, but not to approve cuts going beyond this.

Officials also began to point out that the Government would be heading for trouble if cuts beyond those of 1980–1 were accepted. The British Council had been relatively silent as compared to the BBC but letters were now being received from the academic world and from Members of Parliament. In fact, as it became known that the Council was once more being reviewed, letters poured in to the Council, to Ministers and to M.P.s. These included a most touching letter from Henry Moore to the Prime Minister herself, in which he described what the Council had done for him. He ended his letter:

> The Council continues to support young artists in the way it has supported me in the last thirty years – many of our painters and sculptors will benefit from its encouragement and practical help, and will bring credit to the cultural life of our country (as well as income from abroad). I feel sure, Prime Minister, that money spent on the full support of the British Council is financially profitable to the nation.[4]

In November Sir John Llewellyn was told in confidence that the FCO would not be prepared to go further in the inter-Departmental review than the £39 million option and would accept this only if it was phased over three years to minimise redundancies. In December the House of Lords debated the Government's policy in regard to the functions and responsibilities of the British Council in view of the cuts in public expenditure. On this occasion twelve of their Lordships spoke and there was this time unanimous agreement on the value of the work of the British Council. Lord Eccles expressed a general feeling when he said:

> Therefore, I ask the Government to reassure us this evening that whatever cuts they have decided to make — I do not know what they are — will be extremely short-lived, because this is an instrument which they simply cannot afford to cut down.[5]

The inter-Departmental committee reported at the end of November. They had considered three major options: (1) to maintain the FCO and ODA grants at the 1980–1 level; (2) 'the £37½ million option', which would involve complete withdrawal from a further 4 countries and major reductions (in most cases including the closure of regional directorates) in another 8 and the closure of 14 out of 22 regional offices in Britain; (3) the '£33½ million option', which envisaged a further £4 million savings to be made almost entirely from the FCO vote, that is from the OECD countries and in arts work.

In the Foreign Office it was felt that the cuts which the Council had sustained in 1980–1 went far enough and that beyond this level cuts should be resisted. Since the committee failed to agree on which option or options to propose to Ministers, they recommended that the Foreign and Commonwealth Secretary should circulate the Report to his colleagues, proposing that it should form the basis for early Ministerial discussion. The committee did, however, make one proposal which was to have considerable effect. It recommended that there should be a review of the Council's administration in conjunction with the FCO and ODA to examine the organisation and system of manpower control and its financial control and monitoring. The review team should include some test inspections at home and abroad, should be led by a member of the Staff Inspection and Evaluation of the Civil Service Department and should include a qualified accountant. In short, one more Civil Service Department review.

Following this Report, the Secretary of State for Foreign Affairs sought the agreement of the Prime Minister to assemble a meeting of his Ministerial colleagues represented on the recent review of the British Council to discuss the funding of the Council after 1980–1.[6]

Owing to the objections of the Treasury the British Council had not been privy to the deliberations or progress of the inter-Departmental review, but they had been kept 'discreetly aware of its progress'. Now the Chairman had to be introduced to the recommendation that there should be a new review of the Council's administration in conjunction with the FCO and ODA, to be led by a member of the Civil Service Department.

Some sympathy was felt for the British Council on this matter and at an interview between the Foreign Secretary and Sir Charles Troughton on 7 December, Lord Carrington said that he did not think the Civil Service Department was necessarily the best body to inquire into the operation of a big international concern like the British Council. He wondered whether it would be better for the Board of the British Council to take the initiative by inviting the advice of an outside body and by appointing, after consultation with the Foreign Office, a 'wise man' to look into the ways in which they might maximise revenue. Sir Charles replied that, provided that there was no question of a CSD management review, and that the wise man could be seen to be responsible to the Board, this might be done. However, in spite of this cautious reply, there seems no doubt that Sir Charles jumped at the 'wise man' suggestion. In a letter to Lord Carrington, he said:

I have thought about such an enquiry or review ever since I came here. It has, however, been quite impossible to start one since, from the day I came, we have been in a period of siege and, to mix a metaphor, you cannot start to change the rules in the middle of a battle for survival. I don't think the staff or management would think any time appropriate for an enquiry, having been dug up by the roots not less than twelve times since the war. Nevertheless, if it is done in the way and with the terms of reference I propose, I hope that I could get the support of the staff, the unions, the management and the Board.[7]

Unfortunately this was not the end of the matter. Members of the inter-Departmental review committee felt that a distinction had to be drawn between two proposals – a review of the Council's administration, which would not be an appropriate field for a 'wise man', and a much wider and more radical look at its activities, which might well be.

When this was put to Sir Charles Troughton, he said he felt strongly about a review which would be imposed on the Council by Ministers and conducted by the Civil Service Department, and that this would go down 'incredibly badly' in the Council itself. He said he was not himself a man for striking postures, but he wondered whether, if such an

Inspection were imposed, the Board would want to continue. His own idea which he had formed in the very frank talk he had had with the Secretary of State was that a 'wise man' might undertake both an inspection of organisation and financial control and a more radical look into the Council's ability to become self-financing.

Sir Charles was in fact very much angered at this sudden change in the agreed arrangement. But he decided to 'try and pre-empt such an enquiry by the use of the "wise man" in the context in which I saw him rather than a "wise man" looking at distant horizons'.[8] He wrote immediately to the Foreign Secretary saying that he thought the 'wise man' should be someone of such outstanding ability that no one could question it, and he submitted a list of names of public figures, of which Lord Seebohm's was one. He said that whoever undertook the review would have to be supported by a small team of experts in management techniques and financial controls from outside and he suggested a number of firms which might provide these. The terms of reference he proposed included an examination of the size and constitution of the Board; recommendations which might give it greater control of allocation and of financial resources and the ability to monitor management performance; an examination of the desirability of a three-year financial budget rolled forward annually. 'No one in the private sector could or would run anything on an annual basis.' As far as management was concerned, the inquiry should be concentrated on three areas: the interpretation of financial policy and the implementation of financial controls; the recruitment and allocation of manpower; the desirability of revenue-earning activities and an examination of the quality and skill of financial appraisals and planning to acquire such revenue. 'In my time Council earnings have risen from £6m to £17m.'

Sir Charles then said this:

> What, after a lifetime's experience in various not wholly unsuccessful businesses, I should find difficult if not impossible to accept would be yet another imposed enquiry by people not experienced, in my view, in the elements of successful, competitive survival. I know the staff and the unions would bitterly resent such an enquiry. I do not believe the Board would accept it; and it would, I regret to say, be in my view a very severe criticism of my own ability to achieve standards acceptable to you.[9]

Sweeping on with this mixture of enthusiasm and evident intention to stand firm on the issue, Sir Charles cut the ground from under the feet of the inter-Departmental committee and succeeded in 'pre-empting' the role of a CSD review. By the end of March he wrote to Lord Seebohm, formally asking him to 'come to our aid and be our "wise man" '.[10] Replying, Lord Seebohm said he would need very strong support and suggested that he might be joined by Lord Chorley of Coopers and Lybrand.[11] In April the Foreign Secretary reminded Sir Charles that, when he had secured his colleagues' agreement to the suggestion which 'headed off' the CSD review, it was on the conditions that the CSD be asked to nominate someone to work with Lord Seebohm on certain aspects of his review, and also that the Foreign Office should see his terms of reference and be allowed to make suggestions in regard to them.[12]

Any tendency to rejoice at the success of these manoeuvres was quelled by the decision of Ministers as to the cuts. At a meeting of the Board on 14 February, the Director-General said that the decision communicated to him by the Foreign Office was that there should be a further cut in the Council's core budget (i.e. the grant-in-aid from the FCO and ODA and the amount paid by the ODA for aid administration) of £3.9 million phased over three years to 1983-4. Taken together with the cut already accepted for 1980-1, this amounted to a reduction over four years of nearly 25 per cent. He had been reminded by the FCO that these figures were likely to be affected by future pressure on the aid budget; reductions in the bilateral aid funding might cause a proportionate reduction in the money paid by ODA for aid administration of some £1½-2½ million. In addition, the Council had been asked in the present financial year to absorb 3 per cent of the increase in staff salaries. If this trend continued, the cost to the Council over four years might amount to a further reduction in activity of about £1.5 million and the cost of the necessary redundancies would be a further £1.5 million. The total cut in the core budget was therefore likely to be to a figure of nearer £33 million than £37.5 million.[13]

In response to questions the Foreign Office representative said that the decision on the level of cuts had been taken collectively by Ministers.[14]

The representative of the Staff Side of the British Council expressed herself as dismayed at the cuts which she said were considerably worse than management had led them to expect. She urged the Board to seek re-consideration at the highest level of decisions which seemed to have been taken without any regard for the British cultural and educational interests for which the Council was responsible.[15] So matters stood when John Burgh succeeded Sir John Llewellyn as Director-General of the British Council.

John Burgh was born in Vienna, the son of a lawyer, and came to England with his sister through the good offices of the Quakers at the time of the Anschluss. Later his mother followed her children to England and took a house at Blackheath. He was educated at Sibford, a Quaker school, until the age of fifteen, when, at the beginning of the war, he went to work as a junior clerk in a factory making aircraft parts. After the war he taught in a secondary school at Harrow by day, and attended evening classes at the London School of Economics in the evening. At the end of the year he won a scholarship and continued at the LSE as a full time undergraduate, becoming President of the Union. Today he is a Governor of the LSE and an Honorary Fellow. Before going to the British Council he had worked in the Colonial Office, the Departments of Economic Affairs, Employment, Prices and Consumer Protection and of Trade and in the Cabinet Office. In a private capacity he had acted as Secretary of the National Opera Co-ordinating Committee and Assistant Secretary to the Board of Directors of the Royal Opera House, Covent Garden. He began his appointment at the British Council at an unfortunate time but in the circumstances at the right time. He is a man of great energy and capacity for work, and he is recognised as a first class administrator. Above all he was fresh. The vagaries of Government tend to exhaust all but the strongest Directors-General of those bodies over which it has financial control. John Burgh was knighted in 1981 and will be referred to here as Sir John.

His first act on taking office was to take the Piccadilly Theatre and to address an audience consisting of all members of the staff of the British Council who were able to assemble to hear him. In advance of this meeting many people had doubts of its wisdom, but in the event it seemed a brave and successful manoeuvre and it did much to raise the morale of the staff, at that time exceedingly low. Having paid tribute to his predecessor and referred to the unparalleled difficulties of his last year, Sir John said:

Today I stand before you as your new Director-General. Why have I invited you here, and why am I exposing myself to your critical scrutiny? Quite simply because I think you may be curious to see what the new man looks like and sounds like. And I think you may appreciate an immediate indication of my approach, since I come to you as an outsider unknown to you.

He said that when he had finished he hoped to be asked questions and also that some of his audience would give their opinions about future policies and priorities.

I would also like from the first to try to establish direct personal contact with you quickly. I shall visit offices as much as I can to talk to as many of you as possible on the job. But I would also like to meet you more informally. So, until further notice, I shall be in your Snack Bar or canteen at a specified hour every week ... I hope you will take advantage of this opportunity to meet me personally and tell me what you think.

Having said that the cuts at present proposed could leave a core budget as small as £34 to £35 million in 1983–4, as compared to £46.5 million in 1979, and that cuts of such disproportionate magnitude would be inconsistent with recent assurances by Government and Opposition speakers, both inside and outside Parliament, that the value of Council work to Britain was fully recognised, he went on:

We all accept that we must bear our share of public expenditure cuts. But we cannot do our job effectively if our budget is cut by a quarter or more, while our major European partners, France and Germany, put ever larger resources into their cultural diplomacy ...

We all believe – the Board, staff and management – that the extent of the proposed cuts is caused by inadequate understanding of the importance of our work. If they are implemented, British interest will suffer. We must spare no effort – all of us – to persuade the Government to think again ...

I have one other quite definite view. As you all know, the reputation of the Council overseas is very high. But in Britain itself the work of the British Council is little known. And where it is known it is as often misconceived. We must remedy this situation ... We must make sure that our achievements and successes are known and not hidden under a bushel. I propose to examine immediately what we need to do to bring this about.

The last paragraph gave an airing to what was to be one of the themes of Sir John Burgh's period as Director-General. He believes that the Council should be better known to the British public, particularly to influential members of it, and he has brought much energy to the task of publicising its work.

The proposal that all should work to persuade the Government to think again in fact reflected Board policy. At a meeting on 31 March 1980, the Deputy Chairman, Lord Goodman, asked in what terms the Council's protest against further cuts was being conducted. He strongly opposed acceptance of any more random and arbitrary cuts as a painful necessity, and he said that the Government's own spokesman in the House of Lords had been unable to justify these except on grounds of lack of time for adequate consideration. The need for cuts was not contested, but the cuts must be sensible and discriminating. The case against cutting the Council was unanswerable if properly presented.[16]

On the question of timing a protest campaign, the Chairman said that the advice he received was that this should be delayed until the publication of the Government's White Paper. The deadline for the Council would be the presentation (probably in October) of the estimates for 1981–2.

Long before October – on 3 June – the Chairman secured permission to call on the Prime Minister herself. Sir Charles Troughton has left a note of this meeting from which it is clear that he saw Margaret Thatcher alone, that she asked informed and probing questions, but that she gave him every opportunity to state his case. He told her that the purpose of the Council was to win the minds of people abroad to the British way of life and the great qualities and things we had to offer – our language, arts, professions, institutions, medicine, doctors, accountants, etc. We could now only defend ourselves in the long run by directing people's minds towards what is of value in our way of life and in our attitudes. And he spoke of the great asset of the English language. Then, partly in answer to questions, he told the Prime Minister about the work of the Council and what the proposed cuts would do to it. In the note he made following the interview, Sir Charles said:

> I do not know what will be the result. Very little I fear. *But* she has heard 40 minutes on the Council; she does know that wherever we withdraw, others will gladly pick up the pieces.

On 24 June the Director-General of the British Council received a letter from Peter Blaker, Minister of State at the Foreign and Commonwealth Office. This read:

Following Sir Charles Troughton's call on the Prime Minister, Ministers have reconsidered the level of the Council's Core Budget for the next four years. They have agreed the following figures at 1979 Survey Prices, subject only to the proviso that if the Seebohm Review were to show that there was scope for further staff savings they would wish to review them in the light of its findings.

1980/81	1981/82	1982/83	1983/84
41.4	40.2	39.1	38.0

How the money will be divided between different elements of the Core Budget, including Aid Administration, has not yet been determined. But the figures will enable the Council to engage in its long term planning.

The figures assume that the Council will continue to be responsible for the cost of any redundancies that may still be necessary.[17]

In other words, the cuts were to be spread over four years and to be 18 per cent of 1979 figures, rather than as formerly proposed 25 per cent.

22

The Seebohm Report

Before turning to the Seebohm Report — undoubtedly the most important review of the structure, financial control and administration of the British Council ever undertaken — it is necessary to record two events which occurred as a direct result of the Government's determination to cut public spending. A decision was taken to reduce the number of bodies relying in part on Government subsidy — the Quangos (Quasi-Autonomous Non-Governmental Organisations). Two obvious candidates were TETOC (Technical Education and Training for Overseas Countries) and IUC (Inter-University Council). The degree of overlap between the work of these two bodies and that of the British Council had been under discussion for some years, particularly at the time of the Phillips/Thomas review of the relations between ODA — then ODM — and the Council. Then the Berrill Report made recommendations for rationalising the position and proposed as one option that TETOC and IUC should be incorporated in the British Council. Now the Government's *Report on non-Departmental Public Bodies* (Cmnd 7797) presented to Parliament in January 1980, while promising the continued existence of the British Council, made proposals about both TETOC and IUC. With regard to TETOC the proposal was quite definite: 'This organisation will, after March 1981, cease to exist as a separate entity. Most of the work of TETOC will be transferred to the British Council or in some cases to ODA.'[1] Although less definite in regard to IUC (which, unlike TETOC, was not the creature of a Government Department but of the independent universities), the Report said that it had been decided to rationalise support for tertiary education and that the work for which IUC had been set up — to help in the creation of universities in the emergent Commonwealth countries — had been largely completed. Its present position was reserved, however, until after Ministerial decisions on the future of the British Council.

Negotiations about the mergers went on through the summer of

1980, one of the chief problems being the natural desire of the specialised staff of all three bodies to escape redundancies. In the case of IUC, the new arrangement made it necessary to envisage special relationships being set up between the universities, polytechnics and other institutions and the British Council, and the establishment within the British Council of a recognisable unit (Higher Education Division), staffed as much as possible from existing IUC staff, with British Council officers to co-ordinate and execute programmes of work hitherto the responsibility of the two separate organisations. The Board of the British Council also approved the creation of a Standing Committee, answerable to the Board but acting as a link between the Council and the collective body of universities and polytechnics, the Chairman of this Standing Committee to be elected to the Board of the Council for the duration of his Chairmanship. Negotiations went on during the summer and autumn but in 1981 both mergers were completed.

Lord Seebohm, the 'wise man' who had undertaken to conduct the internal review of the British Council, had a distinguished record of public service. A banker by profession (he had been Deputy Chairman of Barclays Bank and Chairman of Barclays Bank International), he had also been, among many other appointments, Chairman of Provident Life, Finance for Industry, the Joseph Rowntree Memorial Trust and the Seebohm Committee on Local Authority and Allied Personal Social Services, as well as President of Age Concern. He had had a good war service in the Royal Artillery, having been mentioned in despatches. He became a governor of the London School of Economics in 1970.

In a letter to Sir Charles Troughton, he said he would need strong support and that his nominee would be Lord Chorley, a senior partner in the firm of accountants Coopers and Lybrand, who had been a member of the Royal Commission on the Press.[2] The British Council was to be represented by Mr Richard Auty (the author of a paper much quoted here), who was about to retire from a life-time on its staff. Later Dr Harriet Harvey Wood was appointed to act as 'deviller' and to draft the report. The review team was assisted by A. J. Langford of the Staff Inspection and Evaluation Division of the Civil Service Department and by Roger Cook and David Sanderson of Coopers and Lybrand Associates.

Lord Seebohm said that he and Lord Chorley would expect that a review of this kind would be the same as a Government Committee, in which case they would require no personal expenses. Lord Chorley's visits to representations abroad would take place in the course of travel for his business house. Lord Seebohm would expect travelling costs, and the representatives of Coopers and Lybrand seconded to look at Council finances would require reimbursement, which he expected would be a figure of about £2,500.[3] E. J. Rayner of the British Council would act as 'link man'. It was agreed that Lord Seebohm should visit Italy, Poland, and Mexico, while Lord Chorley would be visiting Pakistan, Tanzania and Kenya. All three members of the team visited Greece.

The terms of reference were drawn up by the British Council in conjunction with the Government Departments concerned and were:

TO EXAMINE

1   The role and composition of the Board (and its advisory bodies), its relationship with the sponsoring Department of State and the chief executive of the Council and the extent to which it should monitor the attainment of agreed Council objectives

2   The financial management and funding of the Council in particular:

    a.   the need for flexibility in the management of Council funds subject to Parliamentary and Government accounting requirements and public service practice

    b.   the extent to which the Council's management and financial control systems secure its policy objectives and ensure efficient management of its resources

    c.   the need to ensure that the Council's accounting procedures enable it and its sponsoring department to see how and where money is being spent

    d.   the scope for broadening the financial base of the Council by increasing earned income and private sector participation

3   The Council's manpower recruitment, levels and structure and the extent to which they provide for the efficient and economical staffing of the Council.[4]

In a letter agreeing to the terms of reference, Sir Michael Palliser suggested that the review team might spend some time with Treasury accountants to familiarise themselves with Government accounting procedures and then said:

Finally, we think that the team, throughout their enquiry, should bear in mind that the British Council is an indispensable agent of British cultural diplomacy and technical co-operation. In our view this places on the Council the difficult responsibility of maintaining, despite its independence from Government, the ability to respond to changes and nuances in the overall foreign policy (including aid policy) of the Government of the day. Naturally, this is a two-way process. I think that in the past we have succeeded remarkably well in ensuring a harmonised approach but, as I am sure you agree, it is important that we should continue to keep in step.[5]

Sir Michael added that, although this aspect of the situation was not something that ought to be incorporated in the terms of reference, he thought it should be a central feature of the team's briefing. This was agreed and, after some skirmishing, it was also agreed that A. J. Langford of the Civil Service Department should not only act on demand as a resource for the team on Civil Service practice, but also satisfy himself that the Council's complementing and grading were consistent with Civil Service standards.

The Seebohm Review was the first major examination of specifically British Council problems, all previous reviews having been of the Overseas Information Services generally. The review team interviewed all senior staff at the Council's headquarters in grade B and above, and many in grades C and D; received evidence from present and past members of the Board and Chairmen of the Advisory Committees and Panels; visited one directorate in Britain (Southampton) as well as travelling abroad; had discussions with senior staff in the FCO, the ODA and the Treasury; and discussions with the Council's Trade Union Side.

The report was presented in March 1981. It made 85 recommendations or suggestions. Of these, 6 concerned the Council's relations with Government Departments, 10 the role and composition of the Board, 5 the role of the advisory committees and panels, 12 management below Board level, 22 the financial management and funding of the Council, 9 the scope for broadening the financial base of the Council and 21 the Council's manpower.

Obviously it is impossible to do justice to it here and only recommendations which are broadly based or informative about the structure of the Council can be picked out for comment. Very clearly written and presented, probably the most notable thing about it was the degree of approval it received. It was welcomed not merely by the Chairman and Board who had commissioned it, and by staff of the Council at almost all levels, but in the main by the relevant Government Departments. The Chairman of the British Council reported that in general the view of the Board was a 'very enthusiastic acceptance', while Representatives from all over the world wrote with equal approval. The following is typical of a great many comments:

> I am glad to tell you that it has been given excellent ratings. In general, it is properly informed, perceptive, sympathetic and balanced, and the recommendations are sensible, practicable and constructive. In brief, to a very large extent it matches our own views about the Council and our own prescriptions for evolutionary change.[6]

Several Representatives simply cabled to the effect, 'Very satisfactory. Nil comments'. Equally important, the Report was, if rather more critically, generally well received in the Government Departments.

Some of the most contentious passages in it occur in the first section, 'The Council's Relations with Government Departments'. The authors were critical of both the sponsoring Departments:

> FCO do not appear to have any clearly established set of policies for the Council's work, or any clear-cut policy on the contribution to be expected from cultural diplomacy to the government's overseas representation. The guidance which the Council receives from the FCO appears generally to be short-term and reactive rather than long-term, at the expense of a global cultural policy. We note with satisfaction a recent move by FCO to define more clearly their thoughts on Council policies and priorities, and urge that this initiative should be followed up ...
>
> The relationship with the Overseas Development Administration (ODA) is similarly unsatisfactory. We note the close supervision exercised by ODA at desk level over the aid work handled by the Council, and the amount of consultation and paper work which this involves. ODA have, however, indicated in a paper prepared for the team that they would be willing to relax control to a greater extent if there could be closer identity of view between them and the Council on overall aid policy, and if the Board ... were seen to include a larger proportion of members with relevant experience and expertise.[7]

Having said that they hoped the suggestions they would make for enlarging the scope and competence of the Board would provide a solution to this problem, the review team went on to consider the problems caused by 'banding' of the FCO and ODA contributions to the British Council core budget. The criticism here was that, since banding had produced a higher contribution from ODA, this Department had gradually ceased to think of its contribution as a general one to the Council's professional effectiveness and had become increasingly concerned with whether the spending of their money supported the specific aid programmes laid down for individual countries 'and, by corollary, that (according to ODA) where there is no agency expenditure on behalf of ODA, there should be no ODA contribution to the grant-in-aid'.[8]

The Report discusses the dangers arising from this, the only completely new criticism of the system being that when a developing country ceases to be aid-worthy, the ODA aid element in the mixed funding is reduced or withdrawn without any compensating increase in FCO funding 'at the very time when Britain should expect to benefit from her former aid investment in a now prospering country ... The whole concept of banding appears increasingly artificial at a time when ODA has been absorbed into FCO'.[9]

Important recommendations were made on the role and composition of the Board, which the review committee regarded as too large. They recommended that the Government nominees should be reduced from six to two – one each from FCO and ODA – and that the practice of reserving seats for special interests should be restricted. They were surprised that (apart from former members of the diplomatic service) there were so few members who had seen service overseas; they would have expected to see senior officers from the large international banks, trading houses and academics who had held posts overseas. The Report recommended the election of members with first-hand knowledge of overseas development and the teaching of English as a foreign language, and they hoped that 'by the election of members who sit in more than one capacity, the total number of members could normally be restricted to about 20'.[10]

The review team saw the advisory committees as of great value to the Council and recommended that those which did not meet regularly should do so at least once a year to review and assess the past year's work and offer advice on policy and proposals for the coming year. They also recommended that consideration should be given to nominat-

ing a Board member to represent the Board on each (other than the
Scottish and Welsh Advisory Committees) with the approval of the
Chairman of the committee or panel concerned.

On management below Board level the Committee had this to say:

> The impression given to the team and almost universally accepted
> by those who have been interviewed is that, in the past, decision-
> making has been more by committee (often *ad hoc*) and on the
> principle of consensus, rather than by line managers. The result
> seems to have been considerable delay in coming to decisions and
> sometimes actual absence of any decision ... The first requirement
> is to define the operational line which is accountable for the manage-
> ment of the Council, and to ensure that the service and functional
> departments recognise that they are there to service the line and not
> to give instructions without 'line' authority.[11]

Having said that their recommendations were not intended to diminish
the Representatives' delegated powers, the Report goes on:

> We therefore strongly *recommend* that the line responsibilities of the
> Overseas Divisions and Home Division be firmly established, and
> the necessary authority given to all Controllers and Directors to
> manage their areas of command, to take decisions and to be account-
> able for them. This should not only speed up the work of the
> Council, but save much time now spent in committees and in the
> production of papers.[12]

The section on the financial management of the Council is enormously detailed, running, as has been said, to twenty-two paragraphs.
Probably the most important comment that can be made here is that
all twenty-two were accepted and put into practice over the next two
or three years. Some of the most valuable concerned the introduction
of an 'activity accounting system', in relation to which the Council had
special problems; and one of the most interesting to the outsider was
that the Permanent Art Collection, which was essential to the Council's
work of making British art better known abroad, should continue to
be funded basically from the grant-in-aid, but that the desirability of
selling some items with a view to reinvestment in other works of art

should be examined, provided that relaxation of Treasury rules made this possible.*

One of the most interesting passages concerned the growth of Paid Educational Services (PES). The team expressed themselves as uneasy about the growth of these activities and disturbed that the Council were bidding for a World Bank contract in Indonesia 'without sufficient financial or commercial information on which to make a balanced judgment'.[13] In this case sub-contracting to an American firm was involved, and no information was given to the Board on how these contracts were to be placed, monitored and controlled in the USA. 'Such projects involve large potential liabilities, both financial and of reputation, much management time, and skills which do not all appear to exist in the British Council.'[14] The Committee also thought the growth of these activities should be encouraged only if they contributed positively to the Council's main objectives and were not taken on simply to make money or increase exports.

On staffing, the Report said:

The Council offers an interesting and varied career but not, by Civil Service or Diplomatic Service standards, a financially rewarding one. Prospects for home serving staff are particularly poor, as are those for locally-engaged (LE) staff overseas.[15]

They recommended that 'while the present system of parities with the Civil and Diplomatic Services be retained, they should be suitably adjusted to take account of the Council's special needs and conditions.'[16]

Since the Council does not promote a man unless he is also moved to a post in his new grade, a sharp conflict arises between operational needs, which demand continuity, and good personnel management, which demands fair treatment of meritworthy staff.[17]

Speaking of the locally-engaged staff, the team said that, while overseas Representatives attached the highest importance to their locally-engaged colleagues and relations were almost always excellent, in London their importance got 'lip service' but not always the recognition it deserved.

* The British Council Collection was started in 1938 and by 1984 contained 960 original works and 3,540 graphics and multiples.

It is our view that, particularly at times of retrenchment, special attention should be given to the needs of locally-engaged staff overseas to ensure that their position as equal partners in the Council's operation is respected, and we so *recommend* ...

The terms and conditions of locally-engaged staff are determined by the Diplomatic Service Inspectors on criteria agreed by the Civil Service Department. These are based largely on Embassy and Consulate requirements which are not, however, wholly analogous to those of the Council which frequently depends more on its local staff for positions of responsibility (e.g. nearly all Council accountants are locally engaged whereas in Embassies such posts are held by London-based officers).

We *recommend* that consideration be given to setting up a system of merit and/or long-service awards for locally-engaged staff and also perhaps the creation of a super-grade (or grades) beyond the present maximum of Grade I = Grade F = Higher Executive Officer.[18]

The Report did not escape without any adverse comment. Both the FCO and ODA seems to have been surprised at the criticisms of their relationship with the British Council which they had thought good, while it was pointed out that the authors of the Report had spoken to very few people outside the Council, with the result that they were uncritical and unduly bland in their references to it, while accepting too easily Council views on the Departments with which it had to deal. They recommended pay and grading links, for instance, where these suited the Council, but sought freedom from them when they proved inhibiting.

The most contentious part of the discussions between the Board and the Government Departments following on the Report concerned the question of 'banding'. In particular, ODA officials felt that if the Council wanted to go on requiring funding in countries where 'developmental activity' had ceased, the logical thing would be for a larger amount of mixed money from FCO to be provided. In current circumstances this was simply not feasible.[19]

In the Council itself there was some doubt about the passages on PES where it was felt that the possible dangers outlined had in practice over a fairly large number of cases never arisen. On the whole, however, it was extremely well received on all sides.

Lord Seebohm and his colleagues did not pluck all their recommendations from the air, but, like the Drogheda, the Duncan and most of the other Committees, they gave a firm definition to current ideas and policies. In regard to the role and composition of the Board, their views were very much in line with those of Sir Charles Troughton, while Sir John Burgh was already determined to institute many of the reforms suggested for the structure and administration of the Council.

It is too early to say how history will regard the period of this Chairman and Director-General, but their enthusiastic belief in the value of the Council's work has corrected a spirit of uncertainty in the staff which had existed ever since the days of the Beaverbrook attacks. Neither of the present occupants of the leading roles suffers from uncertainty; on the contrary, they take a fearless pride in the Council and their unashamed promotion of its interests has infected all those who work with them.

In his first two years, Sir John paid much attention to clarifying the purposes of the Council, which he redefined in the following phrase: 'To create an enduring understanding and appreciation of Britain abroad through cultural, educational and technical co-operation.' This phrase, simple it seems to the point of obviousness, has nevertheless acted as a touchstone against which to test the appropriateness of any activity, and it has helped to curb the tendencies to expand in any direction and to undertake whatever is asked.

Sir John should also be remembered for his overwhelming concern for the welfare of the staff. When he arrived, for reasons already described, the opportunities for promotion were much depressed, and there were many bottlenecks on the road to advancement. One of his first acts was to recommend to the Board that £2.4 million be set aside for a Structural Retirement Scheme so that compensation could be offered for early retirement in certain grades, making opportunities for promotion from below. He has shown himself always concerned with the interests of the individual, and determined to make sure that these are weighed against those of the organisation. He created a post to look after the welfare of the locally-engaged staff, and, in the same way, is watchful of the interests of the rather disadvantaged Home Service. The reforms he has set in motion and the care he shows for individuals has created an attitude of mind which should outlast his own reign.

Yet, if the whole of the credit for the reforms carried out after the Seebohm Report cannot be given to its authors, the clarity of their analysis and the wisdom of their recommendations did much to make these possible and, in the circumstances of the time, to raise morale. Not since the days of Paul Sinker has there been so strong a feeling of confidence in the possibilities of developing financial and managerial structures which can stand up to the strains continually imposed on the Council.

Morale had been raised by the manner in which the cuts had been presented. If an 18 per cent cut had been imposed originally, or by any other Government, one must suppose that insurrection would have broken out. Because of the reduction from an even more punishing level by the direct intervention of the Prime Minister herself, all levels of personnel felt they had achieved a victory and received a favour.

In fact the size of the cuts was very damaging. Probably all big bureaucratic institutions tend to grow a certain amount of fat and there was some agreement that a 10 or 12 per cent cut might have been sustained without irredeemable damage. Beyond that it was bound to be serious.

Three factors to some extent reduced the harm. The first was the concession that the savings were to be phased over a period of four years, so that they could be properly planned and put into force. The second, fortuitous and not in itself a matter for congratulations, was the savings made through the enforced withdrawal from three countries – Iran, Malta and later Argentina. The third was the increase in revenue from the direct teaching of English.

The new Director-General announced his intention not to be stampeded into decisions carrying long-term consequences and to establish clear priorities. There was general agreement that the overseas service should as far as possible be protected from damage, and initially only the representations in Mauritius and Costa Rica were voluntarily closed (the latter having been opened only the year before).

A Working Party had been set up to review the pattern of the United Kingdom network, bearing in mind the likely reduction of students and visitors as a result of cuts elsewhere. This network consisted of 25 offices (3 representations, 11 regional directorates and 11 area offices) and 28 local correspondents. It had developed in response to particular needs from the days of refugees and members of the allied forces, through the period when it was asked to provide a modicum of welfare services for all overseas students, to the present day, when it is concerned largely with the administration of students and visitors for whom the Council has a special responsibility. The Berrill Report had commented on the 'lavish scale' of the work done and, although the implied charge was rejected, it was recognised that the needs of the present-day student were catered for in many other ways. The Working Party proposed increased efforts to stimulate 'host' institutions (universities and so on) to take more responsibility for student support services, questioned the need for much of the representational work and made a number of suggestions to improve procedures in the network offices. As a result of its recommendations it was agreed to close all but thirteen of the twenty-five offices, leaving offices in Birmingham, Newcastle, Leeds, Manchester, Nottingham, Cambridge, Oxford, Bristol, Brighton, Edinburgh, Glasgow, Belfast and Cardiff, to be supported by Outposted Student Support Officers (a new post) working with the nearest parent office, mainly on accommodation and welfare matters.

It was agreed to close Tavistock House, where training courses in the use of radio and television for educational purposes had been provided. Finally, a decision was taken to close the Students' Centre at Portland Place in London. There was now no possibility of touching more than the fringe of the vast numbers of students coming to London every year, while the facilities for learning English before arrival and the welfare arrangements made by universities and other bodies made the work of less importance.

For the rest the savings were found from a cut in staff of $19\frac{1}{2}$ per cent over the four-year period, and, most serious of all, by ceasing to recruit, with all the predictable long-term results in the overweighting of certain grades at the expense of others that this would inevitably bring in its train.

Reporting in February 1983, after detailing the cuts described above, Sir John Burgh gave the figure for the reduction in London-appointed posts (personnel) as 427 and locally engaged as 97. 'Simultaneously we have redeployed £1.2m into operational activities.'[20]

Morale was kept fairly high all the time, due, in a greater degree than is probably realised, to the extreme devotion of the Chairman, the Director-General and many of their senior staff, not merely to the Council itself, but to the interests of all its personnel. Pride was taken in the efficiency with which the cuts were operated, and in the improved administration as the Seebohm recommendations were put into force. Satisfaction was felt again when, despite the Government's switch to cash planning in 1982–3, the terms of the 'Blaker Agreement' were nevertheless honoured. Cash planning meant that Government-financed bodies were no longer guaranteed an increase in public expenditure provision for future years, or a Supplementary Vote in the current year, if there was a rise in the cost of the services they provided. In some years this system can be of disadvantage to bodies like the British Council, much of whose costs depend, not on the United Kingdom level of inflation, but on exchange rates and the inflation in the countries in which they work. The agreement in the Blaker letter that the Council's grant should be 'at 1979 Survey Prices' protected it from the adverse results of the new system for the four year period over which the agreement ran.

In February 1983 the Foreign Secretary, Francis Pym, announced in the House of Commons that the Government had decided (apparently in an attempt to repair some of the damage done by previous cuts) to allow more money for scholarships for overseas students coming to Britain. This move resulted from the publication in June 1982 of a study by the Overseas Students Trust entitled *A Policy for Overseas Students* – a publication with which the Council had been closely associated, and to the idea of which the Government had, in May 1981, given cautious encouragement.[21] Forty-six million pounds, described as new money, was made available, partly to particular countries – Hong Kong, Malaysia and Cyprus – partly to ODA to enable them to make more Technical Co-operation and Training awards – and partly, for the first time ever, to the Foreign Office for scholarships of its own choice.[22] These scholarships, it was later decided, would be largely administered by the British Council.

All in all, then, by 1983 it seemed an appropriate time to ask for an increase in funds.

> We are asking for more money not from any sense of grievance, but from a conviction that investment in the Council is crucial to the national interest. For political and commercial reasons we must nurture our overseas connections. Fifty years' investment in the Council, which has produced a flexible, responsive and innovative instrument for cultural, educational and aid relations, cannot be properly exploited without an additional injection of funds.[23]

Money was required for education and training (in the current financial year £2.37 million was being spent on work which was predominantly a continuation of that formerly done by the Inter-University Council), for English language teaching (partly for 'pump-priming'), for the arts, for information technology, for staff training and for enlarged geographical coverage.

The moment, however, was not propitious. In June 1983 there was a General Election in which Mrs Thatcher's Government was returned with a much increased majority of seats in the House of Commons, and the post-election climate was immediately harsher. The previous Chancellor, Sir Geoffrey Howe, went to the Foreign Office and his place at the Exchquer was taken by Nigel Lawson, whose first act was to impose a new round of cuts.

On 25 July 1983, the Chairman of the British Council, Sir Charles Troughton, wrote two letters. One, which was addressed to all members of the Board, said that, speaking to him on the telephone, Sir Geoffrey Howe had said that he would greatly appreciate it if the Council could see its way to offering help to the FCO in the current round of cuts.

> I told him that I would consult the Director-General; John and I have agreed to act as set out in the attached letter. Difficult though this sacrifice will be it is manageable and in the circumstances seems to us to be the right thing to do.
>
> I think you know how concerned I have been about the Council and the cuts. But in the long term I hold the old-fashioned view that if one behaves well one will be rewarded.[24]

The attached letter referred to was addressed to Sir Geoffrey Howe and contained the following paragraphs.

> After you spoke to me this morning I went to see the Director-General and talked the matter over with him. Frankly, we are in a fix. We really have pared to the bone in the last four years — $18\frac{1}{2}$% cut in real terms! But we would like to help nevertheless because we understand the problem. So we offer you £$\frac{1}{2}$m for 1983/84. But this is on the understanding, which I hope you will agree, that this contribution would relate both to the ODA and FCO grant to the Council.
>
> There is one other point. You know of our minimum £7m needs for 1984/85. If the reduction in our 1983/84 grant, which we are now offering, were to be carried forward in 1984/85, we would feel hard done by.[25]

In reply, the Foreign Secretary wrote:

I am writing to confirm that in the revised cash limits to be announced shortly, the British Council Grant-in-Aid (Vote 4) will be reduced by £0.5 m ... The ODA will not be reducing their contribution to the Council's finances.

I can confirm that the decision to reduce all Central Government voted expenditure applies to 1983/84 only. The reduction will not be carried over into the next financial year, but you will appreciate that I can at this stage give no commitments on levels of funding from 1984/85.[26]

The fiftieth anniversary year, 1984, began with a tragedy. Kenneth Whitty, Assistant British Council Representative in Athens and Cultural Attaché, and Diana Economidou, one of the locally-engaged staff, were the victims of a particularly senseless act of violence. On 28 March Kenneth Whitty was driving home with Diana Economidou by his side when a young man stepped out of the traffic and flagged him down. He rolled down the window to speak to the man, who stuck a gun through the window and fired, killing Kenneth Whitty instantly and inflicting wounds on Diana Economidou from which she soon after died. There was no apparent motive for this act, unless it was because the car carried diplomatic plates.

The year also began uneasily in more mundane ways. In his letter to the Foreign Secretary of 25 July, Sir Charles Troughton had spoken of 'our minimum £7 million needs for 1983/84'. In a Newsletter of February 1984 the Director-General reported that the Council had still not received the assurances it needed to enable it to plan its 1984-5 activities at largely the same level as 1983-4. He said the Council was short of three elements and he gave an account of these as follows (arriving at a different total from that given in Sir Charles Troughton's letter, a circumstance not unusual in the financial statements of large organisations): £2.6 million in order to carry forward into 1984-5 the excess of home and overseas inflation granted in a Spring Supplementary Estimate in 1983-4; £1.4 million to cover the increased rent of 10 Spring Gardens following a ten-year review; and £2.1 million to cover the costs of overseas inflation in 1984-5 in excess of the Treasury Inflation Factor (estimate of rising costs).

Negotiations dragged on without a settlement so late into the year that the Chairman, with the support of the Foreign Secretary, was forced to appeal, as in 1979, direct to the Prime Minister. In a Newsletter dated 14 May, the Director-General reported that, as a result,

Mrs Thatcher had directed that £4.0 million must be found for the
Council, to cover the £2.6 million carry forward and the rent of
Spring Gardens.

Sir John Burgh said:

The remaining £2.1 million overseas inflation costs in 1984/85 may
be found when the Council is in a position to substantiate the figures,
although this point is still unclear. We continue to be profoundly
grateful for the outstanding ability of the Chairman to carry the
Council's case with conviction to the highest levels of Government
and for the personal belief of the Prime Minister in the value of the
Council.

He went on to say, however, that a satisfactory permanent arrangement had nevertheless not been agreed by the Treasury. Overseas
inflation continued to rise at 8–9 per cent above the Government's
Factors for home inflation, so that, without a permanent agreement the
Council had to go through protracted and difficult negotiations year by
year. Pay rises and other bills were also running above Government
Inflation Factors, and, since all public bodies are expected to fund such
costs from their cash limits, the Council would in real terms be worse
off in 1984–5 than in 1983–4, the last of the four years of the 18½ per
cent cut.

Sir John said:

Every large organisation can continue to increase its efficiency and
to make some savings without damage to the body as a whole. But
for the Council it is now barely possible, after the heavy cuts of the
last four years, to respond to the new opportunities which are arising
all the time for extending British influence overseas. That is why I
continue to fight for additional funds.

There we leave the British Council in its fiftieth anniversary year. In
all its history there have not been more than a dozen years or so when
it had any more explicit assurance as to the future funding of its activities. Yet it has managed through the devotion and dedication of its
staff, through the demand for its services, above all by the virtue of its
purposes, not merely to survive but to thrive. In the past year British
visitors who have praised the Council's work were headed by Her
Majesty the Queen and included the Prime Minister, Mrs Thatcher;

and it has been more than ever in demand by British Ambassadors and by the representatives of Foreign Governments. The Council's fortunes are tied to those of the British nation, but one may feel some confidence that it will continue to receive the comparatively small funds necessary to exploit fifty years' investment of financial capital and human endeavour.

PART THREE
EPILOGUE

23

A Personal Account of Visits to British Council Offices

No one who has read as far as this can fail to have noticed that, however critical the spirit in which inquirers into the overseas work of the British Council set out, they always return captivated. Even in the early days in the war, when the Council had to recruit staff largely from those left over from the army, and the rate of growth had been out of proportion to the resources available to service it, observers returning from tours abroad always expressed surprise at the success achieved by the overseas offices.

After the war, in one of the most hostile papers ever written about the Council, Montagu-Pollock said that his criticisms did not apply with equal force to the staff overseas. 'The impression gained ... was that it was remarkable how efficiently the Council was performing in the field considering how thin was the guidance from home.' Following this, Lord Drogheda was reported from all over the world as 'being greatly impressed by the work being done by the Council'. From Egypt, the Representative wrote: 'There was very little left for me to do, as he had been considerably impressed by the centres he had already visited, and I could do no more than confirm this good impression. He seemed to be more interested in extension than in survival.'

Dr Hill, who conducted the next inquiry, said this:

At the start of the job I knew no more about the British Council than I had learnt from the Press, and that was more derisory than informative. Before I left the job, I had come to regard the work of the British Council as unquestionably the most effective single thing which our country was doing to present itself overseas.

Following Dr Hill, Dennis Vosper conducted a review of the Overseas Information Services and, although this report has not been published, it is known that he formed a very favourable view of the activities of the British Council overseas. Sir Harold Beeley recommended that the Council should be enabled to expand some of its work and to restore some which had been cut, and that it should receive an increase in the grant of £325,000 to enable it to do so. Sir Val Duncan recommended a shift towards Western Europe and that more of educational aid should be allotted to the British Council. Even the Berrill Team said: 'We are conscious that the Council has established itself in the national life and that it is highly regarded in many quarters overseas'; and finally, in conversation, Lord Seebohm said: 'In the end I fell a little in love with it.'

When I started out to visit Council offices in countries which had been chosen because, in combination, the patterns of work illustrated almost all of its many and varied activities, I knew that, since I was sent not to inquire but to describe, I should have in the end to make a shot at explaining the reasons for the almost complete conversion of my numerous and often sceptical predecessors. Before I attempt to do this, however, I must give some account of all I saw on these journeys.

Originally it was not the intention that I should see much of the Council's work in Europe, where it pursues its traditional roles of English language teaching and cultural exchanges. However, for one reason or another, by being on holiday in the country, or by going to see a special exhibition, I managed to visit Council offices in Milan, Paris, Madrid, Lisbon and Athens before I set out to the farther parts of the world. Later I went to Venice for the Biennale and to Frankfurt for the Book Fair.

In northern Europe the teaching of English is usually undertaken through the ordinary academic processes and British Council work requires subsidy. In Milan and the southern capitals of Lisbon, Madrid and Athens where I first visited, the atmosphere in the Institutes is electric. I have nowhere been present on enrolment day or seen the students queueing for half a mile down the road, but in Milan those already enrolled were being tested so as to be suitably placed when they arrived the following week. As they sat sucking their pens in search of a word, there was no doubt of their commitment to the task.

We travelled — my husband and I — from Florence via Milan to Genoa where we were staying, and in consequence saw our first British Council Institute in Milan, immediately after visiting the famous one in Florence. The experience was, as indeed is that of leaving Florence and entering Milan, comparable to leaving one century and entering another. The offices at Milan had none of the atmosphere or elegance of the Palazzo Lanfredini, and the literature library, at the time being weeded out by a new young librarian, seemed rather short on quality in that middle area so redolent in Florence of the taste of the erstwhile British community — the area, that is, between Agatha Christie (absolutely necessary to the student of English all over the world) and the classics. Yet Milan is a centre of modern design and Meyric Hughes, then British Council Regional Representative, is one of the most talented and experienced of the Council's Art Officers and is now running the Visiting Arts Unit. He met us at the station and we ate toasted sandwiches at a bar while he talked about modern music and painters. I already knew enough of the work and staffing of the British Council to know that he is at the present day a comparatively rare bird.

The Institute is not, I believe, more lavishly equipped than many other Institutes, but we saw for the first time the language laboratories where students use tapes to listen to and then practise speech, and the closed circuit system which allows a student teacher to see himself (or herself) in action and learn from mistakes.

In Lisbon, Madrid and Athens, our next ports of call, there is even now a growing demand for English teaching. This may be direct to the student, to teachers in training or for special purposes — for Government servants, banks, scientific institutions or for industrial purposes. For all these courses charges are made, in some cases the full economic price, in others, as for the Government, on a subsidised basis. A second large source of revenue is the conduct by the British Council of the Cambridge University examinations — for a first certificate in English and a certificate in Proficiency. Here once more there seems to be no end of the growth in demand. In Athens in 1980 8,000 people took the Cambridge examinations; by 1984 this figure had risen to 30,000. The police still turn out on Kolnaki Square on the day the students enrol for English teaching courses, and nowadays they do so for the Cambridge examinations as well.

Because of the surpluses earned by English language teaching, the Council is able to contribute generously to the other aspects of cultural exchange. In Greece, Spain, Portugal and Italy extra scholarships can be offered and there is increased academic exchange. As one Council officer put it: 'We can pay the fares, we can pay subsistence, we can give more bursaries.' In the same way the Council can afford to supplement the initial contribution of the host country towards the enormous costs — perhaps to a Festival — of the larger orchestras, opera or theatre companies.

The most dramatic example of the results of a large English teaching operation is in Spain. The annual revenue (which, it may be remembered, was expected in Sir John Llewellyn's day to reach £100,000) is today in the order of £3 million. A great deal of this is absorbed by costs but there is a surplus which is employed to increase the cultural programme. So keen is the desire for British Council scholarships that the Spanish Government has been offering to support them 'one for one'. In 1984 they have asked for 100 scholarships and have offered to pay two-thirds of the cost if the British Council will provide the rest. There is a rule that the Savings Banks must put 3 per cent of their profits into the cultural life of the country and these Banks are also anxious to pay for scholarships on a basis of one for one. The problem for the Council is that the demand is so big they have not the resources to match the 'one for one'.

In Lisbon I had the luck to catch the Henry Moore Exhibition – jointly arranged by the British Council and the Gulbenkian Foundation and previously shown in Madrid. This was the most comprehensive exhibition of the world's most famous sculptor ever shown. All his art forms were included but the particular feature of the Lisbon exhibition was that, as one walked round the galleries of the Gulbenkian building, looking at the drawings and smaller figures, the larger sculptures could be seen in the gardens through the windows. Thus, the extent of Moore's work and the final expression of it could be seen as one whole.

In the following year I went to Venice to the Biennale, the scene of Moore's first international triumph. It was a lucky year to have chosen because once more an English artist, Barry Flanagan, stood alone. In the charming British Pavilion – built on the hill formed from the bricks of the fallen Campanile and originally the tea rooms of the Gardens – his elegant and witty anthropomorphic bronze hares were arranged to come into view, boxing and dancing and performing acrobatic feats, as the visitor entered the gallery.*

Finally in the autumn of that year I went to Frankfurt to see the Book

---

* Once again on 12 June 1984 the Art Critic of *The Times* wrote:

It is pleasing to relate that the triumph of the Biennale has been the British Pavilion, devoted entirely to Howard Hodgkin: the work itself looked even stronger than one might expect, it is immaculately hung, and the British Council's presentation, documentation and even publicity cannot be faulted. It may sound lukewarm to say that this is a triumph, above all, of sheer professionalism, but, in a context of hopeless amateurishness and sheer incompetence, one can hardly think of higher praise.

Fair. The British Council has a long experience of Book Fairs and there is no doubt of the high reputation of its stand at Frankfurt where it has exhibited since 1950. Because it is the only one which shows an impartially chosen selection from all British publishers, it is valued as much by the publishers themselves as by the buyers, who, having found a book they want, pass on to the publisher's stand to buy it.

Egypt has a particular significance in the history of the British Council because it was from there that in 1934 Sir Percy Loraine wrote a memorandum (quoted earlier) of primary importance in pressing the case for cultural relations; and, secondly, because the Council's first overseas representation opened in Cairo in 1938.

After 1956 nothing remained of the pre-Suez network of Institutes and supported schools. All British property was sequestrated and an entirely fresh start had to be made. The Egyptian authorities were extremely suspicious, not merely of the British generally, but of the former British Council Institutes, which were regarded as sources of propaganda and anti-Government feeling. The Government would not deal with the Council except through the diplomatic mission, and the Council Representative had to be attached to the Embassy as Cultural Attaché.

No teaching of English was possible at first, but the Egyptians were immediately anxious for information services. Council work was gradually built up, at first through advisory visits from British specialists and through co-operation in the training of teachers of English. In 1963 a library was opened in the ballroom of the British Embassy and Council-appointed teachers were accepted at the former Victoria College and at the English School, Heliopolis. Gradually other appointments were allowed – a permanent ELT adviser to the Ministry of Education in 1965, a lecturer in English to Ain Shams University, Cairo. Then summer schools for English teaching were run at Alexandria, the library premises were developed for exhibitions, and, above all, contacts were increased between Egyptian medical schools and the Royal College of Surgeons. A Cultural Agreement was signed in 1965.

In 1967 at the time of the Five Days War the British were once more forced to withdraw, and British property was sequestrated. Hassan Khalifa, at that time Assistant Librarian, gave me this account:

I was left in the Library alone and I remained there just trying to retrieve books that were on circulation at the time to minimise the loss – but strictly speaking we were not officially told to close the Library. So in December 1967 the talks started and on the 17th diplomatic relations between Cairo and London were restored. The Ambassador then was Sir Harold Beeley ... During that time the gate of the Library was opened just for people to return their books and to ask ... when will you open? And the answer will be 'Shortly'. Or as they say in Arabic, In Sh'Allah. If God wills. I started opening the gate bit by bit and I asked the Ambassador to open the Library to the public. He did not object and he said, 'Could you do it?' and I said, 'Yes. Certainly.' ... We had a lot of people coming in. We used to look at the number of people that we received every day. It was of course as I say, opening the gate every day making it a bit wider – opening it wider.

From these beginnings the Council developed the organisation of to-day. It was at no time officially recognised under the Nasser regime and operated from the British Embassy as its Cultural Section until after Egypt's change of direction from East to West, when President Sadat dismissed the Russian Military Mission in 1972. Then, under an Agreement on Technical Co-operation with Britain, the Council was designated a major agent in aid administration, and in 1973 moved out of the Embassy to a waterside villa in a large garden overlooking the Nile at Agowzain. It now operates both in its own name and as the Cultural Section of the Embassy, the Representative holding the post of Cultural Attaché with the rank of Counsellor.

Nowhere better illustrates the development of Council work since its early days. In the first place 80 per cent of its grant-in-aid now comes from ODA, only 20 per cent from the FCO, while the two together are not much more than two-thirds of its total budget, the rest being revenue from its own undertakings or agency work on behalf of ODA and UN. Then, although its aim remains to promote friendship with Britain, the means by which this is to be achieved have significantly altered. When I was there these were defined as to make a contribution to Egypt's technical, vocational and management resources; to assist the development of applied scientific research and the teaching of science; to promote the use of the English language; to assist the library development. It was stated that 'reflecting the Representation's priorities, the arts profile in Egypt is a low one'.

Egypt, like many other developing countries, has a small educated and rich upper class, but considerable over-population, severe unemployment and much overcrowding in schools. The Council is able to earn revenue from the direct teaching of English, which is carried out on a large scale in Cairo and Alexandria (16,700 students registered for courses in 1982-3) while Egypt has the largest Council Library in the Middle East (membership 4,700; issues 44,000 books annually). In the garden of the Council premises in Cairo, a new building houses a unique experiment in the direct teaching of science. When I was there in 1982 this was still new and showing rather disappointing results. I am told that nowadays there is an overwhelming demand for its service.

The Council's main activities, however, follow directly from its expressed aims and are in the fields of technical and vocational education and training in management. In particular, it has been very successful in Egypt in securing contracts for Paid Educational Services, that is for work paid for not by the British but sometimes by the Egyptian Government, more often by the World Bank. There has been no tremendous scheme of the kind of the King Abdul Aziz University in Saudi Arabia, but PES contracts ranged from staff training for the Faculty of Agriculture at Cairo University and courses in Agricultural Management for the World Bank Agricultural Development Project, to training and consultancies for the mining trade, and for the Egyptian Electrical Authority with British Electricity International as the subcontractor.

It is the range and extent of educational and training schemes that surprises the visitor. By the spring of 1982 I was accustomed to the links with universities, teaching of English for Special Purposes, bursaries, visits and study tours, and to the training of teachers and administration of examinations. In Cairo I personally met consultants from various sectors of British higher and further education who were holding courses in carpentry and metal work, training medical students in the use of medical equipment, and, in one case, advising the agricultural advisory service on how to advise. Other things being managed by the British Council included programmes for control of cotton pests; research into rodent control and its aspects for public health; and support for Hydraulic and Sediment Research studies of the Nile.

Despite a certain amount of pirating, there is a very good market for British books in Egypt, estimated at £4 million a year, but until the educational training and scientific programmes were well established a fairly low priority was given to the Arts. Lately, extra staff have been appointed and in the last year or so visits from British musical groups, and from drama and ballet companies, have been organised in conjunction with the Ministry of Culture.

In April 1982 we visited China. A British Council Representation had been re-established there in 1979. A few Chinese students had been sent to Britain in 1972, and in 1975 the Chinese Government asked for two senior lecturers to run courses over a full year in Peking and Shanghai. These were very successful and were followed by further courses in 1976 and 1977. Great impetus was given to the establishment of a more permanent training programme in the spring of 1978 by the visit to China of the British Secretary of State for Education and Science, Shirley Williams. By now the need for rapid absorption of Western technology had decided the Chinese Government to send thousands of students abroad and Mrs Williams was told they wished to send a thousand or so to Britain every year and would pay the costs. In return, Shirley Williams proposed a British English Language Teaching Institute in Peking.

The entry of Chinese students into Britain ran into immediate difficulties because the Chinese had not understood that 'costs' included fees. After the first batch they ceased to send any undergraduates to Britain and concentrated instead on postgraduates and attachments for visiting scholars. Following the introduction of the overseas student fee policy, fewer students came to Britain – under 500 in 1984 compared with at least 8,000 to the USA, 700 to France and about 1,000 each to West Germany and Japan. Until recently the British Council could allocate only twenty-five scholarships annually, although in the autumn of 1983 schemes were introduced by ODA and FCO to provide fees for about 260 Chinese scholars.

The Council entry into Peking was more successful. By what the first Representative, Keith Hunter, calls the 'Robin Hood' principle – that is by appropriating funds from other sources – the Council was able to finance and staff a Cultural Section in the British Embassy (no non-diplomatic presence being allowed). By the time we arrived there in 1982, in addition to the Representative there were his Assistant, Viva Hart, and an extremely able English Language Officer, Alan Maley. All these three and the Representative's wife, Ann, spoke Chinese fluently.

There is a story told to visitors to China that, when the Chinese Government broke with Russia, everyone teaching Russian was told to stop doing so and teach English. Whether true or not, this story illustrates the kind of situation the Council team found on their arrival.

The study of English, by now the first foreign language, appeared also to be an all-absorbing pastime for those of the younger generation with any aspiration to self-advancement. The United States is the dominant influence but there is some affection and admiration for Britain, and among the older people a preference for our language and literature.

The Council has achieved quite a lot with very little. A programme of three eight-week high-level teacher training courses every year has helped and influenced hundreds of Chinese tertiary level teachers; and since 1980 the Council has been recruiting contract British teachers. Today there are thirty of these working in key institutions in Peking, Nanjing, Shanghai, Chengdu, Xi'an, Hangzhou, Wuhan and Guangzhou. Few survive more than two years because they are cut off from Chinese society. They are housed separately, eat separately and are given privileges denied to their Chinese colleagues, an isolated existence which becomes very wearing. In 1982 the British Council achieved a coup. Alan Maley had, in his previous post in France, recruited Katherine Flower to present an English Language Programme called 'Follow Me' on French television. By an arrangement negotiated by the British Council, Katherine Flower was now presented in 'Follow Me' on China Central Television. Overnight she became the best known and best liked foreigner in China, with an audience conservatively estimated at 20 million. Shortly after, Andrea Rose of the Fine Arts Department was invited to do a forty-minute programme on the British Water Colour Exhibition, the effect of which was therefore spread throughout China. Later the English Language Officer Alan Maley was interviewed at length on television, the first time a foreign diplomat had been given such exposure.

The English Language Teaching Resource Centre, housed in the Council offices, gives a service to anyone in China who applies for help, and an English Language Teaching Newsletter goes out to 1,000 teachers three times a year. There have been book presentations, including a major donation to the Ministry of Education of 7,500 English dictionaries, and in 1982 more than £10,000 was spent on building up a collection of English literature.

The large Arts programme is made easy because so many British artistes are anxious to go to China. It is expensive to send theatrical performances there because, although the Chinese pay all expenses in China, they pay no fees. The British Council has therefore paid the fees for television performances, ensuring that the British theatre and ballet companies performing in the main centres are also seen by ten to twenty million people throughout China. A sustained follow-up has been arranged with some of the visiting British, who have returned to work with the Chinese — two examples are Council-sponsored visits by a choreographer and a choreologist after a tour by the Festival Ballet; and the return of Toby Robertson, who directed the Old Vic *Hamlet*, with a designer and lighting expert to direct the Peking People's Art Theatre in a Chinese production of *Measure For Measure*.

Our visit to China was timed to coincide with a performance in Peking by the John Alldis Choir and with the great exhibition of British Water Colours. One or two incidents we witnessed seem worth recording. We went to the first John Alldis concert which was received with rapt attention but not much demonstration until at the end the choir sang a Chinese song, a courtesy very much appreciated. The following morning in a small hall not far from our hotel, the Peking choir sang to the English one. When they finished their concert, the British choir went up and joined them, and together the two sang the Chinese song the John Alldis choir had sung the night before. The pleasure of the Chinese was very touching. The sexes were segregated and one could see them, particularly the women, talking happily and touching their British colleagues. We made friends with one of our own singers, Hugh Davies, and he told me that in the Chinese choir there were at least five voices which would be regarded as of international standard in the West. When I saw him later in England I asked him if the choir in Shanghai had sung as well. He replied: 'Even better', and told this rather sad story. One of the Chinese baritones had asked him if he would take the opportunity of his visit to give him some help and advice about his singing. Hugh had replied: 'But if I live to be a hundred, I'll never sing as well as you do,' and the Chinese turned away in disappointment, believing the opportunity lost for the sake of artificial politeness. John Alldis later returned to China to coach the Peking choir.

We visited the Exhibition of British Water Colours — an exhibition covering two hundred years of British drawing and water colour painting being 'introduced to a country where these arts have been established for well over a thousand years', but, nevertheless, covering an extraordinary range of styles and interests. This exhibition was a great success and attracted large numbers. On the day of our visit my husband and the British Council Representative walked on with the Director of the Gallery in the good old chauvinist way and I lagged behind. Because of the restrictions placed on contacts with foreigners it was perhaps not surprising that no one spoke to the three men in front. I, more un-expectedly, was immediately surrounded by groups of young people wishing to be told which of the modern painters they should be sure to see.

In the spring of 1982 the British Council work was nowhere more interesting and exciting than in Hong Kong, and no part of British Council history is more curious. First established in 1947, by the early 1970s the Council had two offices (one in Hong Kong and one at Star House in Kowloon), but it was not very active and its future was un-certain. In 1972 the staff of the Hong Kong office was much reduced and when Kenneth Westcott arrived as Representative in 1974, his brief was to consider closing the Hong Kong office altogether. Its role was not clear and it often duplicated the work of the Urban Council. Westcott decided to close the office but he received funds from London to conduct a survey, in conjunction with the representatives of various Hong Kong Government Departments, the two Universities and the Polytechnic, on the Use of English in Hong Kong. This showed such a huge demand for English classes that, with the small amount of money he had left from the survey and without waiting for approval from London, Westcott started some experimental classes.

In four rooms rented from a secondary school in the evenings and with the help of three part-time teachers, he enrolled in the first term 200 students, a number which in the following terms jumped to 900. More classrooms had to be rented and it was decided to convert the Hall and part of the Library at Star House into six classrooms and to start day-time courses. By 1977, when the lease of Star House ran out, the number of students had reached 3,500. Three floors were then taken in the Easey Commercial Building in Wanchai, Hong Kong, two floors being converted into classrooms, and one into offices.

In November Peter Cavaye succeeded Kenneth Westcott as Repre-sentative and the first four floors of Easey Commercial Building were taken and converted into a hall, offices, a library and more classrooms. In 1978 the Kowloon office was closed down altogether and the Direct Teaching of English operation was concentrated on Hong Kong Island. By the summer of 1978, 9,700 students were attending classes.

During this time Shirley Williams paid her historic visit to China, and the British Council, not yet able to persuade either the FCO or ODA to increase its budget, was looking round for money to enable it to open there. When the Representative in China spoke of the 'Robin

Hood principle' he meant that, the Hong Kong office having by now covered the whole of its budget from revenue, this budget was borrowed as a 'bridging operation', and together with a small contribution from ODA, was used to open up in China.

When we visited Hong Kong in 1982 student numbers had reached 11,500–12,000 and the teaching staff was about 170. There, as in Spain, one immediately asks the question: if the teaching of English is so highly profitable, why (as is usually claimed) are the British Council classes more desirable than those of commercial schools? The first answer is that, although the British Council charges high fees, it maintains a consistently high standard all over the world. Thus when Hong Kong became the first overseas centre to be approved for the Royal Society of Arts Preparatory Course, this course was made compulsory for all new teachers, while full-time contract teachers had to take the RSA course in Further Education. This is reinforced by compulsory training weeks for all 120 teachers.

The second reason is because of the facilities provided by the libraries. When the library was first opened in Easey Commercial Building 3,000 books of fiction and 3,000 of literature were weeded out and given to secondary schools and to the Chinese University, and, when Oliver Siddle arrived as Representative in 1980, he decided not to duplicate the resources offered by other libraries in Hong Kong but to make a collection which would give information on Britain and have large technology and reference sections.

One's first impression on entering the Hong Kong offices is one of wealth. There is a fine library and an impressive array of modern electronic devices to aid teaching. As it happened, in the only class I visited, there were no materials except illustrated advertisements cut from colour magazines. This class was for young people being trained to teach in primary schools and part of the training was in making their own materials. The chief impression I got was of the charm and brightness of the Hong Kong Chinese. After a while they began an exercise in which one teacher taught, while the others acted as her pupils. An attractive and very confident young lady acted teacher and insisted that I should join the class. The exercise was a simple one for beginners.

'So-and-so, this is a pen. Is it your pen?'
'No, it is not mine.'
'Lady Donaldson, is it your pen?'
'No, it is not mine.'

'So-and-so, is it your pen?'

'Yes, it is mine.'

Presently someone came to fetch me to keep another appointment and the whole class groaned.

'Aren't you going to stay for … ?' – I did not catch what, but obviously some very delightful exercise.

As I went down the aisle between the rows of students, the girl who acted teacher ran after me with a plastic bag in her hand.

'Lady Donaldson', she called. 'You've left your bag behind.'

I turned and looked at it. 'No, it is not mine,' I said automatically.

'Oh! Lady *Donaldson*', the class cried out in unison.

In Hong Kong the Council also runs courses for secondary school teachers of English, and both courses are paid for in full by the Hong Kong Government.

The Arts programme is rather different from that in many places because again so much is paid for by the Government. The City Hall contains a concert hall, a theatre and small recital hall, and there is support for museums and libraries. Every year there is a Festival financed entirely by the Government and by private sources at which leading British companies – the Old Vic, the London Festival Ballet, the Hallé Orchestra – have appeared without any direct involvement by the British Council. The Council seeks to support the Arts programme indirectly by exchange of experts and administrators, through training courses, scholarships and art consultancies. One of the most interesting things it has been responsible for is the Chung Ying Theatre Company. This was begun by Peter Day, a locally-appointed officer with a brief to keep a proper balance between the Council's English teaching operation and the equally important presentation of the arts; and to help create a new, professional theatre company which, beginning as a British project, would eventually leave the Council to become part of the Hong Kong's own theatrical development.

The Council could not alone guarantee the substantial subsidy needed but set out to find partners in the venture. British Airways agreed to help with return passages for actors, director, designer and musical director; the Gulbenkian Foundation covered the cost of the Artistic Director's salary; the Hong Kong and Shanghai Bank made a large contribution, and the Urban Council agreed to present the new company in two productions at the City Hall at fees which would help subsidise the work in schools and the touring and teaching.

The first production, which toured schools, was a 'pruned' version of *The Merchant of Venice* played by five actors, who invited questions at the end of each performance. That production and the workshops which followed it proved such an immediate success that it was obvious that Chung Ying had hit on a winning formula. Word spread from school to school and produced a great demand. Two public perform-ances were then given in the City Hall Theatre — an adaptation of *The Beggar's Opera* and a play for children translated from the German. Two more seasons were organised by the British Council, during which *Romeo and Juliet* was presented as a school production, while public performances included the world première of Orwell's *Animal Farm*, which also toured Malaysia. By the time we reached Hong Kong in April 1982 the Chung Ying Theatre Company had become indepen-dent of the British Council and was subsidised by the Hong Kong Government. Peter Day went with the company and a British director, Colin George joined as Artistic Director. We visited a rehearsal of *Macbeth* played with the maximum attention to the need to be understood.

A venture probably unique to Hong Kong in British Council experi-ence is in Bio-engineering. Bio-engineering has been defined as engineering participation at clinical level in reconstructive surgery and rehabilitation of the disabled, and is, as I understand it, the application of the principles of engineering to the practice of medicine. The work covers not merely such things as the improvement and design of arti-ficial limbs and braces but also muscle transplants and gait analysis in physically impaired children. Oliver Siddle had seen some of this work in Peru and when six clinically significant problem areas were isolated he arranged the visits of six specialists from Britain. Programmes of work on all these problems are now established, and long-term links have been made with the Bio-engineering Unit at Strathclyde Univer-sity in Glasgow and with the Bio-mechanics laboratory at the Royal Free Hospital in London. There seems no doubt that the British Council sponsorship of these projects has been an influence in the development of permanent research centres in Hong Kong.

At Hong Kong airport, where we were both waiting to fly back to England, I met one of the visiting engineers. 'I think the British Council is wonderful', he said. 'I used to think it was just art and I don't go much for that. But now I know what it does, I think it's wonderful.'

So it takes all sorts to make a world.

Thus Hong Kong in the spring of 1982. Following Margaret

Thatcher's visit to China later in the year and the intensifying speculation about its future, depression set in and it became increasingly difficult to cover costs. In 1984 the British Council in Hong Kong, as in
most other countries, requires subsidy from London.

The staff of the British Council are much addicted to using words in
esoteric ways which they then sometimes use to cover more than
one meaning. The uninitiated often have great difficulty in following
what they say, although once the various meanings of a word are
explained, it is usually possible to understand its use in any given situation. In the context of the aid countries, it is necessary for the reader to
have some idea of the uses of the verb 'to administer' in Council terms
and I once asked a member of the staff to define it. She replied that it
could mean anything 'from a mere travel agent trotting out to meet
somebody at the airport' to 'a visit to a Ministry or Institution to talk
to the Director to find out what he saw as the next step in some programme and then reporting back to ODA in London'; saying, for
instance, 'Perhaps a workshop on safety is required'. London, she went
on, might say: 'All right we will recruit you two people on safety', or
they might not be in a position to judge and might recruit a consultant
to see whether this workshop was necessary. ODA would recruit this
person but the British Council would make all the arrangements. After
the consultant had reported, it would be the job of the Council to consult the Minister or Director on the country concerned as to whether
the proposal could be put to the State Government or Government.

She added: 'This is why the man in the field often thinks that the
project is a British Council one, although it is financed by ODA, because the only person he meets is a British Council officer' – a circumstance which sometimes ruffles the peace between the British Council
and the ODA, although not, as far as I could see, among the people
actually doing the work, only among the higher echelons in London.

As far as the activities of the British Council in one place can be exactly
compared with those in any other, Kenya can be used to illustrate the
work in the newly independent African countries; although because of
its long period of comparative stability and its friendship to Britain, it
is particularly favoured.

In these countries the British Council usually has three major roles.
The first is to carry out its own programme of cultural exchange – to
establish a centre and libraries, to administer its own programme of
scholarships and so on. This will usually be a small part of the whole.

The second is to act as Education Adviser on the spot to HM Mission. The third and most important is to act as the agent of ODA in its training programmes, in which role it spends (in Council terms) large sums. At the time I visited Kenya in the autumn of 1982, ODA contributed 90 per cent of the total budget and sent between 400–500 Kenyans to Britain on training programmes every year. In addition to administering recognised ODA projects, the British Council may find and seek approval for promoting others. Consequently, although there is a major effort in the field of conventional education, one learns not to be surprised at anything which comes under the heading of a training programme.

In Kenya the British Council is not involved in any direct teaching but it administers a series of educational seminars for ODA, courses for teachers and so on and it is largely involved in training Kenyans to replace British academics and other specialists in the Kenyan educational system. In addition to this there are six Key English Language Training (KELT) officers working in Kenyan educational institutions and the Ministry of Education. These are recruited and administered by the British Council but financed by ODA. The standard of English is falling and it is their task to try to raise it.

There are libraries in Nairobi, Kisuma and Mombasa and there is a programme of book presentations paid for by ODA. In Kenya I witnessed Sir John Burgh, the Director-General, present the Vice-Chancellor of Nairobi University with a cheque for £40,000 for books.

In 1978 President Moi launched a campaign to make every adult Kenyan literate in five years and, apart from a serious shortage of teachers for this grandiose plan, there was very great difficulty in producing teaching materials. The British Council was asked to help and in 1980 they brought Rachel Jenkins to Kenya as a British Council Specialist Consultant to give advice. Then, using some of her recommendations, the Assistant Representative, who was expert in this field, and the Adult Education Adviser in London devised a programme for training people in methods of writing, illustrating and producing their own teaching materials. As an example, when we visited Nyeri we were shown a primitive little hand-made duplicator on which the teacher produced copies by the old-fashioned method of using gelatine.

An illustrative example of the difficulties created by a combination of British Council knowledge of the programmes on the ground and ODA responsibility for financing them concerns the trouble the Kenyans found in inspecting small projects of the adult literacy programme dotted about in rural areas all over the country since they could not afford the cost or the maintenance of Land Rovers. The Council suggested that they might be presented with some motor cycles. Two hundred motor cycles were then presented by ODA, but, because the suggestion came from the Council in the first place, the Kenyans often speak of them as British Council motor cycles.

It is often difficult for a British Council officer trying to explain his work to the visitor to find anything that he can actually show. One cannot, for instance, inspect the academic links, and, although it is sometimes amusing to sit in on an English language class, one cannot in a short time make any judgment on its quality. On our first day in Nairobi we were able to inspect a training project with both much visual interest and historic links with the past. The opening up of Kenya was a direct result of the building of the railways in the late nineteenth century when, although at that time a swampy area, Nairobi was chosen for the foundations of a permanent settlement for the workshops, owing to the engineering difficulties of extending the project into the Rift Valley. Today in Nairobi there is a Railway Museum where some of the early steam engines still stand and the history of the development is recorded in photographs, maps and so on. We visited this and the up-to-date railway workshops and Training School.

The British Council/ODA have been involved in railways' training for many years, latterly under the Kenya Technical Co-operation and Training programme, which sponsors trainees to Britain in such subjects as engineering, systems analysis, finance, and personnel and industrial relations. In 1979 the British Council gave £1,500 of books to the Railway Training School under the ODA book presentation programme.

While in Nairobi we also visited the Agricultural Information Centre, a British Aid project designed to provide a centre for the production of information on seeds, crops and fertilisers, and on agricultural techniques. Here material, mainly pamphlets, is written, films and slides are made, and regular programmes are put out on the Voice of Kenya (radio programme). This work is for the benefit both of the farmers themselves and the advisory services. The British Council regularly sends staff to Britain for training. We also visited the Veterinary Section of an Agricultural Research Institute, where they were operating a scheme for training newly recruited research workers. These work for six months in Kenya, then for eighteen months or more in Britain and finally return to Kenya for a further six months before taking their degree.

In Mombasa we visited Bandari College (Kenya Ports Authority) where, assisted by ODA and the British Council, the University of Wales has collaborated in a series of port management seminars; the Government Training Institute; the Matuga Development Centre where the Council had organised an exhibition of materials designed for the Adult Literacy Programme; and the Mombasa Polytechnic which had recently received a visit from a British Council specialist consultant to advise on library development and books (£23,500 worth by 1982) under the ODA book presentation programme.

We spent under three weeks in India, visiting Bombay, Madras, Calcutta and Delhi. Consequently, what follows is impressionistic in the extreme and intended only to give some idea of the scope of the Council's work.

India is remarkable in that millions of people are poorer than almost anywhere else in the world, yet sections of the population are highly developed, very articulate and, in the fields of education and research, the equal of their colleagues in the western world. There is an advanced, if not well distributed, educational system and India has developed its own English teaching and training. There are many links through which she has access to new British teaching methods but no great scope for the Council in its traditional roles. Here, what is required is collaboration in research and training to build up Indian industry, technology, medicine and agriculture.

Britain's aid to India is far greater than to any other country. In the four years between 1976–7 and 1980–1 it amounted to £600 million, and, in addition, British funds also reach India through contributions to the World Bank, the United Nations and the European Community. The main source of finance is therefore ODA, and the Council operates as their agent in the administration of the programme of Technical Co-operation with the Government of India. This has a budget of £8 or £9 million – something less than 10 per cent of the total aid programme – and concentrates on training, science, technology, agriculture, management and rural development. In practice, the Council may do no more than bring out a specialist consultant; or, at a higher level, it may initiate some proposal for a small project and, if this is agreed, be responsible for the equipment and the handling of the Indian end. In a large programme of capital equipment it takes part only in the training.

One of the best examples of the very big project is in the coal industry. ODA provides the capital equipment for coal mining on a vast scale – £13 million every year. At Moonidih Mine in Bihar a special training school has a mock face where everyone, from a technician who needs practice to senior managers and safety officers, is trained. The British Council is responsible for all aspects of this training school – 'administering' 130 people who come to Britain every year for training, and the twenty or so consultants who go to India, for whom it explains the job, arranges the logistics and co-ordinates the work with the others concerned. It is not the job of the Council to recruit these consultants; this is done by British Mining Consultants, an overseas arm of the British Coal Board.

I did not see this coal mine but I went to Anna University in Madras, where Professor Rushton from Birmingham University, originally brought out by the Council, advises on water engineering; visited a school for spastic children; learned of research into leprosy, malaria and viral hepatitis; and saw experiments promoting the use of fertilisers. One of the most interesting visits was to India's famous botanist, Professor Sharma, who is doing research into identifying the quality in legumes which produces nitrogen, and attempting to breed this quality into wheat.

In conversation, one of the British Council Science Officers said:

India is a country where they very clearly know what they want from the UK. You very rarely have actually to tell people we have this or that, do you want it? They know what they want ... They have great reservoirs of skilled people, a tremendous amount of brain power ... what they do not have is a very modern system by which these brains can flourish. There are many constraints. Poverty is one of them, the other is tradition ... What they want is people to come in and interact – they miss the contact with the outside world. They're very western oriented, and they get a tremendous satisfaction and help even from a single person coming and talking to them about what's happening in the field of railway modernisation – the course we've just run with the Institution of Engineers last week was Railway Modernisation. We're doing another course next month on air pollution with the Institute of Engineers ... So you have to choose. And one thing we do choose is what the High Commission considers important. Where can British assistance make the most impact both for Indians and for ourselves? Because the Council is working for the mutual benefit of Britain and India.

The British Council in India has a very large proportion of locally-engaged staff – 103 in Delhi as against 9 London-appointed, 64 in Bombay as against 2, 71 in Calcutta as against 2, and 64 in Madras as against 3. It has a relatively small Arts programme except in Bombay, a city rich enough to pay for itself and where the Regional Director is an experienced Arts Officer. The Indian theatre-going public is extremely critical and, as in other spheres, sticks out for the best. But there is much interest in lectures by writers talking about their own work. While we were in India we followed a route taken immediately before us by Angus Wilson, and we were followed by Salman Rushdie. Over the previous year visitors had included Alan Sillitoe, Melvin Bragg, Anthony Thwaite, Michael Holroyd and Antonia Byatt. The locally-engaged Arts Officers are extremely keen. There is a small hall at the Council Centre in Calcutta where I was told there was something going on every evening of the week except at week-ends, and at certain seasons also by day. The entire series of the BBC films of Shakespeare plays has been bought by the Council and the demand for these is so great that they are often shown two or even three times a day.

Yet the most vivid and the most lasting impression I brought home from India was of the great row about the libraries. Although the shortness of my visit does not allow me to pose as an expert, I formed the opinion that the Indian educated classes dearly love a *cause célèbre*, or to borrow further from the French, a *potin*. At that time all their energies in this direction were being expended on the mistaken behaviour of the British Council in relation to their libraries.

The Council has large libraries in Delhi, Bombay, Calcutta and Madras (Bombay, which is the largest, had in 1982 358,000 issues of 18,230 books and 267 periodicals), and also runs nine libraries in association with the Indian Council for Cultural Relations. In 1978 the Council made two rather abrupt changes in its library policy. First it doubled the subscription rates, and secondly it weeded out enormous numbers of books from the shelves marked Fiction and introduced what the Council calls 'a more strongly information-orientated pattern of activity'.

According to the Regional Representative in Calcutta, by no means a protagonist of this policy, something had to be done, since the numbers of people borrowing books was so enormous that they could not get everyone in, and the lists had to be closed. Not only was it costing a great deal, but the library stock was extremely run down, the books used too much, scribbled upon and even torn. Obviously there had to be a change. What the Indians resented was that a kind of moral fervour, what one might perhaps term an 'education-oriented' or 'developmental-targeted' emotion crept in, and the reform of the libraries, actually far less severe in the field of fiction than was believed, was conducted with unnecessary insensitivity and a disregard for Indian opinion. The intention was defined as follows:

> A closer integration of the work of all the libraries ... at the same time as the principal target audiences have been re-defined towards the post-Masters degree and post-doctoral students and above; and away from the older mass supply of books at undergraduate level, and of 'general' interest.

It was to this intention that the Indians objected, even more than to the clumsy implementation of it. The increase in subscription in relation to the rate of inflation was not unreasonable and would probably have been accepted if it had been spread over several years (as it was, it caused a drop in subscriptions of about one-third, the target group appearing to fall equally with the others). In the same way the reduction in Fiction might have caused less trouble if the books had not been re-labelled Modern Literature, so that many people thought they had gone altogether.

The complaint varied from, 'Doctors don't want only to read medicine or engineers engineering' and, 'You pour millions into industry which the ordinary person knows nothing about and yet pinch on the one thing we all care for', to the harsher, 'English literature is the only real British heritage, technology comes from all over the world'. Everyone seemed to be enjoying it very much and the curious thing was that one heard exactly the same complaints in each of the great cities, expressed in more or less the same words. As far as I was concerned, it was grist to a mill I am always grinding, because I believe that, because of the necessity to conform to constant changes of policy and to the cultural standards of the British Treasury, the Council is in continual danger of forgetting the purposes for which it was created.

The distinctive feature of the Brazilian scene (as in other Latin American countries) is still the Culturas. In the 1960s and 1970s, partly as a result of British aid, there took place a rapid expansion of exchanges and training awards in science and technology, and in 1968 a Technical Co-operation Agreement between Britain and Brazil was signed, naming the Council as the principal British Agent. Although British aid projects which the Council managed have now come to an end, a large share of the Council's own funds still goes to science and technology, and in Brazil it has many of those links with scientific, medical and engineering practice and research which have been sufficiently described in this account of the Council's work in other countries. The more traditional roles of English language teaching and training of teachers are here carried out by the Sociedade Brasileira de Cultura Inglesa.

This movement began in 1937 with support from the British Council. (In January of that year our Ambassador addressed a letter to the Foreign Secretary, Anthony Eden, in which he recommended an application from the funds of the British Council of £600 as subsidy to the Anglo-Brazilian Cultural Society, £150 as subsidy to the Sociedade Paulista de Cultura Anglo-Brasiliera, and £50 to be spent on books for the Anglo-Brazilian Cultural Society.) Today there are Culturas all over Brazil, the largest in Rio de Janeiro having 23,000 students and that in Sao Paulo 20,000. There are others in Curitiba, Belo Horizonte, Recife, Uberaba, and new ones spring up all over the country. Sao Paulo has a large new extension to its premises and to enter the basement, where the electronic teaching devices are housed, is something like visiting the BBC. Its Superintendent General, who combines this job with that of British Council Regional Director, and the Director of Studies are the only Council officers still directly involved.

However, it is the job of the Council's English Language Officer to monitor the work in the schools and to stimulate innovation. He organises a training course for Cultura teachers every year and an annual meeting between Cultural Directors. The relationship between the two movements remains very close and the Society of Culturas shows itself increasingly willing to sponsor small British Council artistic events.

The innovation of which Council officers seem most proud is the Ingles Instrumental Project (English for Special Purposes). In 1980 two Key English Language Teachers (KELTS) went to the Catholic University in Sao Paulo and a third to the Universida de Federal de Santa Caterina in Florianopolis to manage a project involving twenty-three, mainly Federal, universities, approximately 150 teachers, and at its maximum about 10,000 students. The purpose is to teach reading skills in the specialised academic texts of any particular field of study.

I find the whole concept of English for Special Purposes difficult to believe in, but in truth it is not different in principle from the system of scholars who work in areas requiring some understanding of dead languages. In any case, the sincerity of purpose and confidence in the method at the University in Sao Paulo, which I visited, is not to be questioned.

In the arts the Council has often only to support local initiative in arranging the visits of large programmes such as symphony orchestras or ballet companies, and smaller groups sponsored by the Council are usually supported by local cultural authorities and increasingly by the larger Culturas.

Finally there is the Sao Paulo Bienal, only second in international prestige to that in Venice and also the scene of Henry Moore's early triumphs. This is regularly supported and in recent years saw a magnificent up-to-date exhibition of Henry Moore's work as well as exhibitions of the work of other British painters and sculptors such as Patrick Heron, Victor Pasmore, William Scott, Peter Lanyon and Eduardo Paolozzi.

In Poland there is nothing exceptional about any of the Council's activities. The important thing is only that it is there – and has been there without a break from 1946.

In Warsaw there is a Library and a small Reference Library, which the Representative would like to expand. There is a Centre for Scientific and Technical Information and a much used Film Library, from which films are lent to educational institutions throughout Poland. All these services are in the words of the Representative 'too popular', the demand being very much in excess of any possibility of supplying it.

In Cracow there is a Reading Room for which the Council supplies all the materials and the University everything else, including the excellent staff – an arrangement with obvious advantages for both.

Every year there are fifteen to twenty training courses for teachers from universities, polytechnics and other organisations, at which those teaching are usually brought out from Britain and are either university lecturers or specialists of the methodology of language teaching.

There is the usual exchange of scholars to Britain and lecturers to Poland. Almost all those going to Britain are graduates or academic staff, many visiting in support of active scientific collaboration with universities. The British have equipment the Poles have never seen but Poland supplies first class scientists.

Three centres are run by the British Council for the Cambridge University examinations and it is hoped to increase these to six or seven.

In addition, there are links between Polish and British universities, partially funded by the Council.

However, the main excellence of the Council operation in Poland is that it is, as the present Representative put it, 'enormously open'. It is well known, he said, to the Polish authorities, to the Polish universities; anybody can walk into the libraries, anybody can go to the film shows. This openness justifies the cliché one so often hears that the British Council is 'a window on to the outside world'.

What then in brief is the reason why visitors to the Council overseas return so much impressed? Even before I left Europe's shores I had come to the conclusion that it is largely because a spirit resides in these offices, independent of the present incumbents and now almost fifty years old.

The British Council has sometimes been compared to the Old Boy Net but this is misleading, because, although also built up over the years, that was based entirely on the fruits of the class system. The British Council is intellectually élitist but socially democratic. It would be absolutely wrong to give any impression that either its conduct of the social side of its work or its influence in the spheres of transport represent more than the outer signs of capacity, but one may use them for the purposes of illustration, since everyone has some experience of these things. The more important sphere is that of entertaining. The hospitality of the Embassies – not only the British – is widely regarded as a little out-of-date; not so much because, as is frequently said, the guest lists draw almost entirely on the establishment, but because the formula of the grand house, the large splendid rooms, the pictures, furniture and glass, above all the butlers and footmen serving down the long vistas of places, is apt in the modern world to be counter-productive. The splendour is necessary, not merely to demonstrate the wealth and power of the country represented but also as a courtesy to the host nation, yet it does not make for ease. All of us, except those long accustomed to it, are a little wary in this atmosphere, a little stiff and formal; and in the less developed countries it can be positively damaging. One gets the impression that outside Europe and America, Ambassadors' wives are accustomed to the difficulty that they cannot place their guests until after the hour for arrival, because so many of those invited will simply not turn up.

The British Council hospitality is given sometimes at receptions – in hot countries held in the gardens – sometimes at small luncheon and dinner parties. The guests include leading men and women from the worlds of education, science, medicine, the press and a smattering of junior government agriculture officials. The food will have been prepared in the house, often by someone inherited from a predecessor, the atmosphere is easy and conversation flows. The best are the luncheon and dinner parties. I remember particularly a dinner given in Nairobi at which two of the guests were young and strikingly handsome women – one a barrister, the other a lecturer at a college of adult education. At these meals the conversation is as uninhibited as it might be at small dinner parties given by members of the same nation.

Then the Council performance on airports is spectacular, although I must repeat illustrative, rather than of the first importance. In Madrid airport our seats had been paid for and confirmed but we were told we could not travel because the Spanish Government had taken over a number of seats in the aeroplane; in Nepal we missed an aeroplane which should have connected with the night flight to London and much depended on our getting seats on a later flight; in Rio de Janeiro my husband's suitcase, battered over thousands of miles of air travel, simply gave up and burst. All these matters were swiftly and successfully dealt with by someone with a reassuring confidence in his own ability to do so.

If the Old Boy Net is not a good analogy, there is undoubtedly a network which has been gradually built up over the years. The London-appointed staff are changed every five years or so, but not all together. A new man simply takes over where the last one leaves off. Most important of all are the locally-engaged staff. Staff of the host nations are employed in the Embassies, but mainly as typists, receptionists and so on. The British Council relies on them for much very responsible work (we have seen their preponderance in India) and above all for its contacts. In many of the countries where it works an understanding of the route through red tape, a personal acquaintance with the man who holds power, is of the first importance. Any member of the London-appointed staff can rely on these contacts from the moment he arrives; anyone who has once been overseas can take up a new post confident that they are there.

The British Council is the only non-Governmental institution in the world which has this almost live accretion of goodwill, this linkage of long established relationships. A member of the staff once said to me: 'The British Council deals in penny packets.' I had never heard the expression, but it is true that a few thousand pounds spent locally may engender more friendships than millions poured in from a desk in London. Wherever one goes with a British Council officer – to a University, Agricultural College, engineering works, centre of adult education; on a personal visit to a famous botanist, or the Director of a Museum or an Art Gallery – there is a convincing relationship between him and the man one has come to see. They are on terms of regular intercourse. 'Ah! I wanted to see you ... '

It is because of these things that all those connected with the British Council so much resent that bludgeon of modern political management – cuts across the board. A few offices may be shut out of some eighty or so countries ... When they are, the locally-engaged staff must be paid off, all the friends of Britain rejected, and an almost living organism, which has taken years to build up, severed from the parent institution.

Something should be said about the British staff of the British Council, if only that it is rather absurd to attempt it. There are so many of them, and as everywhere else in the world, they are all different. Their Deputy Chairman has publicly suggested that they are a strange race of men and women, unambitious, out of this world, giving their lives to an ideal or to others. I have not noticed any of this. They are very much interested in their work and probably dedicated to it, but not more so than scientists, educationalists, research workers, all those people who see more in life than the exercise of power or the acquisition of money. They have good and interesting jobs and, if one can generalise at all, they seem to me to have one thing only in common, and that is the wish to spend a large part of their lives in foreign countries. (I speak of the Overseas Service, the Home Service has no general characteristics.) Two subsidiary qualities as a rule accompany the first – the ability to learn languages and a natural detachment so great that one can happily pull up one's roots every few years, and, leaving all friends and colleagues, go off to rejoice in a new set of relationships.

Most of the Overseas Service are men, for obvious reasons, the chief of which is that it is a great advantage to have a wife. And where better to end this whole account than with the wives of the British Council officers.

It is noticeable how little use the British Council makes of women, although this appears not to be from principle but because of the demands of the service. In other countries there are no British women in the lower Grade G because these jobs are filled by local staff (at home 80 per cent in this grade are women). In the higher grades women fare almost as badly overseas as they do at home. There are about 5 per cent in Grade C and 4 per cent in Grade B abroad, as opposed to none at all at home, and no woman in either service has ever reached Grade A in the whole history of the Council. The women at home are at a particular disadvantage because of the need for the overseas staff to serve for periods at Headquarters.

Yet wives are a different matter. Unpaid but not unappreciated, in the old-fashioned role of housekeepers and hostesses they are an indispensable part of the scene. Many of them seem to share the travel lust of their husbands – I know of one Representative who joined the Council only because his wife saw a chance of visiting a country she wanted to go to – while many are natural linguists. They have splendid houses as a rule and often live in the sun, while they meet at close quarters almost everyone of any interest who passes through. They have interesting hobbies. I met one who rode an Arab horse in the Egyptian desert every morning before breakfast, and many are collectors of local antiquities and experienced guides to the local scene.

There is a belief that it is becoming more and more difficult to persuade intelligent young women to leave their own jobs and accompany their husbands overseas. This may be so, but the world changes in many ways, and two British Council officers have already gone abroad accompanied by their husbands. However, I expect that in spite of what it is popular to believe there will always be a supply of women who opt for the traditional role – particularly those adventurous enough to spend some of their lives in other countries.

Personally, I have to thank a great many British Council wives for kindness and hospitality and for their exceptional talents as guides.

Appendix 1

Chairmen and Directors-General of the British Council, 1934-84

★ = present day

CHAIRMEN

Lord Tyrrell		Sir David Kelly	1955–59
(President 1936–47)	1934–36	Lord Bridges	1959–67
Lord Eustace Percy	1936–37	Lord Fulton	1968–71
Lord Lloyd	1937–41	Sir Leslie Rowan	1971–72
Sir Malcolm Robertson	1941–45	Lord Ballantrae	1972–76
General Sir Ronald Adam		Sir Charles Troughton	1977–84
(President 1955–69)	1946–55		

DIRECTORS-GENERAL

General Sir Ronald Adam	1947–54	Sir John Llewellyn	1972–80
Sir Paul Sinker	1954–68	Sir John Burgh	1980–★
Sir John Henniker-Major	1968–72		

Appendix 2

Members of the Board of the British Council
(Governing Board 1934-5; Executive Committee 1935-76)

Note: The Governing Board continued in nominal existence after the creation of the Executive Committee in 1935, but never met again, although it became larger and more unwieldy. Members of the Governing Board who were also members of the Executive Committee are listed below; those who were members only of the Governing Board are not.

For ease of reference, members are listed under the latest title by which they were known during their period of office (e.g. Sir Eugene Ramsden is listed as Lord Ramsden).

★ = present day. For numbered notes see page 372.

Abbotts, F.	1946–70	Barlow, Sir Alan[4]	1948–57
Abel-Smith, Professor		Beaumont of Whitley,	
Brian	1968–69	Lord	1974–78
Acland, Sir Antony[1]	1982– ★	Bird, R. H.[5]	1980–81
Adams, Sir Philip	1977–82	Birsay, Lord[6]	1963–70
Albemarle, The Countess		Bishop, Sir Alec[2]	1962–64
of (Vice-Chairman		Bliss, Sir Arthur	1947–50
1959–62)	1955–74	Blount, Dr B. K.[7]	1957–66
Alexander, The		Boase, T. S. R.	1950–72
Hon. A. V.	1936–41	Bonham-Carter, Sir	
Antrobus, M. E.[2]	1948	Desmond	1965–68
Attlee, The Rt Hon. C. R.	1936–40	Boult, Sir Adrian	1950–56
Bailey, Harold[3]	1964–67	Bourdillon, H. T.[5]	1964–73
Balfour, Sir Arthur		Bowen, Roderic[8]	1974–80
(Vice-Chairman)	1935	Bown, Professor Lalage	1982– ★
Balfour, M. L. G.[3]	1951–64	Bragg, Sir William[3]	1941–42

Brimelow, Sir Thomas[1]	1973–75	Esher, Viscount	1950–52
Brown, Sir John	1969–81	Evans, Sir Ifor	1950–54
Bulmer-Thomas, Ivor	1948–49	Farrer, The Hon. Cecil C.[3]	1937–40
Butterworth, Professor		Faudel-Phillips, Sir Lionel	1935–41
J. B.[9]	1981– ★	Feather, Lord	1959–74
Caine, Sir Sidney[4]	1957–73	Fell, R.[3]	1968–70
Carstairs, C. Y.[10]	1954–62	Fraser, Colonel Ivor[11]	1937–43
Casson, Sir Hugh	1977–81	Froggatt, Dr Peter[12]	1983– ★
Chadwick, Mrs Owen	1974–81	Gaselee, Sir Stephen[1]	1941–43
Chamberlain, Lady	1936–41	George, Lady Megan	
Chancellor, Sir John		Lloyd[8]	1943–66
(Vice-Chairman 1940–1)	1940–46	Golsby, J. W.[3]	1943–51
Chorley, Lord	1981– ★	Goodhart, Sir Philip	1974–79
Clark, Sir Arthur[2]	1964–67	Goodman, Lord (Vice-	
Clark, William	1964–68	Chairman 1974–6;	
Cockram, B.[2]	{ 1934–36	Deputy Chairman	
	1954–62	1976–★)	1966– ★
Cottrell, Sir Alan	1974– ★	Gordon, Alex[8]	1980– ★
Crawley, Aidan	1949–50	Gould, Mrs B. Ayrton	
Creasy, G. H.[10]	1939–40	(Vice-Chairman	
Creech Jones, The		1947–50)	1947–50
Rt Hon. A.	1942–45	Graham, William	1936–43
Curran, Sir Charles	1973–80	Gransden, Sir Robert[12]	1957–59
Dale, Sir Henry		Grant, Dr Michael[12]	1960–66
(President, 1950–5)	1942–49	Greene, Graham C.	1977– ★
Dawnay, Colonel A. C. G.	1936–37	Greenhill, Sir Denis[1]	{ 1966–69
de Freitas, Sir Geoffrey			1972–73
(Vice-Chairman 1967–9)	1965–69	Grey, P. F.[1]	1954–57
Delargy, Hugh (Vice-		Guedalla, Philip	1935–45
Chairman 1969–76)	1969–76	Hacking, The Rt Hon.	
Denman, G. R.[3]	1971–73	Douglas[11]	1936–37
Derby, The Earl of (Vice-		Hamilton, Sir Horace[13]	1943–46
Chairman 1936–46)	1936–46	Hamilton, Mrs Mary	1943–46
Dunwoody, Dr J. E. O.	1967–69	Hamilton, Dr Walter	1958–70
Eastwood, C. G.[10]	1964–66	Harewood, The Earl of	1956–66
Eccles, H. A.	1968–73	Hargreaves, J. A.	1975–80
Eddy, Sir Montague	1946–50	Harte, Miss W. P.[5]	1973–75
Edelman, Maurice (Vice-		Hendy, Sir Philip	1951–67
Chairman 1950–67)	1950–67	Hollis, Christopher	1952–55
Egerton, Sir Alfred	1949–59	Hornby, R. P.	1970–74

Quirk, Professor Randolph	1983– ★	Thistlethwaite, Professor	
Ramsbottom, J. W.	1934–52	Frank	1971–82
Ramsden, Lord	1934–52	Thomas, Ambler R.[15]	1965–69
Randall, Alec	1940–41	Thomas, Professor	
Reid, Sir Norman	1968–76	Brinley[8]	1966–74
Richardson, W. R.[5]	1943–49	Thomas, Mrs Elizabeth	1982– ★
Riverdale, Lord (Vice-		Thompson, Professor Sir	
Chairman 1936–46;		Harold[7]	1966–80
President 1947–9)	1934–46	Tomlinson, Sir Stanley[1]	1971–72
Robertson, I. M.[13]	1970–78	Trethowan, Sir Ian	1980– ★
Robertson, Lewis[6]	1978– ★	Trevelyan, Sir Humphrey[1]	1962
Rodgers, Sir John	1957–58	Troughton, Sir Charles	
Rooke, J. S.[3]	1973–75	(Chairman 1977–84)	1974–84
Rootes, Lord	1934–64	Tweedsmuir of Belhelvie,	
Rosebery, The Earl of	1943–45 1946–47	The Baroness[6]	1958–62
		Ulrich, W. O.[5]	1977–80
Ross, Lieut.-General Sir		Unwin, Sir Stanley	1934–68
Ronald[12]	1951–57	Walker, James	1941–45
Rowan, Lady	1975–82	Walker, M. A.[5]	1958–60
Ryrie, Sir William[15]	1982–84	Walker, The Rt Hon.	
Sayers, J. E.[12]	1966–69	P. C. Gordon (Vice-	
Sharp, I. L.[13]	1978–82	Chairman 1946–7)	1946–47
Sinclair, The Rt Hon. Sir		Wallace, W. I. J.[10]	1962–64
Archibald	1938–40	Warner, C. F. A.	1948–51
Sinker, Sir Paul (Director-		Welsh, Dr James[6]	1947–53
General 1954–68)	1954–68	White, The Rt Hon.	
Snell, Lord (Vice-		H. Graham	1940–62
Chairman 1941–4)	1941–44	Whitehorn, John	1968–82
Snow, C. P.	1954–64	Whitley, O. J.	1968–71
Stephens, F. J.	1962–68	Wilks, S. D.[3]	1976–80
Stevens, Sir Roger	1964–80	Williams, Sir William	1946–52
Strathcona and Mount		Wills, J. J.[3]	1935–41
Royal, Lady	1973–75	Wood, S. H.[5]	1935–43
Tasker, Anthony	1970–74	Woolcock, W. J. U.	1936–42
Tewson, Sir Vincent	1946–59	Wright, Sir Oliver	1981–82

NOTES

1 Nominee of the Secretary of State for Foreign Affairs (from 1968 for Foreign and Commonwealth Affairs).

2 Nominee of the Secretary of State for Dominion Affairs (1934–47) or Commonwealth Relations (1947–68).

3 Nominee of the President of the Board of Trade or the Secretary for the Department of Trade (from 1940 to 1947 both had the right to nominate to the Executive Committee; the Secretary for the Department of Trade lost his right to nominate under the 1947 revision of the Bye-laws, and his current nominee was nominated by the President of the Board of Trade); from 1970, by the Secretary of State for Trade and Industry.

4 Nominee of the Chancellor of the Exchequer; this nomination was only intermittently exercised and lapsed on the 1976 revision of the Bye-laws.

5 Nominee of the President of the Board of Education (1934–44), Minister of Education (1944–64) or Secretary of State for Education and Science (1964–81).

6 As Chairman of the Scottish Advisory Committee.

7 Nominee of the Lord President of the Council. This right of nomination ceased to exist in the 1976 revision of the Bye-laws, and the current nominee was then elected a member in his own right.

8 As Chairman of the Welsh Advisory Committee.

9 As Chairman of the Committee for International Co-operation in Higher Education.

10 Nominee of the Secretary of State for the Colonies (until 1966 when the office merged with that of the Secretary of State for Commonwealth Relations).

11 Nominee of the Travel Association.

12 Nominee of the Secretary of State for Home Affairs to represent Northern Ireland. This right of nomination ceased to exist in the 1976 revision of the Bye-laws, and the current nominee was then elected a member in his own right.

13 Nominee of the Secretary of State for Scotland.

14 Nominee of the Secretary of State for Wales.

15 Nominee of the Minister for Overseas Development.

Appendix 3

Countries in which the British Council is or has been represented

For ease of reference, countries are listed under their present-day names. Earlier names are given in parentheses, although it is recognised that the territory covered in earlier days may not have been identical with present national boundaries.

* indicates countries in which a Council officer is attached to an Embassy or High Commission (e.g. as Cultural Attaché) and there is no separate Council office.

Aden (Southern Arabia)	1940–51; 1957–67
Afghanistan	1964–80
Africa, East	*see* Kenya
Africa, French North	1943–46
Africa, Portuguese West	1943–44
Africa, South	*1958 to
Africa, West	*see* Ghana
Algeria	1963 to present day
Argentina	1942–82
Australia	1947–54; *1954–59; 1959 to present day
Austria	1946 to present day
Bahrain	1959 to present day
Bangladesh	1972 to present day
Barbados	1944–67
Belgium	1944 to present day
Belize (British Honduras)	1955–74
Botswana (Bechuanaland)	1972 to present day
Bolivia	1941–47
Borneo, North	1961–63
Brazil	1940 to present day
British Guiana	*see* Guyana

British Honduras	*see* Belize
Bulgaria	1940–41; 1947–50
Burma	1946–66; *1978 to present day
Cambodia	1959–71
Cameroon	1969 to present day
Canada	*1959 to present day
Chile	1940 to present day
China	1943–52; *1978 to present day
Colombia	1940 to present day
Congo	*see* Zaire
Costa Rica	1978–79
Cuba	1969–73
Cyprus	1940 to present day
Czechoslovakia	1945–50; *1963 to present day
Denmark	1945 to present day
Dubai	*see* United Arab Emirates
Ecuador	1942–47; 1978 to present day
Egypt (United Arab Republic)	1938–56; 1960–67; 1968 to present day
Ethiopia	1942–51; 1958 to present day
Fiji	1950–66; 1982 to present day
Finland	1945 to present day
France	1944 to present day
Gambia	1945–62
German Democratic Republic	1982 to present day
German Federal Republic	1950–54; 1959 to present day
Ghana (Gold Coast, West Africa)	1943 to present day
Gibraltar	1944–57
Greece	1939–41; 1944 to present day
Guatemala	1943–47
Guinea and Mali	1961–62
Guyana (British Guiana)	1944–74
Hong Kong	1948 to present day
Hungary	1945–50; *1963 to present day
Iceland	1940–47
India	1948 to present day
Indonesia	1948–64; 1968 to present day
Iran (Persia)	1942–52; 1955–79
Iraq	1940–67; 1969 to present day

Israel	1950 to present day
Italy	1939–40; 1945 to present day
Jamaica	1942–67
Japan	1953 to present day
Jordan	1948 to present day
Kenya (East Africa)	1947 to present day
Korea	1973 to present day
Kuwait	1955 to present day
Lebanon	1943–76; 1977 to present day
Lesotho (Basutoland)	1963 to present day
Libya	1957–72
Luxembourg	1944 to present day
Malawi (Nyasaland)	1950 to present day
Malaysia (Malaya, Sarawak)	1948 to present day
Malta and Gozo	1939–79
Mauritius	1950–80
Mexico	1943 to present day
Morocco	1960 to present day
Nepal	1959 to present day
Netherlands	1945 to present day
New Zealand	1947–54; 1960 to present day
Nigeria	1943 to present day
Norway	1946 to present day
Oman	1971 to present day
Pakistan	1948 to present day
Palestine	1940–48
Paraguay	1946–47
Persia	*see* Iran
Persian Gulf	*see* Kuwait
Peru	1946 to present day
Philippines	1978 to present day
Poland	1938–39; 1946 to present day
Portugal	1938 to present day
Qatar	1971 to present day
Rhodesia, North	*see* Zambia
Rhodesia, South	*see* Zimbabwe
Romania	1938–40; 1946–47; *1964 to present day
Sarawak	*see* Malaysia
Saudi Arabia	1965 to present day
Senegal	1973 to present day

Sierra Leone	1943 to present day
Singapore	1948 to present day
Somalia (Somali Republic, Protectorate of Somaliland)	1958–63; 1968–72
Spain	1940 to present day
Sri Lanka (Ceylon)	1950–54; *1954–59; 1959 to present day
Sudan	1947–50; 1957 to present day
Swaziland	see Lesotho
Sweden	1941 to present day
Switzerland	1946–47; 1950–76
Syria	1943–56; 1976 to present day
Tanzania (Tanganyika and Zanzibar)	1950 to present day
Thailand (Siam)	1952 to present day
Trinidad and Tobago	1943–67
Tunisia	1962 to present day
Turkey	1940 to present day
Uganda	1952–73; 1983 to present day
United Arab Emirates (Dubai)	1969 to present day
Uruguay	1942–74
USA	*1973 to present day
USSR	*1945–47; *1967 to present day
Venezuela	1941–74; 1975 to present day
Vietnam	1959–68
Yemen Arab Republic	1973 to present day
Yugoslavia	1940–41; 1945 to present day
Zaire (Congo, Belgian Congo)	1941–44; 1961–67; *1976–80
Zambia (Northern Rhodesia)	1950 to present day
Zimbabwe (Southern Rhodesia)	1980 to present day

Appendix 4

The British Council's Advisory Committees and Panels

This appendix lists the most important of the Council's advisory bodies. It is not entirely comprehensive owing to the patchiness of the early records of the formation and disbandment of committees and panels.

These bodies are all committees unless otherwise stated and are listed in chronological order of formation. In cases where more than one committee was set up in the same year, they are listed alphabetically within that year. Wherever possible, they are listed under the titles by which they are known today, with previous titles given in parentheses.

* = present day.

Title	Date	Chairmen
Books and Periodicals (succeeded by Books and Publishing Panel)	1935–48	John Masefield (1935–36) Stanley Unwin (1936–48)
British Education Abroad	1935–36	Lord Riverdale
Fine Arts	1935– *	Sir Lionel Faudel Phillips (1935–41) Sir Eric Maclagan (1941–51) Sir Philip Hendy (1951–67) Sir Norman Reid (1968–75) Professor Peter Lasko (1975–81) Alan Bowness (1981– *)
Ibero-American	1935–45	Philip Guedalla
Lectures	1935–44	Sir John Power (1935–36) Lord Percy of Newcastle (1936–37) Lord Lloyd (1937–41) Sir John Power (1941–44)

Music	1935– *	Ernest Makower (1935–46)
		Sir Arthur Bliss (1946–50)
		Sir Adrian Boult (1950–56)
		Lord Harewood (1956–66)
		Sir Anthony Lewis (1966–73)
		Professor John Manduell (1973–80)
		Lord Boyle (1980–81)
		Lord Gibson (1981– *)
Students (succeeded by Universities Committee)	1935–46	Sir Eugene Ramsden (1935–46)
		Sir Raymond Priestley (1946)
Near East	1936–39	Lord Lloyd (1936–38)
		Sir John Chancellor (1938–39)
Drama and Dance (formed as Drama Committee; renamed 1980)	1939– *	Lord Esher (1939–51)
		Sir Bronson Albery (1952–61)
		Norman Marshall (1961–68)
		J. W. Lambert (1968–69)
		Sir David Webster (1969–71)
		Norman Fisher (1971–72)
		Alfred Francis (1972–75)
		Peter Williams (1975–81)
		Lady Anglesey (1981– *)
Films	1939–45	Philip Guedalla (1939–44)
		Sir Stephen Tallents (1945)
Resident Foreigners (renamed Home Division Committee in 1941)	1939–44	S. H. Wood (1939–43)
		E. N. Cooper (1943–44)
English Teaching Overseas	1940–44	Professor Gilbert Murray
Medical (formed as panel of the Science Committee; known as 'Panel', 1941–69)	1941– *	Sir Edward Mellanby (1941–55)
		E. A. Carmichael (1955–64)
		Lord Rosenheim (1964–72)
		Sir Francis Avery Jones (1973–79)
		Dr C. C. Booth (1979– *)
Science (known as 'Panel', 1976–82)	1941– *	Sir William Bragg (1941–42)
		Sir Henry Dale (1942–49)
		Sir Alfred Egerton (1949–59)
		Sir Patrick Linstead (1960–63)
		Lord Jackson of Burnley (1963–66)

		Sir Harold Thompson (1967–74)
		Sir Derek Barton (1974–77)
		Sir Denys Wilkinson (1977– ★)
Engineering and Technology (formed as Engineering Panel of the Science Committee; renamed General Science Panel, 1949; Combined Sciences Panel, 1950; Science and Engineering Panel, 1952–76)	1941– ★	Sir William Larke (1941–49)
		Sir Harold Spencer-Jones (1949–52)
		Sir Alfred Egerton (1952–53)
		Professor H. H. Read (1953–64)
		Professor A. R. Ubbelohde (1964–73)
		Professor A. W. Merrison (1973–76)
		Professor G. D. Sims (1976–84)
		Professor R. W. H. Sargent (1984– ★)
Book Export	1942–44	H. Graham White
Law (known as 'Panel', 1967–82)	1942– ★	Viscount Finlay (1942–45)
		Lord Porter (1945–56)
		Lord Evershed (1956–66)
		Lord Diplock (1966–80)
		Lord Ackner (1980– ★)
Humanities	1944–48	Sir John Clapham (1944–46)
		Sir Maurice Bowra (1946–48)
Agricultural Panel (formed as panel of the Science Committee; amalgamated with Veterinary Panel in 1981 to form Agricultural and Veterinary Committee, q.v.)	1945–81	Sir James Scott Watson (1945–57)
		W. G. Alexander (1957–66)
		Sir Frederick Bawden (1967–72)
		Dr H. S. Darling (1972–77)
		I. A. M. Lucas (1977–81)
Universities (superseded by Commonwealth Universities Interchange and Foreign Universities Interchange Committees, q.v.)	1945–68	Sir Raymond Priestley (1945–52)
		Sir James Mountford (1953–61)
		Sir Robert Aitken (1962–68)
Scottish (known as 'Panel', 1947–66)	1947– ★	James Welsh (1947–53)
		Sir John McEwan (1953–57)
		Lady Tweedsmuir (1957–62)
		Lord Birsay (1963–70)
		Dr W. Macfarlane Gray (1970–76)

		Lewis Robertson (1978– *)
Welsh (known as 'Panel', 1947–66)	1947– *	Lady Megan Lloyd George (1947–66)
		Professor Brinley Thomas (1966–74)
		Roderic Bowen (1974–80)
		Alex Gordon (1980– *)
Books and Publishing Panel (formerly Books and Periodicals Committee, *q.v.*; superseded by British Books Overseas Committee, *q.v.*)	1948–58	Sir Stanley Unwin
Commonwealth Universities Interchange	1951–80	Lord Morris of Grasmere (1951–68)
		Professor J. B. Butterworth (1968–74)
		Professor L. C. B. Gower (1974–80)
Veterinary Panel (formed as panel of the Science Committee; amalgamated with Agricultural Panel in 1981 to form Agricultural and Veterinary Committee, *q.v.*)	1951–81	Sir Thomas Dalling (1951–52)
		Sir John Ritchie (1952–67)
		John Reid (1968–70)
		Sir Alexander Robertson (1971–78)
		Professor J. O. L. King (1978–81)
Editorial Panel (subsumed in British Books Overseas Committee, *q.v.*)	1952–58	John Lehmann
English Teaching (formed as English Studies Panel; renamed English Studies Committee, 1957; English Teaching Panel 1976–82)	1952– *	Sir Ifor Evans (1952–56)
		Professor Geoffrey Bullough (1956–63)
		Professor Bruce Pattison (1963–66)
		Basil Fletcher (1966–69)
		Professor Angus McIntosh (1970–72)
		Professor Norman Jeffares (1973–76)
		Professor Randolph Quirk (1976–82)

		Professor Henry Widdowson (1982– *)
Foreign Universities Interchange (became Committee for Academic Interchange with Europe, q.v., 1972)	1953–72	F. W. Deakin (1953–65) Sir William Mansfield Cooper (1965–71)
Soviet Relations	1955–59	Christopher Mayhew
British Books Overseas (formed from Books and Publishing and Editorial Panels; split into Libraries and Publishers' Committees, q.v.)	1959–64	Sir Charles Snow
Libraries (known as 'Panel', 1964–82)	1964– *	Frank Gardiner (1964–71) K. W. Humphreys (1971–75) Professor W. L. Saunders (1975–81) Sir Harry Hookway (1981– *)
Publishers (known as 'Panel', 1964–82)	1964– *	Sir Stanley Unwin (1964–68) Sir John Brown (1969–75) John Boon (1975–81) Rayner Unwin (1981– *)
Academic Interchange with Europe (formed from Foreign Universities Interchange Committee, q.v.)	1972–80	Professor J. S. Watson (1972–78) Dr A. E. Sloman (1978–80)
Agricultural and Veterinary (formed from Agricultural and Veterinary Panels, q.v.)	1981– *	I. A. M. Lucas (1981– *)
International Co-operation in Higher Education (superseded Commonwealth Universities Interchange and Academic Interchange with Europe Committees, q.v.)	1981– *	J. B. Butterworth (1981– *)
Films, Television and Video	1982– *	Lord Brabourne (1982– *)

Appendix 5

Income and Expenditure 1934-84

Year	Grant-in-aid from HM Government FCO	Other	Council's general revenue	Agency expenditure[2]	Total expenditure
	£	£	£	£	£
1934–35			881		881
1935–36	5,000		8,947		13,947
1936–37	15,000		12,922	1,609	29,531
1937–38	60,000		6,095	1,048	67,143
1938–39	130,500		45,965	2,001	178,466
1939–40	330,249		21,110	1,874	353,233
1940–41	433,099		16,712	30,862	480,673
1941–42	611,728		5,944	71,101	688,773
1942–43	966,705		9,146	35,258	1,011,109
1943–44	1,573,958		60,773	11,590	1,646,321
1944–45	2,108,122		120,778	8,160	2,237,060
1945–46	2,179,880	342,490	267,646	24,609	2,814,625
1946–47	2,443,292	434,510	257,646	5,508	3,140,956
1947–48	2,700,206	461,207	274,601	3,500	3,439,514
1948–49	2,408,285	445,472	417,984	3,414	3,275,155
1949–50	2,405,936	639,385	326,088	3,540	3,374,949
1950–51	2,146,003	986,277	376,218	9,347	3,517,845
1951–52	1,906,049	866,991	374,879	53,224	3,201,143
1952–53	1,642,153	820,118	398,477	115,699	2,976,447
1953–54	1,625,090	878,918	373,558	170,835	3,048,401
1954–55	1,643,120	944,637	413,457	183,033	3,184,247
1955–56	1,772,384	1,028,043	407,534	200,015	3,407,976
1956–57	2,173,617	1,064,960	454,178	334,500	4,027,255
1957–58	2,184,108	1,194,163	489,628	380,000	4,247,899
1958–59	2,517,906	1,347,493	512,633	490,000	4,868,032
1959–60	2,961,647	1,880,329	549,499[1]	605,000	5,996,475

Year	Grant-in-aid from HM Government FCO	Grant-in-aid from HM Government Other	Council's general revenue	Agency expenditure[2]	Total expenditure
	£	£	£	£	£
1960–61	3,357,238	2,278,489	585,430	977,000	7,198,157
1961–62	3,721,553	2,710,706	641,070	1,450,000	8,523,329
1962–63	3,738,940	2,925,452	677,021	2,033,000	9,374,413
1963–64	4,347,465	3,490,691	730,673	2,250,000	10,818,829
1964–65	5,170,119	4,532,762	833,633	2,500,000	13,036,514
1965–66	5,500,082	4,532,324	898,393	2,850,000	13,780,799
1966–67	4,079,156	5,884,505	920,985	3,000,000	13,884,646
1967–68	4,238,966	6,118,456	1,090,250	4,975,000	16,422,672
1968–69	4,618,864	6,671,356	1,154,356	5,130,000	17,574,576
1969–70	7,833,091	4,487,715	1,214,580	6,000,000	19,535,386
1970–71	8,745,634	5,121,457	1,403,546	7,760,000	23,030,637
1971–72	9,722,015	6,026,227	1,390,154	8,096,000	25,234,396
1972–73	10,931,338	7,717,812	1,584,023	9,750,000	29,983,173
1973–74	12,028,180	8,653,982	1,860,883	12,824,527[3]	35,367,572
1974–75	14,404,928	10,936,672	2,268,556	15,859,424	43,469,580
1975–76	18,292,238	14,456,135	3,196,758	21,096,523	57,041,654
1976–77	20,476,071	16,316,526	5,317,080	25,056,698	67,166,375
1977–78	20,826,595	18,220,594	7,590,202	30,950,853	77,588,244
1978–79	25,709,993	20,195,357	9,468,206	35,492,865	90,866,421
1979–80	28,927,754	21,523,119	10,897,340	47,913,960	109,262,173
1980–81	31,007,954	24,667,511	12,747,381	54,321,532	122,744,378
1981–82	34,164,805	29,378,769	16,545,067	66,905,579	146,994,220
1982–83	39,531,603	29,444,415	19,899,623	71,473,903	160,349,544
1983–84	41,632,462	31,273,170	23,050,598	77,241,804	173,198,034

NOTES

1 From 1959–60 to 1983–84, donations for special purposes were included in net expenditure from grants from the UK Government and an equivalent amount of revenue is included in the Council's general revenue.

2 This column shows all expenditure as agents for the UK Government, other Governments and foreign institutions. From 1934–35 to 1958–59, donations for special purposes were included in agency expenditure.

3 Only figures for ODA agency money are available for this year. The figure of £12,824,527 is regarded as a reasonable estimate for total agency expenditure in this year.

Notes

References to the files of the British Council and Government Departments now in the Public Record Office, Kew, are identified in the notes by the letters PRO followed by the relevant class and piece number. Files which at the time of writing had not yet entered the public domain and therefore not available to researchers and from British Council archives which, though more than thirty years old, have not been transferred to the Public Record Office are identified as follows:

BC   British Council archives.

FO   Foreign Office archives up to October 1968.

FCO   Foreign and Commonwealth Office archives from October 1968 to the present day.

Where reference is made to British Council publications:

Annual Reports are those of the British Council from 1940 to the present day.

Quarterly Reports are those to the Executive Committee from January 1938 to December 1945.

Home and Abroad is the British Council Staff Journal, from January 1961 to July 1972.

INTRODUCTION

1 *Annual Report*, 1975–6, p. 5.
2 Foreword to *The British Council. Speeches delivered on the occasion of the Inaugural Meeting at St. James's Palace on 2nd July, 1935*, privately printed by the British Council, 1935.
3 Harold Nicolson, 'The British Council 1934–1955', *Twenty-first Anniversary Report*, London, 1955, p. 4.
4 Memorandum on French Policy with regard to propaganda in foreign countries. A Review of the Report of the French Budget Commission on the Estimates for the Foreign Services for 1920, PRO, FO 371/7003, W 814/814/17, p. 3.

5 Memorandum on the Alliance Française, 1933, PRO, FO 431/1, P 1724/19/150.
6 Russell Galt, *The Conflict of French and English Educational Philosophies in Egypt*, March 1933, PRO, FO 371/17034.
7 'Reichstag, Reichshaushalts-Etat für das Jahr 1878–79; Etat für das Auswärtige Amt', quoted in Ruth McMurry and Muna Lee, *The Cultural Approach, Another Way in International Relations*, University of North Carolina Press, 1947, pp. 40–1.
8 16 July 1935, PRO, FO 431/1, P 2512/5/150.
9 *Annual Report*, 1980–1, p. 21.
10 Ibid.
11 Central Policy Review Staff, *Review of Overseas Representation*, HMSO, 1977, p. 223 (quoted later — see especially chapter 19 — as the CPRS *Review*).

I   THE CASE FOR CULTURAL RELATIONS

1 Harold Nicolson, 'The British Council 1934–1955', *Twenty-first Anniversary Report*, London, 1955, p. 4.
2 Ibid., p. 5.
3 R. A. Leeper, 'British Culture Abroad', *Contemporary Review*, vol. 148, August 1935, p. 201.
4 Cate Haste, *Keep the Home Fires Burning*, Allen Lane, 1977, p. 3.
5 A. J. P. Taylor, *Beaverbrook*, Hamish Hamilton, 1972, p. 138.
6 10 May 1929, PRO, FO 395/437, P 732/732/150.
7 Commons *Hansard*, 5th Series, vol. 331, cols. 1929–30, 16 February 1938.
8 Memorandum by Lord Curzon, 26 March 1919, PRO, FO 366/787, 32759.
9 T. C. Heath to Lord Curzon, 31 May 1919, PRO, FO 366/787, 82638.
10 *Report of the Foreign Office Committee on British Communities Abroad*, Cmnd 67, HMSO, 1920.
11 Memorandum by Lord Derby, 1 August 1929, PRO, FO 395/435, P 1140/178/150.
12 Cultural Propaganda, 1919–35, PRO, FO 431/1, introductory memorandum, p. 2.
13 Philip M. Taylor, *The Projection of Britain, British Overseas Publicity and Propaganda 1919–1939*, Cambridge University Press, 1981, p. 139.
14 K. R. Johnstone, 'Sir Reginald Leeper, CBE, KCMG', *Home and Abroad*, 14 (May 1968), p. 53.
15 Taylor, op. cit., p. 139.

16 Report of the British Economic Mission to South America, 18 January 1930, PRO, FO 371/14178, A 1908/77/51, p. 6.
17 Ibid., p. 55.
18 Ibid.
19 Ibid., p. 56.
20 R. A. Leeper's correspondence with his family, now in the possession of Miss V. A. Leeper and deposited in Sydney University Library.
21 Ibid.
22 Ibid., letters of 10 and 16 September 1931.
23 Cultural Propaganda, 1919–35, PRO, FO 431/1, introductory memorandum, p. 3.
24 R. A. Leeper's correspondence, letter of 18 May 1932.
25 Committee on the Education and Training of Students from Overseas; report by the Chairman on a visit to Denmark, Sweden, Finland and Norway, 5 October 1933, PRO, BT 59/16, DC 398/13.
26 Sir Percy Loraine to Sir John Simon, 9 November 1933, PRO, FO 431/1, p. 222.
27 Ibid., pp. 227–30.
28 Memorandum on British cultural relations in the Mediterranean, 3 June 1936, PRO, FO 431/2, p. 5. This memorandum was actually written after the formation of the British Council.
29 Ibid., p. 6.
30 Account given to the author by George West.
31 Memorandum by R. A. Leeper, 18 June 1934, PRO, FO 431/1, P 1887/9/150, p. 21.
32 Ibid.
33 Conversation with Lady Leeper.
34 K. R. Johnstone, op. cit., pp. 53–4.
35 2 June 1934, PRO, BW 82/6.
36 Op. cit., p. 148.
37 Conversation with Lady Leeper.
38 5 November 1934, PRO, FO 395/505, P 3151/150.

2   EARLY DAYS

1 The British Council. Speeches delivered on the occasion of the Inaugural Meeting at St James's Palace on 2nd July, 1935, p. 3.
2 Ibid.

3 Ibid., p. 7.

4 See p. 16 above.

5 Speech to the Manchester Chamber of Commerce, 12 May 1931, reported in *The Times*, 13 May 1931.

6 From a paper by H. P. Croom-Johnson.

7 Memorandum by K. R. Johnstone, 10 October 1936, PRO, FO 431/2, P 3781/15/150.

8 Opinion delivered by Raymond W. Needham, PRO, BW 2/121.

9 The British Council, Statement of Activities, 2 July 1935 to 15 March 1936, p. 4.

10 Memorandum of 18 June 1934, PRO, FO 431/1, P 1887/9/150.

11 Ian Greenlees, *The British Institute, its origin and history*, Florence, 1979, p. 10.

12 Stanley Unwin, *The Truth about a Publisher*, George Allen and Unwin, 1960, p. 418.

13 Ibid.

14 15 November 1937, PRO, BW 2/35.

15 29 July 1935, PRO, BW 82/5.

16 Vansittart to Reith, 26 February 1935, PRO, FO 395/523, P 393/12/150.

17 West to Bridges, 27 May 1936, BC (unreferenced).

18 Ibid.

19 Ibid.

20 A. J. S. White, *The British Council: the first twenty-five years, 1934–1959*, The British Council, 1965, p. 16.

21 14 March 1935, PRO, BW 82/5.

22 18 July 1935, PRO, BW 82/5.

23 11 April 1936, PRO, BW 82/5.

24 Ibid.

25 27 August 1935, PRO, BW 82/5.

26 Rootes to Percy, 20 November 1936, PRO, BW 82/6.

27 K. R. Johnstone, 'The first six years of the British Council 1934–1940', *Home and Abroad*, 4 (November 1962–June 1963), p. 13.

28 13 November 1936, BW 82/6.

29 13 October 1936, BW 82/6.

30 5 May 1937, BW 82/6.

3   LORD LLOYD

1 Colin Forbes Adam, *Life of Lord Lloyd*, Macmillan, 1948, p. 20.

2 Harold Nicolson, *Daily Telegraph*, 22 October 1948.

3 Kenneth Rose, *Superior Person*, Weidenfeld and Nicolson, 1969, p. 96.

4 Forbes Adam, op. cit., p. 64.

5 James Lees-Milne, *Ancestral Voices*, Chatto and Windus, 1975, pp. 194, 9, 43 and 98 (in order of reference).

6 James Lees-Milne, *Another Self*, Hamish Hamilton, 1970, p. 101.

7 K. R. Johnstone, 'The first six years of the British Council 1934–1940', *Home and Abroad*, 4 (November 1962–June 1963), p. 14.

8 A. J. S. White, 'The Council during the war', *Home and Abroad*, 6 (March 1964), p. 16.

9 Ibid.

10 Conversation with Professor West.

11 Quoted in Forbes Adam, op. cit., pp. 262–3.

12 Harold Nicolson, 'The British Council 1934–1955', *Twenty-first Anniversary Report*, pp. 11–12.

13 Rose, op. cit., p. 202.

14 Lord Lloyd, *Egypt since Cromer*, Macmillan, 1934, II, 6 and 4.

15 Ibid., p. 5.

16 Quoted in Forbes Adam, op. cit., pp. 219–20.

17 23 June [1937], PRO, BW 82/5.

18 Leeper to Bridge, 8 July [1937], PRO, BW 82/5.

19 White to Syers, 3 May 1940, BW 2/109.

4 PRE-WAR DEVELOPMENT, 1935–9

1 Lord Eustace Percy to Eden, 8 June 1937, PRO, FO 395/554, P 2485/138/150.

2 Ibid.

3 Eden to Simon, 16 June 1937, PRO, BW 82/5.

4 Philip M. Taylor, *The Projection of Britain, British Overseas Publicity and Propaganda 1919–1939*, Cambridge University Press, 1981, pp. 240–1.

5 Colin Forbes Adam, *Life of Lord Lloyd*, Macmillan, 1948, pp. 284–5.

6 Lloyd to Eden, 22 December 1937, PRO, T161/907.

7 Lloyd to Halifax, 29 December 1938, BC (unreferenced).

8 Ibid.

9 British Council deputation to Lord Halifax, 22 February 1939; Lord Lloyd's speech, BC (unreferenced).

10 Ibid.

11 25 May 1939, PRO, FO 395/642.

12 Hale to Barlow, 11 January 1938, PRO, T 161/907.

13 Tom Driberg, *Beaverbrook*, Weidenfeld and Nicolson, 1956, p. 59.

14 Ibid., p. 307.

15 A. J. P. Taylor, *Beaverbrook*, Hamish Hamilton, 1972, p. 156.

16 Unpublished paper by Richard Auty.

17 Ibid.

18 *Daily Express*, 4 August 1939.

19 *Daily Express*, 24 July 1939.

20 31 January 1940, Lloyd Papers, Churchill College, GLLD 19/16.

5 STRUGGLE WITH THE
MINISTRY OF INFORMATION

1 R. A. Leeper's correspondence, letter of 8 July 1939.

2 Philip M. Taylor, *The Projection of Britain, British Overseas Publicity and Propaganda 1919–1939*, Cambridge University Press, 1981, pp. 41–2.

3 Note of a conference at the Treasury on 17 February 1939, on the future position of the British Council, PRO, T161/907/S35581/06.

4 Waterfield to Hale, 17 October 1939, PRO, INF 1/443.

5 Ibid.

6 Hale to Bamford, 29 September 1929, PRO, T161/981/S35581/06/39/1.

7 Finance and Agenda Committee, 57th meeting, 13 August 1940, minute F97, PRO, BW 69/6.

8 15 November 1939, PRO, INF 1/443.

9 *The Times*, 11 October 1940, p. 5.

10 Minute by Lloyd, 3 November 1940, PRO, BW 2/85.

11 6 February 1940, PRO, BW 69/5.

12 Ibid.

13 Ibid.

14 16 February 1940, PRO, BW 69/5.

15 Minute by Waterfield, 21 February 1940, PRO, INF 1/443.

16 16 February 1940, PRO, BW 69/5.

17 Minute by Waterfield, 21 February 1940, PRO, INF 1/443.

18 Finance and Agenda Committee, 51st meeting, 13 February 1940, minute F2, PRO, BW 69/5.

19 Anthony Haigh, unpublished memoirs.

20 Ibid.

21 Gates to Waddell, 23 November 1940, PRO, INF 1/445.

22 Minute by N. G. Scorgie, 19 November 1940, PRO, INF 1/445.
23 Duff Cooper to Churchill, 7 February 1941, PRO, PREM 4/20/3.
24 Ibid.
25 15 February 1941, PRO, PREM 4/20/3.
26 1 March 1941, PRO, PREM 4/20/3.
27 18 May 1941, PRO, PREM 4/20/3.
28 20 May 1941, PRO, PREM 4/20/3.
29 Memorandum of 21 June 1941, PRO, CAB 66/7, W.P.(41)137.
30 Note of a meeting of Ministers, held in the Lord President's Room on
   1 July 1941, as amended in letter from Harvey to Brook, 2 July 1941,
   PRO, CAB 123/57.

6 WAR IN THE MEDITERRANEAN

1 A. J. S. White, *The British Council: the first 25 years 1934–1959*, The British
   Council, 1965, p. 49.
2 Ibid.
3 Ibid.
4 *Annual Report*, 1940–1, pp. 19–20.
5 B. Ifor Evans, 'Report on British Council activities in Portugal, June 1941',
   PRO, BW 69/7.
6 Op. cit.
7 Report by Lord Lloyd on his visit to Spain, 16 November 1939, PRO,
   BW 2/59, C 18541/16533/41.
8 12 December 1940, BC (unreferenced).
9 Conversation with R. A. Phillips.
10 C. A. F. Dundas to Boyd Tollinton, 20 October 1939, PRO, BW 34/9.
11 A. R. Burn to Lord Lloyd, 23 December 1940, PRO, BW 34/9.
12 3 October 1939, Lloyd papers, Churchill College GLLD 20/12.
13 29 June 1940, PRO, BW 34/9.
14 Ibid.
15 Cairo Office Quarterly Report on general progress with Balkans and
   Greece, 30 September 1940, PRO, BW 34/9.
16 White, op. cit., p. 39.
17 B. Ifor Evans, 'General Report on his tour of the Middle East, 1942–43',
   BC (unreferenced).
18 'Notes on British Council work in the Middle East', 15 April 1943, BC
   (unreferenced).
19 Leslie Phillips, 'The Suffering Grass', unpublished memoirs.

20 Minute from Professor Ifor Evans to A. J. S. White, 1 August 1941, PRO, BW 2/92.

21 17 December 1942, BC (unreferenced).

22 31 October 1940, BC (unreferenced).

23 C. A. F. Dundas to B. Ifor Evans, 17 December 1942, BC (unreferenced).

24 Dundas to Burn, 25 March 1942, BC (unreferenced).

25 Ibid.

26 13 August 1940, PRO, BW 29/13.

27 Ernest Bevin to Anthony Eden, 5 January 1943, PRO, FO 370/733, L382/178/410.

28 Minute by K. T. Gurney, 5 February 1943, PRO, FO 370/733, L603/178/410. A note of the meeting at the British Embassy, Cairo of 1 December 1942 at which these points were made is on PRO, BW 29/13.

29 Ibid.

30 22 February 1943, PRO, BW 2/56.

31 Ibid.

32 Report on British Council work in the Middle East, 1943–45, PRO, BW 29/9.

33 'General Report on tour of the Middle East, 1942–43', BC (unreferenced).

34 Ifor Evans to White, 11 April 1943, PRO, BW 2/341.

35 'General Report on tour of the Middle East, 1942–43', BC (unreferenced).

36 Ibid.

7 LATIN AMERICA

1 Report of tour of South America by Mr Philip Guedalla and Mr A. J. S. White, August–November 1939, Appendix C, PRO, BW 2/143.

2 Ibid.

3 Ibid.

4 Ibid.

5 Ibid.

6 Sir Eugen Millington-Drake, *The Drama of the Graf Spee & the Battle of the Plate*, Peter Davies, 1965, p. 287.

7 E. E. R. Church, 'Latin-American Roundabout', *Home and Abroad*, 18 (May 1970), p. 10.

8 Cadogan to Robertson, 17 June 1941, PRO, BW 2/92; Cadogan's identical letters to Riverdale and Chancellor on the same topic were dated 9 June 1941, PRO, BW 2/92.

9 Chancellor to Cadogan, 4 June 1941, PRO, BW 2/92.

10 White to Robertson, 20 June 1941, PRO, BW 2/92.

11 Stevenson to Robertson, 17 December 1941, PRO, BW 2/92.

12 White to Guedalla, 31 March 1941, PRO, BW 2/92.

13 E. E. R. Church, op. cit., p. 10.

14 A. J. S. White, unpublished memoirs.

15 Francis Toye, *Truly Thankful*, Arthur Barker, 1957, p. 76.

16 Ibid.

17 Ibid., pp. 74–5.

18 Ibid., pp. 48–9.

19 Ibid., p. 79.

20 Ibid., p. 81.

21 E. E. R. Church, op. cit., p. 6.

22 Toye, op. cit., p. 95.

23 Ibid., p. 96.

24 Ibid., p. 117.

25 Ibid.

26 *A Manha* and *Correjo do Brazil*, quoted in *Annual Report 1941–2*, p. 79.

8   HOME DIVISION

1 Executive Committee (39th meeting), 21 September 1939, minute 51, PRO, BW 68/3.

2 John Power, William Graham and S. H. Wood, 'Scheme for promoting social and cultural relations with peoples of other countries resident in Great Britain during the War', 2 October 1939, PRO, BW 2/228.

3 Ibid.

4 Executive Committee (49th meeting), 10 December 1941, minute 57, PRO, BW 69/7.

5 Quarterly Report, April 1940, pp. 18–19.

6 Wood to Chancellor, 2 September 1940, PRO, BW 2/228.

7 Ibid.

8 White to Randall, 28 January 1941, PRO, BW 2/229.

9 Ibid.

10 Minute by Nancy Parkinson, 19 April 1941, PRO, BW 2/229.

11 *Annual Report*, 1941–2, p. 11.

12 Ibid., 1941–2, pp. 11–12.

13 Ian Hay, *Peaceful Invasion*, Hodder and Stoughton, 1946, pp. 63–4.

14 Ibid., pp. 65–6.

15 Ibid., p. 70.

16 Harvey Wood to Parkinson, 1 July [1941], PRO, BW 2/229.

17 H. Harvey Wood, 'Poles Apart', extract from unpublished memoirs.
18 Richard Seymour, 'Developments in the United Kingdom during the Second World War leading to the practice of collective cultural co-operation', June 1965 (unpublished paper commissioned by the Council for Cultural Co-operation of the Council of Europe), p. 18.
19 Ibid., p. 3.
20 Quoted by Richard Seymour, op. cit., p. 25, from the *Receuil des accords intellectuels*, published by the Institute of Intellectual Co-operation, 1938.
21 Seymour, op. cit., p. 29.

9   POST-WAR READJUSTMENT

1 Reginald Davies, 'Policy in relation to the Financial Prospect', 4 January 1943, PRO, T161/1153/S35581/03/43.
2 Ibid.
3 Davies to Wilcox, 3 February 1943, PRO, T161/1153/S35581/03/43.
4 Ibid.
5 Wilcox to Barlow, 1 September 1943, PRO, T161/1153/S35581/03/43.
6 Ibid.
7 Ibid.
8 Eden to Kingsley Wood, 22 June 1943, L3219/116/410, PRO, T161/1153/S35581/03/43.
9 Ibid.
10 Minute by Wilcox, 23 June 1943, PRO, T161/1153/S35581/03/43.
11 Kingsley Wood to Eden, 26 June 1943, PRO, BW 2/342.
12 Ibid.
13 Eden to Kingsley Wood, 5 July 1943, PRO, T161/1153/S35581/03/43.
14 Kingsley Wood to Eden, 10 July 1943, PRO, BW 2/342.
15 Robertson to Eden, 23 December 1943, PRO, FO 370/782, L6529/4874/410.
16 Ibid.
17 Palairet to Cadogan, 10 January 1944, PRO, FO 370/782, L6529/4874/410.
18 Robertson to Eden, 24 January 1944, BC (unreferenced).
19 Robertson to Eden, 7 September 1944, PRO, BW 2/151.
20 Eden to Robertson, 21 September 1944, PRO, BW 2/151.
21 Churchill to Eden, 26 November 1944, PRO, FO 924/17, LC 1589/1589/451.
22 *Daily Express*, 30 November 1944.
23 Robertson to members of the Executive Committee, 28 May 1945, PRO, BW 69/11.

24 Ibid.

25 'Memorandum regarding the Cabinet review of the British Council in 1944/45', 8 March 1950, PRO, FO 924/782, CRA 20/1.

26 Sir Findlater Stewart, 'Report on the British Council', para. 46(8), FO 924/112.

27 'Memorandum regarding the Cabinet review of the British Council in 1944/45', 8 March 1950, PRO, FO 924/782, CRA 20/1.

28 Montagu-Pollock to Palairet, 27 April 1945, PRO, FO 924/113.

29 Montagu-Pollock and Hedley, 'Sir Findlater Stewart's Report on the British Council', 26 April 1945, PRO, FO 924/113.

30 Ibid., para. 6.

31 Ibid., para. 22.

32 Conversation with Professor Grant.

33 Montagu-Pollock and Hedley, op. cit.

34 Ibid., Appendix D.

35 Ibid., Appendix D.

36 Ibid., para. 9.

37 Ibid., para. 10.

38 Ibid., para. 18.

39 Ibid., paras 20–1.

40 Ibid., para. 28.

41 Ibid., para. 29.

42 'The Future of the British Council', CM(17)46. p. 135, PRO, CAB 128/5.

43 Report on the Government Information Services, 12 February 1946, CP (46) 54, para. 32 (3), PRO, FO 924/782.

44 Opinion given by Hartley Shawcross and Frank Soskice, 3 May 1948; PRO, FO 924/266.

45 Definition of the work of the British Council, 3 December 1946, FO Circular 0169, PRO, BW 1/27, P 802/718/907.

46 Annex to Evidence presented to Sub-Committee D of the Select Committee on Estimates, memorandum by the British Council, Reports from the Select Committee on Estimates, 1945–46, HC 158, 170, 171, 190–93, p. 469.

47 Definition of the work of the British Council, 3 December 1946, op. cit.

10   THE RETURN TO EUROPE

1 Law to Robertson, 8 February 1945, EC (62nd meeting), Paper B1, PRO, BW 69/10.

2 Robertson to Law, letters of 21 and 22 February 1945, EC (62nd meeting), papers B2 and B3, PRO, BW 69/10.

3 Ibid.

4 Minutes of EC (62nd meeting), 13 March 1945, PRO, BW 69/10.

5 2 January 1945, Finance and Agenda Committee (109th meeting), paper A, PRO, BW 69/10.

6 Conversation with the author.

7 Ibid.

8 *Evening Standard*, 22 March 1948.

9 *Evening Standard*, quoted in Sweden's *Dagens Nyheter* of 5 March 1941.

10 *Daily Express*, 23 June 1964.

11 *Daily Express*, 4 June 1954.

12 *The Times*, 15 January 1948.

13 Richard Auty, unpublished paper.

14 Ibid.

15 *The Times*, 20 November 1978.

16 Conversation with the author.

17 *Annual Report*, 1946–7, p. 77.

18 *Scotsman*, 16 August 1952.

19 Rudolf Bing, *5,000 Nights at the Opera*, Hamish Hamilton, 1972, p. 85.

20 Third Report from the Select Committee on Estimates (Sub-Committee D), Session 1947–8, HC 99, p. 17.

21 Gascoigne to Bevin, 21 January 1946, PRO, FO 924/418, LC 640/64/452.

22 Shuckburgh to Bevin, 21 June 1946, PRO, FO 924/458, LC 319/234/452.

23 Cavendish Bentinck to Foreign Office, 28 August, 1945, PRO, FO 924/210, LC 3547/1695/452.

24 Cavendish Bentinck to Foreign Office, 6 September 1945, PRO, FO 924/210, LC 3724/1695/452.

25 Extract from unpublished account of C. G. Bidwell, attached to letter from Jardine to Overseas Division C, 8 February 1950, BC, CF/POL/680/1.

26 'The British Council among the warmongers', *Szabad Nep*, 11 February 1950, BC, CF/HUN/680/1.

27 Tunnard-Moore to Witmor, 19 March 1947, PRO, BW 12/1.

28 Dr Neil Mackay, 'Latin-American Roundabout II', *Home and Abroad*, 18 (May 1970), p. 13.

29 A. J. S. White, *The British Council: the first 25 years, 1934–1959*, The British Council, 1965, p. 70.

30 Colonial Office circular 97511/3/48 of 9 August 1948, BC, GEN/682/6.

31 Ibid.

32 Circular letter from Sir Charles Jeffries, to High Commissioners etc., 28 November 1949, BC, GEN/682/6.

33 Jeffries to Gurney, June 1950, BC, GEN/682/6.

34 Harold Nicolson, 'The British Council 1934-1955', *Twenty-first Anniversary Report*, London, 1955, p. 28.

35 Ibid.

36 A. J. S. White, op. cit., p. 88.

37 T. W. Morray, 'India and the British Council', 31 January 1945, PRO, BW 38/1.

38 'Report on a visit to India', January 1947, PRO, BW 38/5.

39 Tunnard-Moore to Sir Angus Gillan, 27 June 1946, PRO, BW 38/5.

40 CRO to High Commissioner, India, 13 December 1947, PRO, BW 38/5.

41 Dr Joseph Needham, 'British Council Policy in China', 7 November 1947, PRO, BW 23/6.

42 A. J. S. White, op. cit., p. 79.

11   FINANCIAL STRINGENCY

1 Conversation with the author.

2 Third Report of the Select Committee on Estimates, 1947-48 (HC 99), p.v.

3 The British Council Review, Final Report by Organisation and Methods Division, H.M. Treasury, November 1950, FO 924/784.

4 *The Economist*, 27 January 1951, p. 181.

5 17 June 1950, PRO, FO 924/843, CRL 160/49.

6 Ibid.

7 Ibid.

8 Ibid.

9 Jeffries to Strang, 15 January 1951, PRO, FO 924/891, CRA 20/3.

10 Troutbeck to Strang, 16 January 1951, PRO, FO 924/891, CRA 20/2.

11 A. S. Fordham, 25 July 1950, FO 924/843, PRO, CRL 160/49.

12 P. Pares, 20 July 1950, PRO, FO 924/843, CRL 160/49.

13 Ibid.

14 Bridges to Strang, 21 November 1950, PRO, FO 924/783, CRA 20/23.

15 Strang to Bridges, 25 November 1950, PRO, FO 924/783, CRA 20/23.

16 Troutbeck to Strang, 2 December 1950, PRO, FO 924/783, CRA 20/23.

17 Record of a Ministerial Meeting ... on 10 January, 1951, PRO, FO 953/1054, P 1012/40G.

18 Minutes of the 8th Meeting of the Working Party on the Future of the British Council, 27 January [1952], FO 924/891, PRO, CRA 20/13/51.

19 Troutbeck to Davies, 27 January 1951, FO 924/892, CRA 20/28/51.

20 Ibid.

21 27 January 1951, PRO, FO 953/1054, P 1012/53.
22 The British Council: Joint Staff Committee, Staff Side Memorandum No. 63, 17 January 1951, PRO, FO 924/892.
23 Ibid.
24 Ibid.
25 Ibid.
26 Shreeve to Troutbeck, 27 January 1951, PRO, FO 924/891, CRA 10/9/51.
27 Minute by Malcolm, 1 February 1951, PRO, FO 953/1054, P 1012/56.
28 Ibid.
29 Davies to Attlee, 2 February 1951, PRO, FO 953/1054, P 1012/56.
30 Ogmore to Attlee, 2 February 1951, PRO, FO 953/1054, P 1012/56.
31 Griffiths to Attlee, 2 February 1951, PRO, FO 953/1054, P 1012/56.
32 Gaitskell, 28 February 1951, PRO, CAB 129/44, CP(51)59.
33 Esher to Adam, 15 April 1951, BC, CF/GEN/680/16a.
34 Memorandum by the Secretary of State for the Colonies, the Minister of State and the Parliamentary Under-Secretary of State for Commonwealth Relations, 22 February 1951, PRO, CAB 129/44, CP(51)53.
35 Minutes of Cabinet meeting, 2 April 1951, PRO, CAB 128/19, CM(23)51.
36 'Future of the British Council', 26 July 1951, PRO, CAB 129/47, CP(51)231.
37 Ibid.
38 Adam to Nicholls, 11 October 1951, PRO, FO 924/897, CRA 20/97.
39 Commons *Hansard*, 10 March 1952, vol. 497, col. 1009.
40 Commons *Hansard*, 2 April 1952, vol. 498, cols 1685–1806.
41 Ibid., col. 1716.
42 Ibid., col. 1798.
43 T. F. S. Scott, unpublished paper.
44 A. J. S. White, *The British Council: the first 25 years, 1934–1959*, The British Council, 1965, p. 89.
45 Ibid., p. 73.
46 R. M. Auty, unpublished paper.

12   THE DROGHEDA REPORT

1 Letter from Nutting, 5 April 1952, PRO, FO 953/1218, P 1012/33.
2 Nicholls to Nutting and Strang, 4 April 1952, PRO, FO 953/1219, P 1012/44.
3 Report of Cabinet Committee of Inquiry into the Overseas Information Services, 11 July 1952, PRO, CAB 130/75.

4 29 July 1952, PRO, CAB 128/5, C.C.74(52), minute 10 (Overseas Information Services).

5 Commons *Hansard*, 30 July 1952, vol. 503, col. 1487.

6 Summary of reports by Representatives on visits by members of the
Independent Committee of Inquiry, BC, CF/GEN/697/15ᵃ.

7 Ibid.

8 *Summary of the Report of the Independent Committee of Inquiry into the Oversea*
Information Services, Cmd 9138, April 1954, p. 3.

9 Ibid., p. 4.

10 Report of the Independent Committee of Inquiry into the Overseas
Information Services, Annex 2 (The British Council), paras. 11–13, PRO,
FO 953/1401.

11 Ibid., para. 15.

12 Ibid., para. 21.

13 Ibid.

14 Quoted from full unpublished report in final draft of Cabinet Paper on
Overseas Information Services, para. 10(6), PRO, FO 953/1403, P 10113/87.

15 Report of the Independent Committee of Inquiry, Annex 2, para. 34, PRO,
FO 953/1403.

16 Ibid., para. 42.

17 Ibid., para. 43.

18 Ibid., para. 44.

19 Ibid., para. 44(i).

20 Ibid., para. 45.

21 Ibid., para. 61.

22 Ibid., para. 62.

23 Ibid.

24 Ibid., para. 63.

25 *Annual Report, 1953–4*, p. 8.

26 14 August 1953, PRO, FO 953/1402, P 10113/57.

27 21 October 1953, PRO, FO 953/1402, P 10113/72.

28 Ibid.

29 Nutting to Eden, 23 October 1953, PRO, FO 953/1461, P 1011/45.

30 Nicholls to Selwyn Lloyd, 29 January [1954], PRO, FO 953/1459, P 1011/
19a.

31 Minute by Evans, 2 February 1954, PRO, CO 1027/69, INF 104/71/01.

32 25 March 1954, PRO, FO 953/1461, P 1011/47.

33 *The Times*, 29 April 1954.

34 *Spectator*, 30 April 1954.

35 Nutting to Eden, 13 May 1954, PRO, FO 953/1463, P 1011/64a.

36 16 May 1954, PRO, FO 953/1463, P 1011/64a.

37 1 June 1954, PRO, FO 953/1464, P 1011/129.

38 Swinton to Maxwell-Fyfe, 18 June 1954, PRO, FO 953/1463, P 1011/95.

39 Nicholls to Kirkpatrick, 25 June 1954, PRO, FO 953/1464, P 1011/130.

40 Nutting to Eden, 6 July 1954, PRO, FO 953/1463, P 1011/103.

41 Reported in a minute by Marett, 12 October 1954, PRO, FO 953/1464, P 1011/123.

42 Norman Brook to Butler, 27 October 1954, PRO, FO 953/1464, P 1011/1269.

43 Ibid.

44 Commons *Hansard*, 8 November 1954, vol. 523, col. 847.

45 On minute by Grey, 11 November 1954, PRO, FO 953/1464, P 1011/135a.

46 Lords *Hansard*, 8 December 1954, vol. 535, col. 303.

47 Nicholls to Nutting, 23 December 1954, PRO, FO 953/1459, P 1011/9.

13   SIR PAUL SINKER: THE HILL REPORT

1 'Sir Paul Sinker', *Home and Abroad*, 15 (December 1968), p. 36.

2 Ibid., pp. 36–7.

3 E. E. R. Church, 'The Director-General', *Home and Abroad*, 1 (January–March 1961), p. 20.

4 Unpublished paper by James Livingstone.

5 Note by Controller Establishments to Chairman, 24 July 1967, BC (un-referenced).

6 Selwyn Lloyd to the Vice-Chancellors of Birmingham, Bristol, Cambridge, Durham, Exeter, Hull, Leeds, Liverpool, London, Manchester, Nottingham, Oxford, Reading, Sheffield, Southampton, Bangor, Leicester, North Staffordshire, Aberdeen, Edinburgh, Glasgow, St Andrews, Belfast and Dublin, 17 April 1956, BC, Executive Committee paper EC(56)31.

7 Report of the Official Committee on the Teaching of English Overseas, Ministry of Education, 23 March 1956, para. 10.

8 Ibid., para. 13.

9 Ibid., para. 14.

10 Ibid., para. 24.

11 Ibid., paras. 25–6.

12 Ibid., para. 37.

13 Ibid., para. 46.

14 Ibid., para. 49.

15 Lord Hill of Luton, *Both Sides of the Hill*, Heinemann, 1964, p. 187.
16 Ibid.
17 Ibid., p. 189.
18 Ibid., p. 190.
19 Ministerial Committee on Overseas Information Services, The British Council, March 1957, para. 5a, BC.
20 Executive Committee minutes, 12 March 1957, BC, EC(57) 3rd Meeting, minute 29.
21 Ministerial Committee on Overseas Information Services, The British Council, Second Report: Five-Year Programme, 27 March 1957, para. 2, BC.
22 Ibid., para. 7.
23 *Overseas Information Services*, Cmnd 225, HMSO, July 1957, paras. 25–30.
24 Unpublished paper by Richard Auty.
25 *Annual Report*, 1955–6, p. 3.
26 Unpublished paper by James McDonaugh.
27 Ibid.
28 Ibid.
29 *Annual Report*, 1957–8, p. 6.
30 Ibid., p. 7.
31 *Overseas Information Services*, Cmnd 685, HMSO, March 1959, paras. 9–11.

14   SIR PAUL SINKER: EDUCATIONAL AID

1 *Report of the Commonwealth Education Conference, Oxford, 15–28 July 1959*, Cmnd 841, HMSO, 1959, paras. 11–20.
2 Ibid., Annex II, para. 19.
3 Report of the Commonwealth Conference on the Teaching of English as a Second Language, held at Makerere College, Uganda, 1–13 January 1961.
4 *Report of the Second Commonwealth Education Conference, New Delhi,11–25 January 1962*, Cmnd 1655, HMSO, 1962.
5 'An open letter to Arthur King', *Home and Abroad*, 22 (July 1972), p. 6.
6 Ibid., p. 16.
7 Ibid., p. 17.
8 Ibid., p. 15.
9 Carmichael to Sinker, 1 August 1961, BC, GEN/682/41.
10 Draft Bill providing for the establishment of the Department of Technical Co-operation, BC, EC(61) 3rd Meeting, Annex I to the Minutes.

11 CRO to Cabinet Office, 23 February 1961, FO, UEE 1063/49.

12 Ibid.

13 Cabinet Office to CO, 27 February 1961, FO, UEE 1063/49.

14 CO to Cabinet Office, 28 February 1961, FO, UEE 1063/49.

15 2 March 1961, FO, UEE 1063/49.

16 4 April 1961, FO, UEE 1063/49.

17 BC to FO, 12 April 1961, FO, UEE 1063/49.

18 BC to CRO, 20 April 1961, BC, GEN/682/41.

19 CRO to BC, 1 May 1961, BC, GEN/682/41.

20 Commons Hansard, 25 April 1961, vol. 639, col. 346.

21 Lords Hansard, 1 June 1961, vol. 231, col. 899.

22 Working Group on Overseas Information Services Review: Note by the British Council, May 1962, BC, CF/GEN/687/42.

15   A SPATE OF REPORTS

1 Circular Letter from Morris Dodderidge to Representative overseas, 2 October 1964, BC, GEN/900/28.

2 Ibid.

3 Educational Recruitment by the Department of Technical Co-operation and the British Council: report of working party to examine recruitment machinery, 1964, BC, GEN/900/28.

4 Note of a meeting at H.M. Treasury on the British Council – Departmental Responsibility for Votes, 10 December 1964, BC, GEN/120/3.

5 Ibid.

6 H.M. Treasury, Report of a Working Party on the Division of Financial Control of the British Council [June 1965], BC, GEN/120/3.

7 Ibid.

8 Ibid.

9 Sir Harold Beeley, Report on the Overseas Information Services, May 1967, para. 47(c), BC, CF/GEN/682/5^s.

10 Report of the Working Party to examine collaboration between the Ministry of Overseas Development and the British Council, June 1966, para. 3, BC.

11 Foreign Office Circular No. 013 to HM Representatives, 21 March 1966, FO, CRA 23/1.

12 Report of the Review Committee on Overseas Representation, 1968–69, Cmnd. 4107, HMSO, 1969 (quoted henceforth as Duncan Report).

13 Commons *Hansard*, 16 January 1968, vol. 756, col. 1577.

14 Duncan Report, p. 5.

15 Ibid., Chap. VIII, para. 28.

16 Ibid., Chap. VIII, paras 38–9.

17 Ibid., Chap. VIII, para. 26.

18 Ibid., para. 26.

19 Ibid., Chap. VII, para. 13(d).

20 Lords *Hansard*, 19 November 1969, vol. 305, col. 953.

21 Interim Report of Official Committee on Overseas Information Services to the Duncan Report Steering Committee, 16 September 1969, SC(Duncan) (69)10, BC, CL/GEN/687/69A.

22 Report by the Chairman of the Duncan Interdepartmental Steering Committee to the Secretary of State for Foreign and Commonwealth Affairs, 4 June 1970, SC(Duncan)(70)21, BC, CL/GEN/687/69A.

23 Report of the Working Party set up to review co-ordination between the Ministry of Overseas Development and the British Council, 1969, BC, GEN/682/41W.

16   PROBLEMS OF ADMINISTRATION

1 'Lord Bridges, KG', *Home and Abroad*, 17 (December 1969).

2 Quoted in a letter from Sir David Kelly to Stephen Bach, 6 October 1958, BC (unreferenced).

3 Ibid.

4 Kelly to Bach, 20 November 1958, BC (unreferenced).

5 Bach to Kelly, 5 December 1958, BC (unreferenced).

6 Ibid.

7 Note by Controller Establishments to the Chairman, 24 July 1967, with additions made on 20 November 1967, BC (unreferenced).

8 Ibid.

9 Fulton to Church, 13 October 1967, BC (unreferenced).

10 Appointments Sub-Committee of the Executive Committee, 9 January 1968, BC, AC(68)1.

11 *Guardian*, 7 March 1968.

12 The British Council: First Report from the Expenditure Committee, together with parts of the minutes of evidence taken before Sub-Committee E of the Estimates Committee in Session 1969–70, HC 304, Q. 1007. The

Estimates Committee had been reconstituted as the Expenditure Committee with different functions before its report on the Council had been issued; the report was, therefore, published by the new Expenditure Committee (with the disclaimer that 'the conclusions presented are not necessarily those which would have emerged from its own deliberations') in April 1971, and is quoted in future as the First Report from the Expenditure Committee.

13 Ibid., Q. 1013.

14 Ibid., para. 30.

15 *The Times,* 7 August 1971.

16 Reported in *The Times,* 22 June 1971.

17 First Report from the Expenditure Committee, Q. 2108.

18 Note of a meeting between Sir William Armstrong, Lady Albemarle and Sir John Henniker on the British Council Career Structure, 25 May 1972, FCO, PC 16/2.

19 Report by Management Services, Civil Service Department, on the British Council, October 1972, MS(SA)53/4/01, paras 2.14–2.16, BC.

20 Ibid., para. 4.3.

21 Ibid., para. 4.4.

22 Ibid., para. 4.5.

23 Fowells to Llewellyn, 13 November 1972, BC (unreferenced).

24 First Report from the Expenditure Committee, Q. 306.

25 Ibid., Q. 308.

26 Executive Committee minutes, 9 February 1972, BC, EC(72) 3rd Meeting.

17   THE COMMON MARKET

1 20 May 1970, BC, CL/GEN/687/78.

2 Cabinet Interdepartmental Study on Anglo-French Cultural Relations, 'Franco-British Centre in Paris: Note by the British Council', February 1971, BC, CL/GEN/687/78.

3 13 July 1971, FCO, PC 16/312/2.

4 First Report from the House of Commons Expenditure Committee, 1970–71, The British Council, Q. 2337.

5 Ibid., Q. 2339.

6 Joint Anglo-French Declaration, 12 November 1971, BC, CL/GEN/687/78.

7 Director-General's Newsletter 72/2, 27 March 1972, BC, GEN/680/22.

8 21 July 1972, FCO, PC 16/312/2.

18   NEW SOURCES OF INCOME

1 Llewellyn to Representatives overseas, 30 August 1974, BC, GEN/120/39.
2 Ibid.
3 Bunting to Perret, 13 January 1975, BC, GEN/120/39.
4 'The British Council – Planning Ahead', June 1975, BC, GEN/120/39.
5 Ibid.
6 13 February 1975, BC, GEN/120/39.
7 26 June 1975, BC, GEN/120/39.
8 'Assessment of the Council's Priorities', 6 October 1970, BC, EC(70)36, para. 9.
9 Working Party on arrangements for funding the British Council, 2nd Meeting, 25 March 1971, BC, GEN/120/31.
10 Ibid.
11 'Assessment of the Council's Priorities', 6 October 1970, BC, EC(70)36, para. 13.
12 'Proposed Revision of the Council's Funding Arrangements', 5 October 1971, BC, EC(71)34.
13 1 November 1971, BC, GEN/120/31.
14 8 July 1976, BC, CM(76) 6th Meeting, minute 8.
15 24 September 1976, BC, GEN/618/32.
16 'British development effort in the Middle East', August 1974, FCO, PC 16/9.
17 *The Times*, 31 January 1972.
18 'PAR: Projection of Britain Overseas', 3 May 1976, para. 4.1, BC, CL/GEN/680/59.
19 Ibid., Annex C, para. 4.3.3.
20 Ibid., para. 3.5.
21 FCO to BC, 2 June 1976, BC, GEN/680/59.

19   THE BERRILL REPORT

1 Commons *Hansard*, 14 January 1976, vol. 903, col. 386.
2 Ibid., col. 387.
3 Ibid., col. 388.
4 29 April 1976, BC, CL/GEN/680/62.
5 6 May 1976, BC, CL/GEN/680/62.
6 Quoted in letter from Naylor to Ellis, 16 August 1976, BC, CL/GEN/680/62.
7 7 July 1976, BC, CL/GEN/680/62.

8 22 October 1976, BC, CL/GEN/680/62.

9 19 October 1976, BC, CL/GEN/680/62.

10 22 October 1976, BC, CL/GEN/680/62.

11 30 October 1976, BC, CL/GEN/680/62.

12 2 November 1976, BC, CL/GEN/680/62.

13 16 November 1976, BC, CL/GEN/680/62.

14 24 January 1977, BC, CL/GEN/680/62.

15 4 April 1977, BC, CL/GEN/680/62.

16 'Review of Overseas Representation; educational and cultural work. Some points for discussion', BC, CL/GEN/680/62.

17 Central Policy Review Staff, *Review of Overseas Representation*, HMSO, 1977, p. ix (the CPRS *Review*).

18 CPRS *Review*, para. 12.22.

19 Ibid., para. 12.28.

20 Ibid., para. 12.30.

21 Ibid., para. 12.49.

22 Ibid., paras. 12.75–77.

23 *Observer*, 7 August 1977.

24 *New Statesman*, 5 August 1977, p. 157.

25 Ibid.

26 *The Times*, 17 August 1977.

27 *The Times*, 13 August 1977.

28 *Bookseller*, 27 August 1977.

29 *Listener*, 2 February 1978.

30 *The Economist*, 6 August 1977, p. 13.

31 Max Beloff, *The Think Tank and Foreign Affairs*, Royal Institute of Public Administration [1977] p. 12.

32 *The Times*, 6 August 1977.

33 *The Times*, 10 August 1977.

34 Lords *Hansard*, 23 November 1977, vol. 387, col. 900.

35 Ibid., cols. 903–06.

36 Ibid., col. 906.

37 Ibid., col. 922.

38 Ibid., col. 934.

39 Ibid., cols 990, 991.

20 AFTERMATH OF THE BERRILL REPORT

1 4 August 1977, BC, GEN/680/62.

2 6 August 1977, FCO, PCB 410/1B.

3 Record of Conversation between the Foreign and Commonwealth Secretary and the representatives of the British Council Staff Side ... Friday 4 November, FCO PCB 410/1E.

4 'Review of Overseas Representation. Memorandum from the British Council Board', October 1977, BC, BCB(77)38.

5 Report of the Defence and External Affairs Sub-Committee of the Expenditure Committee, 13 April 1978, para. 141.

6 *The United Kingdom's Overseas Representation*, Cmnd 7308, HMSO, 1978.

7 Ibid.

8 Ibid.

9 Ibid.

10 10 February 1978, BC, CL/GEN/680/62.

11 Report of the Organisation and Evaluation Project, 23 April 1979, BC, GEN/314/9.

12 26 October 1978, BC, CL/GEN/680/62.

13 Ibid.

14 Ibid.

21 THE 1979 CUTS

1 FCO to BC, 14 August 1979, BC, CL/GEN/680/67.

2 BC to FCO, 15 August 1979, BC, CL/GEN/680/67.

3 FCO to BC, 1 October 1979, BC, CL/GEN/680/67.

4 10 November 1979, FCO, PCB 410/1.

5 Lords *Hansard*, 19 December 1979, vol. 403, col. 1758.

6 7 December 1979, FCO, PCB 410/1.

7 BC to FCO, 20 December 1979, BC, CF/GEN/680/74.

8 14 December 1979, BC, CF/GEN/680/74.

9 20 December 1979, BC, CF/GEN/680/74.

10 27 March 1980, BC, CF/GEN/680/74.

11 3 April 1980, BC, CF/GEN/680/74.

12 24 April 1980, BC, CF/GEN/680/74.

13 14 February 1980, BC, BCB(80) 1st Meeting, minute 2.

14 Ibid.

15 Ibid.

16 13 March 1980, BC, BCB(80) 2nd Meeting, minute 3.

17 24 June 1980, BC, CF/GEN/680/74.

22   THE SEEBOHM REPORT

1 *Report on Non-Departmental Public Bodies*, Cmnd 7797, HMSO, 1980, p. 77.
2 3 April 1980, BC, CF/GEN/680/74.
3 17 July 1980, BC, CF/GEN/680/74.
4 Review of the British Council by Lord Seebohm, Lord Chorley and Mr Richard Auty, March 1981, para. 1.2, quoted hereafter as the Seebohm Report.
5 25 July 1980, BC, CF/GEN/680/74.
6 8 April 1981, BC, CF/GEN/680/74.
7 Seebohm Report, paras 3.2–3.3.
8 Ibid., para. 3.7.
9 Ibid., paras 3.10–3.11.
10 Ibid., para. 4.8.
11 Ibid., paras 5.6–6.7.
12 Ibid., para. 5.9.
13 Ibid., para. 8.8.
14 Ibid.
15 Ibid., para. 9.5.
16 Ibid., para. 9.13.
17 Ibid., para. 9.14.
18 Ibid., paras 9.28, 9.30.
19 Preston to Dodd, 12 June 1981, FCO, PCB 410/5.
20 Paper by the Director-General, 1 February 1983, BC, BCB(83)3.
21 Commons *Hansard*, 20 May 1981, vol. 5, col. 63.
22 Commons *Hansard*, 8 February 1983, vol. 36, cols. 883–92.
23 1 February 1983, BC, BCB(83)3.
24 25 July 1983, BC, GEN/121/2(83–84).
25 25 July 1983, BC, GEN/121/2(83–84).
26 27 July 1983, BC, GEN/121/2(83–84).

Index

Mention of certain subjects (e.g. some Government departments, teaching English overseas, etc.) occurs on almost every page of the text. To avoid unnecessary overloading of the index, entries have been confined to significant references only.